John Hill

Sermons on several Occasions

John Hill

Sermons on several Occasions

ISBN/EAN: 9783743351981

Manufactured in Europe, USA, Canada, Australia, Japa

Cover: Foto ©Lupo / pixelio.de

Manufactured and distributed by brebook publishing software (www.brebook.com)

John Hill

Sermons on several Occasions

PREFACE

TO THE

FIRST EDITION.

THE Author of these posthumous Discourses was well known in this city, (London), having been engaged in the pastoral office over a church of Christ herein, more than ten years; during which time God was pleased to own him for the conversion of many, and for the no small increase and edification of that hill of Zion. But the wise Sovereign of heaven and earth saw fit to remove him in the midst of his years and usefulness; which is the more to be lamented, as there are so few, who, in this degenerate age, appear steady and zealous for the truths and glory of the blessed Redeemer. But nothing can be more suitable on this occasion, than his own words, in one of these discourses: "Christ's cause is in the best "of hands. What! shall the gospel drop, be- "cause we see a flower fade, which we thought "would be very useful and adorning in his "church? That we may know that he is GOD, "he will lay aside an instrument we thought rea- "dy polished for the work, and choose and square "another, which shall do equal, it may be more "service."

The design, however, of this Preface, is not to give a character of the deceased; to attempt this, would be to violate the will of the dead*, and answer no valuable end to the living; but only to inform the reader of a few particulars, which relate to the publication of these Sermons. And, in justice to his memory, it is necessary to observe, that these discourses were not prepared or intended by himself for the press. The modest and perhaps too mean opinion he always had of the best of his performances, prevented his appearing in so public a way while he lived, and his preparing for any thing of this kind after his death. But it being his usual method to write down his discourses in long-hand, with what enlargements he thought necessary on the several branches of his subject, this has enabled his Executor to collect

the

---

* See the Reverend Mr Hall's sermon at his funeral, page 4.

PREFACE.

the prefent volume. His method, indeed, was to indulge a prefent freedom of thought when he was in his work, which occafioned a farther enlargement often, upon his feveral heads of difcourfe, than what he had committed to writing; many of which would have doubtlefs given the ferious reader a greater fatisfaction, if they could have been with certainty recovered: But that the Subfcribers might be affured, that thefe Sermons are genuine, nothing has been prepared for the prefs, but from his own hand-writing.

It is apprehended, that the more nice and critical reader may perhaps obferve too great a coincidence of matter, or at leaft affinity of thought, in fome of thefe difcourfes; which doubtlefs had been much more avoided, if the Author had been the revifer; but in the prefent cafe, all that could be done, was the choofing of thofe fubjects which appeared to be moft diftinct in the main, and to be drawn up with the moft fulnefs and care.

Another, and perhaps the greateft difadvantage, that thefe Sermons will be read with, by thofe efpecially who attended his miniftry, is the want of that lively and graceful manner in which they were delivered; which is the more to be regretted, as the language in which he penned them feems very much adapted thereto.

But notwithftanding thefe things, it is hoped, that through the divine bleffing, which crowns every

every work, these Discourses, many of which were so acceptable and beneficial in their delivery, may be of some farther service in their perusal; and if they shall be owned by the Spirit of God, to the conversion, edification, or comfort of any, it will yield no small pleasure to all that have the good of souls at heart, and especially to those that have been at the pains and care of their publication.

THE CONTENTS.

SERMON I.

The exceeding sinfulness of Sin.

ROM. vii. 13.

Was then that which is good, made death unto me? God forbid. But sin that it might appear sin, working death in me by that which is good; that sin by the commandment might become exceedingly sinful, - - - - - Page 13

SERMON II.

Evangelical Repentance.

JER. xxxi. 19.

Surely after that I was turned, I repented; and after that I was instructed, I smote upon my thigh: I was ashamed, yea even confounded, because I did bear the reproach of my youth, 25

SERMON III.

Christ the Covenant of his People.

ISAIAH xlix. 8.

I will preserve thee, and give thee for a covenant of the people, - - - - 40

THE CONTENTS.

SERMON IV.
Christ the Shepherd of his People.

ISAIAH xl. 11.

He shall feed his flock like a shepherd: He shall gather the lambs with his arm, and carry them in his bosom: and shall gently lead those that are with young, - - - - Page 57

SERMON V, VI, VII, VIII, IX.
God the Judge of all.

HEB. xii. 23.

—— *And to God the judge of all,* - 67

SERMON X.
God's Preventing Mercy opened.

PSALM lix. 10.

The God of mercy shall prevent me, - 118

SERMON XI.
The Preparation of the Heart the Lord's Work.

PROV. xvi. 1.

The preparations of the heart in man, and the answer of the tongue, is from the Lord, - 131

SERMON XII.
Past Tokens of Divine Favour, an Encouragement against present Fears.

JUDGES xiii. 23.

But his wife said unto him, If the Lord were pleased to kill us, he would not have received a burnt-offering and a meat-offering at our hands, neither would he have shewed us all these things, nor would, as at this time, have told us such things as these, - - - 144

SERMON XIII.
Chrift's Redemption from the Law's Curfe.

GAL. iii. 13.

Chrift hath redeemed us from the curfe of the law, being made a curfe for us: For it is written, Curfed is every one that hangeth on a tree, 155

SERMON XIV.
Prefent Difpenfations the Right Way to Glory.

PSALM cvii. 7.

And he led them forth by the right way, that they might go to a city of habitation, - - 166

SERMON XV.
Faith eying the Promifes in Life and Death.

HEB. xi. 13.

Thefe all died in faith, not having received the promifes, &c. - - - - 182

SERMON XVI.
The Nature of Regeneration.

2 COR. v. 17.

Therefore if any man be in Chrift, he is a new creature: Old things are paffed away; behold, all things are become new, - - 194

SERMON XVII.
Evidences of Regeneration.

2 COR. v. 17.

Therefore if any man be in Chrift, he is a new creature: Old things are paffed away; behold, all things are become new, - - 204

SERMON XVIII.
Ministers Christ's Stewards.

LUKE xii. 42, 43.

And the Lord said, Who then is that faithful and wise steward, whom his Lord shall make ruler over his household, to give them their portion of meat in due season? Blessed is that servant, whom his Lord, when he cometh, shall find so doing, - - - - Page 214

SERMON XIX.
Receiving Christ, and walking in Him.

COL. ii. 6.

As ye have therefore received Christ Jesus the Lord, so walk ye in him, - - - 228

SERMON XX, XXI, XXII, XXIII, XXIV.
Faith's Estimate of Afflictive Dispensations.

2 KINGS iv. 26.

——And she answered, It is well, - - 244

SERMON XXV.
God's Charge and Call to a Backsliding People.

MALACHI iii. 7.

Even from the days of your fathers ye have gone away from mine ordinances, and have not kept them: Return unto me, and I will return unto you, saith the Lord of hosts: But ye said, Wherein shall we return? - - - 300

SERMON XXVI.
Caution necessary in the best Saints against the worst of Sins.

1 COR. x. 12.

Wherefore let him that thinketh he standeth, take heed lest he fall, - - - 315

SERMON XXVII.

The Saint's importunity for Zion's Prosperity.

ISAIAH lxii. 6, 7.

I have set watchmen upon thy walls, O Jerusalem, which shall never hold their peace, day nor night: Ye that make mention of the Lord, keep not silence; and give him no rest, till he establish and till he make Jerusalem a praise in the earth, - - - - Page 333

SERMON XXVIII, XXIX, XXX.

The Good-will of Christ the best of Blessings.

DEUT. xxxiii. 16.

——*And for the good-will of him that dwelt in the bush,* - - - - 346

SERMON XXXI.

The Withdrawment of God's Spirit deprecated as the worst of Evils.

PSALM li. 11.

———*And take not thy Holy Spirit from me,* 379

SERMON XXXII.

Believers Pardoned, and yet Chastised.

PSALM xcix. 8.

Thou answeredst them, O Lord our God: Thou wast a God that forgavest them, though thou tookest vengeance of their inventions, - 394

SERMON XXXIII.

The Christian's Duty of dying daily.

I COR. xv. 31.

I protest, by your rejoicing, which I have in Christ Jesus our Lord, I die daily, - - 407

SERMON XXXIV:

The Blessedness of them that Die in the Lord.

REV. xiv. 13.

And I heard a voice from heaven, saying unto me, Write, Blessed are the dead which die in the Lord, from henceforth: Yea, saith the Spirit, that they may rest from their labours; and their works do follow them, - - - 425

SERMON I.

THE EXCEEDING SINFULNESS OF SIN.

ROMANS vii. 13.

Was then that which is good made death unto me? God forbid. But sin that it might appear sin, working death in me by that which is good; that sin by the commandment might become exceeding sinful.

TWO things our Apostle aims at in this context: one is, to shew the use and excellency of God's eternal law; the other is, to set forth the exceeding malignity and vemom there is in man's sin. The law is neither sin to the soul, *ver.* 7. nor death, as in the verse now read. It is given to prevent death: 'I had not known sin but by the law.' To shew a sinner his danger and disease, that he may be quickened to look out after a cure: therefore as *it is holy and just*, so it is also *good*, ver. 12. fit for him even in his fallen circumstances, and designed of God for his benefit and advantage. This is the use of God's law. It was given at first, and it is continued still, for kind and merciful purposes. But such is the cursed nature and malignity of sin, that it turns that which was designed for man's good into evil against him.

him. It sucks poison out of honey, and makes that law, which is given to reveal and condemn sin, an occasion of sin.—' Sin, taking occasion by the com-
' mandment, wrought in me all manner of concu-
' piscence,' *ver.* 8.; and in the text, ' Sin, that it
' might appear sin, wrought death in me by that
' which is good.' Those restraints which God's law lays upon corrupt nature make it more passionate and rebellious. This arises, not from any evil design or tendency in the law itself, but from the desperate wickedness which is in man's heart and nature. Should a sick patient thirst for water more vehemently, because the physician charges him, as he loves his life, to abstain from it; this argues the badness of the man's distemper, not any unskilfulness in the physician, or the impropriety of his prescriptions. In like manner is the holy law of God justified from being the cause or means of man's sin, notwithstanding sin takes occasion by the commandment. Therefore the Apostle, in our text, lays all the blame upon sin itself, and not on God's law, and takes occasion from hence to shew the *exceeding sinfulness* which there is in sin, calling it by its own name, because he can find none other, so vile and expressive, to represent it by; ' Was then that which is good
' made death unto me? God forbid,' *&c.*

In discoursing upon these words, I shall endeavour, by divine assistance, to do the following things:

I. To shew what sin this is which Paul speaks of, and wherein consists its exceeding sinfulness.

II. How or by what means its exceeding sinfulness appears; ' Sin by the commandment be-
' comes exceeding sinful.'

III. Why God suffers the motions of it, in such whom he knows to be his own, to be so exceeding violent and dreadful; ' Sin, working
' death in me by that which is good, that it
' might appear sin.'

IV. Apply the subject.

I. What

I. What is this sin which our Apostle speaks of, and wherein does the exceeding sinfulness of it consist?

As to the sin itself; it is a sin which is inward in the heart, not outward in the life, *ver.* 17.; a sin which produces and gives being to all other sins, and gives strength for the performance; a sin which is all along in the context represented as a person, called therefore, *chap.* vi. 6. *the old man;* a sin which ' dwelleth in us,' *ver.* 17. is ever present with us, *ver.* 21. an inherent, deceitful, tyrannical evil, *ver.* 11. 20. 23. is ever presenting occasion of sinning, and pushing on the soul to acts of sin. What can this be but the sin of our nature; or that perverse bias and propensity to sin, which is derived down to all and every man, as a punishment of the first man's first offence? Therefore it is called *flesh,* ver. 5. ' when ' we were in the flesh,' &c. because it comes to us with our flesh. We are shapen and conceived in it; ' by nature children of wrath,' before we were capable of shewing ourselves in practice children of disobedience. This is what the Apostle calls by way of eminence, *Sin,* ver. 8. ' sin taking occasion by the ' commandment:' That sin, that great sin, that leading, mother sin, which is styled in our text sinful sin, as having in it the seeds of all other sins; and *exceeding,* or above measure, *sinful.* Such is the sin itself; and the exceeding sinfulness of this sin will appear, if we consider,

1. That it is a plague which has infected the whole man. The understanding, what is it but the seat of darkness, misapprehension and error? Rom. iii. 11. ' There is none that understandeth, there is none ' that seeketh after God.' It is hard to detain the mind of man before the Lord. Ten thousand vanities possess our thoughts, and steal away our hearts, when we close our eyes upon the world, and profess to be diligently seeking after God. What is the will, but enmity and rebellion against God? ' Ye will not ' come unto me that ye might have life,' John v. 40.

Why is it poor souls take so much pains to shut out the light, and stifle the convictions of the word? but because 'they love darkness rather than light.' The affections, which are as wings to raise the soul to God and heavenly things, are turned quite downwards, being set on things on the earth. Conscience itself is become defiled by this sinful sin, so that it neither witnesses, reproves, or judges, according to God's direction; but becomes first easy, then remiss, next hardened and seared. Yea, our very memories are drawn over to the corrupt part; like leaky vessels, whatever is good and pure they let out, and keep in little but what is filthy, corrupt and evil. Yea, these very bodies of ours are become vile bodies through sin that dwelleth in us; subject to diseases and corruptions, and are tempters of the soul to sin, and servants of it in all outward acts of sinning, *ver.* 5. ' For when we were in the ' flesh, the motions of sin which were by the law, ' did work in our members, to bring forth fruit un- ' to death.' Other sins mar particular parts of the image of God; but this at once defaces the whole. Do but once see yourselves, and I shall have no occasion to reprove you as the prophet does Israel, with an *How canst thou say, I am not polluted?*—The exceeding sinfulness of this sin appears, in that it has diffused itself through the whole man.

2. It is the cause of all those sins which are in the life.—Then is a man said to be tempted, James i. 14. ' when he is drawn away of his lust, and enticed.' Temptation may vex, but it cannot defile the soul, if it be not entertained. The true original of evil and temptation lies *here*, **within.** ' Out of the heart ' proceed evil thoughts, adulteries,' &c. *This* is the fountain, particular sins are but the streams. Original sin is that root of bitterness, which, springing up in the heart, and sprouting forth in the life, defiles and ruins. Begin your confessions here. If the effects are so ruinous and accursed, what must the cause be?

3. This

3. This sin of our nature is, virtually, all sin; sin in the gross, in all the seeds of it; the combustible matter, which only waits for outward occasions and temptations in the life, to blow it into a flame: it is a body which hath many members, and it is working in order to make provision for them all. Never did any sin appear in the vilest wretch that lived, but thou hast the seed of that sin in thy nature. That it does not break forth in thy life, as it does in his, is owing, not to any betterness in thy nature, but to the power of divine restraints. Thou hadst been that swearer, that drunkard, &c. but that God withheld thee from sinning, as he did Abimelech, 'I withheld thee from sinning against me,' Gen. xx. 6. Corrupt nature is the same in all. There is more wickedness in thy heart than thou yet knowest. Trust it not but with the Lord, for it is 'deceitful above all things, and desperately wicked.' That sin must needs be exceeding sinful, that wraps up in its own nature all other sins.

4. It is more durable and abiding than all other sins; therefore more exceeding sinful. It may change its course in a natural man, but it never loses its power. Saul is amongst the prophets, but Saul is a servant of sin, and a slave to his own lusts, notwithstanding. Change of place, companies, resolutions, will not dethrone this sinful sin; and where it is cast out of the throne, it will nevertheless abide in the heart. All the rubbing, and scraping, that was used of old in the house infected with leprosy, would not do to cleanse it, till stones, mortar and timber were taken quite away, Lev. xiv. This sin of our nature is an inhabitant, which will not be removed, till the house wherein it dwells is pulled down. *Here* sin *dwells;* bless God, Christian, it does not reign. Here is pride, envy, covetousness, sensuality, &c. They may not be always stirring in thee: Nevertheless be not high-minded, but fear; the proud, the envious, the sensual nature, is in thee still. Remember the *howbeit* upon good Hezekiah's

kiah's character, 2 Chron. xxxii. 31. *howbeit,* in the business of the ambassadors of the princes of Babylon, &c. God left him to try him, that he might know all that was in his heart. That must sure be sinful, exceeding sinful, that is more durable and abiding than all other sins.

5. It is exceeding sinful sin, because it is ever encompassing, besetting and warring against the soul in whom it dwells. It envenoms every action, every thought and duty, which proceed from the regenerate themselves. Wherever we go, we carry sin with us; whatever we touch, we leave the print of our sin upon it: it will work where it does not reign, and sadly disturb where it cannot destroy. It is this which makes our thoughts vain, our prayers dead; which mingles leaven with our sacrifices, and brings iniquity into our holy things. It is this which makes the ways of God so often tedious, and forces the soul to cry out with David, the man after God's own heart, ' Oh that I had wings like a dove, then ' would I flee away, and be at rest :' Or with Paul, in his agony and conflict with himself, ' Oh, wretched ' man that I am, who shall deliver me from the body ' of this death !' It is a rebel, a traitor within, which holds a settled correspondence with our adversary, Satan, and divulges, not what passes in our bedchamber only, but what are the most secret burdens, conflicts, distresses, and desires of our souls.

6. It is an hereditary evil.—All men are defiled with it; therefore all are concerned in it. ' In A-' dam all die,' 1 Cor. xv. 22. Hereditary diseases are of all others hardest to cure : but before any can heartily enquire after a cure, they must feel themselves diseased. ' Sin must appear sin.' This brings to consider,

II. How, or by what means, the exceeding sinfulness of this sin appears?—We have shewed, in some measure, wherein it consists; but the weightiest consideration is this, wherein does it appear? By what means is the conviction of its sinfulness brought

upon

upon a man's conscience, so that he shall see himself (as Paul did) a lost, undone man by reason of it. 'But sin, that it might appear sin, working 'death in me, by that which is good, that sin by the 'commandment, might become exceeding sinful.' Here it must be enquired,

1. What this commandment is?
2. How sin becomes, or is made to appear, exceeding sinful by the commandment?

1. What this commandment is? In *ver.* 8. and 9. the Apostle calls it *the law,* 'I was alive without 'the law once;' and he varies the phrase, both here and there, calling it *the commandment,* either as the law consists of commands and prohibitions, thou shalt do this, and thou shalt not do that; or it may be, because, when the Spirit comes by the law to convince of sin, he sets home the conviction upon the heart by some one or other commandment, which the man is particularly guilty of the breach of; as in the context, the particular commandment by which Paul was convinced of the evil concupiscence of his own nature, was the tenth, or last commandment, *ver.* 7. 'I had not known lust, except the law 'had said, Thou shalt not covet.' By the commandment, therefore, we are to understand the whole moral law, which the Spirit of God has given on purpose, and which he ever makes use of to convince of sin. This is the commandment.

2. How is sin made by the commandment to appear exceeding sinful? I answer three ways.

(1.) The law or commandment shews the soul, that it is against God.—It is a depravation of his whole image, a contrariety to his whole will; opposite to his justice, holiness and truth, and enmity to all his purposes of grace and mercy. That law which condemns sin in the act, much more condemns it in the principle. This blessed effect it had upon David: Psalm li. 4, 5. 'Against thee, thee 'only have I sinned, and done this evil in thy sight.' *This evil,* says he; in my nature I am nothing but evil;

evil; prone and inclined to all sin. 'Behold, I was
'shapen in iniquity, and in sin did my mother con-
'ceive me.' This is against God; this first, this
breeding sin; therefore let all my humiliation and
repentance begin here. God's law shews the smal-
lest specks. It opens the inward parts, and shews
the plague-sore within. If the heart be not pure,
every action must be defective. God's law condemns
whatever is wanting in conformity to it. It insists
upon perfection, and purity in principle Whatever
Adam lost for us, that, in every tittle of it, the holy
law of God requires of us. The sin of your nature
may be made light of now; Paul himself, who thus
complains of it, was alive without the law. But
when the commandment comes, sin will revive, and
death will ensue. All your presumptuous confidences,
and vain hopes and expectations, will be slain. God
will bring you to clear his righteousness, in the imputation of Adam's sin, in its guilt and punishment,
and for ever to judge and condemn yourselves. Even
of that generation, that are 'pure in their own eyes,'
and see not the lie in their right hand. Many have
been brought to lie in dust and ashes, on account of
Adam's sin, and, with a covering upon their upper
lip, to cry out, as the leper of old did, *Unclean, unclean*.

(2.) It shews the soul that death which God has
threatened against it.

Sin, in every natural man, has a power to command, work, and lord it over the soul, because of
its reign; and it has also a power to condemn, because of its guilt. 'Sin working death in me, by
'that which is good.—The wages of sin is death.'
The law comes with its threatening and curse, de-
nouncing death and wrath *upon every soul of man
that doth evil*. 'And were by nature the children of
'wrath, even as others,' Eph. ii. 3. That is the dismal peal which it rings in the sinner's ears. The
sting of death lies in that vengeance, and everlasting
destruction, which is to come upon the wicked in a
future

future state. This the law sets open, in all its dreadfulness and misery, when the commandment comes. Men now mince matters. Some that profess Adam and Christ to be two covenant-heads, have so far forgot Rom. v. 21. and Eph. ii. 3. as to assert roundly, that eternal death is no where in scripture, to their knowledge, denounced as the wages of the first man's sin. But this is a thread, a withe, which a broken law snaps asunder, when it shews what an insupportable, powerful, penetrating, abiding wrath, the wrath of the living and just God is, when it urges a poor soul with that awful word, 'As sin hath 'reigned unto death, even so might grace reign 'through righteousness unto eternal life, by Jesus 'Christ our Lord.' Are not death and life opposed? God's grace, and Adam's offence, set one against the other? A soul, however, under conviction of this sin can have no peace, because *man* tells him, by death is meant no more than the dissolution of soul and body; what, says he, must become of this poor soul of mine, when this dissolution comes? how shall I appear before an angry God? who shall deliver me from the wrath to come? No one can give him a dram of comfort, or heart's ease, till he is led to Christ, who ' is come, that we might have life, and ' that we might have it more abundantly,' John x. 10.

(3.) Another way in which the law convinces of the exceeding sinfulness of this, and of all other sins, is by loading and burdening the conscience with a sense of it. It brings God's word and man's sin together: 'My sin,' says the Psalmist, 'is ever before 'me,' Psal. li. 3. The law holds a man fast, so that he cannot shift off conviction, as Felix was willing to do, till a more convenient season. It passes sentence upon the soul, and he begins to feel in part the execution of it. Conscience follows him with a " *Thou art the man.* Thou art the sinner; eternal " wrath is thy due; the wrath of God abideth upon " thee," &c. This leads to the third thing:

But

But before I proceed, think not that the law does this of itself. The law is but the instrument or means of conviction; the Spirit is the great efficient, 'When he is come, he shall reprove the world of 'sin,' John xvi. 10. The law is the glass wherein sin is seen; the Spirit holds it up to the sinner, and causes him to see his own face in it. The law is the hammer; but it is the Spirit that works by it.

III. Why is it that God suffers the motions of sin, in such whom he knows to be his own, to be so exceeding violent and dreadful? In general, it is that the sin of our nature might always appear sin. Paul was a chosen vessel; one that dwelt as near to God as any since Christ tabernacled in our flesh: Whence was it, the motions of sin in him were so great, but 'that sin might appear sin,' &c. By this we may judge of our own frames, and the frames of other believers.

1. Therefore such a fight as this sets and keeps open a spring of repentance towards God always. The sin of our nature is what we are to be humbled for, and to repent of, every day we live. 'Thou 'shalt remember thy way and be ashamed,' Ezek. xvi. 61. There will be no mourning or godly sorrow above, but communion with God is kept up in this frame of soul by the way. Paul's frame was not bad, though his groans were deep, when he cries out, ver. 24. 'Oh, wretched man that I am,' &c.; for he immediately adds, 'I thank God through Je- 'sus Christ our Lord.' Wherefore says the Apostle, Eph. ii. 11. 'Remember that ye, being in time pas- 'sed Gentiles in the flesh,' &c. The promise of God's presence is to the broken and the contrite heart. A sensible, repenting frame of spirit is a blessed frame. 'Blessed are they that mourn.'

2. Another use of the prevalency of corrupt nature in the saints, is to divorce them from their own righteousness, and to flay carnal confidence in them all their life long. When sin appears sin, how precious is a perfect righteousness and an ordered covenant!

nant! How sweet is abundant mercy and reigning grace! 'Grace reigneth through righteousness;' and man is a proud creature. It is no little thing that will keep believers themselves humble. If Paul himself begins to be exalted, a thorn in the flesh is given him. Look to the fury and impetuosity of thy lusts in an unregenerate state, when thou beginnest to be lifted up. Know thy way in the valley, see what thou hast done. Yea, the daily workings of corruption in the best of saints are enough to keep them humble to the end of life.

3. It is to shew the suitableness of Christ as the believer's surety, and to stir us up unto more earnest believing every day. Art thou vile in thy nature? Look to him that is holy, infinitely holy and pure in his. In Christ thy surety there is no sin. In him our Apostle triumphs and glories, and in him only; 'I 'thank God, through Jesus Christ our Lord.' *He* thanks God to purpose for Christ, who daily improves him, and lives upon him, as his sanctification.

4. These workings of sin are of use to make us very watchful in our Christian walk. Where there is godly mourning, there will be godly fear; both are where there is a due apprehension of the sinfulness of that sin that dwelleth in us. No temptation should seem small to an heart so easily ensnared by sin. Great professors are liable to great backslidings and falls, when they are off their guard but a little while. 'Take heed, brethren, lest there be in any 'of you an evil heart of unbelief, in departing from 'the living God.'

USES.—1. Is there so much sin in us? Let this silence all murmurings and complaints against God, under the burden of our afflictions. We are punished less than our iniquities deserve. Do thy trials come on thee soon; look upon sin, blame that. By sin came death, and all the pains, griefs and miseries, that lead to it.

2. Is the sin of our nature so exceeding sinful? then let the youngest lay it to heart. Thou hast, it may

may be, been kept from grofs outward fins; a fpecial blefling; reftraining grace can never be valued enough, next to faving grace. But the plague-fore is within. Has the fin of thy nature brought thee with tears to Chrift? If not, thou mayft be undone notwithftanding. A Chrift is provided for none but fuch as fee themfelves loft. Do not put outward privileges in the room of regenerating grace. Thefe are encouragements to come to Chrift, but not to be put in the room of him. You are not too young to be finners, therefore not too young to need a Saviour.

3. Does fin by the law become exceeding finful? Then the law is a blefling, as well as the gofpel. The one fhews what the difeafe is, the other directs to the only remedy. The one tells thee, how thou are become dead; the other, by what means thou mayft be made alive. The law is a fchoolmafter to bring to Chrift. Though it denounces death and wrath, it is with a defign to lead and guide into the way of righteoufnefs and life. In the gofpel is the righteoufnefs of God revealed. That opens the way of pardon, but the law convinces more of the need of it.

4. See the wifdom of God in making the greateft contraries work together for his peoples good. Even the working of fin in the regenerate, is a means of quickening their truft upon Chrift, and their life in him.—' Was then that which is good made death
' unto me? God forbid. But fin, that it might ap-
' pear fin, working death in me by that which is
' good; that fin, by the commandment, might be-
' come exceeding finful.'

SERMON II.

EVANGELICAL REPENTANCE.

Jer. xxxi. 19.

Surely after that I was turned, I repented; and after that I was instructed, I smote upon my thigh: I was ashamed, yea, even confounded, because I did bear the reproach of my youth.

THESE words refer to the children of Israel as a nation, the subject-matter of this chapter being first spoken for their comfort in their exile state. But they must not be confined to them, or to the Jewish dispensation. 'Whatsoever things were written a-'foretime, were written for our learning, that we 'through patience and comfort of the scriptures 'might have hope,' Rom. xv. 4. The *Old Testament* is as much the word of God as the *New*, and no part of the inspired writings is of private interpretation, since the whole is left upon record, 'that it may be 'profitable for doctrine, for reproof, for correction, 'for instruction in righteousness,' 2 Tim. iii. 16. So far therefore as our circumstances, cases, and conditions, are alike to theirs, which are spoken of under that dispensation, so far may we justly apply the word to ourselves, which was delivered by God to them.

them. Applying this general rule to the words before us, they prefent us with a very juft and beautiful account of the difference which there is in man, in his converted ftate, to what he was before the grace of God had reached his heart. The language of every fincere penitent is the fame wherein Ephraim is reprefented as bemoaning himfelf, in the verfe before my text: 'Thou haft chaftifed me, and I was 'chaftifed, as a bullock unaccuftomed to the yoke: 'turn thou me, and I fhall be turned; for thou art 'the Lord my God.' Thefe words are very moving and emphatical; and plainly do they fhew us, how ineffectual is all the moral fuafion in the world, to bring a foul to Chrift, without the powerful operations of the bleffed Spirit. We flight his promifes, difregard his threatenings, and remain ftupid and fecure even under his afflicting hand, till the day-fpring from on high vifits us, Luke i. 78. "Thou haft "chaftifed me, (faith Ephraim), and I was chaftifed; "but I continued, notwithftanding this, an undaunt- "ed heifer, and behaved under it as a bullock un- "accuftomed to the yoke, till I was enabled by the "bleffed Spirit to cry out with my whole heart, "Turn thou me, and I fhall be turned, for thou art "the Lord my God: I defire none other but thy- "felf." Then follow the words of our text: 'Sure- 'ly, after that I was turned, I repented,' &c.

The eafieft method I can take, is to divide the text into the three following general heads.

> I. We may fee, in Ephraim's pathetic language, the way and manner wherein true grace at firft difcovers itfelf in the man that is born of God. 'I repented.'
>
> II. We are taught the only fpring from whence the amazing change always proceeds. 'Sure- 'ly, after that I was turned, I repented,' &c.
>
> III. We

III. We have further an account of the progress of the *work*, in the hand of the Spirit; wherein the true nature of repentance unto life is particularly described: 'After that I was 'instructed, I smote upon my thigh; I was 'ashamed, yea, even confounded, because I 'did bear the reproach of my youth.'

I. The first thing observable in these words, is the constant way and manner wherein true grace discovers itself, when once it is implanted in the heart: 'I repented, (says Ephraim) surely I repented.' Agreeable to this is the language of the prodigal, Luke xv. 18. 'I will arise, and go to my Father.' Old things are passed away with the man that is born of the Spirit; his change of state is soon made to appear by his change of temper and action: Sin ceases to be the object of his delight; he cannot contentedly dwell with the workers of iniquity; his face is turned Zionward, and his eager steps show how desirable and delightful are *Wisdom's ways* to his renewed soul. The man (as our Saviour expresses it, Luke xv. 17.) is *come to himself*. The image of God is stamped upon his soul; his law is written in his heart; and therefore he cleaves to the Lord with stedfastness, and runs the ways of his commandments, Acts xi. 23. compared with Psal. cxix. 32. Former lusts are lamented over; he is ashamed of the reproach of his youth, and he flies from the temptations of Satan, and the corruptions of his own heart, desirous for ever to have done with sin, and to keep at perpetual distance from all iniquity. 'What 'have I to do any more with idols?' are the words, not of returning Ephraim only, but of every regenerate man in the world, as soon as ever he receives the welcome news of peace and pardon, and tastes the sweetness of that grand promise of the covenant of grace, 'I will be merciful to their unrighteous'ness, and their sins and their iniquities will I re'member no more,' Hos. xiv. 8. compared with

Heb.

Heb. viii. 12. He repents, and would gladly call back again his paſt actions, had he but a power of mending them. He ſmites upon his thigh, as being thoroughly ſenſible, that he has gone too far in ſo vicious a courſe, continued too long at a diſtance from God and the ways of righteouſneſs; laying hold, at the ſame time, of the promiſes of free grace, which the Spirit, as the glorifier of Jeſus, communicates to him, in the day of his eſpouſals. Thus, true grace at firſt diſcovers itſelf. I go on now to conſider,

II. The only ſpring from whence this amazing change doth always proceed: 'Surely, after that I 'was turned, I repented.' Grace firſt enters the heart, before it can be diſcovered in the life and converſation. The God of all grace firſt of all *draws* us, or elſe we ſhall never move towards him. John vi. 44. 'No man can come unto me, except the Father 'who hath ſent me draw him.' We have neither ability nor will to repair to the bleſſed Jeſus; nor do we ſee ourſelves in need of a Saviour, till the eyes of our underſtanding are opened. Great darkneſs is fallen upon our eyes; a double veil is drawn over our hearts; and who but the mighty God can cauſe light to ariſe unto them that ſit in darkneſs and in the region of the ſhadow of death? This he claims as his peculiar honour, his ſole prerogative; and we who believe will readily acknowledge, 'that God, 'who commanded the light to ſhine out of darkneſs, 'hath ſhined in our hearts, to give the light of the 'knowledge of the glory of God in the face of Je- 'ſus Chriſt.' 2 Cor. iv. 6. We ſhould never elſe have known ourſelves, our ſins, or Chriſt Jeſus the great atonement; we ſhould never elſe have been led into our own hearts, or the purity and ſpirituality of the divine law, whereby the offence came to abound, and ſin to appear in its proper light and colours, as exceeding ſinful, Rom. vii. 9. 13. Converted we may be through grace; but convert ourſelves we cannot, for the way of man is not in himſelf, Jer. x. 23.

There

There may be a change in some outward actions, where a principle of life and grace is wanting in the heart; and legal convictions there may be, and often are, to a very high degree, in a sinner, where saving faith is not implanted; but the end of these things sufficiently declares the partiality and unsoundness of their first beginning; for as the Apostle saith in another case, Rom. vi. 21. ' the end of these ' things is death.' Terror and despair on one hand, or presumption and carnal security on the other, are the constant attendants of all legal convictions; and that alone is the repentance which is not to be repented of, which begins with a thorough change of heart. This the Apostle lays down as the ground of our future obedience; and the way in which discriminating grace at first discovered itself in the day of our effectual calling, Eph. ii. 1. ' And you hath he ' quickened who were dead in trespasses and sins.' Had not the same mighty power which he wrought in Christ, when he raised him from the dead, been exerted toward us, we should still have continued in the same conversation which we had in times past, in the lusts of our flesh, fulfilling the desires of the flesh and of the mind. Our *love* of sin would still have remained, though we might have abstained, through the influence of some lower motives, from the *grosser acts* of sin. But quickening grace opens the way to godly sorrow, and this always issues in evangelical repentance, 2 Cor. vii. 10. Surely after that I was turned, I repented. This leads,

III. To a more particular consideration of these words, as containing an account of the progress of this great work in the hand of the Spirit; wherein the true nature of repentance unto life is clearly described.

Here it is necessary to enquire,

(1.) What are the things, in which the soul is instructed by the Spirit; when once a principle of grace is wrought in the heart?

B   (2.) What

(2.) What are the various actings of the soul, in consequence hereof?

1. What are the things in which the soul is instructed by the Spirit, when a principle of grace is wrought in the heart?

This work of the Spirit usually begins with leading the soul into the knowledge of sin; after which he instructs him in the nature of pardoning grace and mercy: Under both of these heads a few particulars are necessary.

First, The Spirit begins his work, with leading the soul to the knowledge of sin: And this in three things.

1. The Spirit shews us the nature of sin, as attended with guilt, whereby we are obnoxious to the curse of the law. So long as we are ignorant of God's righteousness, we go about to establish our own righteousness, Rom. x. 3. Nothing formidable appears in sin; nothing faulty in our vain attempts to wash it away; even our *own* iniquity is a little transgression, and with Ephraim we conclude, that in all our labours he shall find none *iniquity* in us that were *sin*, Hos. xii. 8. Till the Spirit takes the work into his own hands, and lays down the strait rule of truth to our actions, causing our eyes to behold our errors; till he presents Sinai's covenant to our view, attended with the blackness, and darkness, and tempest, with which it was at first promulgated, Heb. xii. 18. Sin will never revive till the commandment comes, Rom. vii. 9. but then we die at once; our hopes vanish, and all our expectations of pardon and life, by our own obedience, fall to the ground. Then we see that it is an *evil thing*, and *bitter*, that we have forsaken the Lord our God, Jer. ii. 19. and know to our sorrow and amazement, what is the just demerit of our many abominations. Indignation and wrath hang over our heads; tribulation and anguish are already begun in our souls; hell does oftentimes fly, as it were, in the face of the awakened sinner, and the terrors of the Lord make him afraid. The curse

curse of the law is continually founding in his ears, and the bottomless pit seems ready opened to destroy him. The guilt of sin, as exposing to wrath and punishment, the Spirit leads the soul first into the knowledge of.

2. The Spirit shews the sinner the defiling nature of sin, as opposed to the holiness of that God with whom he hath to do. As attended with guilt, sin is the object of our fear; as attended with filth, pollution, and defilement, it is the object of our shame. An almost Christian sees sin in the first light, but the man who is altogether such, is the only person that can behold it in the second. We may dread the punishment of sin from God, and be afraid of the *shame of our sins*, should they be known to men; but to *hate* sin, as offensive to the pure eyes of infinite holiness, to loath it, because it is the abominable thing which his soul hateth, this is an attainment which only the renewed soul arrives at. Cain was afraid lest every one that met him should take vengeance upon him for his sin. ' *My punishment is greater* ' than I can bear,' was his constant complaint, and his only concern. But David says, ' wash me tho-' roughly from mine iniquity, and cleanse me from ' my sin,' Psal. li. 2. And Job breaks forth, ' I ab-' hor myself, and repent in dust and ashes,' Job xlii. 6. And to whom God gives a new heart and a right spirit, it is said, they shall remember their own evil ways, and their doings which were not good, and shall *lothe* themselves in ' their own sight, for their ' iniquities, and for their abominations,' Ezek. xxxvi. 31. We never take a view of the holiness of God with a spiritual eye, but we always immediately reflect upon ourselves with shame and confusion of face. Thus it was with the prophet Isaiah, ch. vi. 5. ' Then said I, Wo is me, for I am undone (a man ' cut off) because I am a man of unclean lips, &c. ' for mine eyes have seen the King, the Lord of ' hosts.' The Spirit leads us by the word into a thorough sight of the defiling nature of sin.

3. The Spirit shews the sinner the many heinous aggravations wherewith his sins in particular have been attended. The word of the Lord is a discerner of the thoughts and intents of the heart, Heb. iv. 12. It searches all the inward parts of the belly, Prov. xviii. 20. and unrips the many secret cavities wherein our abominations have been concealed, the brooding-place of sin, where all our vileness hath been hatched, and every lust conceived: And 'Thou 'art the man,' is the awful sentence which every convinced sinner hears and feels, before he turns to the strong-hold as a prisoner of hope. The Spirit thus shews us the plague of our own hearts; and how sad is the sight! how affecting the prospect! when we have no view of the blood of Jesus, or that propitiation which he hath made for the sins of his people. But praised be his name! and adored be the exceeding riches of his grace! the Spirit doth not leave the soul here in this forlorn bewildered state; no, he takes him further, and instructs him.

Secondly, The Spirit instructs the soul in the nature of pardoning grace and mercy, which is the sweetest sound that an awakened conscience can ever hear; the most agreeable message a self-condemning sinner can ever receive. Concerning this,

1. The Spirit instructs the sinner, that the privilege is attainable; that there is forgiveness with God, that he may be feared. Some promise is the soul directed to; some example of sovereign grace appears in his view; or he makes all his goodness to pass before him, proclaiming in the most reviving language, ' The Lord, the Lord God, merciful and ' gracious, long-suffering, and abundant in goodness ' and truth; keeping mercy for thousands, forgiving ' iniquity, and transgression, and sin,' &c. Exodus, xxxiv. 6, 7.

2. The Spirit instructs the sinner in the only way though which his grace and mercy is to be attained; lets him know, that an absolute God is a consuming fire; and directs him to Christ Jesus, who is

the

the way, the truth, and the life. The Spirit is, for this reason, said to glorify Chrift, John xvi. 14. becaufe he takes of Chrift's things, and fhews them unto thofe for whom he died: Of him he always teftifies, chap. xv. 26. and to him he ever leads the returning finner: It is through this man is preached unto you the forgivenefs of fins, Acts xiii. 38. The righteoufnefs we need is already wrought out; our pardon is bought, our reconciliation is procured; Chrift is our peace: This the Spirit fhews, when we are led to the Father by him.

3. The Spirit inftructs the finner into the way through which pardon is *communicated* to him. That it was obtained by Chrift; that it is received by *faith*; and that whofoever will, may take of the waters of life freely. This is the ufe of thofe many and exceeding precious promifes which are upon record in the gofpel; they are all defigned for the encouragement of faith. And let me tell thee, poor foul, that be thy faith but as a grain of muftard-feed, which, fays the Lord, is ' the leaft of all feeds,' Matt. xiii. 32. it fhall in no wife be defpifed; for faith God himfelf by the prophet, Zech. iv. 10. ' Who hath defpifed the day of fmall things?' Weak faith may lay hold of a ftrong Saviour; and a trembling hand often receives a whole Chrift, and pardoning grace and mercy from him. ' Thefe things' (faith the beloved difciple, John xx. 31.) ' are writ-
' ten that ye might believe that Jefus is the Chrift,
' the Son of God; and that believing ye might have
' life through his name.'

4. The Spirit further inftructs the finner, who the perfons are to whom this pardoning grace and mercy are applied. This he teaches, by the abfolute promifes of the word, which reach the cafe of the moft rebellious criminals. When the Redeemer of Ifrael afcended up on high, ' he led captivity
' captive, he received gifts for men, yea, for the re-
' bellious alfo,' Pfal. lxviii. 18. What an emphafis doth the Spirit lay upon that word, ' yea, for the re- ' bellious

'bellious also!' but not a greater than the poor sinner may pronounce it with; the good Lord help some poor soul at this time to lay hold of it! to put in for a share in so great mercy, so invaluable a blessing! Grace and glory were purchased for the chief of sinners; for this is a 'faithful saying, (a truth 'that may be depended upon), and worthy of all ac- 'ceptation, that Christ Jesus came into the world to 'save sinners, of whom I am chief; howbeit, for this 'cause I obtained mercy, that in me first Jesus 'Christ might shew forth all long-suffering, for a 'pattern to them which should hereafter believe on 'him to life everlasting,' 1 Tim. i. 15, 16. Is this a saying worthy of all acceptation? then carry this saying, and this example of grace, both of them to the throne of grace, and give him no rest who sits thereon, till he afresh verifies the one, and confirms the other. These things the Spirit never fails to instruct the man in, when once a principle of grace is wrought in the heart. These particulars I have had opportunity only to hint at; I trust the Spirit, who is the best teacher, will bring them to your remembrance, in your private thoughts, with double sweetness and enlargement. I am now to enquire,

2. What are the various actings of the soul in consequence of these instructions.

These lie all of them very plain in the text before me, 'After that I was instructed, I smote upon my 'thigh: I was ashamed, yea even confounded, be- 'cause I did bear the reproach of my youth.'

First, The soul thus instructed, 'sorrows after a 'godly sort.' This is the first thing in which gospel-repentance discovers itself to be genuine and of the right kind; of which 'smiting upon the thigh,' is very expressive. The phrase is used in another place, by which this passage may be justly explained: Ezek. xxi. 12. 'Cry and howl, son of man, for 'it (*i. e.* the sword of God's anger) shall be upon 'my people: it shall be upon all the princes of Is- 'rael; terrors by reason of the sword shall be upon
'my

'my people, smite therefore upon thy thigh:' "*i. e.* "Give a sign of thy sorrow, a token of thy grief; "that it may appear to others, that *you*, above all "men, are affected with the judgment of the Lord, "which is denounced against Jerusalem."—Sin, my friends, wounds the conscience; mercy and grace melts the heart; and no sooner doth the poor creature become sensible of the one as well as the other, but he becomes like 'new bottles, ready to burst,' Job xxxii. 19. Permit me to call over the former times wherein you were enlightened; how was it with you, when the 'day-spring from on high' visited you? when the Spirit first spoke peace and pardon to the guilty and rebellious? when the Lord addressed you in the language following my text, 'Is 'Ephraim my dear son? is he a pleasant child? for 'since I spake against him, I do earnestly remember 'him still: therefore my bowels are troubled for 'him; I will surely have mercy upon him, saith 'the Lord.' Look into *your* hearts, while I am giving you a description of *mine own*. Did you not then seek a corner, wherein you might hide yourselves from every one, save the great God to whom you made supplication? And how did you act before your offended but gracious Judge? Did not you 'smite upon your thigh,' standing amazed at the riches of his goodness, long-suffering and forbearance; and astonished at your ungrateful carriage, your most unworthy behaviour towards him? Say, poor hearts! whether you did not 'sorrow after a 'godly sort,' 2 Cor. vii. 9. It may be, your tears drowned your voice; but it was impossible they should spoil your prayers. Look but to the 9th verse of this chapter, and you may see your own picture, when you was thus prostrate at the throne of grace; 'They shall come with weeping, and 'with supplications will I lead them; I will cause 'them to walk by the rivers of waters in a straight 'way, wherein they shall not stumble; for I am a 'father to Israel, and Ephraim is my first-born.'

There was the grand occasion of Ephraim's bemoaning himself afterwards, because, saith the Lord, *ver.* 17. 'there is hope in thine end.' The first act of the soul after the Spirit's instruction, is his smiting upon his thigh, or sorrowing after a godly manner. *Secondly,* The soul thus instructed is filled with shame and confusion of face, attended with an utter hatred of the sins he hath been guilty of, 'I was ashamed, yea even confounded, because I did bear the reproach of my youth.' *Shame* is begotten in the soul, but it is of an ingenuous nature. The oftener and more intensely he looks upon the long and black score which grace hath forgiven him, the more is he ashamed, and the higher doth his just indignation against sin arise: an indignation against himself for what is past, and a vehement desire to keep clear of the like offences in his future course. 2 Cor. vii. 11. 'For behold, this self-same thing, 'that ye sorrowed after a godly sort, what careful-'ness it wrought in you, yea, what clearing of your-'selves, yea, what indignation, yea, what fear, yea, 'vehement desire, yea, what zeal, yea, what re-'venge! Lothing of yourselves, always follows admiring thoughts of the sovereign, matchless and distinguishing grace of God. The blood of Jesus is the best glass, wherein to see the filth and defilement of sin. And that man can never be said in gospel phrase to *repent,* who is unaffected with the love of a dying Saviour, or unconcerned at the purity and holiness of a sin-hating God. We shall never indeed smite upon our thighs, till God shews us, together with our sins, his own pardoning grace and mercy. There may be fear, but there will be no love, till we hear him saying, *ver.* 3. 'I have lo-'ved you with an everlasting love, therefore with lo-'ving kindness have I drawn you.' And is this, poor soul, the real matter of thy experience? you may then conclude that Jesus, whom God hath exalted to be a Prince and a Saviour, hath bestowed upon you repentance, with forgiveness of sins. 'That he
'hath

'hath granted unto you repentance unto life,' Acts v. 31. compared with Acts xi. 18.

Thirdly, The soul thus instructed, hath an *abiding* sense of these things. He is not weary of his rags to-day, and pleased with them again to-morrow; humbled for sin now, and wallowing in the same mire and dirt anon: No, 'I did bear (faith E-'phraim) the reproach of my youth.' "Wherever "I went, I carried it along with me; my sin was "ever in my eyes, and mine iniquity was always "before me: I never thought the lighter of my sin, "for its being forgiven me; it was still as grievous, "as hateful and offensive in mine eyes as ever." Happy the souls whose hatred against sin continues; when the edge of their first desires, and the warmth of their first affections are lost! they, who can say at all times, "Lord, I cannot bear to offend thee, "howsoever thou mayest deal with me. I love thy "law, I love thine ordinances, I love thy ways, "though I cannot as often as I wish for, find the "place where my beloved feedeth, and where he "causeth his flocks to rest at noon, Cant. i. 7. Sin "is my burden, my complaint, and my greatest "grievance; though I still find a law in my mem-"bers warring against the law that is in my mind, "and bringing me into captivity to the law of "sin, which is in my members, Rom. vii. 23." This is the fruit of the Spirit's work in thy heart, and argues thy repentance to be genuine and sincere.

Fourthly, The soul thus instructed, is most sensibly affected with those sins to which he hath been most addicted. Heart sins are bewailed by the sincere Christian, and youthful transgressions are never forgotten by him. Our own iniquity is most carefully watched against, and most frequently confessed before God; this pricked us to the heart when first the law entered, and it wounds to the quick afterwards, both under the smiles of his love, and the hidings of his countenance. Ephraim's confession and

prayer

prayer every regenerate soul may join in, and often doth, only with a change of circumstance. Hos. xiv. 2, 3. 'Take away all iniquity, and receive us gra-
' ciously, so will we render the calves of our lips.
' Ashur shall not save us, we will not ride upon
' horses, neither will we say any more to the work
' of our hands, Ye are our gods.' Here he confesses and bewails the sin he had been addicted to, in the most particular and affectionate manner. I was a-shamed, yea even confounded, ' because I did bear
' the reproach of my youth.' This is the time when sins are usually most vigorous and lively. Blessed then are they who in their early part of life, are brought to see their own vileness, and the need they stand in of a Saviour! To be brought to Christ betimes, O! how desirable a thing is it! many sins are hereby prevented, which are often the great burden of old age; and what is still more pleasing, the good ways of God do then sustain no reproach upon our account.

I might add,

Fifthly, The soul thus instructed, always applieth to the blood of Christ for pardon. But this having been in some measure spoken to under a former head, and not expressly contained in the text, I shall wholly wave any enlargement; and conclude with mentioning three or four remarks upon the whole.

REMARK I. Repentance can never be a condition of the covenant of grace; seeing it is itself a blessing of the covenant; and a blessing owing wholly and alone to almighty power and grace. ' Surely
' after that I was turned, I repented.' It is strange we should be so fond of making conditions for ourselves, when we have not the least warrant from God so to do. But vain man would be wise; and in his natural state unwilling to be saved merely upon the footing of grace.

REMARK II. What a mighty change doth grace work in the soul. ' Old things pass away, *and* all
' things become new:' The ruins of the fall are not

repaired

repaired only by Chrift; but the old foundation is wholly removed, and a new one is laid, in which grace alone bears the glory.

REMARK III. See, believer, what doctrines make moft for your encouragement at firft, and for your comfort and fupport afterwards. Hope that maketh not afhamed, can proceed only from Chrift Jefus, who is our hope. And every doctrine which leads not to him, either directly or by confequence, always damps our hopes, mars our peace, and fpoils our comfort.

REMARK IV. We muft look to the fame power and grace that laid the foundation, to rear the fuperftructure and finifh the building. Repentance is a daily work; and we have as much need to fay every day, as we had at our firft fetting our faces Zion-ward, ' Turn thou me, and I fhall be turned, ' for thou art the Lord my God.' The text holds always true; may we be led daily further into the fweetnefs and comprehenfive fulnefs of it. ' Surely ' after that I was turned, I repented; and after that ' I was inftructed, I fmote upon my thigh : I was a-' fhamed, yea even confounded, becaufe I did bear ' the reproach of my youth.'

But I add no more.

SERMON III.

CHRIST THE COVENANT OF HIS PEOPLE.

Isaiah xlix. 8.

—I will preserve thee, and give thee for a covenant of the people.—

IN this chapter we have an account of that everlasting covenant which passed between the Father and the Son, touching the recovery and salvation of lost man. This, as it lies at the foundation of all that grace and mercy elect sinners receive in time, both in their regeneration, calling, adoption and glorification, is necessary to be first considered, before we take a view of the blessings themselves. Christ's dying *for them that were without strength*, in time, depended upon some covenant-settlement and agreement which there was about it in eternity. Therefore God the Father is called in the verse before my text, ' the Redeemer of Israel, and his Ho-
' ly One,' long before the Mediator appeared in the flesh; because the plan of redemption was then laid, and he had sworn by his holiness that whatever was promised our Surety, should be performed. Though despised of man, in his humbled state, abhorred of his own nation, yea a servant of rulers; the day
should

should come when kings should see and arise, princes also should worship: A faithful God would give him the heathen for his inheritance, and the uttermost part of the earth for his possession. 'Thus 'saith the Lord, in an acceptable time have I heard 'thee, and in the day of salvation have I helped 'thee; and I will preserve thee, and give thee for a 'covenant of the people.' That is, "I see beforehand the greatness of thy work, and the need "thou wilt stand in of immediate succours from "heaven, in the faithful discharge of it; but the "time of thy help is fixed; thou shalt no sooner "call, than I will hear; salvation is prepared, and "laid by, ready for thee. I will preserve thee, and "give thee a covenant of the people. I consider "thee as the representing head of all mine elect; I "covenant with thee for them: and as such I de- "liver into thy hands for them all covenant-bles- "sings." Christ is called in our text *the covenant*, not barely because the covenant was made with him on behalf of the elect, but also because the Father designed and set him apart, as well to apply redemption as to obtain it. As he was to have the burden of purchasing promised benefits for sinners; he is to have the honour of distributing and conferring them also: for so it follows, 'I will give thee 'for a covenant of the people, to establish the earth, 'to cause to inherit desolate heritages; that thou 'mayst say to the prisoners, Go forth; to them that 'are in darkness, Shew yourselves.'

In discoursing on these words I shall shew,

I. What this covenant touching man's redemption is.
II. That such a covenant hath passed between the Father and the Son before all worlds.
III. Who the people are, for whom Christ was given to be a covenant.
IV. What are the blessings redounding to the people by this covenant. And so,
V. Apply.

I.

I. I am to consider what this covenant touching man's redemption is. A covenant, in the general acceptation of the word, is an agreement between two parties in any thing, or end, upon certain articles or conditions, which both freely consent to.— Thus it is said of Abraham and Abimelech, that they two made a covenant at Beersheba, Gen. xxi. 32. that is, they entered into a league, or voluntary agreement one with another, to maintain each other's properties, and to see that no one did the other any wrong. Sometimes this was done by swearing in the name of the Lord; as in the case of Jonathan and David, 1 Sam. xx. 42. wherein a solemn appeal was made to God, that he should avenge all insincerity and double dealing, if any should be found in either of the parties. At other times it was done by sacrifice, wherein the beast was cut asunder, and the covenanting parties went between the halves, to signify their wish or imprecation that they might be served as those slain beasts were, if either of them broke the covenant which they made. Thus, Jer. xxxiv. 18. This is the idea of a covenant between man and man: any agreement wherein a proposal is made, upon certain terms and conditions which both parties freely consent to, is called *a covenant.* As when we hire a servant, such and such work we require to be done by him, and for his work we engage to give such and such wages: without the wages, we have no right to his service; without the service, he hath no demand upon us for wages. The thing is settled and agreed upon between both, and this makes it a covenant. Such is the nature of the covenant my text speaks of between God and Christ, JEHOVAH the Father, and JEHOVAH the Son: For, " what is the covenant of grace, " but an agreement between God the Father and " Christ, upon the great concern of our salvation*?"

The

---

* Thus it is well explained in a book called, *Social Religion exemplified,* where there is the most plain, concise, scriptural account of this glorious transaction, that I remember to have met with. Dialogue V. page 29.

The covenant of *grace*, or as others call it, the covenant of *redemption*, is an eternal transaction between the Father and Christ; a consultation and agreement between these two glorious Persons, how man should be saved out of the ruins of the fall, in a way becoming God. Hence we read of the *counsel of peace* that should be between them both, Zech. vi. 13. Peace, reconciliation, and life, to sinful man, was the thing proposed; and it was a thing wisely contrived, therefore called *counsel*. This counsel of peace is said to have been between them both; because it was stipulated, and agreed to, on such and such terms between both the contracting parties. Mercy to lost sinners is shewn upon terms, articles and conditions, which were thus agreed to in eternity: Thus concerning the nature of the covenant. This leads to shew,

II. That such a covenant hath passed between the Father and the Son before all worlds; that such a transaction and agreement is subsisting between them on the sinner's account.

Three things are needful to prove this: That there were terms made, or work demanded; that there were promises given; and that there were mutual trusts between both the glorious Parties; for this covenant was an eternal transaction.

1. That there were terms made, or work demanded of the Mediator, which were plainly these four.

First, That Christ should take the name of his covenant-people upon himself, and become their representing head. This was the first requirement, to represent the persons, and bear all the names of elect sinners; and a great act of condescention in the Son of God it was. Accordingly we read of him, Prov. viii. 22, 23. 'The Lord possessed me in the 'beginning of his way, before his works of old. I 'was set up from everlasting, from the beginning, 'or ever the earth was.' " He pitched upon me in " his everlasting counsel, before creation-work be-
" gan,

"gan, to be the head of the covenant. I was his
"treasure, the only person fit for so glorious a trust."
Hence the Redeemer is called in Old Testament
language, *God's servant*, ver. 3. of Hezekiah: 'Thou
'art my servant, O Israel, in whom I will be glori-
'fied.' This is an address to Christ; and observe,
he is called by the name of those he represented; because he is considered as given 'for a covenant of the
'people.' Agreeable to this, in the New Testament,
he is called the second or last Adam, 1 Cor. xv. 45.
Hence our dying Mediator uses this plea with the
Father on their behalf; 'I pray for them: I pray
'not for the world, but for them which thou hast
'given me, for they are thine. And all mine are
'thine, and thine are mine, and I am glorified in
'them,' John xvii. 9.

Secondly, It was a term or demand upon Christ,
that he should become man. The nature that sinned must obey and suffer, that salvation might be
obtained in a way becoming God: The honour of
God's law, the rights of his justice, the glory of his
holiness and truth, could be secured no other way.
Hence we read concerning Christ, Psal. xl. 6, 7.
'Sacrifice and offering thou didst not desire, mine
'ears hast thou opened; (or, a body thou hast prepa-
'red me, Heb. x. 5.) then said I, lo, I come: In
'the volume of the book it is written of me, I delight
'to do thy will, O my God; yea, thy law is within
'my heart.' This therefore was proposed, this was
required by God the Father, and no sooner required,
than complied with; 'I delight to do thy will.'
Nay, he seems to think long till the day of his incarnation was fully come. His name was put down
according to covenant-agreement, and he was ready.
Again,

Thirdly, In this body Christ was to fulfil God's
whole law. Perfect righteousness though it cannot
be wrought out *by* us, it must be *for* us. The Surety
undertook for our debt of obedience, as well as suffering. Hence God is said to 'have laid help upon
'one

'one that is mighty,' Pfal. lxxxix. 19. One that could go through with the whole of Redemption-work: The Mediator's *ear was bored*, to fignify, that he agreed to perform the whole fervice, and that willingly, which was ' to be obedient even un-
' to death.'

Fourthly, It was a fpecial term of the covenant, that Chrift fhould feal all his obedience with his blood. This was a principal article in the everlafting covenant, and the hotteft fervice Chrift was to perform, and therefore particularly infifted on by the Father. Accordingly he faith, John x. 18. 'I ' lay down my life.—This commandment have I re-' ceived of my Father.' So in Ifa. liii. 10 · When ' thou fhalt make his foul an offering for fin, &c.' He confented in this everlafting covenant to be fin, and a curfe for his people. " I will be furety for " them; at my hands fhalt thou require them." In this view Chrift was ' a Lamb flain from the foun-' dation of the world.' Thefe are the terms of the covenant.

2. In this covenant there were promifes given. Chrift thus firmly and freely confenting, and binding himfelf to perform thefe terms and conditions required; in purfuance hereof the Father makes promifes to him. As,

Firfl, That he would fit Chrift for his work. Ifa. xi. 1, 2. ' There fhall come forth a rod out of the ' ftem of Jeffe, and a branch fhall grow out of his ' roots. And the Spirit of the Lord fhall reft upon ' him, the fpirit of wifdom and underftanding, the ' fpirit of counfel and might, the fpirit of knowledge ' and of the fear of the Lord.' Chrift's human nature was a creature, and fo could not furnifh itfelf with needful gifts for this great undertaking. As united to the Godhead it was preferved from fin, but it was needful that there fhould be alfo conftant communications from the Spirit to preferve and uphold it, and fit it for the fervice to which it was called. Upon this account we read, John iii. 34. ' God
' giveth

'giveth not the spirit by measure unto him.' He needed not this as God, but as man. Hence, Psal. lxxxix. 20. God is said not only to have 'laid help *upon* him,' but to have put help *in* him; 'With my holy oil have I anointed him, with whom my hand shall be established.' "I have set him apart for my service, and filled him with my Spirit." 'He is anointed with the oil of gladness above his fellows,' Psal. xlv. 7. None ever had his work to do, none ever had his supply, to fit him for it: The phrase is taken from the custom of setting apart to the extraordinary offices of Prophets, Priests and Kings: Christ, as Mediator, was called to execute all three; and he was by this unction of the Spirit eminently fitted for every one.

Secondly, The Father promised to assist Christ in his work, Psal. lxxxix. 21, 22. 'With whom my hand shall be established, mine arm also shall not exact upon him, nor the son of wickedness affect him.' Satan had much to do *with* Christ, though he found nothing *in* him, John xiv. 30. He was tempted in the wilderness, and tempted on the cross; earth and hell were both set against him; but from God he received his commission, and from him he looked for protection and strength. Accordingly his human nature was supported by an invisible power; 'He was led by the Spirit into the wilderness to be tempted of the devil,' Matth. iv. 1. but he was not left there to be overcome by him; 'he suffered, being tempted,' Heb. ii. 18. but he never fell by any temptation; even when God's *hand and sword* awoke against him; *everlasting arms* were underneath him; neither force nor fraud could bring him to think hardly of his Father, or to make any stop in the work which God had given him to do. Here was a promise given, that there should be no exacting, nor any affliction, further than what was appointed before-hand, and provision made against it, in the everlasting covenant.

Thirdly,

Thirdly, The Father promised to carry Christ safely and honourably through his work. The work which he had begun he should certainly perform; God was ' at his right hand, so that he could not be moved,' Psal. xvi. 8. ' Behold my servant whom I ' uphold, mine elect in whom my soul delighteth; ' I have put my Spirit upon him.—He shall not fail, ' nor be discouraged, till he hath set judgment in ' the earth,' Isa. xlii. 1. 4. Upon this covenant-promise his eye was fixed, through the whole course of his obedience on earth, and to this he fled in the last article of it. When flesh failed, and spirits failed, his heart, his trust, and his hopes, were neither of them moved. See how he owns relation when the darkest cloud covered him; ' My God, my God, ' why hast thou forsaken me?' Mat. xxvii. 46. I am thine still; thy son, thy servant, thy volunteer; ' mine ear hast thou opened;' why am I thus forsaken? But thou art holy, ' O thou that inhabitest the ' praises of Israel,' Psal. xx. 3. Thy covenant-promises fail not: ' Our fathers trusted in thee:' They trusted, and thou didst deliver them, *ver.* 4. ' I was ' cast upon thee from the womb;' I shall be upheld by thee still. Be not far from me, for ' trouble is near, ' for there is none to help,' *ver.* 10, 11. None other helper I need; none I crave; but help from thee I ask, I demand, I have. The blessed Jesus was not delivered from death, but he was strongly supported in dying. He pleaded the promise which God gave him in covenant, and found it sure. Of this he received the grant before, and he expected and had the fulfilment of it then: ' He shall cry ' unto me, Thou art my father, my God, and the ' rock of my salvation,' Psal. lxxxix. 26.

Fourthly, The Father promised Christ ' a seed to ' serve him;' and great glory after this his work was ended. Isa. liii. 10. ' When thou shalt make his ' soul an offering for sin, he shall see his seed, he ' shall prolong his days, and the pleasure of the ' Lord shall prosper in his hand. He shall see of the

'travail of his foul, and be satisfied, Pfal. cx. 3. 'Thy people fhall be willing in the day of thy 'power,' &c. A blefling this, which comes to him through the covenant, becaufe it was promifed him in it. Pfal. lxxxix. 28, 29. 'My mercy will I keep 'for him for evermore, and my covenant fhall ftand 'faft with him: His feed alfo will I make to endure 'for ever, and his throne as the days of heaven.' This was the 'joy that was fet before him,' for the fake of this 'he defpifed the fhame,' Heb. xii. 2. His children and he fhould one day fee their Father's face with joy, though from him it was awfully hid then. There were becoming wages annexed to this his work: After the crofs was to come the crown. He humbled himfelf, and 'God hath highly exalted 'him, and given him a name above every name,' Phil. ii. 9. There was a perfonal glory put upon Chrift; he ftands in the midft of the throne as 'the 'Lamb that had been flain;' all rule and authority is committed unto him as Mediator: He keeps the keys of hell and of death; and fits as an Advocate in the virtue of that blood which he fhed as a Redeemer. And then there is his glory as Head of his feed: Being given to him in covenant, they fhall be brought by him to take hold of the covenant, (as in the *Pfalm* before quoted, cx 3.) 'They fhall be 'willing:' They fhall be brought to bow before his fcepter; and there fhall be a numerous fucceffion of them; they fhall exceed the drops of morning dew. 'He fhall fee of the travail of his foul, and be fatis-'fied.' It is owing to thefe promifes of the covenant, that the church is built fo firm, that it ftands fo fure. It is the Redeemer's throne, and therefore 'it fhall abide as the days of heaven.' There fhall be a church where his name fhall be known; where his praifes fhall live fo long as there is a world; nay, when the world fhall be burnt up, the Redeemer's throne fhall flourifh ftill; 'mercy fhall be built up 'for ever;' it begins to take place in time, but it runs parallel with eternity. Oh! look for the mercy

cy of our Lord Jesus Christ, that mercy which was promised to him, that mercy which he lives to give you, unto eternal life!

These were the promises given in the covenant.

3. In this covenant there were mutual trusts which the glorious parties reposed in each other. God the Father trusted his Son that he would come in the fulness of time to do his will, in making good the articles of his redemption-work; upon the credit of this, all Old-Testament saints were saved, Rom. iii. 25, 26. God the Son trusts the Father, now the ransom is paid, that upon the condition hereof, he will justify and save all those that remain to be gathered in. Hence it is that the Father is called in this covenant, Israel's Redeemer, and ' his Holy ' One,' ver. 7. And in making it, is said ' to have ' sworn by his holiness' that he will not lie unto David, Psal. lxxxix. 35.

Well; these were the proposals Christ consented to; these were the promises given him in pursuance hereof, and these the mutual trusts between the Father and him: All these things taken together make it appear, that there was such a covenant, and on what account this covenant was entered into, wherein is all our salvation and all our desire. I go on to consider,

III. Who are the people for whom Christ was given as covenant. ' I will preserve thee, and give ' thee for a covenant of the people.' They are spoken of here indefinitely, but in other parts of the word of God, they are spoken of as a definite number, ' whose names are written in the Lamb's ' book of life,' Rev. xiii. 8. Christ took down their names, for whom he agreed in the covenant of life; a needless thing, if all men without exception have life by him. But such whom Christ undertook for, are called ' his seed, his children, his sheep, his own ' people,' formed for himself, in opposition to the whole world that lieth in wickedness. 'Those he intercedes for in heaven. 'And,' faith he, 'I pray for them, I pray not for the world,' John xvii. 9. Chrift covenanted for none in eternity, but fuch whom the Father undertook fhould believe on him in time. 'By his knowledge fhall my righteous fervant juftify many; for he fhall bear their iniquities,' Ifa. lxiii. 11. Would you know particularly who thefe were?

1. They are fuch as are brought to feek happinefs and life purely upon the footing of this covenant. 'This,' faith David with his dying breath, 'is all my falvation, and all my defire,' 2 Sam. xxiii. 5. Such are under grace. All their expectation and hopes are from God's covenant, not their own doings. Covenant-pardon, righteoufnefs, ftrength, fupports, comforts; on thefe their fouls live. God teaches them to renounce all other holds.

2. The 'Meffenger of the covenant' is their delight. Mal. iii. 1. 'The Lord whom ye feek fhall fuddenly come to his temple, even the Meffenger of the covenant, whom ye delight in.' God's chofen is their chofen too. They have ventured their fouls upon Chrift, they cleave to Chrift, they rejoice in Chrift, as the foundation, the fecurity, the life, yea, the all of the covenant. This is a good evidence of intereft in the covenant.

3. They are fuch as have the Spirit of the covenant in their hearts. You may judge whether you have this blefling three ways. Wherever the Spirit is given, he comes as a Spirit of grace and fupplication. Chrift's Father is our Father, and we go to him, in a way of faith and prayer, as fuch. Moreover, he is a Spirit of liberty: Such are alive to God. Though once darknefs, now they are light; though once enemies, now they are friends; though once bound, now they are free. Again, he is a Spirit of fanctification and holinefs. Where there is a living *on* the grace of the covenant, there will be a living *in* the duties of the covenant: 'I will put my Spirit within them, and they fhall keep my ftatutes, and do them,' Ezek. xxxvi. 27. This leads to confider,

IV. What are the blessings redounding to the people by this covenant.

First, By this their *calling* is secured. 'Thou 'shalt say to the prisoners, Go forth,' *ver.* 9. The day of our effectual calling, is the day of Christ's power. God remembers this holy covenant, whenever he quickens and draws a dead sinner to Christ. The price is paid, therefore God is but faithful and just to his Son, in setting the poor captive free.

Secondly, In virtue of this covenant, all grace is treasured up for *thee*, believer in Christ. Look to Jesus! the all of the covenant is comprehended in him; through him grace reigneth. There is your fulness, your stock, your riches. Improve Christ more, and your life will be more comfortable and fruitful.

Thirdly, All fellowship and communion with God is by virtue of this covenant. It is through Christ, as our covenant-representing head, that believers draw nigh to God, Heb. x 22.

Fourthly, In virtue of this covenant eternal life is given; Tit. i. 2. 'In hope of eternal life, which 'God that cannot lie, promised before the world be-'gan.' Thou hast nothing of thine own to plead; but thou mayst plead, 'Christ hath died.' The inheritance is purchased and promised, therefore it must be secure.

These are the blessings redounding to the people by this covenant. Which brings me,

V. To apply or make some uses, by way both of doctrine and practice.

Use I. Christ and his seed are comprehended in one and the same covenant. He was first chosen in order of nature, then *they* were considered and chosen in him; Christ as the head, they as the members; Christ as the root, they as the branches: He stands in the covenant not as a single person, but as the representative head, the common root of all his posterity: 'I have made a covenant with 'my chosen,' that 'mercy shall be built up for ever' for his seed, and my covenant shall be established with them, Psal. lxxxix. 2, 3, 4. The same covenant which is made with Christ as God's chosen is established with his seed. Not two different covenants, but one and the same covenant. For distinction's sake, divines have often considered that part of the covenant which relates to Christ, as undertaking to be our Mediator, performing the conditions, and receiving the special promises made to him, under the name and notion of the 'covenant of 'redemption:' The other part of the covenant, wherein we are considered as having an interest in the blessings purchased by him, they call the 'co-'venant of grace*.' But these conditions were performed by him as *our* surety, *our* kinsman-redeemer; and these promises which he received of the Father all redound to our temporal and everlasting advantage. By the blood of the same covenant he made satisfaction, and we obtain deliverance. 'As for 'thee also, by the blood of thy covenant, I have sent 'forth thy prisoners out of the pit wherein is no wa-'ter,' Zech. ix. 11.

Use 2. That which is a covenant of *grace* to us, is a covenant of *works* to Christ. We are justified purely by the Father's grace, but this was 'through 'the redemption which is in Christ Jesus,' Rom. iii. 24. He paid the price; we receive the reward: Christ's death was the means of our life. He obeyed for us, and suffered for us, or else we must have perished

---

* Upon different views this distinction is maintained by many, as Dr Owen, Mr Charnock, Mr Flavel, Mr Gillespie, &c. It is explained in a sense consistent with the perfections and grace of God. But by others it is made a foundation for God's entering into another covenant with us, whereof faith, repentance, and sincere obedience are made the terms. Our Assembly of Divines therefore considered them as one and the same covenant. "The "covenant of grace (say they) was made with Christ as the se-"cond *Adam*, and in him with all the elect as his seed." Larger Catechism, Quest. xxxi. This question is discussed with great accuracy and judgment in Dr Ridgley's Body of Divinity, Vol. I. p. 362.—373.

perished everlastingly in our sins. Christ received nothing by way of gift, but what he also obtained by way of purchase. By the sweat of his blood he obtained eternal redemption for us, and so 'entered 'into his own glory,' Luke xxiv. 26. 'Ought not 'Christ to have suffered these things, and to enter 'into glory?' There was a necessity for it; because he had consented thus to do in the everlasting covenant; and justice made no abatements, not in a single article. He earned his crown before he put it on. The covenant is a covenant of grace to us, but of works to him.

Use 3. Hence we learn the meaning of those phrases, wherein God is said to make *a covenant* with man. As Jer. xxxi. 31. 'I will, faith the Lord, 'make a new covenant with the house of Israel,' &c. and Isa. lii. 3. 'I will make an everlasting covenant 'with you, even the sure mercies of David.' These words evidently refer to the covenant in my text, which was made with Christ our representative-head. Now how can this covenant be made with us? We have nothing to give God which he hath not a right to demand; and whatever we have, we have received; and what he gives, surely he may require and call back again; on these accounts no covenant can properly speaking be entered into between God and man. But the plain meaning of such scriptures is this; either that God enables us by his Spirit and grace to lay hold on his covenant, to bottom all our hopes of salvation upon it, as Isa. lvi. 4. 'Thus 'faith the Lord, unto the eunuchs—that take hold 'of my covenant,' &c. or else they denote the absolute grant and free bestowment of special blessings upon us. God's covenant with us is a mere promise of absolute grace: thus Jer. xxxi. 33. 'This shall 'be the covenant that I will make with the house of 'Israel, After those days, faith the Lord, I will put 'my law in their inward parts, and write it in their 'hearts, and I will be their God, and they shall be 'my people—and they shall all know me, from the
'least

'leaft of them to the greateft of them, faith the Lord: for I will forgive their iniquity, and I will remember their fin no more.' So again, Ifaiah lix. 21. 'As for me, this is my covenant with them, faith the Lord, My fpirit that is upon thee, and my words which I have put in thy mouth, fhall not depart out of thy mouth, nor out of the mouth of thy feed, nor out of the mouth of thy feeds feed, faith the Lord, from henceforth and for ever.' Here is no condition; all is abfolute and free. No bargaining, no ftipulation or agreement on the creature's part; but it is a mere promife of abfolute grace to us and our feed. This is further confirmed by thofe fcriptures, where God's covenanting is applied to inanimate things: thus we read of his covenant of the *day* and *night*, Jer. xxxiii. 35. Here can be no compact or agreement, but there is an abfolute promife, that they fhall ever continue, to the end of time; and by it is the ftability of this covenant in my text illuftrated. In this fenfe, then, are we to underftand all thofe expreffions either in the Old or New Teftament which fpeak of God, as making a covenant with man.

Use 4. Hence we fee the ground of the falvation of Old-Teftament faints: They were juftified and faved upon the foot of this covenant. The compact was made, though the articles were not fulfilled. Chrift had not fhed his blood, yet 'through the blood of the covenant they were faved,' Zech. ix. 11. The reafon is this: God trufted Chrift, knowing him to be able and faithful; upon the perfonal credit of the glorious Mediator they were received up into glory. And now Chrift trufts the Father as to the reft of his elect, that they in due time fhall be brought to glory; for 'God is faithful who hath promifed.' This fhews us farther,

Use 5. That the fubftance of the covenant was the fame, under both teftaments; only the difpenfation of it varies. The covenant made with Abraham, Jacob, David, &c. was a covenant not of works

works, but of grace. 'I will be a God to thee and 'thy feed after thee,' is pure gospel, not law. Hence faith the apostle, Gal. iii. 8. 'The scripture 'foreseeing that God would justify the heathen 'through faith, preached before the gospel unto A-'braham, saying, In thee shall all nations be bles-'sed.' The way of God's revealing the grace of the covenant under the Old Testament, was in types, shadows, sacrifices, &c. which all pointed to Christ. Now it is in the word, ordinances, promises, &c. The covenant is one and the same, only the method varies.

USE 6. What hath been said shews, why Christ is called in the text *the covenant* of his people. It is because he is all in all in this covenant. To him the terms were proposed, with him the covenant was made; all the concerns of the covenant-people are committed to him; all the blessings that were promised are reposed in him; he is the Surety, Messenger, Prophet, Administrator, Head of the covenant. All grace and mercy comes through his hands. All rests upon Christ; he is the foundation, he bears up the pillars, he supports the whole building of mercy. To whom be glory in the church throughout all ages. Amen.

Two or three practical uses.

First, Admire the love and grace of this covenant: The love of the Father, that he should as it were consult about your salvation, and treat with his Son for you: And the love of Christ, that he should stick at no terms to redeem and save you. The love of both is a love which passeth knowledge.

Secondly, Look more at Christ in every covenant-blessing. Even common mercies have more of Christ in them than we see; our ease was bought by his pain, our comforts by his cross. Receive all blessings *in* Christ; you receive all *for* him.

Thirdly, This may be improved for the believer's comfort, whatever his wants are; it is a sure covenant, an ordered covenant, a full covenant; Christ is thy covenant, therefore in all thy dangers, weaknesses, snares, thou art safe: In all thy wants thou art provided for; in all thy fears thou art prevented. Of thee he asked life, thou didst freely give it, even length of days for ever. So long as Christ thy covenant lives, all will be well. He will ‘ guide thee ‘ with his counsel, and afterwards receive thee to ‘ glory.’

SERMON IV.

CHRIST THE SHEPHERD OF HIS PEOPLE.

ISAIAH xl. 11.

He shall feed his flock like a shepherd: He shall gather the lambs with his arm, and carry them in his bosom, and shall gently lead those that are with young.

IN these words are four things:

I. A description of the church, and people of God, for whom Christ undertakes, under the notion of a *flock*.
II. The character and relation Christ bears to them as such. He is their *shepherd*.
III. What he does for them as such. 'He shall 'feed his flock, like a shepherd.'
IV. How he does it: In a way which is suitable to every one's circumstances and condition.—Of each of these something shall be spoken, as it pleases God the Spirit to help.

I. A description of the church, and people of God, under the notion of a flock.—With respect to God they are called a flock, because they are separated

ted from the rest of mankind in his own eternal purpose, and given to the Lord Christ, to redeem, sanctify, and save them. A flock is a company of sheep, which is the property of some owner: a part of his goods, and substance, which are therefore left in trust with a person qualified to take care of them. The elect, though scattered up and down in the world, are gathered together in Christ: when or wheresoever they live in the world, they are equally given to Christ in the everlasting covenant; he took the charge of all, and will give it up another day with confidence and comfort—' Those that thou ' gavest me I have kept, and none of them is lost,' John xvii. 12.

With respect to the Lord Jesus, the church is called a flock; because he brings them into his fold; calls them out of a natural state, into a state of grace, and fellowship with himself: Rom. i. 6. ' Among ' whom ye are also the called of Jesus Christ.' He applies the fruit of his purchase, and death, and a new nature, John x. 9. ' I am the door, by me ' if any man enter in, he shall be saved, and shall go ' in and out, and find pasture.'

With respect to other men, among whom believers converse, they are called a flock upon a threefold account.

1. As they are helpless. What so feeble and helpless as poor sheep? if the owner takes no care of them, they are lost. Believers are God's heritage, and therefore exposed to the persecuting rage and malice of men. Look through all the ages of the world, and of the church, and you will find the people of God to have been a poor and an afflicted people. Their refuge is on high: Christ is their strength; if they have any quiet among the nations, it arises from him, who ruleth in the nations, or, who cutteth off the spirit of princes. ' Because they ' are not of the world, therefore the world hateth ' them.'

2. They are harmless. There is no evidence we are the sons of God, 'if we are not blameless, and 'harmless, without rebuke, Phil. ii. 15.—A sheep will take injuries; but it is not, like other cattle, prone to return them. Patience under contradiction and reproaches, Christ has taught us by his word and example. 'Anger resteth in the bosom of 'fools:' God takes us off from the very thought of vengeance, claiming that as his own prerogative: 'Vengeance belongeth unto me, I will recompence, 'saith the Lord;' and again, 'The Lord shall 'judge his people,' Heb. x. 30.

3. Sheep are useful, therefore the church is compared to a flock. Wherever a believer is, God's blessing goes along with him. Pharaoh's house was blessed for one Joseph. Paul, in the ship, was the security of all the crew. 'The holy seed is the sub- 'stance of the land,' Isa. vi. 13. The state, yea the whole world would fall to pieces, were it not for a few believers that are in it. Believers are a blessing by their prayers, and a blessing by their example. Whatever *others* do, when *they* act like themselves, they know that they have a generation-work to serve before they fall on sleep; and they are careful to fulfil it.

II. The relation Christ stands in to them, as a *shepherd.* Two things are implied in this relation; care and tenderness.

1. Christ's character as a shepherd, necessarily infers care. Thus Jacob speaks, in his appeal to Laban, whose sheep he kept: 'In the day the drought 'consumed, and the frost by night; and my sleep 'departed from mine eyes,' Gen. xxi. 40. And this is further intimated Psal. xxiii. 1. 'The Lord 'is my shepherd; I shall not want.'

Christ has his eye upon every believer's person, and upon all his wants. Whatever grace thou wantest, for temporals or spirituals, it is committed unto Christ. He has undertaken to keep thee in
all

all thy ways; to be thy guide to death, and thy guide through it. Thy times are all in his hands. Wherever thou art, Christ is, to uphold, if not to comfort thee. John was in Patmos; Jeremiah in the dungeon; the church in the wilderness; but neither of them were alone: Christ supported, fed, and comforted them. He waits to be gracious; 'and his eyes run to and fro through the earth, to 'shew himself strong.' 2 Chron. xvi. 9. It is a blessed word, that Christ sees with his own eyes, not another's, as kings and great men do; nor do these eyes of his walk, but *run*; wherever danger or distress is, there is he: all things in the earth are noticed by him; yea, 'the very hairs of thine head are all 'numbered:' they 'run to and fro,' to denote the diligence of providence; his care is repeated; he looks this way and that. His eyes are not confined to one place, or fixed upon one object; but are always moving about from one place to another: and his care engages his strength: He discovers thy dangers, to prevent them: Christ is wise to see, and strong to save. In darkness, as well as light, his eye is upon thee; when thou art favoured with his smiles, and discouraged by his frowns. The relation of a shepherd implies care.

2. It implies compassion and love. 'He shall 'feed his flock like a shepherd;' *i. e.* he will act towards them with the greatest tenderness, sympathy, and love. His grace comes freely, without grudging; and it is given to his poor necessitous members, without upbraiding. There is a *nevertheless*, with which the good shepherd helps, and saves, and restores his sheep, Psal. cvi. 8. 'nevertheless he saved 'them;' notwithstanding all their sin, unworthiness, provocation; yea, before they repented, or reformed; and that for his name's sake. Though we fail in our duty to Christ, he will not fail in his love to us. He does not always wait for our prayers, cries, or humblings, before he feeds, and chears, and delivers our souls; but does all with a sovereignty like
himself,

himself, for his name's sake. It is well for us, Christ does not always deal by us according to our own rules. The wandering, not the returning sheep, are restored; the needy are fed; the distressed are pitied; the lost found: why? but, because he feeds his flock like a shepherd. His own love is the rule of his acting towards us; not our desires, hungerings, thirstings. The poor sheep know not what their weakness or wants are: they cannot apply to the shepherd; but he goes to them and takes, and delivers his sheep, ' out of all the places where ' they have been scattered in the cloudy and dark ' day,' Ezek. xxxiv. 12. Care and tenderness are implied in the relation Christ bears to his people as a shepherd.

III. We are to consider what Christ does for his church and people as their shepherd: Or what are the branches of his pastoral work, wherein his care and tenderness are made to appear. ' He shall feed:' Feeding, as all agree, is a general word, whereby all is intended that is necessary to be done, for the safety and welfare of a flock: This may be branched out into several particulars, As,

1. Christ, as a shepherd, provides pasture for his church and people. There is no living without food: This Christ has provided for his sheep in rich abundance; and has also taken care, that they shall thrive by it. David expresses the language of every soul that is in health and prospers, Psal. xxiii. 2. ' He ' maketh me to lie down in green pastures, he feedeth ' me beside the still waters.' God's word, every line whereof Christ fills, is pasture, which cannot be eaten bare or burnt up. The more trying the dispensation, the sweeter the word. It was David's delight, else he had perished in his affliction. Go in and out; from public, to private duties, from the closet, or family, to the shop; and then again to the house of God; there is something suitable, and satisfying in God's word: Growth, comfort, reproof, guidance,

guidance, and every blessing the believer needs. So ordinances are pasture: Though mean in themselves, they are sweetly refreshing, when quickened and filled by the Spirit; 'I sat down under his shadow 'with great delight, and his fruit was sweet to my 'my taste,' Cant. ii. 3. The Spirit also, what a precious lecture does he read upon the providential dispensations of God towards ourselves or others, in the church, or the world? Whoever the Spirit has to deal with, he causes them to profit. Sometimes, our crosses become food, and our very tears prove like the spiced wine of the pomgranate. We must have lost our sweetest fellowship, had we been without some of our forest crosses. Mizar-comforts, abundantly recompenced to the penitent Mizar-trials, Psal. xlii. 6. As a shepherd Christ provides pasture for his church and people.

2. He protects against rapine. A good shepherd when he has led his sheep into green pasture, preserves them from the evils to which they are exposed in it. 'Thy servant,' says David, 'kept his father's 'sheep, and there came a lion, and a bear, and took 'a lamb out of the flock; and I went out after him, 'and smote him, and delivered it out of his mouth,' 1 Sam. xvii. 34. There is a lion in that very way, wherein Christ has appointed we should walk: Opposition from without, and from within. Inbred lusts endeavour to make a prey of us; and Satan the destroyer is never off the watch for us. In holy ordinances, are we free from sinful and unruly thoughts? even our very food, is it not poisoned by the corrupt doctrines of seducing teachers? The still waters of the sanctuary are muddied by the out-breakings of corrupt lusts. There are some who climb over the wall, to kill, and to steal, and to destroy. Whence is it any of us escape so many and so subtle enemies; but because we have protection from our good shepherd, 'who stands and rules in the strength of the 'Lord, in the majesty of the name of the Lord his 'God;' so that they who are ruled by him *shall a-*
bide,

bide, Micah v. 4. The whole kingdom of Satan, the strong holds of sin, the high imaginations, and all the strength, and malice of the world, sink before him. Every difficulty which lies in the way thou shalt break through: No; 'but thy king shall 'pass before thee, and the Lord at the head of thee,' Micah ii. 13.

3. As a shepherd Christ brings back them that are strayed. 'Thou restorest my soul,' Psal. xxiii. 3. Much of his tenderness and compassion lies in this: When believers go out of the way, Christ pities and reclaims them. Our infirmities Christ is touched with the feeling of: He cannot bear sin or Satan should worry us too long, and beyond what we are able. Though we fall into sin, the blessed Jesus will not suffer us to continue in it.

Peter was gone back many degrees, else he had not denied him with solemn oaths and imprecations; but a look from Jesus fetched him again. Christ will make thee more humble, watchful, holy and heavenly minded by those temptations which have been a wound to thyself, and a shock to others.

4. Christ, as his peoples shepherd, heals the diseased. 'The diseased have ye not yet strengthened, 'nor healed that which was sick,' is his charge against careless shepherds, Ezek. xxxiv. 4. We have many infirmities, more than we know of: pride, worldliness, vanity of thoughts, looseness of conversation, neglect of ordinances; these Christ heals, besides those wounds, the scars whereof will be carried to our graves, which have been gotten by presumptuous sins. Oh! the love of Christ, were it but duly considered! His holy soul hates every sin; it is an abomination, a wound to him: his sheep are full of sores of this kind, yet he bears with them, binds them up, and heals them with his own hand, and keeps from those sins for which no provision is made in the everlasting covenant. I come now to consider,

4. The

4. The way in which this is done suitably to every one's circumstances and condition. 'He shall 'gather the lambs,' &c.

1. Christ's carriage towards his flock, is according to their ages. Some are babes in Christ; some young men; some fathers; considering them members of gospel churches, of which Christ is the head: View them as constituting the flock, over which he is shepherd, some are sheep, others lambs. Is there any place in his heart tenderer than others, his lambs shall be laid there: A poor lamb is not thrust on with the same speed grown sheep are: No; the shepherd clasps his arms round it, and lays it for the sake of warmth in his bosom: Thus Christ deals with his little ones. Young Timothy was not exposed to those trials at his first setting out into the ministry, like Paul the aged. Christ's yoke is lined with love: It is said of the child Samuel, 'that he 'grew, and the Lord was with him,' 1 Sam. iii. 19. Let none be afraid of making too early a choice of Christ: You cannot be under his rule and government too soon. Wisdom's ways 'are ways of plea-'santness.' Christ deals by young converts, as God did by the children of Israel in the wilderness; he would not lead them through the lands of the Philistines, lest they should see war, and their hearts be discouraged because of the way. Often they have a sweeter relish of the promises, greater enlargement in ordinances, more sensible conquests over their spiritual enemies, than believers of longer standing in Christ.

2. It is according to their strength, or weakness. Such as cannot walk shall be carried; and they that are heavy laden shall be gently led. Comfort yourselves with this, none of the flock shall be left behind. Some may be sheep as to their standing; yet weak as to circumstance and condition. Long and sore outward trials bow down the soul; sharp and frequent assaults from Satan, drink up the spirits: To walk in darkness under apprehensions of God's wrath,

wrath, brings weariness and fainting. Now, Christ suits his grace to such according to their needs. Every grace is given to be tried; none to be overborn. Usually when creatures frown, our Jesus smiles. If the conflict between flesh and spirit be sharp, the conquest is sweet. 'Light cometh in the 'morning,' after a night of great darkness, affliction, and sorrow. One view of Christ's heart, and the secret of his love, reconciles to all past sufferings, temptations, and trials. Thy God will not chasten thee beyond thy strength. That soul can never sink, under whom everlasting arms are. A weak believer is strong when held in Christ's arms, and comfortable when lying in Christ's bosom.

3. It is according to the difficulties or dangers his sheep are in. The bosom is a place of safety, as well as of endearment: This supposes danger. Many of our dangers are imaginary, not real: We cry for grace and comfort, rather for a future store, than for our present use. The promise from which Christ seldom varies, runs thus, 'As thy days, so shall thy 'strength be,' Deut. xxxiii. 25. till thou art called to rough and tedious ways wherein thou canst not walk, before thou expectest to be carried with the lambs, or led with those that are with young. When tribulations abound *for* Christ, thy consolations shall abound *by* him.

USE 1. This doctrine affords a just word of reproof to those who are shepherds under Christ, but act not according to his example towards the flock they are appointed to feed. Knowledge of the state of the flock, is one great, though much neglected branch of a pastor's office.

2. How should souls long to be under the care of this good shepherd? You are exposed to wolves and devils, to all errors and sin, whilst you keep off from Christ; there is no safety for you, but only in his arms; no provision but in his covenant. You may try the husks of sensual pleasures, and creature comforts; but they are not bread. 'I am the bread of 'life.'

'life.' Till you come into Christ's fold, you lie exposed to all danger.

3. How safe are all the saints! None of Christ's sheep shall perish. Though in the wilderness, they shall have safe conduct through it. Christ is with them in every danger, and in every fear. Sheep are not left to graze, and feed by themselves. Thou art weak, but Christ is strong. 'He has received a commandment to save thee, and his own heart is in it. If reconciled, and brought home by his death; much more being reconciled we shall be saved by his life.

4. What a blessed plea is here for the church in dangerous times. Christ will spare his flock, and the land for their sake. If the owner is regardless of them, who should be concerned for them? 'He 'shall feed his flock like a shepherd;' that is plea sufficient. Others may be bent upon ruin, but Christ is exalted to save: 'Say ye to the cities of Zion, Be-'hold your God.'

5. With what boldness may the people of Christ attend upon all holy ordinances. They are designed for your support, till you get above them. 'Fear 'not, little flock, it is your Father's good pleasure to 'give you the kingdom:' Eternal life at last insures every needed blessing by the way. Therefore you may sing with the Psalmist, 'The Lord is my shep-'herd, I shall not want.'

SERMON V.

GOD THE JUDGE OF ALL.

HEB. xii. 23.

And to God the Judge of all.

THESE words at first reading strike terror. It is an awful thing for a sinful creature to appear before 'God the judge of all:' But in Christ Jesus this God is a reconciled God, and so is 'the justifier of all them that believe:' Thus considered, they speak comfort. With this view our apostle mentions them in the text, as bearing a large share in those special privileges which the saints under the New Testament are admitted unto. And with this view I have read them, for the subject of your present meditations: That we may know at what door, more especially, our peace and comfort, and all holy fellowship cometh in; namely, by coming to, and conversing with God, as 'judge of all.'

I shall take up as little of your time as may be, in shewing the connection of these words, or explaining those other privileges which they are here connected with.

It is plain our apostle is comparing the dispensation of the law, with that of the gospel. The giving of the law was attended with 'fire and blackness, and darkness, and tempest,' ver. 18. by which is signified that dread and terror which fills the soul, when conscience is under the arrest of a broken law. There is no enduring that which is commanded. Moses himself 'exceedingly fears and quakes,' ver. 21. The best and holiest saint cannot stand when God marks iniquity. Not that we are to think of Old-Testament saints, that they sought righteousness by the works of the law, or that they were in such a state of bondage and fear, as not to know how this righteousness was to be attained. The law itself was sprinkled with blood, Heb. ix. 19. called therefore the book of the covenant, which the Lord made with them, Exod. xxiv. 8. How often do we hear David making mention of God's righteousness, and that only, Psal. lxxi. 16. pleading pardon on account of it, Psal. li. 1. 14. and expecting to behold God's face in it, at death and judgment, Psal. xvii. 15. Ethan repeats the covenant wherein it was agreed it should be wrought out, Psal. lxxxix. 19. The like may be said of all the Old-Testament prophets and saints. When therefore the present gospel-dispensation is compared with that of the law, it must not be supposed, that believers then were in absolute want of the privileges which we now enjoy; who then could have been saved? but the revelation of these things to believers in common, was not so clear; all types and figures are now done away, so that we under the gospel have not the *shadow* of good things to come, but the very *image* of the things, Heb. x. 1. Amongst these good things this is one of the sweetest and most comprehensive, that 'we are come to God the judge of all.'

In these words are three things.

First, A glorious character by which the great God is described. He is 'the judge of all.' Of all persons and things. Not only a future, but a present judge.

Secondly,

Secondly, There is the interest and favour believers have with this judge. 'Ye are come'—to 'God the 'judge of all.' Coming implies freedom, familiarity and comfort, either in the soul's first approach to God, or in his converse with him afterwards. Thus, Heb. iv. 16. and *chap.* x. 19. believers under the present gospel-state, are *come* to God the judge of all, in opposition to the distance there was, when the law was given: The mount was then railed in, &c. We stand not as they of old, 'without the vail,' but are admitted to look in.

Thirdly, We have intimated, the great and glorious privilege which there is in such converse and fellowship: 'Ye are not come to the mount that 'might be touched, and that burned with fire; but 'ye are come to mount Zion, and unto the city of 'the living God; and unto God the judge of all.'

These heads may be comprised in this one doctrine.

DOCT.—It is one of the choicest and sweetest privileges believers are favoured with, under the gospel-state, that they may have access to, and comfortable converse with God the judge of all.

In discoursing on this doctrine, I will endeavour, as the Lord shall help me, to do four things;

I. Shew, that it is an awful, though a comfortable thing to converse with God the judge of all.
II. How such a converse is begun, between a holy God and *guilty sinners*.
III. In what instances, and by what methods, it is maintained and carried on.
IV. Wherein the privilege of such a converse does consist. And so,
V. Apply.

I. I am to shew, that it is a very awful, though a comfortable thing, to converse with God the judge of all.

Calvin

Calvin thinks this the design of the words, to give a check to believers spirits, which in themselves are apt to grow loose and wax wanton, in view of their greatest and best privileges: Therefore, though come to the city of the living God, the heavenly Jerusalem, where there is rest and safety, and all kind of precious provisions, such as their souls desire; yet are they also come to God the judge of all, who expects an improvement and account all their talents, and will be sanctified by all them that draw nigh unto him. God gives grace that we may serve him 'with reverence and godly fear,' ver. 28.

This, though I do not apprehend it to be the sense of the text; yet is an useful and very necessary premisal, in order to our having suitable apprehensions of the greatness of the privilege therein contained.

It is a solemn thing to draw near to God the judge of all the earth. Abraham thought it so, (Gen. xviii. 27. 'Behold now, I have taken upon me to speak 'unto the Lord, which am but dust and ashes:') And so the saints have ever thought it in seasons of their greatest nearness and fellowship. Never was a soul brought into a state of communion with God, who thought lightly of access to him. Whatever we may do, in our stupid, trifling, secure frames, when the heart is set right with God, when we are in good earnest in holy ordinances, when death and judgment appear in view: To deal with God as a judge; to receive our sentence of absolution from him, with respect to our state and actions; to put in our suit, through the Mediator's righteousness; believer! thou that walkest closest with God, say whether it be not a solemn thing?

Job comes out, with an 'how much less shall I 'answer him,' Job ix. 13, 14. 'If God will not 'withdraw his anger, the proud helpers do stoop un- 'der him. How much less shall I answer him, and 'chuse out my words to reason with him.' Such as are most strong and valiant, who are esteemed as pillars of the earth, (some refer it to the righteous, o-
thers

thers to princes and chief commanders on earth), these
'stoop under him; how much less shall I answer,'
&c. when God pleads, I submit. Every charge of
his against me is just,—' whom though I were righ-
' teous yet would I not answer him, but I would
' make supplication' to my judge, *ver.* 15.

Three or four things will shew us, what a solemn
thing it is, even for believers, to converse with God
the judge of all.

1. The majesty and glory of the great God, makes
it awful conversing with him.

Paul counted it a very small thing to be judged
of man's judgment, 1 Cor. iv. 3. but whoever yet
spake this of God's? When accused by men, David
has a *plea* ready at hand, and Job has an *answer*.
One argues the case with his friends, and till he dies
will not let go his integrity, Job xxvii. 5. the other
carries his cause to God, with a ' judge me, O Lord,
' according to my righteousness, and according to
' mine integrity that is in me,' Psal. vii. 8. But
when God himself takes up the matter, holy Job abhors himself, and repents in dust and ashes, *chap.* xlii.
6. and David, upright and innocent with respect to
those things he is charged with by man, cries,
' Enter not into judgment with thy servant.' Psal.
cxliii. 2. Works may be pleaded at man's bar,
but never at God's. ' Though I were perfect, yet
' would I not know my soul,' is the resolution of
every justified person, in all solemn transactions with
God. It is not Job's single experience, *chap.* xxxi.
23. Destruction from God was a terror to me;
and by reason of his HIGHNESS I could not endure.
When the believer presents himself before the great
and glorious God, he is amazed, confounded, and
left speechless; his dread falls upon him, and his
terrors make him afraid. That great saint who could
say confidently in one verse, ' He also shall be my
' salvation, for an hypocrite shall not come before
' him,' Job xiii. 16. (where Job takes comfort from
God's promise and his own sincerity); yet is forced,

as soon as the words are well out of his mouth, to betake himself to another plea, *ver.* 21. ' Withdraw ' thine hand far from me, and let not thy dread ' make me afraid; then call thou, and I will an- ' swer,' &c. God's majesty and glory makes it a solemn thing for poor sinners, though in a justified state, to have converse with him, as judge of all.

2. God's *omniscience* is another thing, which makes it solemn conversing with God as judge of all, Heb. iv. 13. ' All things are naked and open unto the eyes ' of him with whom we have to do.' The eye of God penetrates as deep as the very heart-roots, the hidden parts; so the word is Psal. li. 6. and, oh! who that considers this aright, can in his best services, and sweetest frames, without the deepest reverence and regard, deal with God the judge of all. Christian! though thou lovest to be searched, yet dost thou not tremble often to think how thou shalt bear the trial? though thou appearest before the bar in another's name, and another's righteousness, art thou not at a loss often to know when and how this righteousness became assuredly thine? whether it was granted to thee by the great judge, to be arrayed in this fine linen, clean and white? or whether with a presumptuous hand thou hast not laid hold of it, and called it thine, without his bidding?

To have Christ in thy mouth, may amuse thyself and satisfy others; but with the judge of all, nothing will do, if Christ be not in thy heart. It is not the *blood shed* merely, but this blood as sprinkled upon thee, which purges the conscience from dead works. And thou art in the presence of the heart-searching and rein-trying God, before whom ' a name to live ' is nothing.'—God's omniscience is another thing which makes it solemn conversing with him as judge of all.

3. The *purity* and *holiness* of God make it a solemn thing for polluted sinners, to have any converse with him. An unrighteous judge puts life into one that has a bad cause depending; but of the judge of all

all the earth, we may say with Abraham, when pleading for wicked Sodom, 'Shall not he do right?' In the best of men there is a principle of self-love and self-flattery, but the holy God accepteth no man's person in judgment. True; thou buildest on the promise, and the grace, and the blood of the covenant, for everlasting acceptation with God: But though at times thou hast comfortable hopes as to thy state; does conscience acquit thee with respect to particular sinful actions? And if a Paul, caught into the third heavens in point of communion with God, if he stands at a distance with an 'O wretched ' man that I am, who shall deliver me!' how can'st thou draw near? 'The body of this death,' Rom. vii. 24. There lay thy hand with trembling and self-abhorence; how is God sanctified in thy heart, while it is so full of evil thoughts, and all manner of abominations? how can an holy God converse as a judge with one that is so every way defiled? These things may sit light upon thy spirit now; but in the day of remembrance, when thy God shall reprove thee, and set them in order before thee, thou wilt find this doctrine an experimental truth, that it is a solemn thing to come to God the judge of all. Once more,

4. The strictness of God's law, which is the rule of judgment, makes it a solemn thing to converse with this great and glorious judge. God judges of all thy thoughts and actions by the same law now, that sentence is to be passed by, in the great day of accounts. Soul! God does not set aside his law to shew thee grace and favour: In this case there is no going in unto the king, 'not according to law,' as Esther did, *chap.* iv. 16. Grace does reign, but it is through righteousness, Rom. v. 21. God's eternal law is so dear to him, that 'heaven and earth shall ' sooner pass away, than a tittle of it' shall be lost, Matth. v. 18. The gospel does not relax, or in any wise make void the law; it only shews how, and by whom this law is fulfilled. The law is the rule of that righteousness, by which believers are justified,

and

and the meaſure of every action they perform in obedience to God. Now lay this law to your pureſt thoughts, your moſt ſpiritual aims, your moſt holy and upright actions, where is your righteouſneſs? where is that in you, which comes up to the meaſure of it? May you not ſtand forth and ſay with the church, Iſa. lxiv. 6. 'We are all as an unclean 'thing, and all our righteouſneſs are as filthy rags, 'and we all do fade away as a leaf, and our iniqui- 'ties like the wind have taken us away?' How then can you ſtand before God, the judge of all, without an awe upon your ſpirits; even under a ſenſe of your acceptance with Chriſt, and your intereſt in pardoning love and grace by him?

A few words by way of Uſe.

1. Is it ſo ſolemn a thing for believers in Chriſt, to come to God the judge of all; how or 'where 'then muſt the ſinner and the ungodly appear?' If David's fleſh trembled for fear of God, Pſal. cxix. 120. who came looking by faith to the man of God's right hand; what paleneſs and dread will ſeize thee, when thou appeareſt before the judge of all, *alone;* without a ſurety to bear thy ſins, a righteouſneſs to juſtify thy perſon, and advocate to pleaſe thy cauſe, before God? Thou comeſt before God, as a creator, a benefactor, a God of mercy, without fear; but ſoul! what wilt thou do when thou ſtandeſt before him as a judge? Not grace, but equity, is the rule of God's proceeding on his judgment-ſeat. What haſt thou to plead? what will be God's language to thee then? Oh! that it were thy concern now! God is juſt; let thy thoughts fix there; *not guilty* thou canſt not plead; and to fall down and cry mercy, will not do; this will be rejected by God, as it is in courts of judicature amongſt men. Think thou heareſt thy judge ſaying, "Open the books:" Law, wilt thou acquit him? Juſtice, wilt thou acquit him? Conſcience, can'ſt thou acquit him? Every one ſays, He is curſed; what then will God ſay, (paſſing ſentence according to law), but 'depart 'thou

'thou curfed?' The law knows nothing of pardon but upon the footing of a fatisfaction: Where then is thy righteoufnefs? without this, God muft deftroy his own law to fave a rebel, a tranfgreffor of it. A righteoufnefs in thyfelf, or in thy furety, thou muft have, or thou art undone for ever. Bleffed fouls who have a Chrift for them, when law and juftice give in their verdict againft them! Sinner here is thy foundation, thy plea; that door of hope which is fet open in the gofpel.

Use 2. Is it fo folemn a thing to converfe with God the judge of all? Then, believer, how feldom art thou in a right frame for duty. You know with what folemnity and preparation they of old attended on God, when giving the law. The people were fanctified to-day and to-morrow, and wafhed their cloaths to be in readinefs againft the third day, Exod. xix. 10. Is there lefs call for preparation and folemnity under the gofpel? are trifling frames, and a worldly fpirit, any part of that liberty we have in Chrift? dare we go to holy ordinances drowned in the cares of this life, reeking in the filth of fome unfubdued luft? with fcarce a prayer before hand, that our hearts may be fet right with God, and our confciences purged from dead works? This is no part of the boldnefs of faith, nor of that felf-purifying, which every man that hath this hope is, or ought to be feeking after, 1 John iii. 3. That God has fet one gofpel-ordinance above another, I no where read; but that any fhould be attended on with carelefnefs and neglect, is moft monftrous and abfurd. Soul! knoweft thou whom thou art before in all the ordinances of gofpel-worfhip? a glorious, all-feeing, holy and juft God; who, though he may, for the fake of Chrift, in whom thy perfon is accepted, forgive thy fins; will doubtlefs, as a vindication of the glory of his own name, take vengeance on thine inventions. You know how Nahab's and Abihu's ftrange fire, was refented by a holy God, Lev. x. 2. You may think more favourably of your own perfons, sons, but God will not cast away his own law to palliate your sins. No wonder you complain of leanness, and bondage, and unprofitableness under ordinances, if you take no more pains with your own hearts, in order to your attendance upon them: preparation is God's gift, but is it given unsought? 'Their hearts shall live that seek God,' Psal. lxix. 32. so the promise runs, and every believer's experience agreeth thereto. 'It was but a little that I passed 'from them,' (says the spouse) 'and I found him 'whom my soul loveth,' Cant. iii. 4. but it was in a way of duty, after long and diligent search.—Believers hearts are seldom in frame for conversing with God the judge of all.

Use 3. Learn from what has been said, the only way to think of future judgment with pleasure and comfort. It is by coming to God, the judge of all, *now*. Of all other things, the thoughts of death and judgment are most awful and affecting. Because we know our turn for both will one day come; and that as our state is found then, our portion will be for ever. True, the bridge of the covenant will carry us safe over this Jordan. A perfect, complete, everlasting righteousness will be a sufficient ground of acquittance in the day of our particular and final judgment: yet canst thou help at times such thoughts as these? Oh should I die mistaken at last! may I not ignorantly be a branch of Christ by profession only? have not many compassed themselves about with sparks of their own kindling? how shall I know that I am really in Christ? that the Lord is my portion, that my judge is my friend, my Saviour, my God! How must such thoughts be answered, and conscience relieved? the best way, as I apprehend, (I hope I have found it so), is to set thyself in the presence of an holy and just God now. Call up thy sins; search the ground of thy hope; order thy cause before him; see how far the covenant of God, the blood, the righteousness, the advocacy of Christ, satisfy thy conscience; and hear what answer God thy judge gives to such a prayer or plea as that is Psal. cxxxix. 23. 'Search me, O God and know 'my heart, try me and know my thoughts, and see 'if there be any wicked way in me, and lead me in 'the way everlasting.' Doth he say, "Deliver him "from going down to the pit? Is not this a brand "plucked out of the fire? Behold I have caused "thine iniquity to pass from thee:" then the case is decided. But is a promise wanting? wait on him still in the way of ordinances, put thyself under his shadow, look to Christ and the blood of sprinkling to plead for thee; though no answer comes at present, it will soon, Hab. ii. 3.

USE 4. What a blessed gospel is that which reveals the only righteousness wherein a poor guilty sinner may appear before God with comfort!

But this leads to the second general; of which the next opportunity.

SERMON VI.

GOD THE JUDGE OF ALL.

Heb. xii. 23.

And to God the Judge of all.

IN the last discourse, it was shewn in four particulars, what a solemn thing it is for believers themselves (who appear in another's name, and another's righteousness) to converse with God the judge of all, *i. e.* the majesty and glory of God; his omniscience, as knowing all our thoughts and all our hearts, all designs and aims; the purity of his nature; and the strictness of his law. This leads to the second general head.

II. How is it that such a converse is begun between an holy God and poor sinners?

I answer,

1. It is begun in the conviction, or sensibleness a soul has, that he is a guilty lost sinner.

God sets up a throne of judgment in the conscience, before he gives any discovery by his Spirit of a throne of grace. He herein deals with man according to the covenant he is under, and the state he is in by nature; this is a covenant of condemnation,

nation, and a state of wrath; 'for all have sinned, 'and come short of the glory of God,' Rom. iii. 23. wherefore God's law, which is the rule of judgment, is laid to the sinner's actions, and he is summoned to give an account for all he hath done against it. Hence the commandment is said to *come*, *i. e.* in its convincing power, and spirituality, in order to work in the soul this sense of guilt, and to bring him for ever to despair of appearing before God in his own righteousness: Rom. vii. 9. ' I ' was alive without the law once, but when the com- ' mandment came, sin revived and I died.' Gen. iii. 9. ' Adam, where art thou?' are words uttered by God, with an intention of grace and mercy, but they bespeak a solemn judicial process which God had first with him, as a guilty fallen creature; " What hast " thou done? what a state is this I see thee in! art " thou become sinful? hast thou lost thy righteous- " ness?" Adam never fled and hid himself from God, before he was sensible of this his state. And there must be a charge of guilt laid, before there can be an act of absolution passed. This communion and converse which sinners have with God the judge of all, is begun in a sensibleness of their own guilt, and lost undone state, before him.

In order to a poor sinner's comfortably conversing with God the judge of all, there must be a free confession of all sin, and a subscribing to the rights of his justice. This is called an accepting of the punishment of one's iniquity, Levit. xxvi. 41. and a clearing and justifying God when we are judged, Psal. li. 4. Confession of sin lies not barely in acknowledgment of the fact, but in a submission to the punishment which is the due desert of it. The poor publican, when he prayed to God for mercy, owned himself the most unworthy of it. He stood afar off and smote upon his breast, saying, ' God be merci- ' ful to me a sinner,' Luke xviii. 13. A soul that is affected with a sense of his sin, owns that God might justly behold him for ever *afar off*, and send him into a state of eternal distance from him. He comes as Benhadad's servant of old did, with a rope about his neck; and says, "Lord! it is a righteous thing "with thee to condemn me for ever. I have no- "thing but what I deserve, if I never taste a drop "of mercy. I must take part with God and justice "against myself, though I should lie in hell to all "eternity." Slight thoughts of sin a man cannot have, who is under the convincing power and condemning sentence of God's law, nor slight thoughts of the law by which sentence is passed. 'For the 'law is holy, and the commandment holy, and just, 'and good,' Rom. vii. 12. So the sinner looks upon it, so he esteems it in his heart, and by making confession of his own vileness and the desert of his sin, he gives glory to God, Josh. vii. 19. God never makes a soul a sharer in the riches of his grace, but he first brings him to acknowledge and submit to the rights of his justice. This is a great thing; look inward, soul! if there be solemnity in any soul-transactions with God, this is one of them. Thou art lost for ever by thy own judgment, never never canst thou make one objection against God! This shews how solemn a thing it is to deal with God the judge of all; yet without this solemn approval of the rights of his justice there can be no comfortable converse or walk with him.

3. In order to a poor sinner's comfortable converse with God the judge of all, there must be an absolute renouncing all righteousness of his own.

Job, though he were perfect, yet would he not know his own soul, chap. ix. 21. "This," says Caryl, "imports, not an affected ignorance, but an elected "knowledge: Job was no stranger to his own soul; "he had studied himself, and was well versed in his "own bosom." But the more he knew of his own heart and actions, the more sin and defectiveness he saw in both. A soul whom God brings into judgment has nothing to plead, fetched from within; a holy law turns a man out a mere bankrupt; all his
valuables

valuables go for nothing. Paul would no more trust his evangelical holiness, than his legal righteousness, as to any hopes he had of appearing in it before God as a judge with comfort, Phil. iii. 8. When the Spirit of God has to do with any soul, sooner or later, he brings him to this: " Lord, judge for thine own " honour, unto thy name give glory." What glory can an holy God and a righteous judge get from a sinner's tears, repentance, promises, yea from faith itself, considered as a work? What is there in all these to satisfy his justice; to answer the demands of his broken law? all procuring causes, terms, conditions in a man's self, are never once heard from the sinner, when appearing before God in judgment. He is altogether an unclean thing, and he absolutely renounces all righteousness of his own, in point of acceptance and plea before God the judge of all.

These considerations necessarily come in, yet are they but introductory to that which follows; therefore,

4. The way to have comfortable converse with God the judge of all, is to come before him in the Mediator's righteousness, and to plead it with him, as thy justifying righteousness. This is included in the two following clauses of my text: ' And to ' Jesus, the Mediator of the new covenant; and un- ' to the blood of sprinkling.' Which are mentioned as other distinct privileges which make up the glory of the gospel-state; whereby is insinuated both the way in which reconciliation was obtained for us, and in what it is applied to us. Christ as Mediator purchased our peace by shedding his blood: thus it is said, 1 Cor. v. 7. ' Christ our passover is sacrificed for us.' And by the sprinkling of it, (as of old on the altar and on the people), believers come to have benefit by it, as to those ends for which it was offered up to God. This righteousness of Christ, God-man, which he wrought out as Mediator and Surety, is what every enlightened convinced sinner pleads and urges before the throne, under the accu-

fations of confcience, the charges of Satan, the arreft of juftice, and the curfe of a broken law.

Now there are in this righteoufnefs of Chrift thefe four things, which make a poor foul's converfe with God the judge of all, (who is found in it, and appeals to it), to be fweet and comfortable.

1. It is a *perfect* righteoufnefs. Law and juftice are both fatisfied with it, or elfe the bleffed Jefus who wrought it out had never been 'juftified in the 'fpirit,' 1 Tim. iii. 16. when he arofe from the dead, which was performed by the powerful agency and operation of the Spirit of God, Rom. i. 4. God had never ftyled himfelf 'the God of Peace,' but that the great Shepherd of the sheep paid into the hands of juftice that full price, which the righteous law demanded, Heb. xiii. 20. Soul! there is grace fhewn thee, that this righteoufnefs of Chrift fhould be imputed to thee; but there was no favour fhown to Chrift thy Surety in working it out: 'God fpared not his own Son,' Rom. viii. 32. Chrift did not compound with God, when he ftood in thy place, and acted in thy room and ftead. No! he paid the utmoft farthing. Thy Jefus never gave out obeying and fuffering, till he could fay by the law's allowance, 'It is finifhed,' John xix. 30. Here lies thy plea, and the ground of thy comfort when converfing with God the judge of all, that the righteoufnefs in which thou ftandeft, is a perfect, a complete righteoufnefs: Oh! It could never be pleadable were it not perfect. On this foundation Job triumphs, chap. xxiii. 7. 'There the righteous' (who are made fo in the Redeemer's blood) ' might difpute ' with him,' (argue their caufe and tell their wants), ' fo fhould I be delivered for ever from my judge.' As though he had faid, " I have no need to fear " God's condemning fentence, fo long as I am inte- " refted in his Son's perfect, juftifying righteouf- " nefs."

2. It is a covenant-righteoufnefs. And a great fhare of our comfort in pleading it with God depends

pends upon this. God himself was the contriver, the deviser of it; out of pure love and grace to sinning man. It is a righteousness of his ordination and appointment, about which a council was called in heaven before all worlds. Zech. vi. 13. The 'counsel of peace shall be between them both.' True, this righteousness of Christ was wrought out in answer to the demands of the old law; but it was agreed upon in eternity, and was accepted, and is imputed, upon the footing of a new covenant. 'I 'have made a covenant with my chosen,' Ps. lxxxix. 3. A perfect righteousness is accepted at Christ's hands for thee; why? not barely because it is perfect, answering to every tittle of the broken law, but also because it was at God's ordination and appointment wrought out for thee. Christ thy surety took upon him thy nature, thy name, and thy sins, by covenant-agreement with the Father. Heb. v. 4, 5. ' No man taketh this honour unto himself, but he ' that is called of God, as was Aaron: so also Christ ' glorified not himself to be made an high priest, but ' he that said unto him, Thou art my Son; this day ' have I begotten thee.' Soul, thou hast here a double plea in one; the glory of sovereign grace, and the Son's righteousness; everlasting counsels are fulfilled, and an eternal law magnified; hence arises a soul's comfortable converse with God as judge of all.

3. It is a righteousness, wherein all the attributes of God harmonize. He is, and he appears to be a just God and a Saviour, Isa. xlv. 21. God is just in punishing sin, merciful and gracious in pardoning the sinner. What a blessed answer is here to all the scruples of a tender conscience: God's truth, God's holiness and justice, can put in no single claim, which the Mediator's blood and righteousness has not fully answered. It is a *speaking* blood: It speaks covenant-promises, faithfulness and honour to God *for* thee; and it speaks pardon, and peace, and grace, and glory from God *to* thee. Oh! glorious righteousness

righteousness of our great Mediator! In this may my soul boast all the day long, in this may I ever live, and claim, and triumph! Once more,

4. This righteousness is unchangeable and everlasting. Through all times, changes, and frames, the Mediator's righteousness continues everlastingly the same. Were the saints inherent righteousness, their faith, sincerity, or gospel-obedience, to be their pleadable title to God's favour, or to comfortable converse with him, we should have it often to seek, when we need it for use. But this righteousness of Christ is ever perfect, present and accepted. ' My ' salvation shall be for ever, and my righteousness ' shall not be abolished,' Isa. li. 6. There may be much change in us, but there is no change in that. It is a garment which waxeth not old; it can be no more sullied than worn out. It is of the same validity, efficacy and acceptation with God now, as it was when our High-priest first entered with it into the holiest of all, and presented it to God the Father with his own hands, in the name and for the use of all his seed.—Soul! whence is it thou hast leanness of frame, and distressing terrors? whence is it thou walkest in darkness and hast no light? Is it because thou hast no righteousness to appear in before God, or is it because thou dost not improve it? is it because thy foundation itself totters and sinks, or because thou standest with but one foot upon it? Thou pleadest Christ's righteousness, but what gives thee boldness so to do? it is thy own frames, thy own graces? these thou makest as steps to help thee to Christ's righteousness, therefore thou comest short of peace and comfort. This righteousness of Christ needs nothing of thine own to make it accepted, or to make it pleadable. David makes mention of it wholly and only, Psal. lxxi. 16. It is a righteousness like its glorious Author, ' the same yesterday, ' to-day, and for ever;' a righteousness which will enter even heaven itself with us, and will dwell for ever round us, and our most glorious covering in the
fight

sight of God, and our everlasting title (as one well expresses it) to all the blessings of eternity; the saints above are always viewed and accepted of God, in this everlasting and unchangeable righteousness.

These considerations, touching the righteousness in which a poor sinner appears before God the judge of all, are living springs of peace and comfort, and of 'a hope which maketh not ashamed.' And thus communion and converse with God as a judge of all is begun.

Use. 1. If there be no coming to God as judge of all, with comfort, but by confessing sin, their state must be sad who seek comfort by hiding or lessening sin. Soul! thou mayst cover thy transgressions as Adam, Job xxxi. 33. but here or hereafter, thy sin will find thee out; God is judge alone. To lessen thy sin, is to approve it, to love it in thy heart; and though thou art innocent of some sins, art thou guiltless of all? Will it be any excuse of one guilty of treason, to plead he has not committed murder? Poor sinner, thou art an utter stranger to God's sovereign grace, if thou hast not been brought under his sentence of judgment. How canst thou expect the benefit of a pardon, when thou art not brought to own thyself guilty?

Use 2. Must a soul be brought to submit to the rights of God's justice, in order to a comfortable converse with him as judge of all? then wo to all such as quarrel with God's judgment. We live in a dark day; many are causing the holy One of Israel to cease from among us, saying of the Lord's ways, 'they are not equal.' They are for framing a God altogether like themselves; a God all mercy, that will destroy none of his creatures; and have set up rules and terms and fitnesses of things (as they term them) for the God and judge of all the earth to walk by. But 'wo to him that striveth with his Maker.' Must God give account of his matters to such as are to be judged by him? shall a condemned man give laws to his judge?

judge? Soul! when thou art brought to see sin in the glass of the law, Adam's *sin* will appear no light thing. 'Judgment is come on all men to con- 'demnation,' Rom. v. 18. God willeth not the death of sinners, considered as creatures, but the wicked shall be turned into hell, and all the nations that forget God. For he does not condemn as a so- vereign from his own arbitrary will, but as a judge. How canst thou expect mercy when thou pleadest me- rit; mercy can never be exercised against law. God will give grace to none but such as will prize it when bestowed.

Use 3. Must all self-righteousness be renounced in order to a comfortable converse with God the judge of all? How contrary is that doctrine which sets up the creature's sincere obedience as a part of our gospel-righteousness? Our sincere obedience is to be renounced in point of justification, though it is to be pressed after, as a part of our gospel-sanctifica- tion. The law requires a perfect righteousness, and the gospel reveals it. As judge of all, God can ad- mit of none other, without setting aside his own and his Son's righteousness. Sincerity is in a man's self; it is inherent, not imputed; whereas the righteous- ness, which is accepted for justification, is *unto* and *upon* all them that believe; not *in* them, Rom. iii. 21. It is revealed *to* faith, not obtained *by* it; and faith itself comes through this righteousness of Christ, so far is it from giving a title thereto, 2 Pet. i. 1. 'To 'them that have obtained like precious faith through 'the knowledge of God our Saviour.' These may be bandied about in controversy, amongst men that are at ease in *Zion;* but they are not of such trifling moment to sinners who have their souls awakened. To the poor sinner who comes with the awful que- stion in his mouth, 'How can man be just with 'God?' must we direct him to Christ, to the grace of God in him; to the blood of the covenant, the righteousness of faith? or must we set him to his own repentance,

repentance, inward qualifications, covenantings, &c. Miferable comforters are fuch, and phyficians of no value, whatever their defign be, or how fincere foever (as the phrafe is) their error may be. A guilty finner needs an all fufficient Saviour and a complete righteoufnefs. And this is the glory of the gofpel, that herein is revealed the righteoufnefs of God ' from faith to faith ;' not to works firft, then to faith; but ' from faith to faith,' as it is written, ' The juft fhall live by faith,' Rom. i. 17.

SERMON VII.

GOD THE JUDGE OF ALL.

Heb. xii. 23.

And to God the Judge of all.

I AM now to confider (as God fhall help) the third general.

    III. In what inftances, and by what methods, this converfe which believers have with God the judge of all, is maintained and carried on.

And that we may proceed with the greater clearnefs, under this general head I fhall endeavour to fhew,

    I. In what particular inftances this converfe with God is carried on.
    II. By what fpecial methods it is promoted and maintained. And as a farther ufe of this head,
    III. By what means it is prevented, or interrupted.

    I. I am to give fome inftances, wherein believers have comfortable converfe with God, the judge of all, through the whole of their gofpel profeffion and walk.

walk. The apostle speaks of it as a privilege attending their state, not a blessing peculiar to some extraordinary frames. It is a believer's settled mercy and daily duty to converse with God the judge of all. And,

First, A great part of this comfortable converse with God, lies in those high and honourable thoughts which believers have of his righteousness, as judge of all.

To a soul that has union with Christ, and access to God by him, God's righteousness is as dear an attribute as his grace. It is a glorious part of his character, Exod. xxxiv. 7. ' He will by no means ' clear the guilty;' *i. e.* not without a sacrifice, a satisfaction: and this their souls acquiesce and delight in. This makes up a part of our Saviour's prayer: ' Oh righteous Father, the world hath not ' known thee,' &c. John xvii. 25. And it constitutes the song of the saints and angels, Rev. xvi. 5. ' Thou art righteous, O Lord, which art, and wast, ' and shalt be.' Devils and damned spirits feel how just God is; but the saints only can acknowledge it, and submit to it with complacency and adoration. And why they? because, in the glass of a crucified Christ they behold God as a just God and a Saviour, Isa. xlv. 21. It is with pleasure they look into the high and righteous demands of God's law, and read over the claims of vindictive justice on the entrance of sin, because they see justice and mercy reconciled in the death of Christ, and grace reigning in a way of righteousness, Rom. v. 21. Believers desire to converse with God as a holy and righteous God, that is of purer eyes than to behold iniquity; nor can they bear to think of God's making any alteration in his law, by way of indulgence to any of their sins. ' Thy word is very pure,' says David, ' therefore ' thy servant loveth it,' Psal. cxix. 140. and *ver.* 20. ' My soul breaketh for the longing it hath unto thy ' judgments at all times.' This is one instance of believers converse with God the judge of all.

Secondly,

Secondly, Another inſtance wherein believers have comfortable converſe with God, lies in their pleading juſtification before God, upon the footing of righteouſneſs. Not of their own rightouſneſs; for as creatures, we are debtors; as ſinners, we are bankrupts, and have nothing to pay: Yet juſtice as well as grace is a believer's plea, becauſe he hath intereſt in the Mediator's righteouſneſs. As guilty ſinners, our plea is pure grace and mercy; as clothed upon with this robe of righteouſneſs, we may appeal to juſtice. Holy Paul, in the views of death and judgment, ſays, 2 Tim. iv. 8. ‘ Henceforth ‘ there is laid up for me a crown of righteouſneſs, ‘ which the Lord the righteous judge ſhall give me ‘ in that day.' There is a twofold juſtice in God; *vindictive* juſtice, in demanding ſatisfaction, and inflicting the whole of the curſe for ſin committed; this believers in Chriſt are delivered from; the debt once paid is no farther demandable: And *renumerative* juſtice; which conſiſts in giving all ſpiritual and eternal bleſſings, upon condition of a full price paid; this every believer has an intereſt in. As a judge God condemned the Surety, and as a judge he acquits and juſtifies the ſinner. Hence he is ſaid, Rom. iii. 26. to be *juſt*, and ‘ the juſtifier of him which believeth in Jeſus: And, 1 John i. 9. ‘ He is faith- ‘ ful and juſt to forgive us our ſins, and to cleanſe ‘ us from all unrighteouſneſs.' The righteouſneſs of God's nature as judge, makes it meet, when the Surety has ſatisfied, that the ſinner ſhould be ſaved. A bleſſed, approved way is this, of maintaining fellowſhip and communion with God. What can diſmay that ſoul, who can realize his intereſt in that juſtifying ſentence, which paſſed upon his glorious Surety, when God raiſed him from the dead?

Thirdly, Another inſtance wherein believers have comfortable converſe with God the judge of all, lies in their referring themſelves to his righteous judgment, with reſpect to their ſtate, their frames, and all their actions.—How often, and how frequently

ly do we hear the Pfalmift pleading, ' Judge me, O
' Lord; fearch me, O God; know my heart; try
' me, and know my thoughts,' Pfal. xxvi. 1. and
Pfal. cxxxix. 23, 24. Of all things, an upright Chriftian dreads moft a miftaken notion of his ftate God-
ward. We are bad judges in our own caufe. What
muft we then do as to our converfe with God, when
things look dark and dubious; the heart finks, the
fpirit faints; and the more we look inward, the
more we are afraid to proceed? Prefent thyfelf before God for his judgment; beg him to fhew thee
thyfelf, to fet before confcience his own law and his
own righteoufnefs, and to lead thee in the way everlafting. Confcience itfelf often needs frefh fearch-
ing, and frefh purging. Many times it fpeaks peace,
not by God's allowance, as when it goes only upon
the prefumptive evidence of paft faith, hopes, experiences and enlargements, without direct acts of faith
upon the covenant and grace of God through the Mediator. This is a falfe foundation where there is a
loofe walk, wherefore the believing foul is earneft
for God's teftimony, and God's fearch; and in this
way only, at fuch feafons, is comfortable converfe
maintained with God the judge of all. It is a fign
of true grace when a heart, not barely abides the
trial, but loves to be tried, Job x. 2. ' I will fay un-
' to God, Do not condemn me, fhew me wherefore
' thou contendeft with me.' Job fufpects fome evil
in his own heart unfeen as yet; " God, fays he,
" does not contend for nothing,—Lord, fhew it me;
" make me know what I am in thy fight; as my
" judge, I fly to thee; as my father, my friend, my
" portion, my all, but I ftand before thee alfo as my
" judge." And when a foul has God's judgment, he
is not afraid of man's. ' God is greater than our
' hearts, and knoweth all things.' This is another
inftance, &c.

Fourthly, Another inftance wherein believers have
comfortably converfed with God the judge of all, lies
in

in a hearty approval of all providential difpenfations to themfelves and others.

This was the church's frame, Ifa. xxvi. 8. 'Yea in the way of thy judgments have we waited for thee.' And a great part of a believer's converfe with God lies in it. Paul fays, Phil. iv. 11. 'I have learned,' ἐν οἷς εἰμι, in the things I am in, 'in whatfoever ftate,' condition, frame I am, 'therewith to be content.' "If I am poor, defpifed, or "if I abound, I fubmit; it is well, 'fhall not the "judge of all the earth do right?' I am not to "meafure God's difpenfation towards his church in "general, or myfelf in particular, by *my* rule. He "is a God of judgment, and bleffed are all they "that wait for him." Man's nature is very apt to quarrel at God's difpenfations: In afflictions, darknefs, foul-difpenfing terrors, &c. we are ready to take God's work out of his hands, and to fit as judges upon the way which he takes: Inftead of this thou art called to bow to God's fovereignty; to reft in his unfearchable wifdom; to be perfuaded of his righteoufnefs; to plead his promifes, and even 'againft hope, to believe in hope.' How doft thou refer thyfelf to God's judgment, if in every diftafteful difpenfation thou art for being thy own choofer? David 'fings of mercy and of judgment,' Pfal. ci. 1. Divine conduct towards him was, in a way of goodnefs and mercy, tempered with wifdom, faithfulnefs, righteoufnefs and truth: There was a judicioufnefs in the whole of God's proceedings, that was not to be fathomed by human underftanding. That is comfortable converfe thou haft with God as judge of all, when from the heart thou art enabled to juftify God in his difpenfations. Once more,

Fifthly, Another inftance of this comfortable converfe which believers have with God the judge of all, is in a way of anticipating, or antedating (as it were) that fentence of abfolution, which fhall be openly pronounced upon them at the laft day.

Some are for deferring the season of a sinner's justification to the last day: But thou, believer, instead hereof, art for bringing the mercy of that blessed and glorious day into possession and enjoyment now; it will be a day 'of finding mercy' to all such who have 'washed their robes, and made them white in 'the blood of the Lamb;' and not as if believers were in a state of suspense and uncertainty as to their pardon, justification, and right to life, till the solemn process of that day commences; no, thou *art* saved, and 'called with an holy calling;' Christ, and his righteousness, and grace, and complete salvation, are as much thine now, as they will be then: Believers 'sit together in heavenly places in Christ,' Eph. ii. 5. Right and title never vary; faith gives present claim, though not present possession. But when this 'Day 'of Jesus Christ comes;' (for so it is called, Phil. i. 6.) the mercy of God's nature, his covenant and promise, will be fully laid open: Believers shall hear the sentence of absolution before men, angels, and devils, declared, attested, confirmed, and shall be put beyond the possibility of a single doubt or fear for ever. Then will Christ thy Surety present thee to the Father publicly, solemnly, once for all, as his trust, his purchase, his spouse, as united to his person, clothed with his righteousness, conformed to his image, and fully prepared in body and spirit for his glory. Paul calls the *hope* of this day *blessed*, Tit. ii. 13. much more will the *appearance* of it be so: And believers have comfortable converse with God, in looking for it, and 'hasting unto the coming of it,' 2 Pet. iii. 12. or, as it is more emphatically in the margin, 'hasting the coming of it.' Faith beholds distant things near, and absent things as present. Art thou, believer, 'in his presence to have fulness 'of joy, and at his right hand pleasures for ever-'more?' Psal. xvi. 11. and no comfort, no triumphs, nothing but dark and dead, and bondage-frames now! Begin the songs of Zion in this strange land: Rev. v. 9. 'Thou art worthy to take the book, and

'open

'open the feals thereof, for thou waft flain, and haft
'redeemed us to God by thy blood, out of every kin-
'dred, and tongue, and people, and nation; and
'haft made us unto our God kings, and priefts, and
'we fhall reign on the earth.'

In thefe inftances believers, in their Chriftian walk heaven-ward, have comfortable converfe with God the judge of all. This leads to confider,

II. How, or by what fpecial methods this comfortable converfe with God is promoted and maintained.

I anfwer,

Firft, By looking often to the everlafting fettlements and grace of the covenant; what God does *in time*, is by virtue of covenant-agreement with his Chrift, and our Surety *in eternity*. Pfal. xcviii. 3. 'I have faid, Mercy fhall be built up for ever—for 'I have made a covenant with my chofen. Fallen finners can never behold the rights of God's juftice, but in the views of the precious provifions of grace and mercy. Rom. v. 21. 'Grace reigns through 'righteoufnefs unto eternal life, by Jefus Chrift our 'Lord.' This is Paul's triumph, in views of himfelf as a finner, and of God as righteous. 2 Cor. ii. 14. 'Now, thanks be to God, who always caufeth us to 'triumph in Chrift.'—Believer, thy triumphs are all in Chrift, but it is God, as a God of grace, which *caufeth* thee to triumph. Thou haft no claim in Chrift, but what fovereign grace has given thee. If thou pleadeft, Lord, accept me, prove me, fave me, it is all upon the footing of an everlafting covenant, and rich and reigning grace. Believers are one day to be *pillars* in the houfe of their God, Rev. iii. 12. *i. e. monumental* pillars, whofe infcription on every fide will be *grace, grace*. If thou art looking for the 'mercy of our Lord Jefus Chrift,' Jude *ver.* 21. in the end, thou hadft need *live* upon grace by the way.

way. This is one method of maintaining converse with God.

Secondly, This comfortable converse with God, is promoted and maintained by the soul's *daily faith* on the person of Christ, as God-man. ' And of Jesus ' the Mediator of the new covenant.' By him is the soul's first access to God, (as has been shewn), and by him is its continual converse. He opened the way to God by his blood, and he keeps it open by his intercession and life. It is Christ's relation to God the Father, which gives us boldness and confidence in calling him our Father. We have προσαγωγήν, manuduction to God as a Father. Christ takes us by the hand and presents us to God, as great favourites do such as they introduce to crowned heads, Eph. ii. 18. Soul! never expect a favourable look from thy judge, without first coming to Christ; there must be a fixing and centering in his person, as Mediator. Thus the whole church as represented are maintaining fellowship with God, Psal. lxxxiv. 9. ' Behold, O God ' our shield, and look upon the face of thine Anoint-' ed.' And hence believers are directed both to abide in Christ, and to walk in him, John xv. 5. Col. ii. 6. This is the well-spring of life, and the way to maintain comfortable converse with God as judge of all.

Thirdly, This comfortable converse with God is promoted and maintained by earnest endeavours after conformity to God in righteousness and true holiness: ' Be ye holy, as I am holy,' 1 Pet. i. 16. This converse lies not in notion or talk, but in heart and walk; whatever you hear of the word of truth, beware lest you rest satisfied with taking the notion into your heads; this destroys thousands: Be the truth ever so sweet, practical, directive, it has no saving avail to the soul, without you have some experience of the power of it in your heart. Many an one can talk of justification, who is under a sentence of condemnation; notionally he is acquainted with God the judge of all, but he has never really conversed with him, as such comfort comes in way of duty; if a man is not concerned to walk acceptably before God, he does but deceive his own soul, when he walks comfortably; wherefore says the apostle, 2 Cor. v. 9. we ' labour that whether present or ab-' sent, we may be accepted of him.' Well-grounded hopes of heaven are so far from encouraging sloth and carnal security in the believer's walk, that they are a constant spur to duty, and a check to sin. ' We ' labour', it is exercising work, ' to keep always a ' conscience void of offence towards God and men :' Yet without this there can be no comfortable communion. God as a judge has accepted righteousness from thy Surety; but this in no wise sets aside his right to obedience from thee a creature. Thou art not without law to God, but under the law to Christ. Have a care of *heart-Antinomianism*, it masks itself under the most sweet, precious, soul-reviving and establishing truths of God. Labour most after likeness and conformity to him.

Fourthly, A believer's converse with God the judge of all, is promoted and maintained by his coming often to the blood of sprinkling. ' And to the blood ' of sprinkling, *i. e.* the blood that is sprinkled. This is faith's grand plea, often its only plea in the soul's coming before God; Heb. x. 19. ' Having ' therefore, brethren, boldness to enter into the ho-' liest of all, by the blood of Jesus, let us draw near.' Not thy holiness of heart, brokenness, humility, or any other grace of the Spirit in thee, gives acceptance to thy person, or entrance to thy prayers; but the blood of Christ thy security, which is sprinkled on thee. It is Christ's blood, the holy One of God; and covenant-blood, shed at the Father's own appointment, and in obedience to his will. It is blood, therefore, which speaks in heaven, where the cause is heard; blood which cries for non-condemnation to all those on whom it is sprinkled. It is Dr Goodwin's observation upon the passage; " Abel's " blood cried for vengeance to come down from hea-
" ven;

"ven; but Chrift's blood cries us up into heaven; like unto that voice, Rev. xi. 12. 'Come up hither;' where I am, let them be, for whom this blood was fhed."—Sirs, why fhould God be a terror to us in our folemn tranfactions with him, as judge of all; when we fee ' in the midft of the ' throne a Lamb, as it had been flain,' Rev. v. 6. Converfe with God as judge of all, is kept up by continued actings of our faith on the blood of fprinkling.

One word to the finner, concludes at prefent.

USE. Haft thou no converfe with God the judge of all now? But thou *muft* hereafter. The midnight cry is coming on, and it cometh as a thief, often without the leaft notice. Oh it is dreadful to die Chriftlefs, fuch cannot but die hopelefs; all that fuch can expect to hear from God, when upon his feat of judgment, is to pronounce that fentence of his holy law, which is againft them now, ' Depart, ye ' curfed.' There is no looking at death and judgment with comfort, but in the Mediator's righteoufnefs.

But I add no more.

SERMON VIII.

GOD THE JUDGE OF ALL.

Heb. xii. 23.

And to God the Judge of all.

WE are now upon the third general head. Under which three things were propofed.

I. To fhew in what inftances believers have thus converfe with God the judge of all.
II. By what means it is promoted and maintained.
III. By what means it is prevented or interrupted.

The *firft* of thefe is finifhed, and the *fecond* has been entered upon,

By what methods is this comfortable converfe which believers have with God as judge of all, promoted and maintained?

Anfwer, *firft*, By looking often to the everlafting fettlements, and grace of the covenant.

Secondly, By the foul's daily faith on the perfon of Chrift.

Thirdly, By earneft endeavours after conformity to God in righteoufnefs and true holinefs.

Fourthly,

Fourthly, By coming often to the blood of sprinkling. We now proceed,

Fifthly, This comfortable converse with God as judge of all, is promoted by the believer's application to God as a Father in Christ; Eph. ii. 18. 'Through him we both have access by one spirit un- 'to the Father.' The character of a judge is awful, but the relation of a Father is sweet and endearing. In a Father there is pitying and sparing mercy. 'I 'will spare him, as a man spareth his own son that 'serveth him,' Mal. iii. 17. Here, believer, is thy mercy, and one great foundation of thy hope in solemn transactions with God. As a Father, God is all love, and grace, and mercy, in Christ; the throne whereon he sits is a throne of grace, so that every uneasy, distant thought, and distressing fear, may be banished from thine heart. Hence Job encourages himself, *chap.* xxiii. 6. 'Will he plead against me 'with his great power? No, but he would put 'strength into me.' Nothing so quickening, so invigorating to a believer in his wrestlings before the throne, as a sense of interest in this sweet and near relation to the glorious Person with whom he is pleading. O let not the consideration of God as a judge, check thy confidence, or straiten thy frame; righteous Judge, and righteous Father agree well together; it was Christ's plea first, John vii. 25. and he has warranted believers to use it ever after. God's righteousness and his power are thine, for thy benefit and advantage, as well as his love and grace; because he judges thee as interested in all his love, as having a right and title to all his grace and mercy, through the suretyship-righteousness of his dear Son. Believer! in all thy converse with God as a judge, approach him as thy Father in Christ. The triumphs of faith begin in God's fatherly relation to his people.

Sixthly, This comfortable converse with God as judge of all, is promoted and maintained by direct acts of faith on the promises of the covenant. Such as respect pardon, sanctification, peace, and eternal redemption. Of these you read, Heb. viii. 10, 11, 12. ' This is the covenant that I will make with ' the house of Israel, after those days, saith the Lord; ' I will put my laws into their minds, and write ' them in their hearts: and I will be to them a ' God, and they shall be to me a people. And they ' shall not teach every man his neighbour, and every ' man his brother, saying, Know the Lord: for all ' shall know me from the least to the greatest. For ' I will be merciful to their unrighteousness, and ' their sins and their iniquities will I remember no ' more.' A believer's life of grace, and his life of hope too, more generally lie in the actings of faith than in the sense he has of his own faith. Therefore peace and joy, even when the soul is said to be filled with them, come in believing, or in a way of venturing, resting upon, and earnestly pleading of the promise, Rom. xv. 13. ' Now the God of hope fill ' you with all joy and peace in believing, that ye ' may abound in hope through the power of the ho- ' ly Ghost.' Soul! thou art much troubled about thy state; at a loss as to thy faith; puzzled and distressed in thy approaches to God as judge of all; thou prayest, attendest ordinances, &c. but complainest no comfort comes in: why? because present faith is wanting in the free promises of pardon by Christ. Thou hast believed heretofore and had comfort: believe again now. Venture, as a guilty, condemned sinner, upon the promise of pardon in the blood of Christ; say, " Lord I believe; this " Jesus I trust; this free grace I fly to; I plead, " Lord, to be dealt with for ever according to the " value of this blood. According to the riches of " this grace, the tenor and free promises of this co- " venant: Lord, it is thine own promise, thy hand- " writing. I come not only that thou shouldst " judge, but judge *for* me; and lead me in the way " everlasting." Brethren, this is the direct way to comfort; going by the way of your own graces,

faith,

faith, experiences, is going about; nor is there a soul that knows what communion with heaven means, but finds this course helpful, when all others fail him. It will bring present support, stayedness and peace, when assurance is wanting: Isa. xxvi. 3. 'Thou wilt keep him in perfect peace whose mind 'is stayed on thee, because he trusteth in thee.'

These are some of the tried ways and methods, by which comfortable converse with God as judge of all is promoted and maintained in the life of a Christian.

I must add one thing more, which though it is not peculiar to that converse which believers have with God as judge, yet it is so fundamental to all communion and converse between God and us, that it cannot be omitted. Therefore,

Seventhly, A daily application to the Spirit, as the glorifier of the Father and of Christ. All the glory of the Father's provision for lost sinners in the person and blood of Christ, and in the grace of the covenant, depends upon the Spirit's revelation of it to and in the soul, Gal. i. 15, 16. It is his work as well as to convince of sin as of righteousness, John xvi. 8. In the one, he sets forth the glorious majesty, and awful strictness of God as a Judge. In the other, he displays the kindness and love of God as a Saviour. In the glass of the law, sinners see the hand-writing of their condemnation: In the glass of the gospel, which the same Spirit presents, the sentence of free justification into life; for therein is 'the righteousness of God revealed from faith to 'faith,' Rom. i. 17. All that access, entrance, acceptation believers have in Christ, with God, as Father and Judge, wherein the very life of communion lies, is it not by the Spirit? 'And the Lord direct 'your hearts into the love of God, and into the pa-'tient waiting for Christ,' 2 Thess. iii. 5. As much as we seem to know the way to the throne, the everlasting unchanging love of the Father, we never come really and truly, so as to partake of his love and grace,

grace, and delight ourselves in it, but by the help of this our blessed director and guide. Not a promise we plead but it is of his shewing, John xvi. 14. Not an argument we use but it is of his framing, Rom. viii. 6. Not a grace we act, but it is of his quickening and exciting, Cant. iv. 16. We cannot so much as feel our own wants, without the Spirit's internal agency and operation. We know not what to pray for as we ought. "Were all the men in the "world," says Dr Owen, "to lay their heads together, "to compose one prayer for the use of any one saint, "but for one day, they could not do it, so as that it "should answer all his wants and necessities." It is the alone proper work of the Spirit. He searches our hearts who knows God's, brings the precept and the promise together, shews both what the doctrine of God's covenant and Christ's righteousness is; and what is the application? O he brings God's Christ and the believer's heart together, and does more to thy settlement, peace, comfort and joy, in one moment, than by all thy endeavours, prayers, tears, marks and evidences of grace, thou art ever able to arrive at through all thy life. When therefore thou art meditating with thyself, how can man be just with God; how shall a sinner that is ever slipping and going astray from the way of his statutes, maintain fellowship and comfortable converse with God the judge of all? add this, as what can put an efficacy into all other rules. Be sure that you apply to God the Spirit, as the glorifier both of the Father and Christ. It is through Christ we have an access, as the meritorious and procuring cause of our fellowship, and by the Spirit as the efficient cause.— Eph ii. 18.

Thus concerning those methods whereby a believer's comfortable converse with God as a judge is promoted and maintained. I am now to shew,

III. By what means this comfortable converse with God as judge of all, is prevented and interrupted?

I answer,

First, This comfortable converse with God is greatly obstructed, when it is apprehended that only the benefits and effects of Christ's righteousness are communicated to believers, and not the very righteousness itself.

The life of all comfort lies in this, that a righteousness is wrought out in obedience to that law, by which man is condemned; a righteousness which every way answers all its demands, and fully satisfies the offended, injured, justice of God; and that this righteousness is to and upon all that believe, as the very righteousness in which their persons stand justified before God. So Paul counted, when he throws away all righteousness of his own, that he might 'win Christ and be found in him,' Phil. iii. 9. It is an error destructive to all peace and comfort in the way of a sinner's dealing with God as a judge, that he has indeed some benefit, some advantage by Christ's righteousness; but that he must not trust to that only for gospel justification and right to life. This righteousness of Christ, say some, is the procuring cause of our justification, but not in itself our justifying righteousness; for the sake of it, God accepts faith, repentance, and sincere obedience, as performed by the creature; and so bestows pardon, grace and favour, and in the end eternal life. These are the benefits, fruits and effects of this righteousness of Christ; but that Christ's righteousness itself is imputed to the sinner, is what they deny. But 'we have not,' I trust, 'so learned Christ.' O Sirs! God has constituted Christ a whole Saviour, beware how you make him a half one. 'I will,' says the blessed Psalmist, 'make mention of thy righteous- 'ness, of thine only, Psal. lxxi. 16. Look to the righteousness of Christ, not barely as procuring favour to thy own obedience and defective performances; (will this give comfort in an hour of temptation and darkness, or afford boldness in the great decisive day? but see it, (soul), plead it, and rely on it, it, as that very righteousness wherein thy guilty soul stands accepted before God, here and hereafter. There is no comfortable converse with God as a judge in any other way.

Secondly, This comfortable converse is interrupted, by supposing that the great God has put all his creatures, believers as well as others, into a state of probation or trial, and that a man cannot be fully persuaded of the safety of his state till the day of his death.—It is true, that God is trying the spirits of men by the preaching of his word; and he is trying the graces of his own people, by afflictions, temptations, darkness, &c. But to say that God deals with men under the dispensation of the covenant of grace, as he did with Adam in innocence, waiting to see how man will improve ordinances, providences, checks of conscience, and promises of life to be obedient, &c. it is to make God's grace depend upon the will of man, and to put an effectual bar in the way of those special saving blessings which Christ has purchased by his death, and God has promised in his covenant. What comfort can a soul have in conversing with God as a judge, if there be always a fear and dread, lest he should remain still under the sentence of condemnation? if his peace depends upon his own frames, graces, and imperfect obedience, is any part of his obedience so perfect as to pass the law's censure? can it be offered to God as a condition, or procuring term of his favour? Brethren! the gospel rather calls men to trust than to trial. It opens a way of present access to God, and acceptance with him, through the faith of Christ, and it speaks to all that sit under the sound of it, by way of invitation and encouragement, that they fly for refuge to lay hold of the hope set before them. Such as are in Christ are ' passed from condemnation,' they are justified, called, and saved; it is not a thing deferred till the day of death and judgment. And, blessed be God, some have said it, and can yet say, ' We know that we are passed from death unto life:

' God

'God hath given us an understanding, that we may know him that is true, and we are in him that is true,' 1 John v. 20. This is another way in which comfortable converse is prevented.

Thirdly, Believers comfortable converse with God is further prevented, or interrupted, by a changing or shifting the foundation of our faith and hope. Some that have begun in the spirit, think to be made perfect by the flesh, Gal. iii. 3. they set out upon a free grace bottom, but afterward turn into their own works; as what gave them boldness before, and recommend them to Christ, whose righteousness they still look to for justification. But free grace, absolute promises, an everlasting covenant, and a perfect justifying righteousness, they are to be always lived upon and improved. What gave life to thy soul in dealing with God at first, must give life still. We walk by faith, the same faith which received Christ's righteousness pleads it. Thy own works were renounced by thee before thou hadst pardon; so they must still before thou hast comfort. Thou camest to Christ, guilty, defiled, unworthy; in thyself thou art no more worthy now, than in the first actings of thy faith, when 'thou wast in thy very blood.' See then that in every duty you perform, every sin you abstain from, every grace you are enabled to act, that by all these you are establishing no righteousness of your own; for 'if righteousness were by the law, 'then Christ is dead in vain.' Pure trust is the way to present comfort.

USE 1. Surely a believer's converse with God must be very precious, when Satan finds out so many ways to prevent and interrupt it. Were it not a great privilege it would be less envied, less obstructed. Christian! God's glory depends much upon thy comfortable frames and close walk with him. The glory of his law, his righteousness, grace, covenant, salvation, all are in a manner lost, when thou art careless in thy frames God-ward. It is as much against the law to seek righteousness by any works of
your

your own, as it is against the gospel. It is faith in Christ which establishes the law, because herein is shewn the righteousness of God's nature, and the high demands of an holy law. God 'spared not 'his own son,' not to *relax*, but to *fulfil* the law. To merit for us, not to put us in a way to merit for ourselves. Be very chary of your comfort, and of every gospel-doctrine that tends to promote it. ' Take ' heed to the things you have heard, lest at any time ' you let them slip.'

Use 2. How needful is a doctrinal clearness in the business of a sinner's justification in the sight of God? Confusion in the mind and judgment, makes confusion in the soul's comfort. A poor creature cannot but be wavering and restless in matters which concern his appearance before God, and transacting with him, who is doubtful in what righteousness to come, whether Christ's or his own: who knows not the perfection and excelling worth of the Mediator's righteousness: who is at a loss as to the way in which it becomes his: whether this righteousness changes as his frames do: whether it may be lost, and he come under a sentence of condemnation again, &c. These things are practical truths, though laid down under doctrinal heads. As Moses said of old, they are not a vain thing, for they are thy life, Deut. xxxii. 46. Upon these three or four doctrines lies all the stress of a believer's faith and hope, viz. " That there is but one rule of righteousness;" that is, the glorious law of God; not two rules, one demanding perfection, the other requiring only sincerity: That there is no righteousness which comes up to this rule, but the righteousness of Christ, God-man; his righteousness more especially as High-priest or Surety; ' Christ hath redeemed us from the curse ' of the law, being made a curse for us,' Gal. iii. 13.: That the only way wherein this righteousness can be made the sinner's, is by God's gracious imputation of it to him; it is *unto* and *upon* him for justification of life: That it can be received no otherwise

wise than by faith; and that the duty of a sinner to whom this righteousness is imputed, and by whom it is received, is to glorify God in heart and life, as the author of his present, and eternal salvation. 'On 'these things,' with respect to a sinner's access to God and walk with him, 'hang all the law and the 'prophets.'

Use 3. Though doctrinal clearness be the way to comfort, yet comfort cannot be enjoyed unless there be an experimental acquaintance with these truths in the heart: If the word be not engrafted in the heart, though it may inform the judgment, it cannot save the soul. The life of faith lies not in the notions of faith, but in the actings of faith, and exercise of it through the whole conversation. A soul that has passed under the sentence of the law, and from a revelation of Christ and his righteousness, has ventured and rested his everlasting all upon him, knows more of justification by faith and communion with God in a way of righteousness, than all the schools or books in the world can ever teach him. By tracing my way in a map of the country I am to go through, I come not a whit nearer my journey's end. I am as far off, as if I knew nothing about it, till I begin actually to travel the road. Communion comes in by walking with God, not by talking of him. It lies in converse with God, not conversation about him. O Sirs! see that you rest not in head-knowledge. The devils know more doctrinally of Christ and his righteousness, than you do; but practical, experimental knowledge, they are eternal strangers to. Look inward to your experience and feeling, when you are talking of your knowledge. The witness of conscience and the Spirit of God to such and such a truth, is beyond all the arguments of men, though scripture arguments, as to thy comfortable converse and walk with God.

But so much at this time.

SERMON IX.

GOD THE JUDGE OF ALL.

Heb. xii. 23.

And to God the Judge of all.

THE doctrinal observation from these words was this,

Doc. It is the great privilege of believers under the gospel-state, that they have comfortable converse with God as judge of all.

In discoursing on which it has been shewn, what a solemn thing it is, even for believers to converse with God the judge of all; how such an awful, yet comfortable converse is begun; in what instances, and by what methods it is maintained and promoted; and considered in three particulars, the last opportunity, how this sweet and comfortable fellowship or converse with God is prevented or interrupted. *First*, When believers look no further to the righteousness of Christ, than that they may have some benefit by it; not considering that it is the very righteousness, wherein their persons and graces stand everlastingly accepted. *Secondly*, When it is supposed that God has put men under the new covenant, into a state of probation and trial, as Adam was under the old covenant, and that full justification cannot be had till the day of one's death. *Thirdly*, It is greatly obstructed, by changing or shifting foundations. Many, with the Galatians, begin in the spirit, but seek to be made perfect by the flesh: Set out upon free-grace principles at first, and go about to establish their own righteousness, in point of converse with God afterwards.—We go on. There are three other mistakes, which believers easily fall into, whereby their comfortable converse with God as judge of all, is greatly interrupted.

First, When the sentence of God, passed upon them in their justification, is made a variable and partial thing. He that is justified, is 'justified from ' all things,' Acts xiii. 38. If any guilt be left upon the sinner, he is undone; for he is not delivered from the law's curse. But all that sin and guilt which was born by thy Surety, God, as a righteous judge, remits unto thee: And what sin and guilt of thine was it, which God laid upon Christ? Isai. liii. 6. ' All thine iniquities, and all thy transgressions, ' in all thy sins,' Lev. xvi. 21. Not a single omission to the end of life, not any one infirmity attending thy duties, was left out of the number. Christ's suretyship-righteousness, and God's act of justification, extended equally alike to all sins; it is upon this account there is no place left for condemnation, Rom. viii. 1. And believers by faith in Christ, being brought into a state of pardon, God does not as a judge acquit and absolve them to-day, and condemn and curse them to-morrow. He that is justified once is justified always. There is a perpetual worthiness in that righteousness which believers plead, and in which they stand; although in their own person and duties there are manifold, and, as they apprehend, growing imperfections. Where righteousness is once imputed, sin shall never more be marked, *i. e.* God will not, as a judge, enter into judgment with us for it. How else does he act in faithfulness to Christ our Surety, ' who was deliver-

' ed

'ed for our offences, and raised again for our justi-
'fication?' Rom. iv. 25. A soul must be separated
from Christ, or he cannot be 'separated from the
'love of God that is in him,' Rom. viii. 39. This
love may be tried, but it can neither be lost nor
changed, because Jesus Christ, and his righteousness,
'are the same yesterday, to-day, and for ever. Mes-
'siah was cut off, to finish the transgression, and to
'make an end of sins, and to make reconciliation
'for iniquity, and to bring in everlasting righteous-
'ness,' Dan. ix. 24. Believers frames may vary;
sometimes straitened in duty, sometimes enlarged;
sometimes it is light in the soul, sometimes darkness.
But variable as thy frames are, the ground of thy
comfort abides ever the same. Sense of pardon may
be lost, but our gracious and covenant God never
makes void the title. God's salvation is one thing,
the joys of this salvation quite another; therefore
David prays, Psal. li. 12. 'Restore unto me the joy
'of thy salvation, and uphold me with thy free spi-
'rit.' Liberty, as to a believer's state, is well consistent with bondage in his frame: We read of some,
who 'through fear of death, were all their lifetime
'subject to bondage,' Heb. ii. 14. Yet they are
called children, for whose sake Christ took part of
flesh and blood. Nevertheless, under fresh guilt
contracted there must be faith acted afresh in God's
promises, and the Mediator's righteousness, for the
application of this pardon. What is done in heaven will not satisfy or quiet the soul, unless it be
acted over again in the sinner's conscience. There
is no living upon those promises, in which there is
no visible interest. Do not think justification is a
discontinued and partial thing.

Secondly, Comfortable converse with God as judge
of all, is much interrupted, by putting the graces
and comforts of the Spirit in the room of Christ,
and the actings of our faith on him. It was truly
said by holy Mr Rutherford, that "deadness *to* good
"and gracious works, and lively activity *in* the per-
"formance

"formance of them, seldom meet together." Faith is the noblest of all graces, because it empties the soul of all self-dependencies, and fixes it on Christ, in whom is all righteousness, grace, acceptation, and fulness. It is called 'precious faith,' 2 Pet. i. 1. eminently on this consideration, that it leads the sinner in all his guilt, fears, temptations, trials, duties, to precious, all-sufficient Jesus. It enriches us not, at any time, otherwise, than as a vessel which holds the treasure. Be it grace, life, strength, comfort, peace, or joy, which thou findest at any time in believing, faith derives them all from Christ. What, if thou canst not *see* Christ to be thine, canst thou *trust* him? If thou canst not *rejoice* in Christ; canst thou *mourn* after him? He appears in thine eyes the chief amongst ten thousand, and altogether lovely, and thou venturest thine *all*, for time and eternity, upon this suitable, glorious, and all-sufficient Saviour. Why here is the object of faith, and here are the actings of faith: And let me tell thee, soul! God is better pleased, and more honoured by such an humble, emptied, depending, though sorrowful frame, than he would be with thy choicest comforts, and the sweetest exercise of every grace, wert thou in the actings of these graces to be forgetful of the Mediator's righteousness: There is no stedfastness in frames, no worthiness in inherent righteousness; these are not to be pleaded before the throne; 'Christ is all, and in all.' For this reason is the church's frame commended, that she came up from the wilderness, 'leaning on her beloved,' Cant. viii. 5. There cannot be a surer method taken to prevent, or interrupt the soul's comfortable converse with God as a judge, than by magnifying the fruits of faith above the object; setting up grace and comfort above Christ, and pure faith in him. Once more,

Thirdly, This converse with God as a judge, is by nothing more interrupted, than by a careless and loose walk; where there is little or no respect to

God's commandments, there will be a dread of his presence. The completeness and eternal acceptation which there is in Christ's righteousness, and all the aboundings of the Father's grace in him, will give no comfort in dealing with God as a righteous and strict judge, while a soul is conscious of indulged sins. In the greatest privacy, sin brings shame. ' Let ' us draw near with a true heart, in full assurance of ' faith,' Heb. x. 22. Sincerity is neither our legal righteousness, nor our gospel-perfection; but it is a good inward evidence of interest in that righteousness of Christ, which is both. 1 John iii. 21. ' Be-' loved, if our heart condemn us not, then have we ' confidence towards God.' The truth of faith must be judged of by the fruits of faith; these appear ' in ' all goodness, and righteousness, and truth,' Eph. v. 9. Communion with God, if there is not an aim at conformity to him, is but a delusion, which will one day swallow up the soul in everlasting horror and despair. ' Blessed are they that do his command-' ments, that they may have right to the tree of life, ' and may enter in through the gates into the city,' Rev. xxii. 14. Dost thou keep a knee for Baal, or a bow for Rimmon? is there allowed guile in thy heart, as to this or the other pleasurable or gainful sin? Conscience condemns thee now; and ' if our ' heart condemn us, God is greater than our hearts, ' and knoweth all things.' Many a poor believer knows it to his cost, when he has ventured to go out of God's way, that he has stood trembling, as on the brink of the grave, when approaching his throne, and has scarce dared to pray for his free Spirit. Freedom through Christ, with God thy judge, can never stand with liberty to any sin.

Thus concerning those ways and methods by which converse with God is maintained, and by what means also it is prevented or interrupted. This leads to the fourth general head laid down:

IV. To

IV. To shew what a blessed privilege such a comfortable converse is, in the whole of believers course heaven-wards. Wherein the privilege of such a converse does consist.

'Ye are not come unto the mount that might be
'touched, and that burned with fire, nor unto black-
'ness, and darkness, and tempest; but ye are come
'unto mount Zion, and unto the city of the living
'God, the heavenly Jerusalem; and to an innume-
'rable company of angels; and to God the judge
'of all.' Such a converse is a blessing which can never be enough prized: For,

First, This blessed converse makes all other comforts blessings. Sinner! whatever thou possessest, thou possessest it under the curse, unless God is thy friend and portion in Christ Jesus. All things are ours upon no other ground or tenure, than that we are Christ's, 1 Cor. iii. 22. There is a fatal sting, not only in the vanities and sinful pleasures of youth, but even in the necessary comforts and enjoyments of life: Eccles. xi. 9. 'For all these things, God
'will bring thee into judgment.' Must I leave all these comforts, husband or wife, children, trade, honour, inheritance; and lie down in the grave, and wake in hell! It is an awful thought: Felix himself *trembled*, when Paul pressed it home upon his conscience, God giving power and efficacy to the word, Acts xxiv. 25. Ah! Sirs, there are many that tremble at the thought of judgment, who yet put off the day of judgment: But why should you, when the doctrine you have heard, gives you so sweet a view of the great judge of quick and dead? God is a Father, a Friend in Christ. Once in Christ, and safe for ever. Every thing is a blessing, and comes as such, when sin is pardoned, and interest is given in the blood of sprinkling. "All this, and heaven "at last!" may the believer say,—'Thanks be un-
'to God for his unspeakable gift.'

Secondly, This comfortable converse which believers have with God, sweetens all their afflictions and crosses. No trial befals thee, but it was put into the covenant. It comes from the hand of God as a reconciled Father, for thy profit and purging; not from his hand as a sin-revenging judge, for thy punishment. Under every changing dispensation, thou mayst sing of mercy and judgment: What is a terror to others, is a song of praise, and matter of rejoicing to thee. ' I will praise thee, O Lord; ' though thou wast angry with me, thine anger is ' turned away, and thou comfortedst me,' Isa. xii. 1. It is easy to kiss the rod, when thou art persuaded it comes in love. There is no wrath in the cup of affliction, be it ever so bitter. Christ was made thy curse, that thou through him mightest everlastingly inherit the blessing. Thy Surety has drained the curse and wrath of an angry God, and instead thereof hath put into thine hand the cup of salvation, Psal. cxvi. 15. Sweetly and comfortably may believers talk with God of his judgments, when they are persuaded from his covenant, and promise, and oath to their Christ and them, that whatever befals them, it comes in mercy.

Thirdly, This comfortable converse with God makes duties and ordinances sweet; why should there be terror and fear, where there is no enmity, no distance? True, the law admits of no approach to God, because it insists upon perfect, personal obedience; but the grace of God's covenant, and the righteousness of his Son, lay all things open to the believing soul. This is an hope by ' which we draw ' nigh to God,' Heb. vii. 19. It is spoken of that nearness which is granted in all gospel-ordinances. Thou mayst come boldly to the throne of grace, because the great High-priest of thy profession lives to make thee welcome: Thy judge has received a full satisfaction for all thy sins, and is become a Father, a Friend, through the blood of Christ. Would prayer, and all other holy ordinances be dreaded, had we

right

right notions, I should say, had we present sense of our fellowship with God, as judge of all?

Fourthly, This comfortable converse with God makes all reproaches we receive from men sit easy upon us; Psal. xxxi. 14, 15. 'I trust in thee, O 'Lord; I said, thou art my God; my times are in 'thine hand.' Here is the godly man's refuge in all times of unjust judgment from the sinful world. God, who has justified thy person, will plead thy cause. An appeal to the court above is ever heard. 'It is God that justifieth; who is he that condem- 'neth?' Rom. viii. 33, 34. Soul! Canst thou stand before God? Be not afraid of the sentence of man. 'Commit thy way unto the Lord, trust also in him; '—and he shall bring forth thy righteousness as the 'light; and thy judgment as the noon-day,' Psal. xxxvii. 5, 6.

Fifthly, This comfortable converse with God, secures against the threats, the wiles, and hellish designs of Satan. The prince of this world is judged: Whatever he does against thee (believer!) thy comfort or salvation, it is by permission from thy God, thy Judge, thy Father: He must ask leave before he smites Job, or sifts Peter. When thy God checks him, he must leave off his pursuit and depart. This God, to whom thou comest with such freedom of access, is judge of men and devils; and he has judged for thee beforehand in his eternal counsels; and according to his eternal plan, all his actual dispensations are measured. Not a wile or stratagem of Satan's, but it is put down in God's covenant, with the grace thou needest at such a season, and also the blessed issue of it. His fiery darts may pierce, but they shall not stick in thy heart; envenomed they are, but thy God, thy judge, will not suffer them to poison thee: Thy Jesus is above, 'who is touched 'with the feeling of thy infirmities;' so that thou mayst come boldly with all thy temptations and fears, and leave all to the cognizance and wise direction of God the judge of all. Once more,

Sixthly,

Sixthly, This comfortable converse with God makes death and judgment without terror. Doth the law acquit thee now? it will never condemn thee then. A serpent without a sting may affright, but it cannot injure. When thou puttest off thy earthly tabernacle, thou art going to thy Judge and thy Father: To thy judge, not to hear a sentence of condemnation against thee, but to receive thy crown and kingdom. Thy cause hath been tried here; the law hath discharged thee, justice hath discharged thee; and will God falsify his own word, or make void his Son's righteousness? When believers die to time, they are immediately with Christ; ' This day shalt thou be with me in paradise,' Luke xxiii. 43. Sirs! you die in his arms, your departed spirits committed to him, he presents to the Father. This took away all Paul's fears, and winged his desires. 2 Tim. i. 12.—' I know whom I have belie-
' ved, and am persuaded, that he is able to keep that
' which I have committed to him against that day.'
And chap. iv. 6. ' I am now ready to be offered,
' and the time of my departure is at hand. Hence-
' forth, there is a crown of righteousness laid up for
' me, which the Lord, the righteous judge, shall
' give me at that day.' Death and judgment are no terror to the believer in Christ; when the person and righteousness of the Mediator are before him. He knows already his blessed sentence, and the security his Jesus has given him; and he shall not be deceived. Rev. i. 17, 18. ' Fear not, I am the first
' and the last: I am he that liveth and was dead;
' and behold, I am alive for evermore, Amen: And
' have the keys of hell and death.'

Thus concerning the privileges of this comfortable converse with God, as judge of all. I shall now conclude the subject with,

1. A few directions to them that are in so happy a case.

2. Two or three words to ungodly sinners.

First,

First, A few directions.

DIR. 1. Live more upon the purposes and covenant of your God. Salvation is not a thing of yesterday; your Jesus is ' a Lamb slain from the foundation of the world;' and your sentence of justification was as early determined and ascertained in this your glorious and appointed Surety. 2 Tim. i. 9. ' Who hath saved us, and called us with an holy ' calling; not according to our works, but according ' to his own purpose and grace, which was gi- ' ven us in Christ, before the world began.' Be conversant with that grace which was intrusted with Christ for you, before all worlds were.

DIR. 2. Be much in the actings of your faith upon the Mediator's person and righteousness. This is the way to confirm your title (as to the sense of it in yourselves) and increase your comfort. Come to ' the blood of sprinkling;' when you cannot see it to be blood sprinkled upon you. A believer's life is a life of trust; it lies more in bonds and promises, than in present enjoyments. In one word, it is *in Christ*, not *in yourselves*. ' The Lord is my portion,' saith my soul; therefore be much in the actings of faith upon him.

DIR. 3. Admire and adore the love, the everlasting love of Christ the Mediator of the covenant. All the Father's love and grace towards you is in Christ. As all of us were sinners, we must all have been sufferers, had not the blessed and beloved Jesus offered himself in our room, and consented to stand in our stead. ' Ye know the grace of our Lord Je- ' sus Christ.' Need I say, prize and value it; cast your crowns at his feet; begin the song below, to which your harps will everlastingly be tuned above; ' Unto him that loved us, and washed us from our ' sins in his own blood, and has made us kings and ' priests unto God and his Father, to him be glory ' and dominion for ever and ever. Amen.' Rev. i. 5, 6.

DIR. 4.

Dir. 4. Endeavour to live a life, as of truſt, ſo of praiſe. Much thou haſt received already, though much is ſtill wanting; Chriſt and his righteouſneſs are preſent to thy faith, though heaven is not to thy enjoyment: 'Through him we have acceſs to God 'by one ſpirit,' Eph. ii. 18. and indulged complaints are a very unbecoming frame, in one that hath ever come to God the judge of all with comfort. 'Who-'ſo offereth praiſe, glorifieth me; and to him that 'ordereth his converſation aright, will I ſhew the 'ſalvation of my God,' Pſal. l. 23.

Two or three words to ungodly ſinners.

1. Haſt thou no thought of appearing before God as a judge? Is no account, doſt thou think, taken of all thy ſins and allowed tranſgreſſions? Why, doſt thou come to God's houſe, that thou mayſt compliment conſcience, if thou art apprehenſive of no judgment to come? Man! thy falſe vows and promiſes, thou makeſt in a day of affliction, thy vain wiſhes, prayers, and ſometimes tears, ſhed under an awakening diſcourſe, ſhew plainly there is a judgment to come. Therefore,

2. How art thou provided againſt this judgment? thou dareſt not deſpiſe thy Judge when thou art before his bar: *Not guilty*, thou canſt not plead, when both the law and conſcience witneſs againſt thee: Mere mercy will ſtand thee in no ſtead when thou art under the arreſt of juſtice. Promiſes of future amendment will be of no avail; what *good* haſt thou now to counterbalance thine evils? A broken deſire, a ſabbath's attendance on God's worſhip, a little alms, an hereafter repentance. Soul! were God to call thee away this night, couldſt thou plead theſe before thy judge? Thou art afraid to truſt it now, much more to plead it then. Let me aſk further,

3. Is it not beſt to be at ſome certainty and ſettledneſs in matters of eternity? thou provideſt againſt poverty and old age, becauſe they *may* come; but death and judgment *muſt* come: 'There is no diſ-'charge in that war.' Before God the judge of all thou

thou muſt appear *hereafter*, if thou comeſt not to him *here*. Let me therefore leave with you theſe three words of advice.

1. Beg of God to convince thee of ſin. Saying I am a ſinner, will never recommend a Saviour: Till thou feeſt thyſelf *the* ſinner, the chief of ſinners, thou wilt always think it time enough to hear of Chriſt, death and judgment.

2. Aſk to be led into a heart-acquaintance with Chriſt and his righteouſneſs. ' We preach Chriſt;' but God muſt teach thee the worth of Chriſt, and thy need of him ' Aſk, and thou ſhalt receive:' It is time enough to complain when thou art denied.

3. Venture then in God's ſtrength upon the Chriſt and the righteouſneſs the goſpel reveals. Thou haſt been a great ſinner, but Chriſt is a great Saviour. Thy ſins, though never ſo many and great, are the ſins but of a creature; his righteouſneſs is the righteouſneſs of God. Thy judge will never deſpiſe thee becauſe of thy ſins, if thou art made willing to accept this righteouſneſs: ' If any man thirſt, let ' him come to me and drink.' The promiſes, though not univerſal, are indefinite, that no ſinner may think himſelf beyond the reach of mercy. Wo to them that ſtill deſpiſe this Chriſt and his ſalvation. The judge is at the door, eternity comes on apace; and ' who among you can endure devouring fire, or ' dwell with everlaſting burnings!'

SERMON X.

GOD'S PREVENTING MERCY OPENED.

PSALM lix. 10.

The God of Mercy shall prevent me.

IT is a good observation of Dr Hammond's upon the title of this and two or three foregoing Psalms; "They are called 'Michtam of David,' "David's golden Psalms, his jewels; because the "several preservations which are here recorded, "were exceeding precious to him." Those blessings in the bestowment whereof God eminently displays his wisdom, power, love, and faithfulness, are precious; our meditations of them, and of God the giver of them, are always sweet. What was the special providence which gave occasion to this Psalm, you have in the title of it, ' When Saul sent and ' they watched the house to kill him.' By what means he escaped, he does not tell us, but attributes his delivery to God only, of whom by prayer he sought it. Prayer is our best weapon against our enemies; the best of all means, and first to be used for any deliverance. And there are two pleas which he makes use of; one was, that God was *his God*, ver. 1. the other was the *power* and *strength* of his
enemies.

enemies. It is a blessed thing to have the covenant to fly to, in all times of straits and troubles: there is always an anchor-hold of hope there. *My God,* is such a plea as infinitely over-balances all other things. He has engaged himself to do his people good; and it is time for him to work when the enemy exalts himself. The church's enemies are never so near destruction as when they think they have nothing to do, but take, and divide the spoil. We may plead God's promise, and the enemy's power too; both are a ground of hope to a believer in Jesus. The Psalmist was sure of mercy upon these grounds; he knew he was safe, because God was his God, and the God of his mercy; ' the God of my mercy shall ' prevent me.' Some read it ' hath prevented me;' others, ' doth prevent me;' and others, as in my text, ' shall prevent me.' Each of these senses are exceeding sweet, and full. Take it in the first sense, ' hath prevented me,' and it implies thus much, that the Psalmist never was in any difficulty, temptation or fear, but God was beforehand with him; having always the mercy ready which he stood in need of; and had given it in due season, and that when he least expected it, and it may be was least prepared for it. Take it in the second sense, ' doth prevent,' it argues the Psalmist's ground of confidence when all present appearances were gone: as if he had said, " God is of one mind, his thoughts are thoughts of " peace, and not of evil; he may vary his provi- " dence, but his heart is the same as ever; why " should I fear? why should I not hope and rejoice? " for my God is a tried God, he is working for me " even now. He prevents my fears, and he will " prevent my failing." Take the words, as they lie in my text, and it comes to the same thing: " God sees all my enemies designs, and he is ready " for them: my prayer is heard, and sure I am, de- " liverance will come, though I know not the time " and way of it."

My

My design, under the Spirit's influence, is to look into my own heart and yours, and shew you what wonders of providence and grace God, as ' the God ' of our mercy,' has caused to pass before us. In discoursing on these words I shall inquire.

I. In what sense, or in what respects God is ' the ' God of our mercy.'

II. How, as the God of our mercy, he doth prevent us.

III. Apply.

I. I am to inquire in what respects God is said to be the ' God of his peoples mercy.' And it seems to include in it these three things:

1. That all the mercy, which is in God's nature, is for his saints. It is a great word, that, 1 Pet. v. 10. ' the God of all grace.' God has in him all sorts of grace, and all degrees of grace for his saints. He hath pardoning, quickening, strengthening, comforting, and preserving grace. His mercy is rich mercy, abundant mercy, inexhaustible mercy, sure mercy. A man's riches are his glory; God glories in his mercy; it is his delight, he rests in it, and so may we, because there is an infinite inconceivable fulness of it in him: ' With thee is the fountain ' of life.' All that we have here, all that we can enjoy of it to eternity, are but as the streams; and the more you draw, the faster it springs up. There is no want nor any end in the mercy of the Lord to his people. ' For I said, mercy shall be built up ' for ever,' Psal. lxxxix. 2. God distributes and parcels out this mercy, that we may conceive of it the better; hence he is called by the apostle, ' The ' Father of mercies,' and the ' God of all comfort.' 2 Cor. i. 3. What mercy soever you need, God has it to give. Ask as high as you will, you shall not be denied; God's mercy is proportioned to, nay, it infinitely exceeds all our miseries: and a pleasing consideration it is. God is not called the Author of our mercies, but the Father of them, to shew how freely they come from him; they are his bowels,

he

he is pleased with them, as the father is with his own child; dwell on the name, it is a sweet one, the 'Father of mercies.' In my text, David grasps all this mercy, lays hold of it as his own mercy: the 'God of my mercy shall prevent me.' That is one sense.

2. It supposes farther, that there is a portion of mercy laid by, in the purpose of God, for every saint: A portion of mercy which he may call 'his 'own.' This, some understand to be Christ's meaning to Paul, 2 Cor. xiii. 9. 'My grace is sufficient 'for thee;' *i. e.* tha tgrace which I have allotted for thee, thou wilt find sufficient. I knew what thou wouldst need in my eternal counsels; I have made provision before hand; I have taken care thou shouldst have enough. And this doubtless, says the great Dr Goodwin, is Paul's meaning in that speech of his, Philip. iii. 12. 'I follow after, if that I may 'apprehend that for which also I am apprehended 'of Christ Jesus.' It is a word of great force, 'I 'follow after;' I pursue with vigour, as one that follows the game. I cannot rest satisfied with the grace I have, but am always looking for more. Whence was this, but because Paul knew the largeness of God's heart, and the infinite merit of Christ's blood; there was more grace yet behind, and he could not be at rest till he had received it all. This is the happiness even of heaven itself; to apprehend, attain, possess that, for which also we were apprehended of Christ. Poor soul! thou art often put to it, to believe for this or for the other mercy; thou feest nothing. Now thou shalt be eased under this trouble, and carried through the other difficulty: 'All 'these things are against *thee*;' that is the language of *sense*; but *faith* tells thee quite otherwise. Every one of these trials is the way to some signal mercy, some signal support, some signal comfort which was laid by for thee, against the trial came. Every son, every child shall have his portion; grace for that duty, that trial, that darkness and distress, was settled

tled upon thee in God's purpose, and ordered for thee in the everlasting covenant. That is another sense of the phrase in my text, ' The God of my ' mercy.' But,

3. The words suppose farther, that God has taken it upon him, as his charge, to keep this portion of mercy for his people. Whatever it be, soul, it is in trust for thee with him. Every saint may apply to God, as the God of every mercy which he needs. ' God is my defence, and the God of my mercy: ' unto thee, O my strength, will I sing,' ver. 17. If this will not bring a man to praise, nothing will. To have a faithful friend to go to, under new and unexpected difficulties, is a signal blessing: our friend, it may be, and our father's friend; a great support this, under losses, crosses, and troubles: but what is a faithful *friend* to a faithful *God?* who has wisdom and power equal to his love and mercy! whom none can resist, none can surprise, none can beguile, or draw from our interests! what a blessed foundation of consolation is this! God knows his title; he remembers his covenant; ' he will give ' grace and glory;' why? because it is one of his glorious titles, ' the God of thy mercy.' He would not answer his name was he not to answer thy prayers, to set thee above thy fears, and to deliver thee out of all thy distresses.

Two brief remarks, and I proceed to the second head.

REMARK I. What a happy man is every Christian. How can he be poor who has God for his portion, and all the mercy in his nature for his supply! who is provided for ever, and his inheritance is in such hands that it can never be wrested from him? Col. iii. 3. ' Your life is hid with Christ ' in God,' Not bare life, but all the necessaries, the pleasures and comforts of life, ' hid with Christ ' in God.' When two such securities fail, then complain.

REMARK

REMARK II. What pity it is Christians live no more like themselves; amongst men, one is blamed and another, because they do not live according to their income. Their estates are large, but their spirits are mean; "They are of a poor little spirit." Charge no man else, but condemn thyself. God is thine, his mercy thine; and yet thou art ever fearing, ever complaining, but seldom thankful. What have you lacked yet? the 'God of your 'mercy,' he hath not always prevented you? why then shouldst thou limit him in any of his dispensations? The Psalmist knew that God had done it, and would do it again for him; and from this consideration, that he was the 'God of his mercy,' he rejoices before hand: 'The God of my mercy 'shall prevent me.' Which leads to the second thing.

II. How, or in what respects does God (as the God of his peoples mercy) prevent them.

The word *prevent*, sometimes signifies to 'meet 'one in the way, or rather, to 'come before one, '*or* be before one' in a thing; as when you know your friend's wants, such is your love and kindness to him, that you give him what he needs, before he asks it: This is to *prevent* him. As it is said of the Father, when applied to by the Mediator, Psalm xxi. 2, 3. 'Thou hast given him his heart's 'desire, and hast not withheld the request of his 'lips; for thou preventest him with the blessings of 'goodness,' &c. God may be said to *prevent* his people as 'the God of their mercy,' in the five following respects:

1. God gives them the greatest blessings, notwithstanding their ill-deservings. What were we in our natural state but the children of wrath and servants of sin? Our care was about nothing else, than fulfilling the lusts of the flesh, and of the mind; and yet the God of our mercy pitied us then; then he said unto us, *live*, Ezek. xvi. 6. 'And when I pas-
'sed by thee, and saw thee polluted in thine own
'blood,

'blood, I said unto thee in thy blood, Live,' &c. There was nothing lovely in us, but there was love in God towards us. Again, Isa. xlviii. 8. 'Yea, thou heardst not, yea, from that time that thine ear was not opened, for I knew that thou wouldst deal very treacherously, and wast called a transgressor from the womb'—and yet chosen; and yet called, and made partaker of a divine nature! The Lord loved us, because he would love us: gave us Christ; gave us his Spirit, gave us the name and privilege of sons, notwithstanding all our vileness, and gave us all 'without any upbraiding!' Had God marked iniquity, alas! where had any of us been? But our deservings are not the rule of God's mercy, he *prevented* us beforehand; and he has prevented us ever since; our many slips and falls afterwards, the vanity of our minds, the carnality of our frames, our loose and careless walk, our sad and dreadful backslidings, the turning away of our hearts from God, he provided against them all; he gives the greatest blessings notwithstanding our ill-deservings.

2. God *prevents* us as the God of our mercy, because he gives the greatest blessings, notwithstanding our *unpreparedness* to receive them. Rom. ix. 16. 'It is not of him that willeth, nor of him that runneth, but of God that sheweth mercy.' Were God to wait till man had prepared himself for divine grace, who would be saved? Were his thoughts and ways as man's are, he could never shew mercy; for there is not a soul that receives it but has stood it out against him. The law is engraved in our very natures: 'What must I do to be saved?' is the language of the natural mind when convinced of sin, until Christ is discovered to him, by the Spirit, as 'the end of the law for righteousness,' Rom. x. 4. And all other means are tried, before Christ is trusted. You, that were scripture-proof and sermon-proof, did not God *prevent* you when you came to him? he *found* you in your own way, though he did

not

not *leave* you there. You came, it may be, to ridicule the preacher; to have matter to oppose the truth; to hear some new thing; or it may be were forced by your parents or masters against your desires, to attend public worship.—And there God (who only can persuade Japhet to dwell in the tents of Shem) *met you*, and you heard words whereby you must be saved. Was not this *preventing* you? Ask Zaccheus what preparation there was in him for Christ; it was curiosity not conscience that made him climb the tree; but Christ knew him to be a vessel of mercy, and now the fountain is set open, ' Zaccheus! make haste and come down; for to-
' day I must abide at thy house,' Luke xix. 5. Ask the Samaritan woman, what preparation there was in her for Christ; he was first at the well, and sat there waiting, John iv. 6. What brought him there? a design of pure love and mercy to her soul; ' he
' must needs go through Samaria,' *ver.* 4. There was a lost sheep to be gathered, and Christ can have no rest till he finds her. O! there is a blessed *necessity* in *our* preaching and in *your* hearing ' when the
' day of salvation cometh.' Christ comes out to meet you, and says, ' Turn unto me; I am the
' strong-hold, O! ye prisoners of hope:' God prevents us, in our *unpreparedness*.

3. God *prevents* his people, with respect to *their prayers*. Either he is beforehand with them in asking, or he gives them what they never thought of asking. How sweetly at some times does he by his Spirit bid us pray, as having the blessings beforehand ready to give. Hence we find it, as Psal. xxvii. 8. ' When thou saidst, Seek ye my face; my heart
' said, Unto thy face, Lord, will I seek.' He bespeaks a prayer; calls us by the secret whispers of his Spirit to go and pour out our souls unto him. And how do we find it then? why, ' then shalt
' thou call, and the Lord shall answer; thou shalt
' cry, and he shall say, Here I am,' Isa. lviii. 9. Even while we are yet speaking, the blessing comes,

Isa. lxv. 24. the decree goes forth and grace comes freely, Dan. ix. 21.

Again, God often gives, as he did to Solomon; he gives what you ask with an exceeding overplus, 1 Kings iii. 12, 13. he asked only 'a wise and discerning heart;' God gave him 'riches, and honour, and long life besides.' So you ask direction in his way, or submission to his will; and the very blessing you were content to part with at his call, is often returned to you, and is then doubly sweet; you have more than you ask. Say then, believer, whether the God of your mercy does not *prevent* you. But our *prayers* are too little observed, or else our praises would not be so few.

4. God prevents us as to our *fears*.

Isaiah li. 12, 13. 'Who art thou, that thou shouldst be afraid of a man that shall die, &c.—And forgettest the Lord thy maker, that hath stretched forth the heavens, and laid the foundations of the earth? and hast feared continually every day, because of the fury of the oppressor, as if he was ready to destroy; and where is the fury of the oppressor?' What a sweetness is there in these words! We are often upon the rack for nothing; we slay ourselves by our own disquieting fears; but we need fear none but ourselves: the oppressor whom we feared, becomes a friend; his heart is changed; he is another man, or else his power is restrained; he *dies* perhaps for your sake, as has often been the case of cruel persecutors. God has heaven and earth at his command; and 'no weapon formed against thee shall prosper,' Isa. liv. 17. If you have God's call to any work, never doubt of his presence to attend you in it. 'Fear you not their fear,' Isa. viii. 12. your God, your rock, your refuge, your defence is above; and he will perfect that which concerneth you. Infinite wisdom is never at a loss; he usually worketh with, but he can as easily work without means. Remember whatever friend dies, whatever comfort

comfort goes, ' your Rock liveth.' God preventeth our *fears*.

5. And lastly, God is pleased often to *prevent* his peoples *desires, hopes,* and *expectations*.

Eph. iii. 20. ' Unto him that is able to do ex-
' ceeding abundantly above all that we ask or think,
' according to the power that worketh in us, unto
' him be glory,' &c. God is abundant in mercy and truth; we cannot go to the bottom of a promise, but God will not leave us, who has given us that promise, till he has done all which he hath spoken to us of. Why is he *faithful*, as calling us into the fellowship of his son Jesus Christ? 1 Cor. i. 9. but because all the love he bore us in Christ, all the mercy he settled upon us for the sake of Christ, he will assuredly bring us to the full enjoyment of.—But alas! what are our thoughts about these things, if compared with what infinite wisdom, and power, and everlasting love have laid up for us! ' The love
' of Christ passeth knowledge.' Should God bid you ask or think for yourself, it is best to refer the matter back again to him. O! when we have thought our utmost, what is this, to what God gives? Say with the church, ' Thou shalt choose our inheri-
' tance for us.' Thus, concerning the several respects in which God, as the God of our mercy, *prevents* us. Two or three words by way of use.

Use 1. Observe these things. This is the close of a long and beautiful description of God's providence towards his church and the world. Psal. cvii. 43.
' Whoso is wise, and will observe these things, even
' they shall understand the kindness of the Lord.'
An heart-affecting sense of God's goodness is a great mercy. The kindness, care and love of God are often unseen, because his dispensations are not observed.

2. Trust God more. That is the use of former instances of his mercy. What! received so much mercy, and doubt still! this is shameful unbelief.

3. The great concern is an interest in *Christ*. God shews no mercy out of the Mediator. Whatever you have heard or known of God as a God of mercy in a providential way, you are never the nearer heaven, unless you have a covenant-interest in him; this is your safety, and this your best claim to any thing that is his.

4. Give God the glory of his own mercy. Suitable returns are expected where so much mercy is so freely given; praise him with your lips; honour him in your lives; walk humbly with God; walk fruitfully before men. And let no man call the mercies of God *small*, that is out of hell, and has the least hope of heaven.

SERMON XI.

THE PREPARATION OF THE HEART THE LORD'S WORK.

PROVERBS xvi. 1.

The preparations of the heart in man, and the answer of the tongue, is from the Lord.

THERE is hardly any thing profeſſors are more at a loſs about in our day, than what we call preparations for holy exerciſes. Some will ſcarce allow themſelves any time to think of the duty they are about to engage in, when drawing nigh to God in ſolemn ordinances; others, by their preparation-days, and preparatory duties, ſeem rather to make a *God* of ordinances, than by the help of ordinances to draw nigh unto him. Suffer me, therefore, in a ſhort diſcourſe, to open to you the nature of that preparation which the goſpel requires, and the way and manner in which it is to be obtained; that you may not, on the one hand, ruſh into God's preſence, as a horſe doth into battle, without either care or fear; nor, on the other, venture to come before him in a dependence on your own doings, leſt haply (Ephraim like) you be ' counted an empty vine.'

The words which I have read, are a general proposition, which holds true in every state, circumstance and condition of life. They respect in general all the purposes, contrivances and designs of a man's heart, whatever be the subject it is fixed upon. The word rendered *preparations*, is a military term, and signifies, either the marshalling of an army; or else it refers to the ordering or ranging the loaves of shew-bread according to divine appointment, Lev. xxiv. 6. Taking it in this sense, it gives us to understand thus much, that the putting in order the frames and motions of our hearts is of the Lord, and him only. Some indeed, vary the words and sense, reading them thus: " *The preparations of the heart are of man*, or in the power of man; he has a freedom to lay his own schemes as he pleases, *but the answer of the tongue is from the Lord;* he shall speak not what he hath purposed and contrived, but what the Lord hath appointed." And thus our English Expositor glosses upon the place, " Man purposeth, but God disposeth." This seems rather a strain upon the words, for why is it not as much in the power of man to speak, as think? Both are alike natural acts, and both ' are from the Lord.' He teaches us to order our thoughts, and to order our words, for that is plainly the sense of my text. Applying the general proposition to a particular instance, the doctrine from the words is plainly this.

DOCT. All our fitness for duty, and our assistance in it, is from the Lord.

In discoursing on this proposition, I shall only resolve two queries, and then apply.

I. How doth God prepare the heart for duty?
II. How doth he assist and enlarge it?

I. How doth God prepare the heart for duty? The frames of our heart in duty are as much his gift, as are the blessings bestowed in answer to the request of our lips. Preparation for duties is two-
fold.

fold. I will a little explain that. There is preparation which divines call habitual, and there is also actual preparation for duty.

That which is habitual, respects our state. When a poor soul is clothed with Christ's righteousness, and hath the graces of the Spirit implanted in his heart, he is then habitually prepared for duty. That which is actual represents our frames, which my text intends, and consists in a suitable exercise of those graces, which the Spirit hath implanted in the heart of a regenerate soul. There is a going forth of the soul towards God in the way of faith, repentance, love, joy, &c. It is a frame of spirit suited to whatever duty God calls us forth to. There is in the soul a desire after God, a delight in him, and a tendency of soul towards him. Thus the Psalmist expresses himself, Psal. lxiii. 1. ' O God, thou art my God, ' early will I seek thee, in a dry and thirsty land, ' where no water is.' Here was a heart prepared to meet God, his inward desires and prayers were agreed; so ver. 8. ' My soul followeth hard after thee:' There was restlessness till he had enjoyment; nothing but God could satisfy him. Our habitual and actual preparation for duty, is all from him.

This being premised, the question returns, How doth God assist and enlarge in it?

1. He calls off our vain and wandering thoughts, and so fixes our hearts for duty, as the Psalmist expresseth it, Psal. lvii. 7. ' My heart is fixed, O God, ' my heart is fixed.' Our vain thoughts are the cause of our daily complaints. The Christian hates them, but he cannot himself get rid of them. Psal. cxix. 113. ' I hate vain thoughts, but thy law do I ' love.' The more we know God's law, the better we shall love it; and the more we love it, the more we shall hate those spiritual wickednesses in the heart, by which contempt is cast upon it; our heart-sins are our worst enemies. Poor soul! say what thou wouldst give to be delivered from the vanity of your own mind, your roving fancy, disturbing distracting thoughts?

thought? Do you not find then a *law*, that when you would do good, evil is present with you? The more eagerly you strive to get out of yourself, the more violent Satan, and a wicked heart oppose it? Cannot we give in our testimony to Paul's experience? 2 Cor. iii. 5. ' Not that we are sufficient of ' ourselves, to think any thing as of ourselves.' There is an indisposedness, we have no aptness, or bias by which we are that way inclined of ourselves. Our thoughts make a mutiny within, they rebel against God ; it is necessary they should be sent off, when we profess to draw nigh unto him. Thus the Psalmist prayeth, and thus God in effect promiseth, for all our sufficiency is of him: Psal. xix. 14. ' Let the ' words of my mouth, and the meditation of my ' heart, be always acceptable in thy sight, O Lord, ' my strength, and my Redeemer.' Never let us seek God's face, without seeking his strength. A man may be whole days and weeks in preparing himself for some solemn ordinance, and yet come unprepared at last, without God's strength. Power belongeth unto the Lord, power to dislodge our vain thoughts, and power to quicken our dead hearts, and our poor lifeless frames.

2. God further prepares for duty, as he works in our hearts an holy fear and reverence of his majesty, when we come before him. There is a two-fold fear scripture speaks of; one is slavish, it leads to bondage, and brings torment: the other is filial, or child-like, which proceeds from love, and is influential into the whole of obedience. It consists in an holy awe of his greatness, and glorious majesty ; we dare not trifle before him, nor behave ourselves lightly. A sense of God's presence with us, and a just apprehension of his infinite perfections, will lead us to sanctify the Lord in our hearts, so that we dare not indulge our formality before him. ' God is ' greatly to be feared in the assembly of the saints, ' and to be had in reverence of all them that are ' about him,' Psal. lxxxix. 7. Whence comes this
fear

fear and holy reverence? Doth man difpofe and frame his own heart thus to fear God? No, it comes from God's grace given to him; Heb. xii. 28. 'Wherefore we receiving a kingdom which cannot 'be moved, let us have grace, whereby we may ferve 'God acceptably, with reverence and godly fear. 'Let us have grace;' how fhall we obtain it? Why, afk it of the God of all grace, 'who giveth liberal-'ly, and upbraideth not. My grace is fufficient for 'thee,' 2 Cor. xii. 9. It is fuited to our times and our wants; *my grace*, but *ours* too; it is defigned for us; it is given to us. Given! for what? to help us in every time of need, Heb. iv. 16. O! we need this grace to fear God. Humbling grace, that we may be low before him, under a fenfe of our own wants, and our own fins; or elfe we fhall never be exalted by him. It is a blefled turn given to our fpirits, when they are thus difpofed to fear the Lord.

3. God prepares for duty, by giving us the favour of paft experiences, and by giving us prefent defires, after communing with him, Cant. i. 3. 'Becaufe of 'the favour of thy good ointment, thy name is as 'ointment poured forth, therefore do the virgins 'love thee.' Chrift's love is beyond all other de-lights. If ever we have enjoyed his prefence, his name and every thing which appertaineth to him will be precious. Though he hides his face, we fhall feek after him till we find him: Former experiences quicken and enliven our prefent defponding frames. O! there is a favour in Chrift's good ointments! The fpoufe found it fo, and even believers find it fo. But fay you, "What muft I do when my heart is "out of frame; when I have gone aftray like a loft "fheep; how can I go back to Chrift again? My "heart hath not the liking to him it once had; the "ftrength of my love, my defires, my delights is a-"bated. Strangers have devoured up my ftrength, "and I am not fuitably affected with it, thoroughly "humbled for it. What muft I do now?" To this the text gives a fweet and encouraging anfwer, 'The 'preparations

'preparations of the heart in man, and the anfwer of the tongue is from the Lord.' Art thou repenting, art thou defiring, and waiting for thy beloved? Is his name precious, his perfon, his righteoufnefs, his love precious? Why, in this very frame he is preparing thy heart for himfelf, and making a way for the out-goings of his love to you. Here is a favour arifing from communion once enjoyed though now loft: 'Draw me; we will run after thee.' Here is fenfe of diftance from Chrift, but there is alfo defire of union with him. Draw me, to thyfelf, nearer thy prefence, thy everlafting embraces. I can be eafy with abfence from my beloved no longer; draw me, elfe I move not. 'Draw me, we will run after thee.' It denotes eagernefs of defire, fwiftnefs of motion, and a ready affection to Chrift. Here is an heart prepared for duty. How? By the free Spirit of God, as giving the favour of paft experiences, and prefent defires after communion with God.

4. God prepares for duty often by fudden, unexpected enlargement of fpirit. We are furprifed into mercy. Faith is raifed, hope aboundeth, love to Chrift is inflamed, repentance and godly forrow are fet to work; and all before the foul is aware of the mercy. Thus we read, 2 Chron. xxix. 36. 'And Hezekiah rejoiced, and all the people, that God had prepared the people; for the thing was done fuddenly.' O! poor doubting foul, look into yourfelf, I am fpeaking your experience and my own, both at once. Have you not found the frame of your heart, at times, change in a moment? One gale of the Spirit hath fet all the fpices a flowing out. You have a dead time, it may be, the evening before the Lord's day, and life and liberty when you are in God's courts. One look from Chrift melts you down prefently: you are overcome with his love; he fets you as a feal upon his heart, as a feal upon his arm, fo that, or ever you was aware, you are with God. Now all thefe things worketh that one
and

and the self-same Spirit, dividing to every man severally as he will. His motions are free, he acts when, and where, and how he pleaseth. Thus the truth of the text is confirmed by these several particulars.

I proceed now to enquire,

II. How doth God help us in our speeches before him; for as the preparations of the heart in man are from the Lord, so is in like manner the answer of the tongue. Now this the Spirit doth also four ways.

1. He reveals to us our own wants, gives us some especial errand to go with to God. General expressions are a sure sign of prison frames. Prayer is a great burden, when we have nothing in particular to pray for, when we are neither affected with our sins, nor our mercies, our temptations, afflictions, nor even our present barren frames. In this the Spirit helps, Rom. viii. 26. ' Likewise the Spirit also helpeth our ' infirmities, for we know not what we should pray ' for as we ought.' He reveals our wants, that we may make them known to God. Sense of want is the spring of desires; there is an holy contention and earnestness in the soul, when he feels his burdens, and has conscience affected, and bowed down under his guilt and infirmities. How will a poor soul wrestle with God, when he knows himself to be in want, and sees where his help is! Alas, we may speak with our mouths, but our words drop short of heaven, if we speak not with our hearts. Did you never observe great labouring and little enlargement? Doubtless you must. Men pray as if they were to be heard for their much speaking, some, as if they were to be heard for their fine speaking : But alas! there is nothing of the Spirit in this. Our own gay plumes will not serve us for a covering, nor are they ornamental in prayer. He prays to the best purpose, whose heart is moved, who comes to unload himself

upon the Lord Christ, to cast all his burdens upon one mightier than he. Prayer is blessed work then, when a man knows what he should pray for as he ought; long prayers without this, are the dullest part of all our worship.

2. God helps in the answer of the tongue, as he gives us arguments and pleas to use in prayer. For this we have expressly the promise of the Spirit, John xiv. 26. 'But the Comforter, which is the Holy 'Ghost, whom the Father will send in my name, he 'shall teach you all things, and bring all things to 'your remembrance, whatsoever I have said unto 'you.' We have treacherous memories and deceitful hearts. We forget God's perfections and promises, and our own experience, even when we are calling upon him. Not one word to say at some times before the throne, though we have just before been reading many a sweet promise. If we know what we want, we know not how to plead for the bestowment of it. Well, but the blessed Spirit secretly suggests what we should say to God, when standing before him. He orders our cause for us, and fills our mouths with arguments, Job xxiii. 4. puts a force into our pleas, and life and vigour into our hearts. How will a poor soul dwell upon a promise in prayer, when the Spirit gives him to taste the sweetness of it. There is much preaching in prayer, sometimes little pleading, many vain repetitions, but few of the Spirit's arguments. Our language will be scriptural, when our frames are spiritual. The answers of the tongue are just as the dispositions of the heart are. It was a sweet frame of the Psalmist, Psal. v. 3. ' My voice shalt thou hear ' in the morning, O Lord; in the morning will I ' direct my prayer unto thee, and will look up.' He knew God would hear him, because the Spirit helped him. Do you ask in what? I answer, in *directing* or *marshalling* his prayer before the Lord; for so the word signifies, as has been before observed. His mouth was filled with arguments, and his heart big
with

with expectation; he looked out beforehand, knowing he should speed, because God had enlarged his heart to plead. We should not lose so much of the comfort of our prayers, were we more observant of the return of them. Time forbids me to enumerate all these pleas. Every perfection is a plea, every promise is a plea, every passage of our experience is a plea; the blood and righteousness, the covenant engagements and performances of Christ, are all pleas in prayer; so is this present life, the gift of the Spirit, and the graces implanted in our hearts, &c.

3. He further helps us in and after prayer, by making intercession in us with groans which cannot be uttered. Of this you read, Rom. viii. 26. 'Likewise 'the Spirit also helpeth our infirmities, for we know 'not what we should pray for as we ought; but the 'Spirit itself maketh intercession for us, with groan-'ings which cannot be uttered.' Many persons words go beyond their hearts; but the true Christian, the more he speaks, the more he leaves unspoken; there is something still remaining, which he can never say out; he sighs and groans that he falls so short in his best duties; but he can go no further, only he longs and waits for that day when full perfection shall come, and he shall be filled with all the fulness of God. Christian, let me come close to your experience: Have you not sometimes felt most, when you have said least? Fears have stopped your mouth, but they have given vent to your heart. God has brought you into his banqueting-house, and nature has found it enough to support under the larger discoveries of grace. You have been in the spouse's condition, sick of love, the sweetest frame earth can admit of; such seasons you have felt, though they are very rare; they come not often, that they may be prized the more when enjoyed; however, thus much you can say by them, that the Spirit hath, in such sweet intervals, helped your infirmities, in and after duty, with groanings which cannot be uttered. Once more,

4. The Spirit helps in prayer, as he guides and directs the soul to ask but for those things which God means to give. He regulates their desires by the promise, and makes the will of God, whatever it be, their satisfaction and delight. ' He maketh in-
' tercession for the saints according to the will of
' God,' Rom. viii. 27. O! it is a blessed thing to look on all our mercies, as promised, and to see, at the same time, Christ, in whom all the promises meet. To have our wills and affections swallowed up in the will of God, is the top of the saints attainments here. By God's promises we know what his purpose and will is; and therefore, says the Psalmist, and with him every upright-hearted soul will join, ' Remember the word unto thy servant, upon which
' thou hast caused me to hope.'

Use 1. Cannot men prepare themselves for duty, *after* grace is received? much less can they prepare themselves for grace, while in an unregenerate state. This is to make man the first mover in his conversion to God, whereas he must have life before he can have motion. The scripture-account of man in his natural state, is, that he is dead in trespasses and sins, darkness itself, enmity against God, and such as cannot be subject to the law of God, till *born again*. Dead Lazarus was quickened and made alive before he was able, at Christ's call, to come forth: And God, says the apostle, 2 Cor. iv. 6. ' Who com-
' manded the light to shine out of darkness, hath
' shined into our hearts.' We must distinguish between a thing which is good only as to the matter of it, and a thing which is good in all the circumstances. To read the word, attend ordinances, pray, and think of one's former state as dangerous and sinful; these are good things, as to the matter of them, and yet many go thus far, who are strangers to a work of grace in their hearts. Herod did many things, and heard John Baptist gladly; yet afterwards cut off the head of the preacher whom he delighted to hear: Good works (which the scripture

esteems so), flow from the new heart; we must also distinguish between that which is a duty in man, and a debt in God. It is every man's duty to read, hear, meditate, pray, &c. which are usually put amongst what are called preparatory works; but let no one dare to say, that he who doth these things lays God under an obligation thereupon to give grace. There is ground of hope, from the promise, that such as 'ask, shall receive,' and such as 'seek shall find;' but whatever we receive from God, comes as a free gift, Rom. ix. 16. Further, it is one thing for God to prepare his own way into the soul; another for corrupt nature to prepare itself for grace. There is a beautiful order in the Spirit's work, but nothing preparatory, that man can do towards God's making him a partaker of his own grace.

Use 2. Are the very *disposings* of our hearts from the Lord, so that we cannot think a good thought abstracted from his gracious influx; what shall we then say to those great things which he has done for us in a way of providence and grace, and to those far greater which he hath promised to do? surely these are of the Lord. Before Israel could be settled in the promised land, they must pass through the brick-kilns in Egypt, and a red sea, and an howling wilderness, and a swelling Jordan. Our way to heaven lies through many trials, temptations, snares and sorrows. That thou hast been supported and comforted under every affliction, kept from falling by temptation, or recovered when fallen; that thou hast emerged from under so many corruptions; that Christ is still thy sanctuary, when pursued by justice; thy anchor hold of hope under outward pressures, or inward conflicts; that thou art helped to feed on Christ, to fetch all from him; that death is unstung, the grave perfumed, and a mansion prepared for thee above, against the time when this earthly house of thy tabernacle shall be dissolved; What great things are these? Every one of them is

J from

from God. 'Every good gift, and every perfect 'gift, cometh down from above.' Say with the Psalmist, Psal. cxv. 1. ' Not unto us, O Lord! not ' unto us, but unto thy name give glory, for thy ' mercy, and for thy truth's sake.'

Use 3. Are the preparations of the heart in man, and the answer of the tongue from the Lord? This may give a lift to humble doubting believers, under the sense they have of their indisposedness for duty. Thou complainest of a wandering, proud, hard and unbelieving heart, in holy duties; how shall it be bettered? By keeping from them. This is not the rule of judgment in natural things; such as would be warm do not use to keep away from the fire. When Christ has promised his presence, there believers should expect his fellowship. If thy heart be wandering, God can fix it; be it hard, God can soften it; one sight of Christ, as pierced for thee, will lay thee mourning at his feet, Zech. xii. 10. ' They shall look and mourn.' Sense of thy unbelief, is a sign thou believest. Whatever are your doubts, your fears, your sins, carry them to the cross of Christ.

Let me only caution against three things, and I close.

First, Against known omissions. The gift that is in us must be stirred up, if we would have it preserved; means are appointed that they may be used, not lived on. The better the digestion, the keener the appetite: Our desiring the word depends very much on our taste of it, 1 Pet. ii. 2. The more prayer is used, the better will it be loved. The very spirit of prayer hath been lost by a restraint of the duty. Do not think a few closet petitions, and confessions on the Lord's day, will bring down blessings from God, when he has been unapplied to in the closet all the week besides.

Secondly, Much more should you beware of conscience-wasting sins. Nothing so much straitens the heart, as allowed guilt, in this sense. With the pure, God

God will shew himself pure, but with the froward, he will shew himself *unsavoury*. Expect no heart-preparation for duty, but in an holy endeavour to walk with God. To the presumptuous wicked, God saith, ' What have you to do to declare my sta-
' tutes ?'

Thirdly, Take heed of a dependence on gifts, in your approach to God. If duties are not filled with grace, they are good for nothing. The preparations of the heart are from God, when there is an whole trust and delight in him. Then is God's aid justly denied, when we venture to engage in holy duties without the help of his Spirit. Even faith itself doth no otherwise enrich the believer, than as it is a vessel which holds the treasure. Remember Paul's confession, ' For me to live is Christ,' &c.

SERMON XII.

PAST TOKENS OF DIVINE FAVOUR, AN ENCOURAGEMENT AGAINST PRESENT FEARS.

JUDGES xiii. 23.

But his wife said unto him, If the Lord were pleased to kill us, he would not have received a burnt-offering and a meat-offering at our hands; neither would he have shewed us all these things, nor would, as at this time, have told us such things as these.

THERE is nothing difficult or hard to be understood in the connection of these words with the preceding context. The person who appeared to Manoah and his wife, was looked upon by them to be no other than a created angel, till the flame of the offering went up towards heaven from the altar, and the angel of the Lord ascended in the flame. Whether fire came down from heaven, or whether it came out of the rock to consume the sacrifice, is not certain : but the angel of the Lord ascended in the flame of the altar, to shew the acceptableness of the sacrifice ; and that it was made so, by his carrying it into heaven, and presenting it unto the Father. Christ as Mediator perfumes the services and sacrifices of his people with the odours of his own obe-

dience

dience and righteousness. Hereby Manoah knew that it was JEHOVAH, the second Person of the Trinity, who condescended to be Mediator, and Messenger of the covenant; not a created angel. His reflection upon it was strange, but not new or uncommon: 'We shall surely die, because we have 'seen God.' His wife argues much more justly, in the words of our text, 'If the Lord were pleased to 'kill us,' &c. Death could come from no hands but God's; and the tokens of his favour can never be intended as evidences of his wrath. This reasoning of her faith is built upon three considerations:

First, The acceptance of their offering. God would never accept the offering, if he did not love the person.

Secondly, The discovery of those secrets wherein their own preservation, and the deliverance of the whole nation were concerned. That Sampson should be born; how he was to be educated and instructed, that God would save Israel by his means: From which, excellent Mr Henry makes this good and pithy conclusion, " We need not fear the withering " of those roots out of which such a branch is yet ' to spring."

Thirdly, The time of this discovery is a great argument of hope, 'at this time he would not have 'shewn us such things as these;' a time when visions were very rare and unfrequent; a time when they seemed, as a nation, to be abandoned of God, being left in the hands of the Philistines forty years. At such a time to receive these precious visions of the kindness and care of God, was an argument, that they should live, and execute what God had given them in charge. 'But his wife said unto him,' &c. This is the connection and sense of the words, as referring to Manoah, and the Lord's appearance to him. But as no scripture is of private interpretation, every believer has a warrant to apply them for his own use, so far as his case is parallel to this in the text. Thus considered, the words give us the following observation.

OBSERV. Such whom God has distinguished with tokens of his favour, shall never be left to perish under the displays of his wrath. In discoursing on this observation, I will endeavour to shew,

I. What are those tokens of God's favour, which every believer has been distinguished withal.

II. What are those things which God is *even now* shewing them, under all their *darkness* and *fears*.

III. Why they who have been, and are so blessed with the tokens of God's favour, shall never perish under the displays of his wrath.

I. Let us enquire what are those tokens of favour which have been shewn every true believer. 'Neither would he have shewed us all these things,' refers to past experiences of the Lord towards them, and instructions they had received from him. Saints have past experiences to turn to, under present doubts and terrors. Is it no token of God's favour, that you have been kept alive unto your calling? that you was not suffered to drop into hell before you had any knowledge of the way to heaven? Believer, art thou preserved from the gates of hell to the glory of heaven? Had death seized thee in thy unconverted state, thy portion had been appointed thee everlastingly with hypocrites and unbelievers: And how near has thy own intemperance, it may be, and excess brought thee to it? There is a preservation *to* calling, as well as a preservation ever *afterwards:* 'Jude,' ver. 1. 'preserved in Christ Jesus, and called.' Miraculously are we preserved to the day of our natural death, through a world of dangers and deaths; so are we, to the time of our spiritual life. Manasseh and Paul are triumphing in heaven, one that God spared him till his affliction in Babylon; 'before this Manasseh knew not the Lord,' 2 Chron. xxxiii. 13. The other, that he knew not Christ when, he

persecuted

persecuted the church, and wasted it. Had Paul known Christ then, he had committed the unpardonable sin. (Paul had never preached Christ, much less been a witness of his resurrection): O! the wonders of providence towards the saints, before ever they are acquainted with the ways of grace! Ever account it one of thy chief mercies, that thou was kept alive unto thy calling.

Secondly, It is a token of a distinguishing favour that thou hast not received the gospel of 'the grace 'of God in vain,' 2 Cor. vi. 1. The gospel has been welcomed not only to thy house, but to thine heart. Thou knowest it; at least thou desirest to know it, not more in the sound, than in the favour of it. Many a sincere soul is complaining, O! 'that all things were become new;' and yet 'old 'things are passed away.' He fears he has no life in Christ, yet all his desire is towards him: cries out, he is lost, and yet he 'has found him, of whom 'Moses in the law and the prophets did write,' John i. 45. and ventures himself wholly upon the Lord Christ for acceptance, and eternal life. There has been a day of God's power, wherein Christ and his soul were made one. A divorce has been given to sin, and to his own righteousness; he can yet say, 'What have I to do any more with idols?' And can there be sense where there is no life? Did ever any one desire whom he did not love? or can any man love an object he does not know? God's work upon the heart is best known, not by the present operations, but by the after effects. Lydia's attention to the things spoken by Paul, sheweth her heart to be opened of the Lord, Acts xvi. 14. The blind man would not deny that he saw, because he could not tell every circumstance which attended the miracle of opening his eyes, John ix. 25. If thou knowest the worth of thy soul, and darest not venture it but with the Lord 'Jesus Christ, 'thou hast not received the grace of God in 'vain.'

Thirdly. It is a token of diftinguifhing favour, that thou haft at any time feen the truth of thy own grace. As thy God hath his hiding times, fo there are alfo times of finding; Pfalm xxxii. 6. 'For this fhall every one that is godly pray 'unto thee in a time when thou mayeft be found.' The eleven difciples though they doubted, as foon as a word came from Chrift's mouth, they all believed, Mat xxviii. 17, 18. That blefled Lord Jefus who at firft begets hope in the breaft of a broken, contrite finner, always fecretly fupports it, and often revives it. The fun is not out of the firmament becaufe it is hid under a cloud. There is a gracious promife made, Mal. iv. 2. which there are few believers who have not at times tafted the fweetnefs of: 'But unto you that fear my name, fhall the 'Sun of righteoufnefs arife with healing in his 'wings; and ye fhall go forth, and grow up, as 'calves of the ftall.' Chrift has wings to enlighten, warm, and heal. Difconfolate foul! thy Surety and thy Saviour is the *Sun* of *righteoufnefs*. Sometimes light comes fuddenly, after the longeft night of darknefs. God has often accepted thy gifts, when thou haft thought him defigning at that very time, by greater withdrawments, to punifh thy fins. Many a prayer begun in diftrefs has ended in delight. The Angel of the covenant has afcended, in thofe very frames thou haft thought low and legal. Thy God has raifed thee out of thy depths, and fet thee on thy high places.

Fourthly. It is a token of diftinguifhing favour, that thou haft been kept from falling by temptations, or that thou haft been recovered when fallen. Afflictions have purged thy drofs, and brightened thy gold. Unruly thoughts have been often quieted by divine confolations. Satan has been fuffered to ftir thy corruptions, but not to deftroy thy faith. Many a true believer has been ready, through the power of temptation to draw back; but by the power of grace has been kept from
turning

turning back. 'He restoreth my soul;' where is the Saint that is an utter stranger to that sweet experience of the holy Psalmist? Thy God has restored thee, and healed the wounds in conscience which thy backslidings have made. Hast thou had Demas's temptation, and been delivered from his fall? Hast thou sinned with David, and has the Lord put away thy sin? Surely God hath no mind to destroy thee, he would never else have thus reached forth his hand to save thee. Thy fears may be great, when thou lookest inwardly to thy little strength, and to the power of thine enemies: But thy Redeemer is mighty: 'The 'Lord of hosts is for us, the God of Jacob is our 'refuge.'

Fifthly, It is a token of distinguishing favour, that thou hast been kept close to the appointed ways and means of comfort, under all thy complaints for want of comfort: The spouse was directed where to go, and whom to inquire of, if she would find her beloved; Cant. i. 8. 'Go thy way forth by the foot- 'steps of the flock, and feed thy kids beside the 'shepherds tents. The waters of life and healing 'run through the sanctuary,' Ezek. xlvii. 12. And so do the streams of joy and gladness. If die thou must, it is best to die sacrificing. It is a special remark of Eliezer, Abraham's servant, Gen. xxiv. 27. 'I being in the way, the Lord led me to the house 'of my master's brethren.' To be out of the way of duty, is to be out of the way of comfort. The disciples went to the mountain appointed of Christ, in order to meet with Christ. Mary, though weeping, stood at the sepulchre, and soon heard her own name called by her beloved Jesus. Thomas was not with the disciples when Christ appeared, and you know what he lost by it. It is a mark of distinguishing mercy to be kept in the *way* of comfort. *Manna* never was esteemed so light bread as in our day. Ordinances are attended on, it is to be feared, by many, more to keep up the form, than to revive the power of godliness. So much for the first general.

II. What are those things which God is even now shewing the Christian under all his darkness and fears? 'Neither would he have shewed us all these 'things, nor would, as at this time,' &c.

1. Believers see a loveliness in Christ's person, when they cannot discern interest in his love. Their doubts are not about Christ's suitableness and sufficiency, but about union to this suitable and sufficient Saviour. 'O! thou whom my soul loveth,' will force itself out, at some times unawares; even when they have numbered themselves amongst such as never knew his name. They stagger at the promise, and yet venture upon Christ in the promise. Heman contradicts, in the first words of his complaint, all that he objects against himself, both as to his state and frame afterwards, Psal. lxxxviii. 1. 'O 'Lord God of my salvation, I have cried day and 'night unto thee. In the Lord have I righteousness 'and strength,' is not often uttered in full assurance of faith; but it is spoken as the fixed resolution and utmost desire of every true believer. In Christ they seek it, and they will never seek it in any other. There is a joy that so glorious a method of salvation is found out for others; that God's name is glorified, and his law honoured by God-man; though they, as they have fallen by their iniquity, should perish in it. Shall a soul perish to whom Christ is lovely? 'If the Lord pleased to kill thee, 'he would not have shewed thee such things as 'these.'

2. Believers have strong desires after the truth of grace, when they most complain under the want of it. Sorrow and godly mourning flow from love, as well as joy and praise. One supposes the object desirable

firable and lovely, though abfent; the other fuppofes the object prefent. Chrift was no lefs dear to weeping Mary, than he was to believing and rejoicing Thomas. In his darkeft hours a believer will be a feeker, whether or not he finds the beloved of his foul whom he feeks after. 'With my foul,' fays the church, 'I have defired thee in the night; yea, 'with my fpirit within me will I feek thee early,' Ifa. xxvi. 9. Like Ruth of old, the believer will take no denial, chap. i. 16. 'Intreat me not to leave 'thee, or to return from following after thee; for 'whither thou goeft, I will go; and where thou 'lodgeft, I will lodge.' A Chrift, and an heaven at laft, will recompence the foul for all his waiting. There will always be David's wifh under thy greateft apprehended wants, 2 Sam. xxiii. 15. 'O that 'one would give me drink of the water of the well 'of Bethlehem, which is by the gate!' O for one fight of Chrift, who is of more worth to me than ten thoufand worlds! This is a prefent token for good, under all thy doubts and fears; nothing but an whole Chrift will content thee.

3. When believers cannot find fin mortified; it is their defire and prayer, that it may be rooted out. It is more on account of indwelling fin, than any worldly affliction and forrow, that you hear the Chriftian crying with David, Pfal. lv. 6. 'O that 'I had wings like a dove! for then would I fly a-'way and be at reft.' It is by flight doves fecure themfelves, not by fight. A believer's aim is levelled at the root of fin. Paul fpeaks the whole language of his heart, Rom. vii. 24. 'O wretched man 'that I am, who fhall deliver me from the body of 'this death!' Sin is always thy burden, and the nearer to Chrift, the heavier the weight feels. There are the feeds of all fin in thee; but no fin is allowed to reign in thee. Though thou often doubteft the conqueft, yet thou art ever maintaining the conflict. This is a bleffed token under all thy jealoufies

fies and fears, that God is not pleased to kill thee. Once more,

4. Weak as his hope is, a believer dare not cast it away in his darkest seasons. It is the language of his heart, 'Yea, though he slay me, yet will I trust 'in him.' If he cannot go to the throne as sanctified in Christ, and called; he will fall down at the footstool, as a perishing sinner. There is a fulness in covenant-promises, when there is a saplesness and withering in his best frames. 'Jesus Christ is the 'same yesterday, to-day, and for ever.' The grace of hope may vanish, the object of hope continues ever present. The less a believer sees in himself, the more readily and eagerly he ventures on Christ. Believers often doubt their faith; but when matters are put close, not a soul of them is willing to part with his hope.

I am now to shew,

III. Why such who have been, and are blessed with such tokens of God's favour, shall never die under his wrath.

1. This would argue God to be wavering and imperfect like ourselves. The great God may alter his way, but he never changes his heart. What God hath begun, he will perform, because his work is perfect. The great God never acts inconsistently with himself.

2. Were God to accept thy offering, and destroy thy person, what becomes of his faithfulness to Christ the Mediator? Christ purchased, and he intercedes for the weakest grace. Was his blood shed in vain? or did he intercede for nought? 'Him the 'Father heareth always.' The grace we receive from the Father is a debt to Christ, though a free favour to us.

3. Should God kill us, after such grace shewn us, one in whom the Spirit inhabits would be lost:

'The

'The Spirit is given to believers to abide with them
'for ever.' Often thou mayſt not know that thou
liveſt, but thou canſt never die, becauſe the Spirit
hath taken poſſeſſion for Chriſt.

Believers may loſe the Spirit's comforting pre
ſence, but not his quickening, becauſe he never
quits poſſeſſion which he hath once taken.

4. God would loſe the triumphs of his own grace:
'Grace reigns through righteouſneſs unto eternal
'life.' Grace in us is a creature, but it is kept alive
by the grace in God's heart, which is infinite and
everlaſting. 'Grace, grace,' will be the language
of heaven; but 'becauſe he was not able to deliver
'and ſave them from my hands, he has left them to
'periſh for ever,' will never be the triumph and
mockery of hell.

A few Uſes.

Use 1. See what uſe you are to make of paſt experiences. Carry them about with you by faith,
that you may turn to them in time of need. They
are a treaſure which will be ever precious. Tried
caſes are out of doubt. Theory may amuſe, but
experience only can ſatisfy and comfort. So much
mercy your God, your Jeſus, will never beſtow in
vain.

Use 2. Be humbled for the weakneſs of faith, in
ſo great a multitude of experiences. It is a moving
queſtion Chriſt put to his diſciples, 'Wherefore do
'ye doubt?' a God ſo able, ſo wiſe, ſo gracious, ſo
faithful; a Saviour ſo near; a heart ſo crowded
with mercies, one miracle after another miracle, in
implanting, preſerving, reviving grace, wherefore
ſhould we doubt?

Use 3. Labour to encourage ſinners by your taſte
and experiences of mercy. You were not rejected
in your ſuit for mercy; why then ſhould they doubt
in their deſires for the ſame bleſſing? 'With the
'Lord there is plenteous redemption.'

Use 4.

Use 4. Bleſs God for Chriſt, all your offerings go up with acceptance on this altar. The grace of the covenant he made the purchaſe of; and to him appertaineth the beſtowment of all covenant bleſſings: Neither portions, nor offerings are accepted, but through his blood. ' By him therefore, let us offer ' the ſacrifice of praiſe to God contniually, that is, ' the fruit of our lips, giving thanks to his name,' Heb. xiii. 15.

SERMON XIII.

CHRIST'S REDEMPTION FROM THE LAW'S CURSE.

GALATIANS iii. 13.

Christ hath redeemed us from the curse of the law, being made a curse for us: for it is written, Cursed is every one that hangeth on a tree.

IN this context the apostle is establishing the great doctrine of justification by faith, without the works of the law. This he does by many arguments; as, that 'such as are under the law, are un-
' der the curse,' ver. 10. That which condemns a man, it is a vain thing for him to look for justification and life from. The law curses every sinner, because he is a transgressor of it; 'one who has not
' continued in all things written in the book of the
' law, to do them.'

Again, The scripture reveals another way of justification and life, that is, faith: 'The just shall live
' by faith.' Such as are accounted just in the sight of God, trust in another for that righteousness which makes them so.

Besides, this would set aside the great end of Christ's death for such as believe; he died to redeem

deem them from the curse of the law, that Abraham's blessing might come upon them through him, or by faith in him. To trust therefore to one's own doings, or to plead them before God, as the reason of our justification in his sight, is to make the death of Christ, and our redemption by it, a vain thing. 'Christ has redeemed us from the curse of the law, 'being made a curse for us.' There is a poor convinced sinner's hold, and his only hope. The sweetness and marrow of the whole gospel is comprehended in this: it is a truth which faith looks to in every ordinance, in every providence. That I may a little open and explain it at this time, as it shall please the Spirit of Christ to enable me, I would briefly do these four things:

I. Inquire what is this *curse* of the law, which believers are by Christ redeemed from.
II. How, or by what means is this redemption brought about? 'being made a curse for us.'
III. Who is this great and glorious Redeemer? 'Christ hath redeemed.'
IV. Who are redeemed? He hath redeemed *us* from the curse of the law, being made a curse for us.

I. What is the 'curse of the law,' which believers are by Christ redeemed from? To this I answer,

1. Believers are redeemed from the sentence of condemnation, which as sinners they are liable to, and are under in their unjustified state. 'There is 'therefore now no condemnation to them that are 'in Christ Jesus,' Rom. viii. 1. There is not a man or woman present, but considered as in Adam their first root, and covenant head, they lie under the sentence of condemnation. All of us are separated from God, by our fall in him; Rom. iii. 23. 'For 'all have sinned, and come short of the glory of
'God,'

'God.' That is the first branch of the curse. Adam fell under it as soon as ever he had sinned, 'Dying thou shalt die,' Gen. ii. 17. Many other things appertain to the curse, but this is the main and principal of all. Spiritual death seized him at once; he was in a state of alienation from God. 'I heard thy voice,' says he, 'in the garden, and I was afraid, because I was naked, and I hid myself,' chap. iii. 10. Sin and guilt, shame and fear go together. A man is dead in law, when the sentence of death is passed on him; though he may live, it may be many months, or years afterwards. The law has in it, first, a command, next a promise, then a threatening or curse. 'If thou dost well, shalt thou not be accepted?' thou shalt live in the things thou dost: but 'if thou dost ill, sin lieth at thy door;' the law condemns and curses thee. O! that poor sinners did but see their misery in a Christless state. 'They that are under the law, are under the curse;' which believers in Christ are redeemed from.

2. Believers in Christ are delivered from the wrath and vengeance of God, which is consequential upon this curse. We read of the 'second death,' Rev. ii. 11. which consists in the destruction of soul and body in hell; this is a part of the law's curse, of which death natural is scarce the shadow: therefore it is with a 'Depart, ye cursed,' Matt. xxv. 41. This is what the law renders as 'the wages of sin,' Rom. ii. 8, 9. Alas! what are all the trials in life, yea, what is death itself, if compared with the wrath of an holy and an angry God, that is to be endured everlastingly afterwards,' 2 Thess. i. 9. O think, what 'a fearful thing it is to fall into the hands of the living God! Tophet is ordained of old,' &c. Isai. xxx. 33. Forbearance is no remission; wrath is treasured up, when it is not poured forth. Every sin thou committest, every idle word, adds to the treasure of God's wrath against thee another day. Thy very blessings, sin turns in-

to curses. The curse of the law will be wholly executed hereafter. This curse believers are redeemed from, which leads,

II. To consider, How, or by what means this redemption is obtained. The text says, Christ took away the curse of the law from us, by taking it upon himself, 'Christ hath redeemed us,' &c. The word signifies to *buy out*, as one does a thing which he gives the full price and value of. Thus Abraham is said, in the purchase he made of a burying-place for his beloved Sarah, to have weighed to Ephron the silver which he had named in the audience of the sons of 'Heth, four hundred shekels of silver, 'current money with the merchant,' Gen. xxiii. 16. The satisfaction Christ made to justice was full and complete, every way proportionable to the wrong which the sinner had done; 'current money,' such as neither law nor justice could refuse; 'Christ hath 'redeemed us from the curse of the law, being made 'a curse for us.'

Two things are to be considered by us here,

1. That Christ endured the very curse which the law denounced against the sinner. And,

2. That in his enduring the curse, he acted as the sinner's surety, putting himself in the sinner's room and stead.

1. In this humbled state Christ endured the very curse, which the law denounced against the sinner, 'being made a curse for us.' He was first made sin, then a curse, 2 Cor. v. 21. From the cradle to the cross, he was 'a man of sorrows, and acquainted 'with grief; numbred with the transgressors;' counted a deceiver, a sinner, a devil, from the very first of his public appearance among men: Yea, 'neither did his brethren or kinsfolks believe in him. 'He is,' saith the prophet, 'despised and rejected 'of men.' Isai. liii. 3. 'A worm, and no man,' Psal. xxii. 6. The curse he is said to be made, in our text, is not the curse of the *judicial* law, merely

according

according to which a malefactor was after his stoning to be hanged on a tree; but it is the curse of the *moral* law. That punishment seems designed on purpose to represent the blessed Jesus as accursed of men, and accursed of God. He hangs between heaven and earth, as unworthy of either. The Father poured into that cup whereof he drank, all the vengeance and wrath which was due to our sins: ' It ' pleased the Lord to bruise him.' It is an expressive passage, Psal. cx. 7. ' He shall drink of the ' brook in the way.' It was the brook *Cedron*, over which Christ passed, in order to his beginning his conflict in the garden. Into this brook all the uncleanness and filth of the temple was cast; this was also the common receiver of those accursed things, which the good kings of *Israel* destroyed. Doth it not sweetly suggest to thy thoughts, that all thy guilt and defilement was emptied upon Christ? All thy curses light upon him? He made a way through that torrent of wrath and curses, which would have everlastingly separated between thee and glory? He was made thy curse. Why else do we hear the sword of justice laid under an express command, to awake and smite him? Why is his soul troubled and sore amazed? The fire of God's wrath forces great drops of blood from him in a cold night, which fall in clots to the ground, Luke xxii. 44. Could David say, ' Yea, though I walk through the valley of the sha' dow of death, I will fear none evil;' and doth the dear and only Son of God die under amazement? He that never saw a frown on his Father's face before, complains now that he is forsaken of him? ' My God, my God, why hast thou forsaken me?' Paul glories in the suffering of the cross; Christ bows and groans, yea, he roars under his. ' Why ' art thou so far from the voice of my roaring?' Psal. xxii. 1. Whence, O whence is this, that the head dies in distress, while the members die in triumph? Christ's soul is full of horror and darkness, trembling and astonishment, when many of them have

have the oil of joy for mourning, and the garments of praise for the spirit of heaviness? The cause of all you have in the text. Christ ' in redeeming ' thee from the curse of the law, was made a curse ' for thee. The chastisement of thy peace was up- ' on him.' There was no need the dear Redeemer should go down into hell, to suffer the punishment of the damned there. The avenging wrath of God seized him, and he endured it here: Here, even here on earth, when he hung on the accursed tree, ' the sorrows of death compassed him, and the pains ' of hell gat hold upon him:' The crown of thorns which he wore without, was a badge of that curse of the law, and that weight of wrath he endured within. Christ endured that very curse of the law, which was denounced against the sinner. The punishment of loss and sense, he suffered at one and the same time.

2. In his enduring this curse, he acted as Surety and substitute for the sinner. Thou contractedst the debt, thy Redeemer paid it. Thou committedst the sin, thy Redeemer endured the curse. ' He restored ' that which he took not away,' Psal. lxix. 4. Christ knew no sin of his own, though he was made sin for thee. In his own person he was the just, the holy One of God, the beloved of the Father. There was of old a transferring of sin and guilt upon the sacrifice, by the offender's laying his hand upon the head of the beast that was to be slain. It is out of the creature's power to lay sin upon another; ' the ' soul that sinneth, it shall die :' But it is not besides the right and prerogative of God, the great Lawgiver, to accept a ransom; provided the glory of his holy law, and the rights of his justice can be secured by his so doing. Herein God commendeth his love to sinners; herein he hath also declared his righteousness. The law is so honoured, justice so satisfied with the suretyship-performances of our great Mediator, glory so redundant to the whole name of God, his justice, holiness, and truth, as well as

his

his pity, grace and mercy, as could not have been in any other way whatever. Christ accepted our names with all our guilt in the everlasting covenant, and consented to bring in for us everlasting righteousness; I will be Surety for them, at my hands shalt thou require them. Hence the law discharges the principal debtor, and comes upon the Surety. Sinners are wholly insolvent; but our Redeemer is mighty; all the riches of heaven are laid up in him. He acted in all he did and suffered in our name; how else could any curse light upon him? ' He was ' made under the law, to redeem them that are un- ' der the law.' He never broke the law, therefore lay under no obligation to satisfy it; but upon his own voluntary consent, to answer for crimes which we had done. ' For us,' is in our room and stead, as we read, ' an eye for an eye, a tooth for a tooth.' Christ obeyed, and suffered, not only for our good, but in our stead: as our Redeemer and Surety, in obedience to the law's commands, he fulfilled all righteousness, and bore all the curses which the law threatens, ' That we might receive the adoption of ' sons,' Gal. iv. 5. But I pass on to consider,

III. Who this great and glorious Redeemer is. *Christ* hath redeemed us from the curse of the law.

Two things are intimated to us here;

1. That as to the Redeemer's person, he is God-man. *Christ* includes them both. He is a man, that he may have somewhat to offer; as God, he could neither obey nor suffer; he is God, that he may give an efficacy, an infinite value to his obedience and sufferings. The Redeemer of old was to be the near kinsman of the redeemed! ' I am the ' near kinsman,' says Boaz, Ruth iii. 12. Howbeit, there is a kinsman nearer than he. Our blessed Redeemer is *next* of kin to us, ' Forasmuch as the chil- ' dren are partakers of flesh and blood, he also him- ' self likewise took part of the same,' Heb. ii. 14. God in our nature. ' Without controversy, great is ' the mystery of godliness, God was manifest in the
' flesh.'

'flesh.' The wrath and curse of God, who can bear, so as not to sink under it, but God only? The sword of justice must have been smiting and smiting for ever, had it fell upon any other, save the man God's fellow. He shall swallow up sin and death, and be the destruction of hell itself; Why? Because he is the Lord of life and glory, God equal with the Father: 'The Lord said unto my Lord, Sit thou at 'my right hand,' Psal. cx. 1.—7. Hence he is mighty to save, and the church triumphs in him under all the challenges of law and justice, Rom. viii. 33. 'Who is he that condemneth, it is Christ that 'died.' God purchased the church with his own blood. Part with that article of your creed, and you sell your salvation. If Christ be not the great *Jehovah*, the only living and true God, 'your faith 'is vain, your hope is vain, ye are yet in your sins.' The curse remains to be endured, and it is so heavy, that it will sink the noblest creatures God ever made under darkness, despair, and wrath, to all eternity.

2. As to his office and work, he was *set apart* thereto by the Father. The word signifies, that he was *anointed* to his redemption-work, as kings, and priests, and prophets, were anointed to their work of old. God called him to it, and prepared him for it. All the obedience and sufferings of Christ, though he was God, would have been of no avail for the salvation of fallen sinners, had not the Father authorized him by covenant to be their Surety, and substitute, to act in their persons, and names, in time. I have made a covenant with my chosen, Psal. lxxxix. 3. The imputation of our sins to Christ, and his righteousness to us, depend upon this blessed and ordered covenant. 'Lo, I come;' says Christ in eternity, and he speaks the same in time, but it is 'to do thy will, O God;' to engage in that service to which thou hast appointed me. His call to this work, is one ground of his acceptance in it; redemption-work is not a thing of yesterday; the thoughts, purposes, and covenant of God, were

concerned

concerned about it from everlasting. 'I was set up 'from everlasting, from the beginning,' Prov. viii. 23. And when the Mediator came into the world, the Father recognizes his call. He brought his first-begotten into the world, and faith, 'Let all the an-'gels of God worship him.' God girded him for his service in the hottest instances of it, and gave the Spirit to sustain human nature in it, not by measure. It remains, that I offer a word or two on the last general.

IV. Who are the redeemed? Christ hath redeemed *us* from the law.

Two things are implied in that,

1. That the *elect*, as well as others, by nature are under the curse. The *us* here spoken of, are considered, first, as sinners, then as believers, *ver*. 9. 'They which be of faith, are blessed with faithful 'Abraham.' Paul takes himself in, as well as the believing, though deceived *Galatians*. Christ hath redeemed *us* from the curse of the law; therefore we are alike under the curse, children of wrath, even as others. We come into the world under the covenant of works, which is a covenant of condemnation; for all have sinned, and come short of the glory of God. Every natural man, as such, is in the flesh, and before he can be in the spirit, the law is sent to convince of sin, and to shew him his condemned, abhorred state without Christ. How is this consistent with his being previously delivered from the curse, as though electing grace had set him at liberty from the condemnation of an holy law?

2. It is *faith* in Christ as a *Surety*, which gives deliverance from the curse of the law; that deliverance I mean, which is the foundation of my present peace, comfort, and access to God. 'The just shall live by 'faith;' we seek righteousness by faith. Faith receives the blood and righteousness of Christ, and pleads it before the throne, as my righteousness. A gift at a distance will do no good, I must draw near and apprehend it, and receive it. Hence believers are

are represented as 'fled for refuge, to lay hold on 'the hope set before them.' On this depends our pleadable interest in the sacrifice, and righteousness of the Redeemer. I cannot say 'Christ hath redeemed me from the curse of the law,' till I have been enabled to accept of him, and trust in him as a Redeemer. Right to salvation depends upon Christ's redeeming from the curse of the law; right to claim it, to take comfort from it, depends upon our faith in this blessed Redeemer.

Inferences.

1. Hence we see why Christ is so suitable to a poor, convinced, humble sinner. It is because he has satisfied all the demands, and born the whole curse of a broken law: "Surely, shall one say, in the Lord "have I righteousness." O the name, the precious name of *Christ!* it is an ointment poured forth. Others may glory in riches, wisdom, honour, things which seem to have somewhat in them: But all his glorying is in Christ; of him are ye in Christ. "That's my all, says the poor soul; here is all I "need for time and eternity." 'The Lord is my 'strength, and my song, he also is become my sal-'vation,' Isai. xii. 1.

2. Hence we see what a blessing the gospel is. 'Christ hath redeemed us from the curse of the law;' there is the whole gospel in miniature: No man can be saved by the law; doing, to obtain life, is quite shut out of the question. Soul? canst thou suffer too? Canst thou bear infinite wrath? Canst thou endure everlasting burnings? What avails expecting life from the law's commands, unless there is a way found out for redemption from its curse. It is the gospel which brings news of Christ, pardon, salvation. The law is not of faith; it speaks not one syllable but of doing; is ever commanding, and cursing. O! sweet doctrine of the cross of Christ! Who that knows himself will not glory in it continually? 'I am not ashamed of the gospel of Christ,' &c.

3. Has Christ redeemed from the curse of the law? comfort thyself, poor soul, he will redeem from the power of sin and death. 'Sin shall not have domi-
'nion over you, for ye are not under the law, but
'under grace.'

4. Is the law satisfied? it cannot condemn. 'God
'is just to forgive us our sins.' The price, the full price is paid and received. Death has lost its sting, 1 Cor. xv. 56. the grave its power, afflictions by the way all their bitterness, since Christ hath redeemed thee from the curse of the law. Once more,

5. Live to him who is thy glorious Redeemer. Take his yoke upon thee; let none of his commands be grievous; act out of love to Christ in all you do; abhor the sin he hates; think what it cost him to deliver you from wrath, and let this set you at the greatest enmity against all sin. 'Ye are bought with
'a price, therefore glorify God in your body, and
'in your spirit, which are his,' &c.

SERMON XIV.

PRESENT DISPENSATIONS THE RIGHT WAY TO GLORY.

PSAL. cvii. 7.

And he led them forth by the right way, that they might go to a city of habitation.

THESE words, if you consider them in their connection with the context, are a beautiful description of the goodness, care, and loving kindness, which God manifested towards the people of *Israel*, in their passage through the wilderness unto the land of *Canaan*: But we have sufficient warrant to apply them to the particular circumstances and condition of every true believer. This present evil world is more than once compared to a wilderness; and a variety of instances might be produced, wherein the land of *Canaan* is spoken of, as typical of that rest which remaineth for all the people of God. Taking the words then, in this sense, I shall consider them in the following method.

I. I shall consider the happy place to which every true believer is taking his journey. This is styled a 'city of habitation.'

II. Consider

II. Confider the intermediate space, through which he is to pass, in his way thitherward. This is represented in the 4th verse to be a *wilderness*; a solitary way.

III. Shew, that herein God leads his people by the *right way*, that they may go to this city of habitation.

IV. Conclude with some remarks.

I. I am to confider that **happy place**, which every true believer is taking his **journey** to. This is styled a city of habitation. The Christian is a sojourner in this present evil world, as the children of Israel were in the land of Egypt: 'We have here no continu-
' ing city;' this is not our rest; it is polluted: It is not an inheritance befitting the great God to bestow upon the vessels of mercy, his chosen sons: It is not a place worthy of them, whom the King of glory delighteth to honour. The apostle observes, Heb. xi. 16. ' They desire a better country, that is, an hea-
' venly;' and God, for this very reason, is not ashamed to be called their God, because he hath *prepared* such an one for them; an ' inheritance in-
' corruptible, undefiled, and that fadeth not away,' 1 Pet. i. 4. Worthy the relation which he stands in to them, as their God and Father, their portion, and exceeding great reward.

A rational appetite can acquiesce in nothing less than an object, which is **full of real** and durable goodness; neither can any **one** enjoy **true** happiness, before he is in the possession of this invaluable blessing. For this reason, nothing here can satisfy our appetites; nothing can be fully commensurate to our desires on this side the grave. All creature-comforts, are only **cisterns, yea** ' broken and leaky cis-
' terns, that can **hold no water;**' these can therefore never yield us the blessedness we need. On this side Jordan, we dwell only in tents and tabernacles, which are in perpetual motion from one place to another,

nor

nor can this whole world afford us a place of settled rest, a city of habitation.

Moreover, when we are led to 'the rock that is 'higher' than we, and are enabled to lay hold on him, who has promised, that those that love him shall inherit substance; our faith is so weak, and the power of unbelief so exceeding prevalent, that we soon lose our hold of him, and our feet wander upon the dark mountains: our best frames are very uncertain and precarious; our faith, that heaven-born grace, how frequently are its actings and exercise impeded, by the contrary principle of unbelief, which dwelleth in us: how often do we hear the most serious and humble Christian, lamenting that it is not with him as it was in months past, when the candle of the Lord shined upon his tabernacle; and sometimes complaining with the Prophet, Lam. iii. 1, 2. 'I am 'the man that have seen affliction by the rod of his 'wrath; he hath led me, and brought me into dark-'ness, but not into light.' And when this principle of faith, by which we walk in our absent state, is deduced into the most lively actings, and most vigorous exercise, it takes in but a small degree of the beauty and excellency of the Lord our righteousness, and but little of the glory of our future inheritance: Wherefore those that live most heavenly in this present evil world, confess themselves to be but strangers and pilgrims upon the earth: they cannot trust in their present frames, nor rest in their present attainments, but desire to be forgetting the things that are behind, and are 'reaching forth unto those 'things which are before, where Christ sitteth at the 'right hand of God,' Phil. iii. 13.

There is always something wanting, to render our happiness perfect, and our blessedness complete; till we are introduced into 'his presence, where there is 'fulness of joy,' and are set down 'at his right 'hand, where there are pleasures for evermore,' Psal. xvi. 11.

And

And bleſſed be God, there is prepared for us a better world, wherein dwells righteouſneſs: Chriſt Jeſus by his death, has not only procured for us a freedom from condemnation, but a right, and title likewiſe, to the inheritance of ſons. God the Father has tranſlated us out of the kingdom of darkneſs, brought us into the kingdom of his dear Son, and hath given us his Spirit, as the earneſt of our inheritance, until 'the redemption of the purchaſed 'poſſeſſion, unto the praiſe of his glory,' Eph. i. 14. This was ſettled upon us from everlaſting; for this we were born in time, and for it are we in this life prepared; and when we have ſerved our generation-work by the will of God, we ſhall be received into it, where we ſhall ever be with the Lord, and ſerve him day and night in his temple. Thither, as our forerunner, Chriſt Jeſus is for us entered; and where he is, there ſhall alſo his ſervants be; the members never ſhall, indeed they never can be ſeparated from their glorious Head; where he is, they muſt be alſo. Nor can we for this reaſon be in any danger of having our hopes diſappointed, or our right and title to this inheritance loſt, while the Captain of our ſalvation has engaged, not only to conduct us through this vale of tears, but to introduce, and ſet us down in this heavenly bleſſedneſs, that reſt which remaineth for the people of God.

Fully to ſpeak the bleſſedneſs, or tell the glory of this city of habitation, is a work that infinitely exceeds the capacity and comprehenſion of thoſe that dwell in houſes of clay. We muſt enter within the gates of the new Jeruſalem, and taſte the pleaſures of the heavenly ſtate, before we can ſpeak the glories of it, or even conceive how great they are. It doth not yet appear, what our inheritance is, or what we ſhall be when we come there. The Holy Ghoſt makes uſe of various ſimilies taken from ſenſible objects, to deſcribe this heavenly bleſſedneſs by: and though they are but faint emblems, and give us only a ſhadowy repreſentation of the glory of the new Jeruſalem,

Jerusalem, yet are they most pleasant and delightful. How great a satisfaction does it afford to the weary pilgrim, or the man that has borne the burden in the heat of the day, to hear of a rest, to which he shall soon arrive? a city of habitation, where he shall for ever dwell? a crown of glory, which he shall ever wear? an inheritance, incorruptible, undefiled, and that fadeth not away, which he shall eternally possess? And this is the lot not only of some, but of all God's children; they shall not always be tossed with tempests and not comforted, nor groan in this present tabernacle being burdened: the time cometh, nay it is even now at the doors, when the earthly house of this our tabernacle shall be dissolved, and we shall be brought to the building of God, and receive a place in that house, which is not made with hands, eternal in the heavens, 2 Cor. v. 1. There shall we be delivered from all our enemies, and get rid of all these fears which attend us in our present state. ' These are they which came out of
' great tribulation, and have washed their robes, and
' made them white in the blood of the Lamb. There-
' fore are they before the throne of God, and serve
' him day and night in his temple; and he that sit-
' teth on the throne shall dwell among them. They
' shall hunger no more, neither thirst any more, nei-
' ther shall the sun light on them, nor any heat.
' For the Lamb which is in the midst of the throne,
' shall feed them, and shall lead them unto living
' fountains of waters; and God shall wipe away all
' tears from their eyes,' Rev. vii. 14, 15, 16, 17. This is the city of habitation.

But this leads us to consider,

II. The account we have of the intermediate space, through which the believer is to pass, in his way to this city of habitation. And this is styled in *ver.* 4. (to which our text refers), a wilderness, a solitary way. ' They wandered in the wilderness in a soli-
' tary way; they found no city to dwell in.' The

way

way to the new Jerusalem lies through the present evil world, which may be fitly compared to a wilderness in the following respects.

1. This present world is a state of distance, and in this respect it may be fitly compared to a wilderness. We are here a great way off from our Father's house, and sometimes from our Father's company too. We walk here by *faith*, and not by *sight*; and not only so, but we often lose the sensible actings of our faith. How often are we seized with a spiritual languor and deadness, as though we were wholly indifferent whether we enjoy communion with Christ or no? How often do we let down our guard, and walk like men thoughtless of the blessings we have received from God, and the obligations we are under to him? and at other times, how often, with the children of Israel, do we doubt the faithfulness, dispute the power, and call in question the loving-kindness of the Lord? By these means we grieve the Holy Spirit, and cause our God and Father to vail his countenance, and hide his face in thick darkness; he refuses to say unto our souls, 'I am thy salva-
' tion;' or to shew us the least glimpse of his glory. Then all things are black and dismal in their appearances towards us, and we lose the peace we before enjoyed. What then can be the consequence of his departure from us, but a restless and uneasy, a dark and benighted frame of spirit! So long as we lose our God, we must alway be unsettled and unhinged; while he is at a distance from us, we can never find peace and rest to our souls. The throne of grace, that peculiar privilege of the true believer, we can never exercise a holy liberty and boldness at, whilst he is withdrawn; the intimacy drops, our communion ceases, fear and shame attend us, when we are conscious to ourselves that we have offended our God. We then look for peace, but lo it is far from us, and d fire comfort, but we cannot behold it. How sad an l melancholy seasons these are, every true believer can bear witness; thus he walks in
darkness

darkness and distance, till the Father of mercies, and the God of all comfort, is pleased to unvail his face, and give a fresh discovery of his forgiving love and grace through Jesus the Mediator; he is the spring, the fountain of all our blessedness, and from him all our fruit is found. Our present state is a wilderness, as it is a place of distance.

2. This present world through which we are passing, may be justly styled a *wilderness*, as it is a solitary and barren way. It is a lonely and solitary way which we are travelling in; the path is strait and narrow, and few there are that walk therein. The world is no more our friend than it is our home; the true Christian, therefore, who is born from above, whose conversation is in heaven, and who is daily travelling thitherward, is the object of their malice and envy, or else the subject of their banter and ridicule among whom he converses. The soil of this present evil world is barren and unfruitful; it presents before our eyes many objects, which are an hindrance to us in our way; but it is entirely desart and barren, with respect to any help it affords us in our progress. It produces little else than briars and thorns, which have a tendency only to entangle and wound the feet of those that pass through it. The many afflictions with which the people of God are exercised in the present life, are as a constant clog to the wheels of their souls, which makes them drag on very heavily; and were they not sometimes favoured with a view of their rest which remains for them, they would be almost ready to despair of getting safe out of this vale of tears, which they have therefore too great occasion to call a waste howling wilderness, a solitary and barren land.

3. This present world through which we are passing, is also properly compared to a wilderness, as it is likewise a dangerous way. A wilderness is a place not only barren and unfrequented, but is generally full of pits and wild beasts, &c. which render it exceeding dangerous. For this reason it is styled a

' terrible

'terrible wildernefs,' Deut. viii. 15. ' wherein are
' fiery ferpents and fcorpions, and drought; where
' there is no water.' We are called to pafs through
an enemy's country; this world is very much under
the influence of our greateft and moft inveterate enemy.
The devil is ftyled the prince of the power of the air,
and the generality of this world's inhabitants are his
willing flaves and vaffals. Whilft therefore we are
paffing through his territories, he will be fure to
gain all the advantages he can againft us. No foon-
er do we enlift ourfelves under the banner of Chrift
Jefus, but Satan and the world immediately join in
a league againft us; as though they were refolved
to rob the Redeemer of his fpoil, and pluck thofe
who are the purchafe of his blood, out of his hands.
There is a rooted enmity between the feed of the
woman, and the feed of the ferpent. Satan has an
inveteracy againft every one that bears the image of
Jefus, ' like a roaring lion he continually walketh
' about feeking whom he may devour,' 1 Pet. v. 8.
And like an old ferpent he conceals his wiles, that
he may get the greater advantage againft us. We
are, in this life, never free from his temptations; he
is always either contriving a temptation againft us,
or prefenting it to us. And that we do not oftener
fall into the fnares which he lays to entrap us, is
owing to the care and vigilance of our Great Leader,
and the grace which he is pleafed to communicate
to us out of his fulnefs.

As for the world; ' the luft of the flefh, the luft
' of the eyes, and the pride of life,' how prevalent have thefe been to draw afide the believer from
the God and Guide of his youth! thefe Philiftines
are often upon us before we are aware of them, and
there is an unbelieving heart always within, which
is as conftant fuel to the fire of temptations from
without. So that were not God pleafed at particular times to open our eyes, and let us fee, that they
who are for us are more than they which are againft

us, we should be ready to conclude against ourselves, as David did, 'I shall surely one day perish by the hand of Saul.'

On these accounts the present state is compared to a wilderness, which is the intermediate space over which we must travel to the city of habitation. 'We wander here in the wilderness, in a solitary 'way, we can find no city to dwell in, hungry and 'thirsty, our souls faint within us.' This brings us to the third general.

III. To shew, that herein God leads his people by the right way, to the city of habitation.

The people of God are every one of them near to him as his right hand, and dear to him as the apple of his eye. His love was from everlasting fixed upon them, and therefore his care and loving-kindness are ever exercised towards them. He may bring his people into the wilderness, but he cannot, in consistency with the perfections of his nature, or the promise of his grace, ever leave them there. They may, and often do seem to lose their hold of him; but he never does, he never can lose his hold of them. 'For the Lord's portion is his people; Ja-'cob is the lot of his inheritance; he found him in 'a desert land, and in the waste howling wilderness: 'he led him about, he instructed him, he kept him 'as the apple of his eye,' Deut. xxxii. 9, 10. There is no getting to *Immanuel*'s land, but by the way of the wilderness; which, though it is not our rest itself, yet it leads us to our rest; it fits and prepares us for it; and the afflictions which we meet with therein, serve also to make the heavenly blessedness the more desirable now, and delightful hereafter. God may therefore often lead us in a rough and unpleasant way, but he always leads us in the right way. Let us only take a view of three particular seasons, wherein we are most apt to question the loving-kindness of

our

our God, and we may by them determine the happy issue of all the rest. As,

1. Let us begin with the melancholy state and condition of those, from whom God hides the light of his countenance. These are often ready to object against themselves, that they shall never 'see the 'goodness of the Lord in the land of the living.' Methinks I hear them complaining, with the church of old, 'My way is hid from the Lord, and my judg- 'ment is passed from my God.' And condemning themselves for hypocrites, and temporary believers, because of the uncertainty of their frames, and the unfruitfulness of their lives. They are for the present bewildered, as those that have lost their way. They have no sensible communion with Christ, no present discovery of the love of God, to take comfort in; and the terrors of the Lord often make them afraid. But notwithstanding their fears, 'this is the 'right way, wherein God leads us to the city of ha- 'bitation.' Were the reconciled countenance of a covenant God and Father always to be lift up on us, we should be apt to prize the comforts we receive immediately from him, more than the glorious Person who was the purchaser and is the bestower of them. Were he never to hide his face, we should live upon the streams rather than the fountain; we should be too ready to say with the three disciples, 'Lord, it is good for us to be here;' without pressing after any farther manifestations in a better world. We should be ready to make a stop at the banks of *Jordan*, or at least, we should pass that river with reluctance, indifferent in our desires after what remaineth to be received by us in the heavenly world. In a word, God is pleased to give to us at some times a glimpse of our future glory, that he may excite our desires after the farther enjoyments thereof; and at other times is pleased wisely to with-hold his hand in this respect, that we may be willing, when he calls us, 'to depart, and be with Christ, which is

'far

'far better.' This then, though it be a way lefs pleafant to us to walk in, is neverthelefs the right way to the place where our hearts and treafure are both of them lodged : by this means we are made to long after, and then are led to the city of habitation.

The fame may be faid,

2. Concerning the various outward afflictions with which the believer is exercifed. They are all of them, let them arife from what quarter foever, ufeful to us, and neceffary for us. God never fends an affliction to us, but when he fees it needful for us; and he never removes it from us, before it has anfwered the end for which he at firft fent it. Outward afflictions are not accidental things, they come not by chance, but are fent to us by a wife and merciful Father, who caufes them to anfwer the end for which he fends them. By them we are purged from our drofs and tin; grace is tried and refined in the furnace of affliction, and they who have tafted that the Lord is gracious, are hereby more conformed to his heavenly image, made partakers of his holinefs, Heb. xii. 10. and more prepared for his heavenly kingdom. Afflictions are a furtherance to us in our way heaven-ward, not an hinderance to us; though when we are exercifed therewith we often conclude ourfelves to be in a defert and defolate land. We muft be firft of all prepared for glory, before we can, in confiftency with the perfections of our God, be received into it: and this is the end, and proves the bleffed iffue of our prefent afflictions, 2 Cor. iv. 17. Hereby then it further appears that God leads his people the right way, though it may be a rough way, to a city of habitation.

3. The temptations of Satan every one of them anfwer the fame general end. He is indeed ftyled, with an emphafis, 'our adverfary,' 1 Pet. v. 8. But he oftentimes proves, contrary to his own defign and our expectation, our great friend. The powers of darknefs are fuffered to dwell amongft us, for the

fame

same reason that some of the Canaanites were left among the people of Israel; that is, to try us, and shew us how weak we are without Christ; and how strong we are, when we depend upon that grace which is treasured up in him. By all the advantages they gain against us, they only render us the more distrustful of ourselves, and the grace which we have already received makes us the more in love with Christ Jesus, our glorious Head, in whose strength we overcome them; and more desirous of that city of habitation which God has prepared for his people, where we shall join the heavenly host in saying with a loud voice, ' Now is come salvation, and strength, ' and the kingdom of our God, and the power of his ' Christ: for the accuser of our brethren is cast ' down, who accused them before our God day and ' night,' Rev. xii. 10. Thus we see how God leads his people by the right way, that they may go to a city of habitation. I might have been much more large, but time confines me to generals. Let us therefore proceed now to the fourth thing proposed.

IV. To conclude with some practical remarks on what you have heard. And,

1. Has God prepared for his people a city of habitation? how great then is that grace, how free and sovereign is that love, to which this was originally owing. All that we have in time, and all that we expect to enjoy to eternity, proceed alone from this spring; this is the original fountain from which they all flow. The vessels of mercy were prepared from all eternity *to* glory, though they are prepared *for* it only in time. And to what can this unspeakable privilege be owing, or into what can it be resolved, short of the sovereign and distinguishing grace of God? This it is alone that makes us differ from others: Considered in ourselves, we were equally the objects of the anger and resentment of an Holy God,

with

with those who are 'reserved in chains of darkness 'to the judgment of the great day:' and had not the free grace of God found out an expedient for our salvation, we must equally with them have suffered the vengeance of eternal fire; 'but God, who 'is rich in mercy, for the great love wherewith he 'loved us, even when we were dead in sins, hath 'quickened us together with Christ; (by grace ye 'are saved), and hath raised us up together, and 'made us sit together in heavenly places in Christ 'Jesus. That in ages to come he might shew the 'exceeding riches of his grace, in his kindness to-'wards us, through Christ Jesus,' Eph. ii. 4. 7. Grace acts like itself, it gives us all things freely. God deals with us as the ' God of all grace:' for he gives us both grace here, and glory hereafter, and no good thing will he with-hold from them that walk uprightly. He first of all makes us his sons, takes us into the number of his family, and gives us a right and title to the privileges of his house in our justification; and in our sanctification he gradually prepares us for the more immediate enjoyment of himself in that better world; and then he calls us home to the glorious inheritance itself, ' the city of ' habitation' which he had settled upon us before all worlds. And who of us can take but a slight view of these things, without crying out, as the Apostle does, 1 John iii. 1. ' Behold what manner of love the Fa-' ther hath bestowed upon us, that we should be call-' ed the sons of God!' Our eternal predestination to glory, and our actual preparation for it, are both of them owing wholly, and alone, to his free and sovereign grace; and to this shall we everlastingly ascribe it, when we come ' to the general assembly, ' and church of the first-born, and to the spirits of ' the just made perfect.'

2. Are we to pass through the wilderness to this city of habitation? How much need have we of a guide to shew us the way, and how thankful should

we be to him who has undertaken to perform this kind office for us? Were we left in this wilderness-world without a guide, our condition would be above measure deplorable, and our ruin unavoidable: we should then fall into the pits and snares, which our enemies have made for the intanglement of our feet, and the destruction of our souls; they that are more mighty than we, would assuredly prevail against us; we should be led captive by Satan at his will; there would be no withstanding his temptations; no escaping his malice and fury, or resisting those whom he employs against us in this desolate and dangerous way. But through grace this blessing we have: Christ Jesus is styled the 'Captain of our 'salvation,' and he faithfully discharges the office, which he has engaged to perform as such. He not only undertook to purchase salvation by his death, but to apply it likewise by his life; he goes before us continually as our Guide and Leader, and marks out the path which we are to take; he communicates to us suitable help and refreshment, while we are in our way; restores our souls when we have gone out of the way, and preserves us from the fury and violence, as well as the craft and subtlety of our many enemies. He is 'a pillar of cloud to us for our co-'vering by day, and a pillar of fire for our guidance 'by night.' He is always at our right hand, so that we shall not be greatly moved. Here lies our safety, and the strong ground of our hope, that we shall not fall short of our rest, or lose the prize we are so earnestly contending for. Christ himself is our life, and the length of our days; who has graciously promised that he will never fail us nor forsake us. May we therefore begin the work of heaven before we come there, daily sacrificing the sacrifices of praise unto him, even the fruit of our lips. Using the same language here, as we hope to use for ever hereafter. 'Unto him who has loved us and washed us from our 'sins in his own blood, and hath made us kings and 'priests

'priests unto God and his Father; to him be glory
'and dominion for ever and ever, Amen.' Rev.
i. 5, 6.

3. Is the way of the wilderness the right way to a city of habitation? How easy should this make us under all the temptations, trials and afflictions with which we are now exercised. 'All things are for 'your sakes, that the abundant grace might through 'the thanksgiving of many redound to the glory of 'God,' 2 Cor. iv. 15. And that all things might appear in the end to have been working together for good. This should make us willingly submit to the various trials we meet with in our passage. There is a crown of glory reserved in heaven, for all those that shall continue faithful unto death. A city of habitation, where the wearied pilgrim shall rest; rivers of pleasure, where he shall be refreshed and delighted. There he will have an ample amends for all the difficulties he has been exposed to in the present life. The view of this recompence of reward will make death itself pleasant, and hang out a lamp sufficient to enlighten even that dark valley.

4. Can none get admission into this city of habitation but the 'redeemed of the Lord?' ver. 2. Let this lead us to Christ Jesus, the only person 'who is 'of God made unto us wisdom, righteousness, sancti-'fication and redemption,' 1 Cor. i. 30. Him hath God exalted with his right hand, to give repentance unto Israel, and forgiveness of sins, Acts v. 31. No one can save us from our sins, but he whom God hath set forth to be a propitiation for sin, through faith in his blood. Hither then must the convinced sinner fly, as his only city of refuge; on his righteousness must we all depend for a right and title to life; and his Spirit alone can fit and prepare us for it. If we have not on us Christ's perfect righteousness, we are not his people; none but they who are arrayed with this fine linen, clean and white, shall be thought worthy to enter into this city of habitation.

tion. Let us therefore be importunate with God to lead us unto Chriſt, and enable us to believe in him to the ſaving of the ſoul. Such he has purchaſed glory for, and he lives to prepare them for it : there, as their forerunner, he is for them already entered; and thither, as the Captain of their ſalvation, will he at laſt bring them, and preſent them faultleſs before the throne of his Father's glory with exceeding joy.

SERMON XV.

FAITH EYING THE PROMISES IN LIFE AND DEATH.

Heb. xi. 13.

These all died in faith, not having received the promises, but having seen them afar off, and were persuaded of them, and embraced them, and confessed that they were strangers and pilgrims on the earth.

THIS chapter is styled by our old divines a little book of martyrs. It gives us an account of the lives and deaths of Old-Testament saints; and by what means their lives were so honourable and exemplary, and their deaths so comfortable and triumphant. It is by faith, that a believer both does and suffers the whole will of God, till he is put into the actual possession of promised glory. ' These all died ' in faith:' More is implied in the phrase, than is expressed. It denotes the duration or continuance of faith, till the dying time came. Faith carries a believer through every duty, difficulty, trial, every dark passage in life; and it never leaves him when he comes to die. Every thing else leaves him, but faith. Riches, honours, friends, senses, life itself, leaves him, but faith sticks by him, and carries him

safe

safe where he longs to be. Nay, the expression seems to be more emphatical. In the margin it is, these all died *according* to faith. That which had borne them up under so many storms and fears and distresses, heretofore, is their great dependence and only refuge now. They are not afraid to die, as they had lived, *believing*. God's promise and power, his covenant-love and grace, his Christ and salvation, are the same things in death as they are in life. These Old-Testament saints died not only *believers*, but *believing*; in the profession, and in the act and exercise of faith. True, they ' had not received ' the promises,' had not seen Christ in the flesh, nor Canaan, which is a type of heaven and glory ; this was the trial of their faith ; it lay as an obstacle in the way of believing ; but it serves as a commendation of their faith, that notwithstanding it held out, and acted to the end of life. As they lived, so they died ; upon the same blessed principles, and in the same sweet and happy frame ; hugging themselves in the promises, and venturing their eternal all, with confidence and comfort, in a dependence thereon. ' These all died in faith,' &c. What I chose the words for, is to shew, as enabled, how faith acts towards the promises of God in a believing soul, living and dying. The method is plain in the text.

I. What is it to die in faith?

II. What is faith's great support in a living or dying believer?

III. How faith acts towards these promises in a believer living or dying. And to apply:

I. What is it to die in faith?

It is a great question, a man's all depends upon it. To die mistaken in this, is to die mistaken for ever. Therefore,

1. It is not to die barely in a profession of faith. To die owning Christ and his cause ; bearing witness to the truth ; encouraging and exhorting our

dear

dear Christian friends and brethren, 'that with 'purpose of heart they would cleave to the Lord;' this is sweet dying. Thus Jacob died, David died, Simeon died; who with Anna the prophetess spake of Christ to all them that looked for redemption in Jerusalem. What I would guard against is a bare name to live; a notion and zeal for truth, which too many professors rest in. Light in the understanding and judgment, where there is no renewal of the heart. O! Sirs, death divests us of all forms 'Hail, Master!' will not do in the other world. Be whatever you will besides, if you are not in Christ, you have no part in what my text speak of: 'These all died in 'faith.' If you have not received Christ, all your praying and prophesying in his name will turn to no account, when you stand before his bar. You may read your doom already, Matt. vii. 23. 'I will 'profess unto them, I never knew you; Depart 'from me, ye that work iniquity.' It is not what a man believes *of* Christ that saves, but his believing *in* him, yielding up himself only and wholly to him. To die in an outward barren profession of faith, is not to die *in faith*. Nor,

2. Is it necessary always that there be a transporting joy, arising from a sense of interest in Christ, in order to a believer's dying in faith? Our blessed Lord died in faith; yet, poor distressed soul! for thy comfort be it spoken, he died forsaken: 'My God, my God, why hast thou for- 'saken me!' Here was strong faith, but no comfort, no joy. Christ triumphed over death, but not in dying. A man may die in faith, when he doth not die in feeling. There may be no assuring sense of God's love, and yet a strong and firm dependence on his promise. The strength of faith is most where there is least of sight; every believer finds the path of life: 'Thou wilt shew me the path of life,' Psal. xvi. 11. but every one does not see it, as he walks through Jordan. Many a soul goes to Christ dying, just as he comes to him, when he was

first

first quickened and made alive to God, that is, by a solemn determined act of trust and reliance. Even strong faith does not exclude every degree of fear. Therefore,

3. To 'die in faith,' is to die trusting Christ, and commending our souls to him by faith. All faith includes trust, though it is not necessarily connected with joy. The liveliest example of dying in faith we have in the blessed Jesus, who is the author and finisher of our faith; Luke xxiii. 46. 'And when Jesus had cried with a loud voice, he 'said, Father, into thy hands I commend my spi- 'rit,' &c. It is an act of pure trust. Faith not only sees that beyond the grave which will comfort, but it can cling about its God, and close with Christ in a promise, when it feels the ground of all sensible comforts sinking underneath it: The nearer to Christ the more forcible and vehement is the soul's desire to him, and the acting of its trust in him; it is working after its God all along in life, seeking him in one ordinance and another, and always pressing after further and more sensible communion with him; and when death comes, it gathers up all its strength, and throws itself into the Redeemer's arms, with a 'Lord Jesus receive my 'spirit.' "O! present this soul of mine faultless: "I venture my all upon thy promises and righte- "ousness, blessed Redeemer; O! keep that which "I am committing to thy trust." It is a sweet simile, a pleasant writer illustrates this by, "As a river, that after many turnings and windings, at last pours itself with a central force, a mighty and rapid stream, into the bosom of the ocean; so does the soul pour itself as it were into the hands of its God, empties all its trust upon Christ, knowing and being persuaded, that he is able to keep that which is committed to him, though it cannot say at the same time in full assurance, I know that into Jesus I have believed." True, these are the triumphs of faith in a dying hour. Many of the blessed Patriarchs,

archs, in our text, rode triumphant to glory. Moses died 'upon the mouth of the Lord;' so many render that expression, Deut. xxxiv. 5. With a kiss of love, his soul was sweetly drawn out of his body. Jacob sung a song of praise to the God which fed him all his life long, even 'the angel which 'redeemed him from all evil,' Gen. xlviii. 16. And multitudes of the heirs of promise since, have seen themselves 'sitting together in heavenly places in 'Christ,' when they have been dying out of time, and entering within the borders of the invisible world. Faith often brings heaven down into the soul, before it carries the soul up into it. But yet the very nature of faith lies in trust and dependence; and that believer who dies trusting dies in faith, as well as he who dies triumphing. So much for our first general.

II. What is the great support of a believer, consider him either as living or dying? The text says, the *promises* are so, though the blessings contained in them are not received. 'These all died,' &c.

Two things faith sees in the promises, which support and comfort the soul, though the promised blessings are not received.

1. It sees God's Christ; and,
2. God's heart.

1. God's Christ. This was the reach and aim, and the support and comfort of Old-Testament faith. All the promises are but one and the same thing diversified. Christ, and salvation by and in him, is the substance of all the promises: 'All the pro-'mises of God are in him Yea,' and in him 'Amen.' Be the promise in itself never so sweet, so suitable, and engaging, if Christ be not even in it, it is a dry breast, a well without water. How is the curse taken away? is the first inquiry of a poor guilty sensible soul: 'How can man be just with God?' A sight of Christ in the promise is the only satisfying resolve. He is called therefore the *rest* and *refreshing*

freshing of his people: 'This is the rest wherewith 'ye may cause the weary to rest, and this is the re- 'freshing,' Isa. xxviii. 12. Let a poor soul see Christ, tell of him, of peace with God, interest in the covenant, special guidance here, and of everlasting life and glory hereafter, all is well. He can believe and stay himself upon the promise: Why? because there is nothing to hinder the performance of the promise. Christ hath died, therefore God is just in justifying the ungodly; Christ was made *sin* and a *curse*, therefore God is to his people a *blessing* God. Christ hath triumphed over death, therefore in Christ's name, and by virtue of relation to him, believers can sing, 'O death, where 'is thy sting!' Or if the clouds be thick and dark in a dying hour, they can trust Christ to be their guide through death; 'yea, though I walk through 'the valley,' &c. Psal. xxiii. 4. The faith on which they lived is a tried faith; and they can venture upon the same bottom into eternity, that has carried them safe and comfortable through the storms and tempests of time. That which makes faith so precious, so relieving to the soul, is because its hold is on Christ, its refuge only in him. Faith sees God's Christ and salvation in the promise: therefore in the absence of promised good, it supports and relieves the soul.

2. Faith sees God's heart in the promise. What is a promise but an expression of the love of God's heart in word! 'For thy word's sake, and accor- 'ding to thine own heart, hast thou done all these 'great things,' says David, 2 Sam. vii. 21. That is the secret in all God's promises, and none but a believer can spell it out. Faith looks to God's everlasting covenant-love in every promise. Is the rod, says the afflicted saint, put into the promise? then it is good for me that I am afflicted; it would never have been ordained in everlasting counsels, were it not for the b. st. O! I will kiss the rod: 'Not my will, but thine be done.' Must faith have

a trial? love and patience be tried? Has my Father and my God promised strength equal to my day? It is well. There is love in fixing the trial, or else God would have given no promise to bear me up under it: Love in the pain, as well as love in the promise. And 'is it appointed for man once to 'die?' it is the chosen way to my Father's house. Then says the soul, as once God did to Jacob, Gen. xlvi. 3. 'Fear not to go down into Egypt; I will 'go with thee.' Thy God will not leave thee at last, he will go down with thee to the chambers of death, and see thee forthcoming thence. Thy Jesus loves and pities thee dying, and orders thy pains, and tells thy groans, and every sigh of thy faith, he stands ready to receive and present it to the Father. God's heart is in all the strokes of his hand. Faith sees God's Christ, and his heart in the promises, and therefore acts on these promises, and supports and refreshes the soul by them, though the good promised is not as yet received.

III. How in *particular* faith acts towards the promises in a believer's support, living or dying?

This is expressed in three words. 'These all 'died in faith, not having received the promises, 'but having seen them afar off, and were per- 'suaded of them, and embraced them.'

1. Faith sees the promises *afar off*. It does not require the presence or existence of the thing, but only the promise of it. Abraham saw Christ's day and rejoiced; Jacob was filled with that salvation he had been longing for: 'I have waited for thy 'salvation, O Lord.' David had all his desire in a believing view of Christ, and that well-ordered covenant, which God had made with him in Christ. The things themselves were far off. Christ was not manifest in the flesh till many hundred years after; but faith beheld these things as present in God's counsel, his covenant, his word of promise, and fixed and centered in them. Is any thing too

hard for God? Did his promise ever fall to the ground? Is he not truth itself? Are not all his paths judgment? This is the reasoning of faith. It sees things far off in the power of God, the truth of God, the providence, and covenant of God. Hence 'Abraham against hope believed in hope; 'he staggered not at the promise through unbelief;' had not a dispute, one secret demur against the command of God, because 'he judged him faithful who had promised.' Poor believing soul! thou art passing through a wilderness full of dangers, snares, temptations, sins; what use dost thou make of thy faith? Does it not at times lift thee up and set thee on high, so that thou seest the way to be right, though it be rough and uneven? Hast thou no discoveries of the unsearchable riches of Christ? The suitableness and fulness of covenant-provisions? That thou are complete in Christ, free from Satan the tempter, as well as the tyrant? delivered from all pain, and sin, and death? made a pillar in the house of thy God, where there is no going out? Canst thou point to no seasons, wherein God made thee as it were of his secret? shewed thee what he was doing before all worlds were? How he set up Christ as the head of his chosen seed; put thee into him, blessed thee with all spiritual blessings in him; and has put the Spirit of his Son into thine heart, so that thou art able to cry, 'Abba, Father?' What is this but to see things afar off? This may be accounted foolishness by an ignorant and profane world; but herein lies the life and sweetness of true religion, and the power of God in his saints.

2. It is persuaded of these things. They are realities, though invisible to every one but the man who has the eyes of his understanding enlightened. This persuasion is twofold. First, Of the things themselves, then of the soul's special interest and propriety in them.

1. This

1. This persuasion relates to the things themselves. Gospel-principles, gospel-doctrines, privileges, duties, they are inlaid in the soul as well as gospel-promises. A believer will sooner lose his life than sell God's truth; and this persuasion arises not from conjecture, opinion, reasoning, nor merely the authority of the speaker, but from that taste and feeling which he has of the things themselves. 'If 'so be they have tasted that the Lord is gracious,' 1 Pet. ii. 3. There is no disputing against taste; thou hast a wicked and rebellious heart, which is ever annoying thee with some vain or vile thought in holy duties: Can any man persuade thee against original sin, or the remains of corruption in the saints after conversion to God? It is to speak against thy very feeling. So thou hast felt the power of sovereign grace in conversion, the strength of divine consolations under distress and darkness; thou hast known what a sure hold the righteousness of Christ is, and the everlasting covenant, and the Redeemer's intercession above. Thou hast been fed and sustained by the promises all thy life long; they are the issues of the love of God to thy soul, from duty to duty, in all states, circumstances, and conditions. Thus God opens his heart to thee, and melts and cheers, and refreshes thine. Can any one persuade thee these blessed doctrines are false, these precious promises but mere imaginary delusive things? Thou hast an answer in thy heart more ready than words can ever be to express it; thy soul recoils within thee; thou even sinkest to hear thy God and his grace so far abused. Thou art persuaded of these truths, these blessed promises, not to begin, after so long experience, to learn thy creed over again.

2. This persuasion refers to the sense which a believer may have of his interest in them: This is not common to saints as such; it is but at special times and seasons, given and taken away by God, for wise and gracious ends. Therefore, for the present I

pass

pass it over, and come to the third thing, wherein faith discovers itself in acting upon the promises, that is, ' It embraces them ;' the word signifies ' to salute,' a metaphor taken from the manner of parting between two dear and intimate friends : Two things are implied in it.

First, Intimate acquaintance. The saints of old were very chary of God's promises, they were searching and digging into them to know ' what, or what ' manner of time the Spirit of Christ, which was in ' them, did signify,' 1 Pet. i. 11. Hence it is that one saint tells God's covenant and his own experience to another, Abraham to Isaac, Isaac to Jacob, &c. The things were familiar to them, their whole soul was in them : Thus should believers live in the frame of meditation on God's promises. If new promises are wanting, go back to those of older date, bless God for them, and your experience from them. A believer, when he is taking his leave of the promises, takes a sweet farewell of them ; though he is going to walk by sight, yet he bears a noble and just testimony to the promises, as to their use and sweetness, in his walk by faith. These, says he, have been my song in the house of my pilgrimage; my refreshment, and pleasant pools in Bacca's vale. I love them now, though I shall have no more need of them henceforth for ever. O ! my dear friends, whom I leave behind, value and live upon these precious promises. Acquaintance is one thing intended by them.

Secondly, But principally, is meant endearing affection.

The will chooses them, cleaves to them, and if any delight a believer has, it is in them. ' O how ' love I thy law ; how precious also are thy thoughts ' unto me, O God ! how great is the sum of them !' Such are precious interjections ; a man's whole soul is wrapped up in them. Persuasion of interest, some humble, desponding saint may want ; but not a soul present who wants an hand or heart to embrace the promises:

promises: When the Spirit whispers any one to his soul, he catches hold of it, is afraid of looking off it, is humbled and amazed God should thus manifest himself to him, rejoices in it, and throws away a whole world for it. Try a believer in his darkest frames, and you may soon know how his heart stands affected to Christ in the promise; offer him all that can be thought of in time, and he had rather had a promise of forgiveness, sanctification, freedom from temptation, victory over death, and eternal life afterwards; he despises all in comparison of the promises, be his fears never so great in life or death, away his soul goes to the promises, he clasps them in his arms, and many a saint has dropt the tabernacle, pleading and urging them before a faithful God. But I shall close all with a word or two by way of use: And,

Use 1. Did all these 'die in faith?' Have you this faith? It is sad to have faith to seek when you need it to use. They died in faith, and they lived by it too; it was a tried faith they lived and died by. How stands it with thy soul *now*; bring death and judgment near; what thinkest thou of Christ? If thou art a stranger to Christ, thou art a stranger to faith. Hast thou given up thy soul to him *now?* Then thou mayst trust him with body and soul both another day. It is a fruitless wish, that of ' Balaam, Let me die the death of the righteous,' &c.

Use 2. How little just ground is there for a believer in Christ to fear death? The love of God, the covenant of grace, the care of Christ, the being and stability of the promise, the life of faith, all last till death. It is an enemy, it is true, but thy last enemy, a destroyed enemy, an enemy which thou hast a thousand promises thou shalt triumph over; therefore cast not away your confidence, which hath great Recompence of reward. Thy God is faithful, thy redeemer liveth: his word is a sure covenant of faith, and an anchor of hope in life and death.

Use 3.

Use 3. What a flight character do moſt of this world leave behind them; though thou dieſt rich, honourable, eſteemed, eaſy, what is this to dying in faith! It is a poor thing, if all the world have to ſay of thee when thou art gone, " ſuch an one died worth ſo much." No matter how thou dieſt, lingring or ſuddenly, young or old, provided thou dieſt in faith; leave theſe things to the covenant order of thy God. 'Bleſſed are the dead that die in ' the Lord,' whenever is the time, whatever the place, or the means of their death. All taken notice of in our text, is ' theſe all died in faith.'

Use 4. What need have believers of the help of the bleſſed Spirit in life and at death? The ſpiritual eye is his gift, and all ſpiritual perſuaſion is his work: Scripture arguments will be of no avail if the Spirit of God does not make the application. It is not enough to propound arguments, and leave a ſoul to its own choice. All the world cannot bring a ſoul to believe till God open the heart. The Spirit convinces, not barely by informing the underſtanding, but ſecretly drawing the ſoul; 'Draw ' me, we will run after thee.' Apply more frequently and more earneſtly to God the Spirit; try your ſtate by your affections; they embraced the promiſes as well as they were perſuaded of them. What is thy love fixed upon? Where is thy heart? What doſt thou moſt favour? How is thy obedience, thy courſe, thy walk here? Moſt men go by their light, but the rule Chriſt gives is their life and converſation: Knowledge will carry a man but a little way to heaven. 'Theſe things if ye know, happy are ' ye if ye do them.'

Use 5. Think more of home, and live more above life: If you profeſs to be heirs of God's promiſe, live above the croſſes and comforts of life too. Thoſe in my text, who all died in faith, ' confeſſed that ' they were ſtrangers and pilgrims on earth.'

SERMON XVI.

THE NATURE OF REGENERATION.

2 Cor. v. 17.

Therefore if any man be in Christ, he is a new creature: old things are passed away; behold, all things are become new.

IN Isaiah's prophecy God promises, when Messiah's kingdom is spread throughout all the world, and all nations shall flow unto him, that he will create ' new heavens, and a new earth, and the
' former shall not be remembered, nor come into
' mind,' Isa. lv. 17. This is in part fulfilled in every true believer, in whose heart the kingdom of Christ is set up, his image formed, and all things that are contrary thereunto are in some measure passed away. ' The tabernacle of God is with men;' (as it is expressed in a parallel place; Rev. xxi. 3, 4.) ' and he will dwell with them, and they shall
' be his people; and God himself shall be with them,
' and be their God.' This is called new heavens, and a new earth, because it is what the believing sinner was an utter stranger to before. Unregenerate sinners are darkness, Eph. v. 8. being ' without Christ,' that is, in a state of distance and separation from him;

him; 'they are aliens from the commonwealth of 'Israel, and strangers from the covenant of promise; 'having no hope, and without God in the world.' Farther, these new heavens and this new earth are said to be created; because the same almighty power which went to the producing this visible world out of nothing, is necessary to produce a principle of spiritual life in the heart of an unrenewed sinner, yea, the soul thus renewed is said to be a new creation; because every part of the man is changed through this one act of God's almighty power and grace. 'Old things are passed away; behold, all 'things are become new.' The apostle lays a special emphasis upon it: it is spoken, either by way of attention, implying the care believers ought to take when passing a judgment upon their state God-wards. That is to say, " Do not deceive yourselves; a par- " tial change will not suffice to denominate a man " to be in Christ Jesus: *Old things are passed away*; " *behold, all things are become new.*" Or else it comes in by way of admiration and astonishment, as in Rev. xxi. 5. ' And he that sat upon the throne ' said, Behold, I make all things new;' intimating the wonderful display which there is of the sovereign power and grace of God, in the renovation or new creation of a dead and self-destroyed sinner. Therefore ' if any man be in Christ, he is a new ' creature,' &c.

In farther discoursing on these words, I shall endeavour to do the following things:

I. Shew what the new creature is.
II. How it is produced.
III. In what way it discovers itself.
IV. How it evidences a sinner's union to Christ Jesus.
V. The improvement.

I. I am to shew what this new creature is. And,

1. It lies in a change of the whole man: 'If any 'man be in Christ, he is a new creature.' Whatever sin has defaced in man, grace restores. The salve goes full as far every way as the sore. Is the understanding darkness? 'God, who commanded the 'light to shine out of darkness, shines into the heart, 'to give the light of the knowledge of his glory, in 'the face of Jesus Christ,' 2 Cor. iv. 6. Is the will stubborn and averse, even to enmity itself, against the law of God? 'Thy people shall be willing in the 'day of thy power,' Psal. cx. 3. The cords of love are as sweet as they are strong. Are the affections disorderly, impure, sensual, devilish? the 'fruit of 'the Spirit is in all goodness, righteousness and 'truth,' Eph. v. 9. A new heart and a new disposition always go together. 'A new spirit will I 'put within you,' Ezek. xxxvi. 25. Grace also sanctifies the memory and purges the conscience, making even the members of our bodies, those servants of sin, 'instruments of righteousness unto ho-'liness,' Rom. vi. 13. When God renews the man, he as it were new-makes him. 'Behold, I create "all things new,' Rev. xxi. 5. Spirit, soul, and body partake of the change. He is born again; raised from the dead; *metamorphosed*, as the word signifies, Rom. xii. 2. or, as we render it, *transformed* by the renewing of the mind. Though the same faculties of understanding, willing, judging, &c. continue, there are new qualities put into them, they are put into another mold, put into a new frame, whereby they have sustained so great a change as justly denominates the man on whom this change passes, 'a new creature.' Even as our bodies will be raised the same bodies they were sown, bone will come to its bone, dust will find its dust; yet the qualities will be so altered, as the bodies shall be no more earthly, corruptible, or mortal bodies, but be raised spiritual, immortal, and such as shall no more return

return to corruption, 1 Cor. xv. 44.—This new creature lies in a change of the whole man.

2. It is a change which is inward in the heart, 'That which is born of the flesh is flesh; and that 'which is born of the spirit is spirit,' John iii. 6. It lies in the inward disposition and inclination of the mind; not merely in the outward act of the life. Hence it is called, 'The hidden man of the heart,' 1 Pet. iii. 4. and the 'inward man,' 2 Cor. iv. 16. And God is said in creating it to take away the stone out of our flesh, and to give us an heart of flesh, that is, a tender, sensible, melting, obedient heart; apt to receive whatever impressions God is pleased to make upon it, Ezek. xxxvi. 26.—It is a new nature, not a new name; a new principle, not a new notion. Our Lord compares it to a well of water in the soul, which 'springeth up into everlasting life,' John iv. 14. They sadly mistake it, who suppose that it consists in any thing external. Here lies our great business, in looking inward. 'Create,' says David, 'in me a clean heart, O God!' Psal. li. 10. Clean hands or mere outward reformations avail nothing without this. The new creature is a change that is inward in the heart.

3. It is a change which is after the image of God. In this man was created at first, and after it he is renewed.—Eph. iv. 24. 'That ye put on the new 'man, which after' (or according to) 'God is crea- 'ted in righteousness and true holiness.' The new creature is a 'partaker of the divine nature,' 2 Pet. i. 4. The beauty of the Lord our God is upon it, himself being the glorious pattern, according to which the draught is taken, and the gracious principle of sanctification in the heart is delineated. Hence Christ is said to be 'formed in the soul,' Gal. iv. 19. because every renewed man bears a similitude and resemblance of his person; 'being 'righteous, as he is righteous; and pure, as he is 'pure,' 1 John iii. 3, 7. The same mind, the same disposition and spirit which was in Christ, is in him,
Phil.

Phil. ii. 5. Wherever there is really the Spirit of God, there muſt be the life of God. The new creature is acted by the ſame principle and with the ſame views God himſelf is; becauſe it is ſhaped after his image. In regeneration God does not only ſhine *unto* the ſoul, but he ſhines *into* it; communicating himſelf not merely by way of outward diſcovery, as the ſun communicates light to the world; but by way of impreſſion, ' Holineſs unto the Lord' is written within. This makes a man not only differ from others in the world, but differ from himſelf: though he has ſin in him, he has alſo Chriſt in him; a new as well as an old man, according to which all his thoughts, words, deſigns, actions, are framed; notwithſtanding he may at ſome times miſs his aim, and ſee very little of the divine likeneſs either in himſelf or them. But ſome ſtamp of the form into which he is delivered he will bear, though it be hard at times to make it out. The change in the heart of man is after the image of God.

4. It is ſuch a change which is fundamental to all ſpiritual actions. Hence it is compared to ſeed, which being caſt into the heart, is productive of life and motion in the whole courſe of outward obedience: ' His ſeed remaineth in him,' 1 John iii. 9. It is compared to a root, from whence all the fruits of righteouſneſs ſpring. Thus of the ſtony ground-hearer it is ſaid, that ' he had not root in himſelf,' and therefore endured but for a while. Finally, it is compared to a well of water, ' which ſpringeth up ' into everlaſting life.' It is ever ſending forth freſh ſtreams, and ſpringing up towards God, from whom it derived its being, and from whom is its continuance and ſupply. All theſe expreſſions ſuppoſe the new creature to conſiſt in a vital principle implanted in the ſoul from whence all living actions flow, ſuch as faith, repentance, and all the graces of the Spirit.

II. We come to ſhew how the new creature is produced in the ſoul. And this, according to the words

words of the text, is by creation: 'If any man be 'in Christ, he is a new creature.' By this expression three things are set forth:

1. That the new creature is a work of almighty power. It is to create a new world in the soul; to set a man against himself; turning him 'from darkness unto light, and from the power of Satan unto God.' To roll the stone, not from the heart, as the angel did from the sepulchre, but to take it out of the heart; therefore it can be wrought by no power less than divine. Our apostle heaps words upon words, when endeavouring to set it forth, Eph. i. 19. 'That ye may know what is the hope of his calling, and what is the exceeding greatness of his power to us-ward who believe, according to the working of his mighty power.' There is an almightiness of power necessary to bring a man to believe; power which is great even to an hyperbole; the same power which was requisite to raise Christ from the dead.

2. It is a creation, because it is an immediate act of God's power, without the help of any instrument: 'Where wast thou,' says God to Job, 'when I laid the foundations of the earth? Declare if thou hast understanding,' Job xxxviii. 4. 'He stretcheth forth the heavens alone, and spreadeth abroad the earth by himself,' Isa. xliv. 24. The old creation would admit of no instrument, or helper; no more does the new. Man is not more passive in his first formation, than he is in his regeneration. Life is infused, not acquired. There is no intermediate state between death and life; though the principle of grace may be where it is not immediately discovered, yet it cannot be where it is not implanted. Motion always supposes life. The word does not give life; no; this is the peculiar work of the Spirit of God; but it is a means of exciting vital actions, such as faith, repentance and submission to Christ, &c. when the soul is quickened and made alive: 'Faith cometh by hearing, and hearing by the word of God.' There are no pangs in the new birth,

though

though there may be many struggles, pains and fears, before a soul has sensibly turned unto God. Life is an immediate thing; it is breathed into the soul in an instant, though it may not be instantly perceived; it is sown as seed in the ground, which is done at once, though it may not immediately spring up. It is produced immediately without the help of any instrument, therefore called a creation.

3. This change upon the heart is called a creation, because it is produced out of nothing, as the first creation was. Saul, by the help of his own natural abilities and the common influences of the Spirit of God, became ' another man,' 1 Sam. x. 6. but we no where read that he became a *new* man. The work of grace in the heart is not educed out of the principles of nature, but immediately by an act of almighty power produced by the Spirit. There is nothing in the heart of an unconverted man, which affords matter for the Spirit of God to work upon; nothing but what opposes him in his work: ' The ' carnal mind is enmity against God. By nature we ' are dead in trespasses and sins.' *First*, God makes the root good, then the fruit; how? by taking away the old, corrupt, degenerate vine, and planting wholly a right seed, Jer. ii. 21. Hence he promises in the new covenant, ' to take the stone out of the ' flesh, and to give an heart of flesh,' Ezek. xxxvi. 27. Grace is not grafted upon the old stock; root and branch are both new. Nothing in man was disposed to this great change; nothing in man could contribute thereto. Matter and form are both of God's producing: ' Behold, I create all things new.' This should have led to the effects of the new creature, or those operations of the soul whereby it is to be judged of. But it is needful first to improve what has been said.

INFER. I. What has been said may serve for the conviction or reproof of four sorts of men.

1. Such as rest in a performance of outward duties. It is not a new form, but a new heart, that
God

God looks at. Herod did many things, and heard John the Baptist gladly; but outward duties would not make an atonement for heart-sins. 'My son,' says God, 'give me thine heart.' He judges of the duty not from the deed done, but from the principle from which it proceeds. O! dare not to draw nigh unto him with your lips, while your hearts are far from him. God had respect unto Abel, to his person first, and then to his sacrifice. Sirs, see that your persons are in a state of reconciliation with God; that his law be written in your hearts; and his image drawn upon your souls: 'Be ye renewed in 'the spirit of your minds.'

2. What has been said reproves such as trust to outward privileges: 'He is not a Jew, who is one 'outwardly.' The choicest privileges are nothing, if they lead thee not to look after the inward man of the heart. Think not that I am degrading the promises and covenant of our God; God forbid. If it be asked, 'What advantage hath the Jew above the 'Gentile;' such as are born under the visible administration of the covenant, above others that are 'aliens from the commonwealth of Israel?' I answer; much every way. Thou hast God's own word, his covenant, his oaths to plead: 'I will be a God to 'thee, and to thy seed after thee.' Thou mayst plead thy parents faith, tears, prayers, hopes, and all of them as founded upon the covenant of thy God. Only do not rest in them. Grace is a personal thing: Thou canst not be saved by thy parents faith, though thou mayst make a plea of it in thy prayers to God. The new nature is God's gift; it comes not through thine or their desert. Seek it earnestly, because thou hast such encouragement in the promises of God, and in a way of asking thou shalt receive.

3. The doctrine reproves such as trust to outward restraints. A man may be cleansed from much filthiness of the flesh, yet not renewed in the spirit of his mind. Paul was a strict Pharisee, yet a great sinner. The Lord restrains many a one, as he did Abimelech,

Abimelech, whom he does not renew: To leave fin will not do, if thou doft not lothe it. It is a great blefling to be kept back from prefumptuous fins, but let not this be put in the room of regenerating power and grace. Begin thy judgment at the heart; there the Spirit of God always begins his work.

4. It reproves fuch as place their religion in convictions, gifts, or fome ftirrings which they find in their affections to God, and to his good ways. There is a legal 'repentance which is to be repented of:' Thus Judas repented, and Cain repented, but neither of them were renewed: Efau fought the blefling with tears, but was rejected: Yea, Balaam himfelf defired to die the death of the righteous. There may be ftirrings of affections, proceeding not from a love of what we afk, but from a fenfe of the danger of what we fear. Balaam loved his own fins better than Ifrael's God, as much as he defired to die Ifrael's death. Sin muft be hated not merely out of love to felf, but out of love to God; not merely as it expofes to wrath, but as it defaces his image, and contradicts his will.

II. This doctrine may be improved by way of direction and encouragement to fuch as believe. By way of direction; and this is twofold: *Firft*, This will help you in your judgment of yourfelves. Grace muft not always be judged of by comforts. It does not depend upon extraordinary revelations, affurances of pardon, joys unfpeakable, &c. Often the kingdom of Chrift within, is like that without, which cometh not with obfervation. One fays, 'Here is 'Chrift, and there is Chrift:' This is the way to comfort, and that is the way. But all your comfort is nothing without heart-purity. Communion with God confifts as much in conformity, or likenefs to him, as in fenfible enjoyment of him. Chrift was loved by the fpoufe, defired, fought for, when not enjoyed. 'Thou haft,' fays Chrift, 'ravifhed my 'heart with one chain of thy neck;' when a little before

before the spouse was complaining, 'I sought him, 'but I found him not.' Christ loves his own image when the believer cannot see it

2. As it helps in judging of yourself, so of other Christians. Were I asked, where does Christ dwell? I would answer, in the humble, holy, contrite heart, in the heavenly submissive soul: Great names have not always great grace. Elijah was sent to a poor widow woman of Zarephath. As it was said of old, when Christ was marked out to John the Baptist, John i. 33. so would I say now: 'Upon whom thou 'shalt see the Spirit descending and remaining, the 'same is he:' That is the renewed man. There Christ dwells, be he poor or rich; has he little learning or none; great parts, reading, genius, or but a small measure of either. The new creature is after the image of him that created him.

3. By way of comfort.

Has Christ created thee anew, he will perform his words to thee, and his work in thee: 'The path 'of the just is as the shining light, which shineth 'more and more unto the perfect day.' There is a perfection of parts, if not of degrees: The water rises up as high as the spring from whence it flows. It is the fruit of everlasting love to thee, and it shall spring up unto everlasting life in thee.

SERMON XVII.

EVIDENCES OF REGENERATION.

2 Cor. v. 17.

Therefore if any man be in Christ, he is a new creature: old things are passed away; behold, all things are become new.

IN discoursing on these words we proposed to do four things:

I. To shew what the new creature is.
II. How it is produced.
III. In what way it discovers itself.
IV. How it evidences a sinner's union to Christ.

The two first have been discoursed upon already; and we proceed to the

III. In what way the new creature discovers itself; or what are those operations of the soul, and those outward effects whereby it is to be judged of. ' Therefore if any man be in Christ, he is a new ' creature: old things are passed away; behold, all ' things are become new.'

1. Where

1. Where the new creature is, the old things of sin and ungodliness are passed away, and in the room thereof comes newness of life. A man is as his walk is. Such as are born from above, will endeavour to have their conversation in heaven, Phil. iii. 20. 'I have,' says the Psalmist, ' chosen the way of ' truth,' Psal. cxix. 30. A renewed man may fall into some way of sin, but he does not choose it, and he does not walk in it. The apostle lays it down as the very first thing visible in a godly man's character, that he is purged from old sins, 2 Pet. i. 9. It is his daily prayer, ' Search me, O God, and know ' my heart; and see if there be any way of wicked-' ness in me. Ephraim shall say, What have I to do ' any more with idols?' Hos. xiv. 8. This is called, ' the reproach of his youth,' Jer. xxxi. 19. for which he ' was ashamed, yea, even confounded.' Beloved lusts are most abhorred, when once Christ is formed in the soul. It is said of Naaman the *Syrian*, he was a great man, rich and mighty, and honourable, *but* he was a leper, 2 Kings v. 1. Quite otherwise of the new creature, 1 Cor. vi. 11. ' But ye are wash-' ed, but ye are justified, but ye are sanctified, in ' the name of the Lord Jesus, and by the Spirit of ' our God.' Canst thou live in any old sin? Thou hast ' but a name' that thou livest. The same fountain cannot send forth sweet waters and bitter. Paul the persecutor prayeth, when with Ephraim of old he is turned, ' and preacheth the faith which once ' he destroyed,' Gal. iv. 23. ' Zaccheus' the publican ' stands, and says, Lord, the half of my goods ' I give to the poor; and if I have taken away any ' thing from any man by false accusation, I restore ' him fourfold,' Luke xix. 8. The rugged jailor, when a believer, becomes a new man; he washed the stripes which he a little before laid upon the apostle Paul and Silas, Acts xvi. 33. If there be not a new conversation, there can be no new nature.

2. Where the new creature is, that old darkness and blindness which was once upon the mind is

passed away, and he has new apprehensions of things, and a new judgment concerning them: Ephes. v. 8. 'For ye were sometimes darkness, but now are ye 'light in the Lord; walk as children of the light,' The apostle Peter calls it 'a marvellous light,' 1 Pet. ii. 9. because of the wonderful effects produced thereby.

Before, he had heard of God 'by the hearing of 'the ear; but now his eye seeth him,' Job xlii. 5. His spotless purity, strict justice, almighty power, they are known so as to be realized by him. "Con-"version," says Dr Preston, (by it he means rege-"neration, or the new creature,) "is wrought, not "always by making us know new things we knew "not before, though this is true in some, but by "knowing things *otherwise* than we did before." The renewed man is guided not by opinion or reasoning, so much as by spiritual sense and experience. 'O! taste and see that the Lord is good,' Psal. xxxiv. 8. Thou art taught of the Spirit of God, what to judge of God, of sin, of thyself, of Christ, of the world, of heaven; and none teacheth like him. Thou knowest God can by no means clear the guilty; thou hast felt the power of his anger. Thou hast seen the plague of thine own heart, and the spirituality of the holy law. 'Paul was alive with-'out the law once; but when the commandment 'came,' and God shined into his heart, 'sin revived, 'and he died,' Rom. vii. 9. The great things of God's law were once strange things, but now they are glorious things. Does any one put the question, What is thy beloved more than another's beloved? Thy answer is ready, 'He is altogether lovely.' A crucified Christ is 'both the power of God and 'the wisdom of God.' Paul counted all things loss, for the excellency of the knowledge of Christ his Lord; so dost thou. Once the righteousness of Christ was a riddle to thee; thy proud heart was enmity against it; now it is thy life: 'Surely shall 'one say, In the Lord have I righteousness and
'strength:'

'strength:' In this thy soul makes her boast. The promises were once dead, insipid things; thou wert aiming to live by doing; now there are 'exceeding 'great and precious promises.' Thy treasure is above; thy inheritance lies beyond time; all here is vanity and vexation of spirit. To be with Christ is thy aim living, and desire dying: 'Wherefore 'henceforth know we no man after the flesh; yea, 'though we have known Christ after the flesh, yet 'now henceforth know we him no more,' ver. 16.

3. Where the new creature is, the old enmity is taken out of the heart, and a new bent and inclination given; 'Thy people shall be willing in the day 'of thy power,' Psal. cx. 3.

They are willingnesses or free-will offerings; wherever God gives a spirit of life, together with it he gives a spirit of love. Grace makes men servants, because friends: 'They shall come and sing 'in the height of Zion, and flow together to the 'goodness of the Lord,' Jer. xxxi. 12. It is a metaphor taken from waters, which glide along naturally, where there is a free passage. 'Doeg was de- 'tained before the Lord,' 1 Sam. xxi. 7. he must attend, and could not help it; that which was *his* burden is the renewed soul's desire and delight. 'O! when shall I come,' says David, 'and appear 'before God!' Psal. xlii. 2. There is a law in his mind, as well as in his members. Thou canst lay thine hand upon thine heart, and say with Paul, 'I 'would do good;' or appeal with Peter, 'Lord, 'thou knowest all things, thou knowest that I love 'thee.' Whence is this, but from the new heart which this God has given thee? God himself calls this, 'putting his laws into our minds, and writing 'them in our hearts,' Heb. viii. 10. A man's spirit is cast into the form and figure of the law. Thus God gives thee to *will*, and by a powerful excitation of this blessed principle, works in thee also to *do* of his own good pleasure.

4. Where

4. Where the new creature is, there are new affections.

'Who will shew us any good?' is the cry of nature: 'Lord, lift thou up the light of thy counte-'nance upon us,' is the language of grace. Once thou sawest no beauty in Christ, wherefore shouldest thou desire him; now the Psalmist speaks thy whole soul; Psal. lxxiii. 25. 'Whom have I in heaven 'but thee? and there is none upon earth that I 'desire besides thee.' If the renewed man hopes, Christ, and the promise of eternal life by him, is some way or other the object of it: 'The Lord is 'my portion, saith my soul, therefore will I hope 'in him,' Lam. iii. 24. If he fears; it is self and sin, and the wicked one. It is an ingenuous not a slavish fear, which he is actuated by. A fear of God, which breeds watchfulness, reverence, and care; not torment. God's law, his house, and his saints, are the objects of his love. O how I love thy law! and when he hates, 'it is the work of them that 'turn aside to lies.' His zeal is for Christ and his precious cause; and his moderation respects the recreations and cares of the present life; not gospel-doctrines, or gospel-holiness. The new nature does not take away natural affections, but rectifies them; it places them upon suitable objects, and regulates them when they are so placed. The renewed man seeks God in the creatures, and loves the creatures for God and Christ's sake.

5. Where the new creature is, a man's aims and ends are new: 'For me to live is Christ,' Phil. i. 21. Regeneration brings a new form upon a man's soul, because it bringeth a new end into it: 'Be ye trans-'formed in the renewing of your minds,' Rom. xii. 2. A natural man's life is in his pleasures and his sins; self is the principle from whence he acts, and to which he acts: 'I am become rich,' says Ephraim, 'I have found me out substance,' Hos. xii. 8. He may perform some duties, and abstain from some sins, but the bane lies here all this while, 'he brings 'forth

'forth fruit unto himself,' Hof. x. 1. Joash did that which was right in the fight of the Lord, not because he loved God or his ways, but because he was afraid of Jehoiadah. Thou performest this or the other duty; why? because thou hast a godly father, or master, thou art afraid of displeasing. A man's course may be changed when his heart is not; but a believer's ends and aims are become new. This leads me to consider,

IV. How it is, that the new creature evidences a sinner's union to Christ. ' Therefore, if any man be ' in Christ,' &c.

1. Where the new creature is, the Spirit of Christ dwells; and the Spirit of Christ dwells in none but such as are his. Both these ideas are expressed in one verse, Rom. viii. 9. ' Ye are not in the flesh, but ' in the Spirit, if the Spirit of God dwell in you: ' Now if any man have not the Spirit of God, he is ' none of his.' The Spirit of God visits many with his common motions, whom he does not renew by his saving power. All common convictions are from the Spirit: ' When he is come, he will convince the ' world of sin.' But the apostle speaks of his abode in the soul, as an habitation which he hath fitted and furnished for himself. Is the Spirit welcome to thee as a convincer? Dost thou love to hear thine own sins reproved? Are sanctification and holiness thy delight? Art thou fearful of grieving the Spirit of God by heart-sins? Is no duty pleasant, where the Spirit of God is not interested? Dost thou seek to be taught, and led, and ruled by him? The Spirit dwells in thee; how? as the glorifier of Christ in all thy humiliations, prayers, dependencies, hopes. The Spirit leads thee to Christ for support and supply, for righteousness and strength, for quickening and comfort; why? because he is of God made unto thee ' wisdom, righteousness, sanctification and re- ' demption.' Thou art united to Christ, therefore the Spirit leads thee to rest upon him.

2. The

2. The new creature evidences union to Christ, because it brings a sinner into communion with him. Christ is the Head, believers are the members; Christ is the Root, we the branches; Christ is the Surety, we the redeemed and saved by him: But how is it sinners come to be partakers with Christ in his death, and in his resurrection? but because they are quickened by him, and so admitted into a state of friendship and fellowship: ' You hath he quickened who ' were dead in trespasses and sins,' Ephes. ii. 1. Shew me the new nature, and I will shew you the new name; whether regeneration or justification be first, or whether they are privileges bestowed at one and the same time, it matters not to enquire at present; the scripture is express, that one is the evidence of the other: Rev. xxii. 14. ' Blessed are they ' that do his commandments, that they may have ' right to the tree of life, and may enter in through ' the gates into the city.' Sanctification, the principle whereof is implanted in the new creation, gives a right of evidence; justification is that which gives a right of claim. ' They have washed their robes, ' and made them white in the blood of the Lamb. ' Therefore are they before the throne, Rev. vii. 14, 15.

INFER. 1. Hence learn, why the duties of unregenerate men are unaccepted with God; thus praying, thus hearing, thus alms, are vain oblations; why? because they flow from a corrupt principle, and the end is bad. Self is thine aim in all that thou dost, not God. The new creature is wanting, therefore all thy good works are dead works. Jehu's zeal was a vain boast, though a commanded duty, because it was against Ahab's house, which stood in his way to the kingdom, not for God's glory. In Asa's character there's a *nevertheless* which takes the dark spots out of it, though there were many: 1 Kings xv. 14. ' The high places were not remo- ' ved; nevertheless Asa his heart was perfect with ' the Lord all his days.' For the want of this A-
maziah

maziah is condemned, in whom that defect was not: 2 Chron. xxv. 2. 'He did that which was right in the fight of the Lord, but not with a perfect heart.' God looks first at the heart. If there be no new nature, the old channel may be changed, but the old corrupt fountain is not made pure.

INFER. 2. This accounts for the falling away of some, who once made a great shew in the flesh. The stony-ground hearers received the word with joy; Saul himself is one among the prophets; and some that were enlightened, and had tasted of the heavenly gift, and were made partakers of the Holy Ghost, are said yet 'to have fallen away,' Heb. vi. 5, 6. Whence does this arise? Not from any possibility which there is of losing a principle of grace, when it is implanted in the heart, but from those mistakes which are made between nature and grace. Nature, as corrupt, may be restrained or elevated, lifted above itself in some instances, where it is not changed. Those hearers, which received the word with joy, are therefore said not to have endured, 'because they had no root in them,' as you heard before. The light they have that fall away is partial, falls only upon the understanding, but does not shine into the heart. They had a power of working miracles, by reason of the Holy Ghost *with* them; yet never experienced the power of the Holy Ghost in his saving work *in them*. They had a taste of the word of God, so as to distinguish it, when they heard it preached; but not that desire and relish of it, which new born babes have that grow thereby, else no temptation would have prevailed with them to part with it. It was with them as with many of our hearers; they hear of the danger and misery of sin, of the power and grace of Christ, of the promises of the gospel, &c. and Christ is desired as a Saviour from wrath and the curse: For a while they pray, and read, and hear, and, Ahab-like, walk softly: These are new duties, yet they may flow from an old corrupt heart; wait for a while, and all this goodnefs is as the morning cloud, and the early dew, which paſſeth away. Men *fall* not *from* grace, but becauſe they have *no* grace; ' grace eſtabliſhes the ' heart.'

INFER. 3. Are old things paſſed away, and all things become new? Alas! how many are there that miſtake this new creation! Thou mayſt have had great terrors and great joys, and yet be an unrenewed ſinner ſtill. Satan can transform himſelf into an angel of light: Great gifts, and great repute, and yet remain dead in trefpaſſes and ſins. ' Lord have we ' not propheſied in thy name? and thou haſt taught ' in our ſtreets; yet, Depart from me, I never knew ' you.' The queſtion turns here, Are old things paſſed away? When the children of Iſrael were terrified with God's appearance of old, then they ſaid, ' All that the Lord hath ſaid will we do, and be o-
' bedient: O,' ſays God, ' that there was ſuch an ' heart in them!' Exod. xxiv. 7. It is not enough to begin well, to promiſe well: Saul was as ready at promiſing as any of you are: When Samuel met him, he ſaith, ' Bleſſed be thou of the Lord, I have ' performed the commandment of the Lord.' He loved the miniſters of God, though he loved his own ſins. May I not ſay to ſome as Samuel did to Saul, ' What meaneth then the bleeting of the ſheep in ' mine years, and the lowing of oxen that I hear?' 1 Sam. xv. 14. What hath the new nature to do with heart-idols, with filthineſs of fleſh and ſpirit, with a vain walk, or a fruitleſs converſation? What fruit haſt thou in thoſe things whereof ye once profeſſed yourſelves aſhamed? Is not ' the end of thoſe ' things death?' If ye have received Chriſt the Lord, walk after him, and walk in him: ' Be ye followers ' of Chriſt as dear children.'

INFER. 4. What amazing grace does God ſhew in forming the new creature? ' Behold, all things are ' become new.' Admire the ſovereign power and grace of God: ' You hath he quickened, who were ' dead in treſpaſſes and ſins,' Eph. ii. 1.

INFER.

INFER. 5. Let such who are longing after the new creature seek to God, and trust in him. It is a creation. God can as easily speak grace into thy heart, as into another's: ' Such were some of you;' the vilest sinners: ' But ye are washed.' The more desperate thy case, the more extraordinary thy cure, and God will be the more glorified by it.

Let but God put forth an act of his exceeding great power, and thy dead soul shall live. He gives it as an encouragement to poor souls in that very chapter where he promises the new heart: ' Yet for ' all these things he will be enquired of by the house ' of Israel to do it for them,' Ezek. xxxvi. 37.

SERMON XVIII.

MINISTERS CHRIST'S STEWARDS.

LUKE xii. 42, 43.

And the Lord said, Who then is that faithful and wise steward, whom his lord shall make ruler over his houshold, to give them their portion of meat in due season? Blessed is that servant, whom his lord when he cometh shall find so doing.

IT is needless to spend much time in looking into the occasion and connection of these words. From the suddenness of his coming to judgment, and the uncertainty we are under as to the time of it, our Lord recommends watchfulness as the best expedient to prevent the danger of a surprise: Peter hereupon puts the question to Christ, whether he intended this as a general exhortation, wherein all his disciples were concerned; or only as a special direction to his apostles, and to those who should afterwards succeed them, in the work of the ministry. My text is our Lord's answer; wherein is shewn sufficiently what is the true meaning and extent of his former discourse; and particular application is made in the parable, to apostles and ministers of the gospel, as such.

Every

Every servant has his account to give: We must all appear before the judgment-seat of Christ: But stewards have the greatest of all others, because their trust and their charge is greatest. Their Lord has made them rulers over his houshold; not as princes, who exercise sovereignty and dominion, but as stewards, whose chief business it is to make provision. We are your guides, not your lords. Ministers, to serve you in the things of Christ and salvation; not masters, to prescribe laws and ordinances, to which the gospel is a stranger; and to sting and vex you, because in conscience towards Christ, and fidelity to his word, you cannot comply with them. This is our trust and our charge: How hard to execute it well! To be faithful and wise in all our ministrations; circumspect and exemplary in the whole compass of our walk and conversation! Therefore are the words of our text brought in by way of interrogation: 'Who then is that faithful and wise 'steward?' That is to say, they are very rare, and hard to be found: Christ has few such servants; his family, his churches, few such stewards. Some there are through grace: The Lord increase their number! In farther opening of the words for your * instruction and my own, as the Lord is pleased to help, I would do four things:

I. Open the work of an evangelical pastor, as here described.

II. Shew what are the qualifications of such a pastor; whereby only he is fitted for his work, and like to prove successful in it: 'Who then is that 'faithful,' &c.

III. Lay before you some quickening motives to stir you up to constancy and diligence in your work.

IV. Close this solemn charge and exhortation, with some things by way of encouragement, to support you in it. 'Blessed is that servant,' &c.

I. Give

---

* This Sermon was preached at the ordination of the Rev. Mr Richard Cooper at Melburn in Cambridgeshire, July 18. 1745.

I. Give me leave to present to your view the work and duty of an evangelical pastor. You are a *servant* to Christ, Matt. xxiv. 45. 'Who then is a 'faithful and wise servant?' Nor think this a mean blessing; the greatest honour a creature can have, is to be owned of God as his servant: The dignity of angels themselves lies in their services: They are 'principalities and powers,' Eph. iii. 10. but in all this they are 'ministring spirits,' Heb. i. 14. You are a servant to Christ, a steward to his houshold; souls, and the gospel which is the proper food and provision of souls, are committed unto you. 'Let 'a man so account of us as of the ministers of Christ, 'and stewards of the mysteries of God,' 1 Cor. iv. 1. Therefore,-

1. Feed the houshold. The duty of a pastor is to feed; of a steward to provide. This requires good heed: Acts xx. 28. 'Take heed to all the 'flock, to feed the church of God.' That is not food which is not proper for nourishment. Taste the word first yourself, which you distribute to others. A sermon, be it ever so well studied, is never well preached till it is preached to our own souls. Present sense, experience, digestion, enjoyment, put a glow into our word, and a relish into our doctrine, which can never be mimick'd by industry or art. 'The land,' say the spies of old, 'which we pas-'sed through to search it, is an exceeding good 'land,' Numb. xiv. 7. Let the name, and grace, and Spirit, and love of Christ, whose servant you are, triumgh in every sermon: Recommend him to your people, as a sanctuary to protect them; as a propitiation to reconcile them; a treasure to enrich them; an advocate to present their persons and services unto God: As wisdom to counsel; as righteousness to justify; as sanctification to renew; as redemption to save; as an inexhausted fountain of pardon, grace, comfort, victory, glory. This is food; 'I am the bread of life; feed the houshold.'

2. Defend

2. Defend the truth. A steward, to whom is committed the oversight of the household, should be the first in espying any danger which is like to befal the family. The keeping of the faith was the apostle's duty, so he speaks of it as his glory: 'I have finish-'ed my course, I have kept the faith,' 2 Tim. iii. 7. That doctrine which lays the creature low, which exalts free grace, and promotes holiness both in heart and life, esteem every line of it precious. The faith of the gospel is worth striving for, because it is the food of your own and other souls: It is the foundation on which we build for eternity. The springs of our spiritual life are gone, our strength for duty, our hope of glory, if Christ be not God; if justification be not of grace; if we are not chosen to salvation as the end, to sanctification as the means; and as we are chosen by sovereign grace, if we are not kept by almighty power. Deny the importance of these, or any other gospel truths, and it is the same as if you disbelieve the truth itself. That is not worth having, which is not worth owning. There is a practical way of preaching (as they phrase it) some men are famed for, which is to drop the Christian faith, and to sink below some heathen moralists. 'But thou, O man of God, flee these things.' Defend the truth.

3. Administer all appointed ordinances. These are a part of the provision our Lord has made for the nourishment of his household, and are proper means for the building them up in knowledge, faith, holiness, and comfort. A steward is his lord's representative in the family; you act in Christ's name, and represent his tenderness, love and care, as well when you are visiting your flock, enquiring into their spiritual estate, their knowledge, growth, conversation, and holiness; when, like our great High-priest, you are bringing their names, temptations, doubts before the throne; as well as when administring the two seals of the covenant, baptism and the Lord's supper; or exercising office, power and authority, in

admitting

admitting and excluding members. Appearing in the pulpit and at the table of the Lord is the least part of your work, as ruler over Christ's houshold. His family on earth are a company of tempted ones, who need exhortation, reproof, comfort, in a more personal and particular way than can be given from the pulpit. By frequent visits you slide into their hearts, and draw out their whole souls, or ever they are aware: By prayer with them, and for them, you make their doubts, fears, comforts, your own. Some of the sweetest senses you are helped to give of scripture, you will find the issue and result of the conflicts, experiences, and love-visits of other saints. The apostle Paul himself expected to receive some spiritual gift from the believing Romans, as well as to impart it to them, Rom. i. 12. Nothing will render you more like to Christ, than a compassionate suffering with all the members of the church in all their afflictions, trials, and disconsolations, inward or outward. 'Who' says blessed Paul, 'is weak, and I 'am not weak? who is offended, and I burn not?' 2 Cor. xi. 29. This will prove you an evangelical pastor, and that the sheep are considered by you as your own. Administer all appointed ordinances.

4. Teach and guide by example, as well as by doctrine. He is represented as an evil servant whose conversation is corrupt, how pure soever might be his doctrine, *ver.* 45. We must be like the star, which did not only light the wise men, but led them to Christ. He who by his wicked life buildeth again those things which by his holy doctrine he destroyed, maketh himself a transgressor, and stands condemned out of his own mouth. 'Be thou an example to the 'believers in all things,' is a part of the charge given to Timothy, 1 Tim. iv. 12. The sins of the priests will make the offerings of the Lord to be abhorred by the people; the greatest part of men being in this respect like sheep, who go rather as they are led than as they are taught. The word loses its awe and reverence where the preacher is off his guard,

guard, and walks at large; we cannot expect that other men should follow our doctrine when we ourselves forsake it. An holy life justifies the doctrines which are according to godliness. Our calling should set us far from sins, because it sets us near to God. Be not like the Rechabites, who were scribes to make evidences for other mens lands, but had none of their own; 1 Chron. ii. 55. compared with Jer. xxxv. 8, 9. Rather with the priest under the law, offer first for thine own cleansing, then for the peoples; consider the Lord our God is holy. Teach and guide by example as well as by doctrine. So much for the work itself.

II. Let me hint at some things relating to the qualifications of such a pastor: 'Who is that faithful and wise steward?' Pastoral faithfulness respects four things:

Sincerity in the person; purity in the intention or aim; diligence in the work; and impartiality in the administration.

1. Sincerity in the person and frame. Abraham's heart is said to be faithful towards God, because it was upright before him, Neh. ix. 8. Gen. xvii. 1. compared. He can have little care or concern for others souls, who has no sense of the worth of his own. If there be no oil in the vessel, it cannot shine long in the lamp; you will find your own heart one of the hardest texts you have to preach on. Our work is spiritual; but, alas! so often are not our frames. Gifts may make us useful to others, but without the present exercise of grace in duty, how many times are we a burden and terror to ourselves? Delight in God is that which gives us sweetness, rest, and complacency in duty. Keepers of the vineyards have a vineyard of their own to keep; and believe me, brother, abounding in public services and employ, will never atone for neglects in our private and personal communion. Our Lord found some time, early in the morning, or late at night,

for

for special communion, when he preached all day publicly to the people. The sweetest fruits the soul feeds on all his lifetime are those he gathers from his own vine; sincerity in the person and frame is included in this faithfulness.

2. Purity in the intention and aim. Those builders of old are said to have dealt faithfully: no reckoning was made with them, because they acted out of a principle of pure zeal to God and his house, without any respect had to bye and base ends. We err at our first setting out, if we are acted by any other, than that noble principle recommended to Timothy, 2 Tim. ii. 15. 'Study to shew thyself ap-
'proved of God.' If the eye be not to Christ alone in our preparations, inward debates, visits, conversation, our eye is not single. The fear of man bringeth a snare; so does the love of lucre and applause. The scourge of tongues is in God's hands; if it lashes, it cannot hurt when there is peace within: Leave events to God; live above creature-supplies. Your great Lord, who has sent you into his vineyard, has promised to give you whatsoever is right: You and I were never gainers when we have been for taking the right of judgment out of Christ's hands. Christ did all his services from a principle of love and desire to please God. 'Wherefore,' says blessed Paul, ' we labour, that whether present or ab-
'sent, we may be accepted of him.' If our great Lord approves, no matter who condemns us. Purity in intention and aim is an ingredient in pastoral faithfulness.

3. Diligence in our whole work is comprehended in it. The wicked servant is called *slothful*, Matt. xxv. 26. It is an extensive care which the stewards of Christ's household have devolved upon them. There is work for our heads, hearts, and hands: " Nor is it," says Mr Flavel, " so much the ex-
" pence of our labours that kills us, as the loss of
" them; we can seldom find our work as we leave
" it: Sin and Satan unravel all we do." Ministers,

above all others, had need to 'be diligent in busi-
'ness, fervent in spirit, serving the Lord.' Those
who are called daily to lay out had need take care
that they lay up. Paul's advice to Timothy is,
'Meditate on these things, give thyself wholly unto
'them,' 1 Tim. iv. 15. You will find it in spirituals, as it is in temporals, 'the diligent hand ma-
'keth rich.' He that makes no preparation beforehand what he shall say to his people, tempts God to
come out of his ordinary way to his assistance; as
he that trusts wholly to his own preparation, makes
a God of his gifts. Then, my dear brother and
friend, is the Spirit trusted by us on the Lord's day
with the greatest boldness, when we have been waiting on him in a way of duty, with the greatest application in the week. 'Peter had been toiling all
'night, and had caught nothing, when Christ met
'him, and commanded to cast the net on the right
'side of the ship.' Diligence is a branch of that
faithfulness recommended in our text.

4. Pastoral faithfulness respects that impartiality
which should attend all administrations. 'Timothy
'is charged before God, and the Lord Jesus Christ,
'and the elect angels, that he observe all the things
'that were left in trust with him, without prefer-
'ring one before another, doing nothing by partia-
'lity,' 1 Tim. v. 21. He that acts for the glory of
Christ will endeavour always to walk in his Spirit.
All the souls of his saints are equally dear to the
blessed Jesus: Let them be so to you. Think it no
disturbance to be interrupted in your studies by the
objections and fears of a young convert, or the sad
complaints of a distressed believer. Those breaks and
parentheses in our work, are often the sweetest part
of it: Bear with their ignorance, weakness, yea their
very impertinencies: To shew moroseness or impatience is to turn that which is lame out of the way,
and to push the diseased which are rather to be healed. Remember, " He that winneth souls is wise."
Prefer the truth of God, and the conscience of duty

before the favours of men: Cowardice in a minister is baser than in a soldier, by how much our warfare is more honourable. A faithful reproof will get more love and honour at the last, than a sinful and fawning dissimulation. Though Paul reproved the dissimulation of Peter, yet Peter praiseth the wisdom of Paul: 'Our beloved brother Paul, according to 'the wisdom given unto him, hath written unto 'you,' 2 Pet. iii. 15. In a word, we are much more in danger to wrong the souls of men by our oil than by our salt, by our promises than by our reproofs. Faithfulness respects that impartiality which should attend all our ministrations: 'Who is that,' &c. A few things concerning his *wisdom*, which is a second qualification. This respects the following things.

1. The choice of your subject.
2. The phrase or diction in which they are delivered.
3. The season in which they are to be treated on.
4. That gravity of deportment whereby you appear as an example to the believer in all things.

1. Ministerial wisdom and prudence respects the choice of your subject. Hence the steward in my text is called in 2 Tim. ii. 15. ' A workman that ' needeth not to be ashamed,' as knowing how to turn his hand to every branch of business which lies before him. The meat God has provided is of various sorts, of which a wise steward will divide and cut up to every one his proper portion. The word of truth consists of law and gospel, promises and terrors, grace and duty. Some are Christ's sheep to be brought into the fold; others are gathered in, and are to be built up; among those are babes, who are to be fed with milk, namely, plain easy gospel-truths concerning pardon, righteousness, acceptance to life, which are both suitable, and easy of digestion: Strong men are to be fed with stronger meat, ancient things, such as the everlasting love of God towards his elect in Christ, the person, offices, and headship

headship of the Mediator: These are things which best suit their age and standing in the church of Christ: Wandering souls are to be settled; secure sinners roused; backsliders threatened; such as are weary and heavy laden, to be raised up. Our Lord's first public sermon in the synagogue was unto such. Herein lies your ministerial skill, in giving to every man his *demensum*, (as it is expressed in our text), that portion of meat which is allotted him, which his present circumstances, state, condition, and relation in life call for. The apostle calls the elders of the church at Ephesus to witness, ' that he ' had kept back nothing which might be profitable ' to them,' Acts xx. 20. Such as stand in God's counsel, dare not but declare all his counsel. This ministerial wisdom respects the choice of your subjects.

2. It respects the language in which they are to be delivered: See that this be, *First*, wholesome. *Secondly*, plain.

1. Let it be wholesome: Sound speech that cannot be condemned; never preach the law without Christ: As it was delivered, so let it be preached in the hands of a Mediator. At the same time you discover the disease, point to the physician: ' Behold ' the Lamb of God' (says John the Baptist) ' which ' taketh away the sins of the world.' If you speak of repentance, see that you speak of it as a part of the obedience of faith: Gospel-repentance flows from an apprehension of grace and mercy through a Mediator. And when you talk of faith, though it be the creature's act, be sure you speak of it as God the Spirit's work: ' Unto you it is given to believe,' Phil. i. 29. Know no terms or conditions of the covenant, save what Christ has fulfilled; salvation from first to last is a free gift. Finally, lay down the necessity of good works, as evidences to justify our faith before men, while you direct to the righteousness of Christ only, as that which justifies the

person in the sight of God. Let your language be wholesome.

2. Let it be plain. Aim not to shoot over your peoples heads, but rather if it be possible to affect their hearts. Choose rather to be profitable than fashionable in preaching. It has cost some more pains to study plainness, than it has done others to study politeness. Remember delights of fancy hinder wounds of heart. Never affect to show your learning, for that appears most beautiful, as it is ever most useful, when it is most concealed: That surely is the best key that fits the lock and opens the door. Our art does but spoil the edge which there is upon the words of God's Spirit. Let your language be plain. The wisdom my text speaks of respects the language in which gospel-truths are to be delivered.

3. It extends itself to the season in which they are to be treated on. Present truths which are struck at in our day are to be vindicated; and present sins, which professors are prone to run into, are to be reproved. O! there is a fatal neutrality and indifferency prevailing amongst professors, both as to doctrine and practice. A change in our *creed* has made a sad change in our *holiness*. Moderate principles have been an inlet to all that irreligion which is in some families, and to the dreadful declensions which are in churches. Whenever the person, righteousness, grace, and Spirit of Christ, are neglected in your preaching, you may bid farewell to the power of vital godliness in your own and others souls. Guard against lukewarmness, that bane of true godliness. If God be God, serve him; if Baal be God, serve him. Brother, you may shew the good temper of a Christian, while you are fighting the good fight of faith, and keep the good profession you have made this day before many witnesses. Ministerial prudence will direct to the season in which particular truths are most necessary, and likely to prove most useful. There are many things good in themselves;

but,

but, as Hushai said of Ahitophel's counsel, 'they 'are not so good at such a time or season:' But a word fitly spoken, that hits the case, the time, the occasion, and circumstances of persons and things, is 'like apples of gold in pictures of silver,' as pleasant to the ear as they were to the eye.

4. This wisdom concerns that gravity of deportment which is necessary to conciliate a respect for your person, and a regard for your ministrations. Thus our Saviour's sweetness allured, and John the Baptist's gravity, made even an Herod to fear. A mixture of both is most amiable and becoming the steward of Christ.

III. By way of motive to a due attendance to your whole work. This takes in two things which are suggested in the text.

1. You are not your own, but Christ's, and the church's. A steward is wholly another's: Hence ministers are called *vessels*, 2 Cor. iv. 7. not only to signify to us, that we can convey nothing more than we have received, (a truth to be every day thought on); we are not fountains, but mere cisterns; but to shew also that what they receive is not for themselves only, but for others. Brother, you now belong not to Christ only, but to this particular church and branch of his family. You are set as a ruler over this part of his household by your own consent, and solemn investiture of you in the Lord's name into office. Your reading, knowledge, gifts, graces, trials, comforts, are for their use and benefit. It would be sacrilege in you to keep any thing back; yea there is a true and sober sense, in which it may be said of gospel-pastors, that their very souls are not their own; and it was no compliment, (as one paraphrases it upon that passage), but a lively image of the very heart of the apostle, when he told the Thessalonians, 1 Thess. ii. 8. 'So being affectionately desirous of 'you, we were willing to have imparted unto you,

'not the gospel of God only, but also our own souls,
'because ye were dear unto us.' You are not your
own, but the church's.

2. Christ will one day come and demand an account of your whole trust. Stewards are accountable to them by whom they are put in trust. We shall be judged at last not as ministers, which is an office of honour among men, but as servants, which imports a work of trust. Our God values no man by his greatness, place, honour, reputation and office, but as he has been instrumental in his service, and as he has kept and husbanded his talents. Precious time, how art thou squandered away! But we should have no loose founds, no vacant hours, did we look more to the day when our Lord shall come. It is an awful thought, must I who have been employed in that great work of saving souls be now myself a cast-away? I, who have shone as a star upon earth, be now shut up for ever in horror and darkness? I cannot conclude without leaving two things, by way of encouragement and support, under this awful and important trust.

1. If you are faithful now, you shall be blessed at last: Your great Master has a crown of glory in his hands, as the gift of grace. If you work for him, you shall appear with him. All your labours, tears, desires, prayers, will one day be published before angels and men, and your own souls saved with the souls of your dear fellow members and brethren in Christ in the day of the Lord Jesus. Look forward, and encourage yourself beforehand with the great apostle's words, 2 Cor. i. 13, 14. ' For we write
' none other things unto you, than what you read
' or acknowledge, and I trust you shall acknowledge
' even to the end: As also you have acknowledged
' us in part, that we are your rejoicing, as ye also
' are ours in the day of the Lord Jesus.'

2. Your Lord will feed you, while you, as a steward, are dividing a portion to others. The steward has

has a table of his own provided for him by his Lord. Your springs are all in Chrift; though ftreams fail, there is all-fufficiency in the fountain. We look here and there, and are fometimes diftreffed on all hands, in our great and important work. Chrift calls us off from our trials, ftraitnefs and fears, to look on him: 'Lo, I am with you alway unto the end of 'the world.' With him I leave you, dear brother, to fupport, guide, comfort, and eftablifh you to the end. To whom be glory in the churches through‑out all ages. Amen.

SERMON XIX.

RECEIVING CHRIST, AND WALKING IN HIM.

THE work which is allotted me in the courfe of this day's fervice *, is, more efpecially, to addrefs the members of this Church, with refpect to that duty which they owe to Chrift, to one another, and to the worthy perfon whom they have publicly received this day to be their paftor: And the word which lays the foundation of our meditations, and which calls for our diligent regard now and all your lives long, you have upon record in

COLOSSIANS ii. 6.

As ye have therefore received Chrift Jefus the Lord, fo walk ye in him.

THE defign of our apoftle in this context, is to fortify the church at Coloffe againft the fophiftry and guile of feducing fpirits. The mind of man is prone to affect novelty, even in the things of God; and as this is ufually the lure by which the churches are drawn away from that fimplicity which

is

---

* This Sermon was preached at Bocking in Effex, July 5 1744, at the ordination of the Reverend Mr Davidfon.

is in Christ, our apostle, by way of caution and exhortation, lays down two things: One you have ver. 3. ' in whom are hid all the treasures of wis- ' dom and knowledge.' In Christ and his Gospel there is always something to be found new, entertaining, and delightful, as well as supporting and satisfying to the soul. ' And this I say, lest any man ' should beguile you with enticing words,' ver. 4. The other you have in the words of our text, wherein the apostle calls to remembrance their first faith and hope in Christ, as an encouragement to their abiding in him still. Old truths are tried ones. There is no reasoning men out of their experience and feeling. ' As ye have therefore received Christ Jesus ' the Lord, so walk ye in him.'

In discoursing on which words, I shall attempt the four following things:

I. Shew what it is to have received Christ Jesus the Lord.

II. What it is to walk in him.

III. When a church, or particular believers in it, may be said to walk in Christ, as they have received him.

IV. Close with some words of direction and use, which are peculiarly suited to the service and solemnity of this day.

I. I am to shew what it is to have received Christ Jesus the Lord. I answer,

First, Receiving of Christ supposes a thorough conviction and sense which the soul has of its need of Christ. A man must see himself a sinner, before he can be a believer. Gospel-churches are made up of none but real or professed believers; but it is one thing to be joined to the Lord, another thing to join ourselves to a church. We offer ourselves to the fellowship of a particular church, as called and sanctified in Christ Jesus; but we first come to Christ, and betake ourselves to him, as lost, perishing, undone

done sinners. 'The whole need not a physician, but they that are sick,' Matth. ix. 12. He that does not see himself condemned, will never sue for a pardon. It is the wounded spirit which seeks after healing; therefore we flee for refuge to lay hold on the hope set before us, because we see ourselves in danger of death, from the avenger of blood that follows us close at the heels: Christ is lifted up in the Gospel, and presented in the promise, for poor perishing souls to look unto, and believe in for life and salvation. 'As Moses lifted up the serpent in the wilderness, even so must the Son of man be lifted up; that whosoever believeth in him should not perish, but have eternal life,' John iii. 14, 15. In believing, the soul looks on itself as a poor, needy, fatherless, friendless creature, and stays itself on sovereign grace and mercy: 'We have believed in Jesus Christ, that we might be justified, Gal. ii. 16. This supposes an apprehension we had, that we were under condemnation. The strongest believer was once a sinking, perishing sinner. 'A Syrian ready to perish was my father,' Deut. xxvi. 5. Receiving of Christ supposes a thorough conviction.

Secondly, Receiving Christ supposes some knowledge of his person and offices. Faith has for its great object the person of Christ; not barely the doctrine or mystery of Christ, *ver.* 2. Hence the Colossians, in our text, are said to have received Christ himself, and to look for whole salvation from him. There must be a 'seeing the Son,' John vi. 40. an understanding and knowing him well, who he is, before there can be any faith in him. Man! when thou believest, thou ventureft thine all with the blessed Jesus. It therefore behoves thee to consider well, before thou trustest thyself, and thine eternal concerns in his hands: If Christ be not God, he can be no Redeemer, no Surety, no Saviour; a mere man cannot be a rock, a precious corner-stone, a sure foundation for faith to build on. What our Apostle speaks of Christ's resurrection, may be affirmed

firmed of his perſon, 1 Cor. xv. 14. 'If Chriſt be
'not riſen, our preaching is vain, and your faith is
'alſo vain.' If he be not God, let him die, and riſe
and aſcend; as to the juſtification of a ſinner by
his righteouſneſs, it is nothing. And if Jeſus be
not alſo Chriſt, God's appointment and ordinance
for the ſalvation of loſt ſinners, the poor, burdened
ſin-diſtreſſed ſoul draws back; faith cannot act
without a warrant. Chriſt is received as the Father's gift in all the glories of his perſon, and the
ſufficiency of his ſatisfaction: John iv. 10. 'If thou
'kneweſt the gift of God and who it is that ſaith
'to thee, give me to drink; thou wouldſt have
'aſked of him, and he would have given thee li-
'ving water.' Faith acts upon the promiſes, becauſe theſe are declarations of God's mind and will,
with reſpect to Chriſt Jeſus and that ſalvation which
is in him. There muſt be a learning before there
can be a receiving: 'Thoſe things which ye have
'both learned and received, do,' Phil. iv. 9. God
the Spirit teaches the believing ſoul who Chriſt is;
what he has wrought; that he alone can deliver
from going down into the pit; and alſo that he is
willing to ſave loſt, returning ſinners; and none
teacheth like him.

Thirdly, Receiving Chriſt ſuppoſes an hearty approval of the Mediator's perſon, and the ſoul's full
content to be his. Faith lies not ſo much in the
underſtanding as in the heart; 'With the heart
'man believeth unto righteouſneſs,' Rom. x. 10.
Chriſt is propheſied of as the 'deſire of all nations,'
Haggai ii. 7. This implies choice and delight. The
ſinner is never gained till the will is won. Faith
takes Chriſt out of the promiſe, and receives him
into the heart: 'That Chriſt may dwell in your
'hearts by faith,' Eph. iii. 17. Brethren, there are
many bidders for theſe hearts of ours, pleaſures, pro-
fits, riches, honours, eaſe from trouble; theſe the
fleſh and the world bid. Yea, but who, ſoul! will
deliver thee from the wrath which is to come?
Who

Who will give thee peace with God? Pardon in thine own bosom, durable riches and righteousness, true liberty here, and pleasures for evermore hereafter? Christ the Lord can do this and more: 'I that speak in righteousness,' says Christ, 'am mighty to save. I will cause them that love me to inherit substance; I will fill their treasures.' Whom wilt thou choose? To whom wilt thou cleave? whose shall thine heart be? A soul touched by divine grace sticks not to say, "I choose Christ, "I yield myself to Christ, *Ashur shall not save us, "we will not ride upon horses, neither will we say "any more to the work of our hands, Ye are our "gods*, Hos. xiv. 3. Duties shall not save me; "this world shall not satisfy me; as for the lusts "of the flesh and of the mind, which I lived in "before, I renounce them for ever." A world for Christ, when he is beheld in the glory of his person, and the perfection and suitableness of his righteousness: The soul chooses Christ and separates itself from all other things; not works, but grace, not his own duties, tears, repentance, but Christ alone. Receiving Christ supposes an hearty approbation. Once more,

Fourthly, Receiving Christ includes in it an entire trust in his person for all good, for pardon, righteousness, acceptance with God, and eternal life, Eph. i. 13. 'In whom ye trusted after that ye heard 'the word of truth, the gospel of our salvation.' Faith acts properly in a way of trust, dependence and affiance; it is called therefore a looking unto Christ, Isa. xlv. 22. alluding to the Israelites of old, who looked to the brazen serpent, not out of curiosity to see what it was made of, but with earnestness of desire and expectation to be healed by it. A coming to him with appetite and affection, as an hungry man does to his meat, and a thirsty man to his drink, John vi. 35. 'I am the bread of life, he 'that cometh to me shall never hunger, and he 'that believeth on me shall never thirst.' A committing

mitting ourselves to him, 2 Tim. i. 12. Because the soul makes an adventure of its concerns for time and eternity into his hands. Finally, it is called a leaning, resting, staying; alluding to the rite of transferring sin from the offender to the beast, by laying his hand upon the head of the sacrifice. The soul, when it has thus received Christ, sends as it were law and justice both to him, for a satisfaction and payment. 'It is Christ that died,' therefore the soul's trust and his life is wholly in him; hence believers are described, Jude ver. 21. 'As looking 'for the mercy of our Lord Jesus Christ unto eter-'nal life.'

So much for our first general, what it is to receive Christ Jesus the Lord. I am now to consider,

II. What it is to walk in him. Walking is a metaphor, whereby is signified the whole of a believer's life and conversation while he is here: Thus 2 Cor. v. 7. what is called a walking by faith, is expressed, Gal. ii. 20. by 'a living the life we live in the flesh, 'by the faith of the Son of God.' In general, two things are implied in it.

First, That the life of a believer is an active life.

Secondly, It is a progressive life; he is ever going forward.

First, The believer's life is an active life. You have always something to do, or something to bear. Every relation in life calls for suitable duty; seasonable fruit, and abounding fruit, our God expects from his trees of righteousness. A Christian has no time in which to be idle: You have always a deceitful heart within to watch over, 'keep thy heart 'with all diligence;' and a subtle devil and ensnaring world without, to resist and overcome; an holy and a jealous God to please, and a holy calling to walk worthy of. Thy watch and thy walk last so long as thy life lasts, and blessed is he that endures unto the end! Some that set out well in God's ways
are

are soon wearied; but the Christian's life is an active one, there is no standing still in our Christian course.

Secondly, It is a progressive life; it is a believer's duty and desire to go forward: 2 Pet. iii. 18. 'Grow 'in grace and in the knowledge of our Lord and 'Saviour Jesus Christ.' 2 Pet. i. 5. ' Add to your 'faith virtue, and to virtue knowledge.' Whatever grace you have exercised, whatever gifts you have attained, think there is something farther to be learned, to be received, to be done still. Rest not in any past experiences, frames, enlargements, comforts, but press forward: Walking is a constant and progressive motion; the mark is yet before you, and you are but pressing towards it till your journey is ended, and some of your sorest conflicts, your roughest way may come at last: As you have received Christ, so walk in him; well, this is intended by the word *walk*. But,

What is it to walk in Christ Jesus the Lord? I answer,

1. To walk in Christ, is to converse every where like those who acknowledge Christ, and are subject to his government; who are under the law to Christ. ' He is thy Lord, and worship thou him,' Psal. xlv. 11. As he is the author and object of our *faith*, so is he the sovereign commander of our *duty* and *obedience*. The man in Christ Jesus is not his own: He waits for Christ's warrant, he asks his counsel, and listens to his call in every purpose and in every action; be he at home or abroad, in company or alone, in the family, the closet, the church or the world, the language of his heart is, " My Jesus, " my God, I am still with thee: Lord, what wilt " thou have me to do?" The apostle calls this, *ver*. 8. ' a walking after Christ,' because he is Lord and Lawgiver in his own house, ' which house are ' we,' Heb. iii. 6. Not the inventions or opinions of men, but the command of Christ is wholly to be regarded in what concerns the faith and order of
gospel-

gospel-churches. Receive nothing in point of doctrine or discipline which will not bear the preface of Paul's profession, 1 Cor. xi. 23. ' For I have recei-
' ved of the Lord that which also I delivered unto
' you. We have no dominion over your faith, but
' are helpers of your joy; for by faith ye stand,'
2 Cor. i. 24. Faith has Christ Jesus the Lord for its object. not the will and pleasure, the smiles or resentment of any man: To walk in Christ is to converse every where like those who acknowledge Christ, and profess subjection to him.

2. To walk in Christ is to act every grace, and perform every duty in the strength of Christ. Grace in us is supported and kept alive by the grace which is in Christ; there our stock is, and thence our fruit is. ' From me is thy fruit found,' Hos. xiv. 8. Christ is the believer's root, and then may we be said to be rooted and grounded in him, when he is our trust for ever; when the whole of our dependence is upon him for the acceptation of our good work, not barely for the purging of our dead works; as well when our God smiles as when he frowns.
' In thy name shall they rejoice all the day, and in
' thy righteousness shall they be exalted,' Psal. lxxxix. 16. Our spiritual joy is in Christ's righteousness, not in the best and sweetest frames of our own hearts: His strength is made perfect in our weakness: Hence it is that our souls at any times dwell at ease, and we are set upon our high places. That abiding in Christ, recommended to his disciples, John xv. 5. consists not in a bare not going off from Christ: Under all our complaints of decays and want of fruitfulness, sure we have not left Christ; the root abides, though the leaves drop off: But it is to be ever nigh Christ, in his spiritual company, either desiring or receiving some fresh communications from him; duty will not content, if there be not communion with him in it, either desired or enjoyed. As a church of Christ value those gifts most which are most savoury and spiritual,

spiritual, which have the least of a man's self in them, and the moſt of Chriſt. A little grace when drawn into exerciſe by the eternal Spirit will weigh down many gifts: To walk in Chriſt is to act every grace, and perform every duty in the ſtrength of Chriſt.

3. To walk in Chriſt, is to intend and aim at the glory of Chriſt in all occaſions and concernments of life. 'For me to live is Chriſt,' ſays the Apoſtle, Phil. i. 21. the bleſſed Jeſus is glorified in an holy and exempary life before men. Thy faith is ſecret, but thy fruits are viſible and open. When a believer acts like himſelf, every one is the better for him with whom he converſes. Therefore is the path of the juſt compared to the ſhining light, becauſe others ſee by it; ſee what ſin, and what holineſs are; what peace and what pleaſure there is in wiſdom's ways; and that in keeping God's commandments there is a great reward. Chriſt cannot be truly loved where his goſpel is not loved. To walk in Chriſt is to walk worthy of him, *chap*. i. 10. Jeſus is the mark at which he aims in all the affairs and concernments of life. I am now to ſhew,

III. When a church, or particular believers in it, may be ſaid to walk in Chriſt *as* they have received him.

1. To walk in Chriſt, as we have received him, is to be convinced of our *daily* need of Chriſt, to have the ſame powerful impreſſive ſenſe of our need of him, we once had. When the day-ſpring from on high firſt viſited us, and the terrors of the Lord made us afraid, O! how plainly, how forcibly, how feelingly did we ſee our need of a Saviour, of ſuch a Saviour as Chriſt is! Then we haſtened, we ran, we fled unto him. Hell was open before our eyes, and law and juſtice ſeemed puſhing us in. How ſweet was news of a pardon then! how ſweet a promiſe! and how beautiful the feet of him that brought it!

it! There was no halving it then: We needed an whole Saviour, a prophet to teach, a priest to atone, a king to rule and govern. Christ Jesus the Lord was received as such, and received with all the heart, Acts viii. 37. And whence is it we walk no more in Christ as we have received him now? Surely, because we have lost that powerful impression of our wants we then had; unacquaintedness here breeds indifferency towards Christ's person and his gospel. A spiritual appetite is wanting where this manna is lothed as light bread.

2. To walk in Christ, as we have received him, is to continue and increase in our first love to him. To be sensible of the worth of Christ, with the same warmth and fervour of spirit we were first sensible of our need of him. O! the love of our espousals, and the kindness of our youth! How precious was the dear Lord Jesus to us then! when we first viewed him bearing our sins, buying our pardon, conquering our rebellion, opening our understandings, healing our consciences; he acted towards us as Christ Jesus the Lord? Our access to God was by him, all peace and joy of our consciences was in him: Had any asked us at that time, what think you of Christ? We should have found a tongue readily to confess, and with believing Thomas cry out, "My Lord and my God;" or with the church, "He is altogether lovely." Love to gospel-truths can never die, so long as there is an abiding love to Christ's person, in whom all of them centre. Watch very narrowly here. See that your love to Christ does not abate or grow cool. The church of Christ at Ephesus is blamed, not that they had lost all love, but because they had lost their first love, Rev. ii. 4.

3. To walk in Christ, so as we have received him, is to keep up our communion with him, with the same earnestness and vehement desire we once had. Time was when Christ was never missed in an ordinance, but we sought him with tears. Duty

was scarce performed, if his comforting presence was not enjoyed. Experience then taught us the meaning of that, and such like scriptures, Psal. lxxxiv. 2. 'My soul longeth, yea, even fainteth for 'the courts of the Lord, my heart and my flesh 'crieth out for the living God.' Creature comforts are all dead things; none but a living Jesus, a living God, can refresh and satisfy the soul that is newly converted to Christ. Now we can go to God's throne when we find relief no where else; but then God and Christ had our *first* trust, and our *first* suit: Not so much his goods, as his presence, were desired and delighted in. Our visits at the throne of grace were visits of love: Did we but see Christ and our interest in him, we could leave it with him to supply all our present wants. Thus it was with Job, chap. xxiii. 3. 'O that I knew where I might find 'him!' And the church, Canticles i. 2. 'Let him 'kiss me with the kisses of his mouth.' Christ was so wrapped up in their hearts, that when they speak of him it is without naming him, imagining every one besides must know whom they meant as well as themselves. Look after your spirits; watch the frames of your hearts; all declensions begin there.

4. To walk with Christ so as we have received him, is to walk with an holy indifferency towards the world and the things of it. Once Christ was portion enough. The world was rather feared as a tempter, than desired as a friend. Not how shall I be great and honourable here, but how shall I be happy hereafter, was the first thought and the first care: 'Seek first the kingdom of God and his righ- 'teousness.' Christ is substance; all other things are at best but shadows, and often they prove thorns. Once more,

5. To walk in Christ as you have received him, is to behave yourselves in a less selfish way; to shew a greater concern for the salvation of others, and a more disinterested regard for the prosperity of Zion. David on the saddest occasion his soul ever knew,

when he was moſt full of his own private concernments, yet drops a word for poor Zion : Pſal. li. 18. 'Do good in thy good pleaſure unto Zion.' He remembers the church amidſt his greateſt grief, as well as prefers her proſperity before his chiefeſt joy. Once we could not bear the thought of going to heaven alone. Were *we* taught by Chriſt as a prophet? We could not help recommending to him other ignorant, unthinking, unenlightened ſouls. Did we find righteouſneſs and life with him as a prieſt? This and the other relation, friend, ſervant, &c. were brought to the throne, and left with him, with an "O that this Iſhmael might live before thee!" He that conquered our wills, we knew well could change theirs. Religion will never flouriſh in the churches or in our hearts, till there be more of this public, unſelfiſh ſpirit found with us: You cannot but ſhew a tenderneſs for the ſalvation of others, if you love and live upon this ſalvation yourſelves.

Thus I have ſhewn what it is to receive Chriſt Jeſus the Lord; what it is to walk in him; and what to walk in Chriſt as we have received him. It remains,

IV. To ſpeak ſome things by way of direction and uſe, as ſuited more eſpecially to the ſervice and ſolemnity of this day.

Give me leave therefore with plainneſs and freedom to drop a few words to you as a church of Chriſt concerning your walk with Chriſt, and with one another; and your behaviour towards him, whom you have choſen to be your paſtor in the Lord.

As to your walk with Chriſt and one another:

Firſt, Be often reviewing your own experiences. Aſk, how was it with me in months paſt? And ſee whether preſent deſires anſwer preſent mercies. Labour to taſte the truths; you know experience begets hope, which maketh not aſhamed. Judiciouſneſs in the things of ſalvation depends not upon

bare

bare reasoning, but on spiritual sense and experience; there are spiritual sensations which believers can never be persuaded out of. The heart is best established with grace, Heb. xiii. 9. If the word be not mixed with faith, it will not profit, it is but a dead and lifeless thing. Our first experiences are of use to us all our lives long.

Secondly, Press after inward vital godliness. If Christ be received into the heart, he rules there. Religion lies not in talking of Christ or for him, but in walking in him; of all other decays be most afraid of inward decays; dread a barren notional knowledge of experimental truths. The Apostle prays, 1 Thess. v. 23. 'That the whole spirit,' that is, the frame, tendency and disposition of the soul, might be preserved blameless. It was God's command to Abraham, 'Walk before me, and be thou 'perfect,' Gen. xvii. 1. Christ Jesus our Lord has eyes that are flames of fire; such act always as under Christ's eye, who are tender of his glory: If religion be kept alive in the soul, it must be watered at the root: Be sure always, that while you seek God's face, you seek his strength; duties are lifeless, ordinances lifeless, because Christ is not enough interested in them: We are apt to go to Christ too much by the way of frames, to trust in part in our own graces, and in part in Christ our Saviour and head. But in every duty let Christ be all; then the believer acts most honourably, and walks most comfortably when he brings forth fruit in Christ.

Thirdly, Hold fast the pure word as ye have been taught; and labour after establishment in the faith. Gospel-churches are the repository of gospel-truths; therefore the church is called the 'pillar and ground 'of truth,' 1 Tim. iii. 6. Because here the truths of God are published, supported, and defended. Here they are to be found as in their proper seat and place: Christ has left his truths with you as a trust, keep them with faithfulness and care; beware of an indifferent, lukewarm, neutral spirit; in many places,

places, that has been the ruin of the gospel and the bane of the churches; first goes the purity of a church, then its being. Hold fast the truths of God, they are your treasure, your glory, your crown; take nothing upon trust, whoever be the preacher, but search the scriptures. The noble Bereans received the truth as well as those in Thessalonica, but they tried it first. It is a shame for men in years to be babes in knowledge, ever doubting, wavering, unsettled; it is the commendation of the Church at Ephesus, Rev. ii. 2. 'Thou hast tried 'them which say they are apostles, and are not; 'and hast found them liars.' We believe, says Peter, and are sure that thou art the Christ the Son of the living God. So the Colossians, in our text, are said to have been ' knit together in love, and unto ' all riches of the full assurance of understanding; ' to the acknowledgment of the mystery of God, ' and of the Father, and of Christ,' chap. ii. 2. And there may be this assurance of understanding where there is a doubting of interest.

Fourthly, Look well to your discipline and order, and be stedfast in it: The safety of a church, as well as the beauty to it, lies much in their order. Need I say, the eyes of all are upon you? Take the greater heed to your steps, and trust more fully on your God; if the discipline of Christ's house be disregarded, the doctrine will go next. Receive none into your fellowship but those who appear to have received Christ, whatever temptations you may have from their circumstances in life; our God is holy; partiality will sooner or later breed confusion. See that every officer is found faithful in the discharge of his duty to Christ and you. To some this may be strange doctrine, but it is true; it is commanded the Church, Col. iv. 17. ' That they say to Ar-' chippus, Take heed to the ministry which thou ' hast received in the Lord, that thou fulfil it.' Keep the power which Christ has given you; sovereign rule and judgment are committed to no man. Christ hath left the keys in your hands, that is, the power of admitting and excluding members; how can you anſwer it to him as your Lawgiver and Lord, if you reſign them up to any other? In one word, provoke to love and to good works; be of good comfort, be of one mind, live in peace, and the God of peace ſhall be with you.

As to your conduct to your paſtor, whom you have this day received among you in the Lord, you owe him,

1. Your love, 1 Theſſ. v. 12, 13. 'We beſeech you brethren, to know them which labour among you, and are over you in the Lord, and admoniſh you; and to eſteem them very highly in love for their work's ſake.' His work is great, make it pleaſant; add not to his labours, by adding to his trials. Where love is mutual, joy will be ſo, 2 Cor. i. 14. 'As alſo ye have acknowledged us in part, that we are your rejoicing, even as ye alſo are ours in the day of the Lord Jeſus.' If you receive a benefit, you cannot help loving the inſtrument of its conveyance. Nothing but love can hide faults, and is there any man who liveth and ſinneth not? The treaſure is put into earthen veſſels. Do not expect your miniſters to be more than men; when you find perfection in yourſelves, you may condemn your brethren in whom you do not ſee it. You owe your paſtor love, hearty, undiſſembled, conſtant love; if you have not a love to his perſon, there will ſoon be a prejudice againſt his miniſtry; and where there is prejudice againſt a man's miniſtry, there can be no profit by his labours. It is ſad to hear as critics, not as Chriſtians; remember one day the word is to judge you, as forward as you may now be to judge the word.

2. You owe your miniſter your prayers. His furniture is in Chriſt the Lord, as your ſtrength is; let your prayers be fetching it in for him, from day to day. It is a bleſſed thing when there is a ſtock of prayers going up from the church daily for their paſtor. This relieves our ſpirits oftentimes,

when we can scarce pray for ourselves. Brethren, as our work is greater than yours, our temptations and corruptions often are not fewer. Pray hard, that we may preach well and walk well. The peoples prayers are the pastor's best books. Some have known how it has been in this respect with the people by their straitness or enlargements in the closet. Pray over what ye see wanting or faulty, before you talk of it to others : It is a truth of common observation, those who complain most of a ministry pray least for it : What is lacking in your prayers, you may expect to find wanting in your provision. Once more,

3. You owe him support. We receive that which comes from you as a bounty, but we may claim it as a debt. For it is written, ' Thou shalt not muz-
' zle the mouth of the ox that treadeth out the
' corn.' Of all subjects this is the most disagreeable to me to treat on, and I hope there is no occasion for enlargement. Love commandeth the whole man, both honour and support will be given to them by whom you receive Christ Jesus the Lord. You cannot but love the food by which you live ; and if the food be sweet, you will scarce grudge the charge of it. Only walk in Christ Jesus, as ye have received him, and it will put a lustre upon every part of your conversation both towards God, and to all men.

And now, brethren, I commend you to God and to the word of his grace, which is able to build you up, and to give you an inheritance among them that are sanctified.

But I add no more.

SERMON XX.

FAITH'S ESTIMATE OF AFFLICTIVE DISPENSATIONS.

2 KINGS iv. 26.

——*And she answered, It is well.*

SHORT words, soon spoken; but to have a suitableness of heart to them, is one of the highest attainments of faith. To be sure, 'It is well;' we think so, when all things go according to our wish, when there is nothing in Providence that crosses our desires, that thwarts our designs, that sinks our hopes, or awakens our fears: Submission is easy work then; but to have all things seemingly against us, to have God smiting in the tenderest part, unraveling all our schemes, contradicting our desires, and standing aloof from our very prayers; How do our souls behave then? This is the true touchstone of our sincerity and submission: 'Here,' as it is said, Rev. xiii. 10. 'is the patience and faith of the saints:' this shews what they are made of, what they are within; but instances there are many in the book of God, wherein we find this sweet frame prevailing; as Abraham, Job, David, and the Shunamite in my text,

text, than whose story we meet with few things in providence more affecting. If you look back a little, you may see what were her circumstances, and those of her family. She was a 'great woman,' says ver. 8. and that she was a 'good woman,' the whole context shews. Her husband and she wanted but one thing to make them as happy as the vanity and uncertainty of all human affairs would admit of: They had enough of the world, and they seem to have had the enjoyment of it; for when Elisha, to requite her kindness, asks, 'What shall be done ' for thee? Wouldst thou be spoken for to the ' King,' &c. she answers, ' No. I dwell among ' mine own people.' " I seek nothing greater than " what I have:" only (as Gehazi learnt from her) they wanted a child to comfort them *now*, and to inherit what they had when they *were gone*. God in a miraculous way gives their request. This child grows up, and was, no doubt, the delight of its parents. Just at the time of life when children are most engaging, before they are capable of doing any great thing to grieve their parents, God lays his hand suddenly upon him, and takes him away. The dearest comforts are but short-lived, and the dearer they are when living, the deeper they cut when they are removed. Many of you can judge, what the loss of a son, an only son must be, and when there is no hope of a Seth instead of Abel. But behold, ' he taketh away, and who shall hinder him?' Well: What does the mother do now? One would think all her hope was cut off, and all her comfort dried up: No, it is far otherwise; the same power that gave him could raise him; in faith of this she lays him upon the prophet's bed, and makes all the haste to him she could. She concealing what had happened (as it is probable) from her husband, he objects to her going to the prophet, ver. 23. ' Wherefore wilt thou go to him to-day? It is nei-
' ther

'ther new moon or Sabbath *. And she said, It
'shall be well.' Faith sets aside every obstacle:
"It shall be well; the end will be peace;" 'God
'is with me, and he will make all things work to-
'gether for good.' Commentators, in general, make
very light of this, and her answer to Elisha's message in my text. Some suppose she has a reserve in
her breast, when Gehazi asks after her family, that
this *well* only refers to her husband and herself.
Others think it is but a transition to something farther, which she was in haste to say: As if she had
said, "All is well, do not hinder me, I have urgent
"business with your master Elisha, and cannot stay
"to talk farther with you upon any matters." This
is the sense which most annotators incline to, which,
I confess, I the more wonder at, because all agree,
that the Apostle's words in part refer to this story,
Heb. xi. 35. ' Women received their dead raised to
' life again.' How they received them is there specified; namely, by or 'through faith:' Faith, not
as some carry it, in the prophet, but in the persons
who had their dead restored to them; or else there
would have been no need to make mention of any
by name. Now wherein this woman's faith appeared, my text and context make manifest. Here was
a dependence upon God's promise, an abiding by
that. God had promised her a son; a son not to
lose him, but to have comfort in him; and as if she
had said, "As for God, his work is perfect, he does
"not use to raise his people's expectations for no-
"thing; to give, and immediately take away again:
"My son is dead, but God, all-sufficient, liveth;
"why should I mourn as though I had no hope?
"As for God's power and faithfulness, there is no
"abatement in them." Therefore she makes no
preparation for his burial, tells her husband nothing
of

---

* It appears by this, that the prophets were stated instruc-
tors of the people; their houses were a kind of school or synagogue, unto which the people resorted at these times to be
taught their duty, and to be resolved their doubts.

of his death, but seeks to God by the prophet, and expects help from him. See how she expresses herself: 'Is it well with thee?' (says Gehazi) 'Is it well with thy husband? Is it well with the child? And she answered, It is well.' Here is the greatest submission in the deepest distress: Her son, her only son, the son of all her love, the son of her old age, he is taken away with a stroke, and yet all is well. There is nothing amiss in the dispensation; had she been to choose it, she would not have had it so, but as God hath chosen it, it is well, it is best; she has nothing to object. Here are submission and faith both discovered in their sweetest exercise; submission to what God hath done; faith in what he is able to do, and in what she believed he would do: 'By faith women received their dead raised to life again;' so that the words, thus explained, afford us this plain and useful observation.

OBSERV. Faith in God's promise and power, will bring a man to submit to the sorest and most trying dispensations of his Providence: Or thus,

Faith, where it is in exercise, will teach a Christian to say of all God does, 'It is well.'

In discoursing on this proposition, I will endeavour,

I. To shew what submission is, or how and in what sense we are to understand the expression in my text, 'It is well.'

II. What are the grounds of Christian submission, or whence it is the soul thinks and says of all God does, 'It is well.'

III. What are the blessed fruits and effects of this submission.

IV. Whence it appears that this submission flows from faith, as being in lively and vigorous exercise. The Shunamitess, in my text, believed, as Heb. xi. tells us, and therefore says to every question proposed, 'It is well.'

I. What

I. What is submission to the will of God? To prevent mistakes, we will consider a little what it is not, and then what it is. Therefore,

1. This *well* does not suppose there is nothing in providential dispensations, which to flesh and sense appears evil. Submission quiets under an affliction, but it does not take away our sense and feeling of the affliction. The Apostle speaks what is every believer's experience, Heb. xii. 11. ' No chastening ' for the present seemeth to be joyous, but grievous.' Whatever be spoken of the good of it, it presents itself unto us with a very different face; it is matter of present grief and sorrow to them that are chastised; nor are we blamed for our feeling and sense of it. Our blessed Lord himself wept at the grave of his dear friend, John xi. 35. And at the approach of his last sufferings, ' his soul was exceed-' ing sorrowful, even unto death,' Matt. xxvi. 38. ' yet he was led as a lamb to the slaughter; he open-' ed not his mouth:' there was patience and quiet submission under all his sorrows, while nature had some vent, for groans are sometimes an easement to our grief. Thus it is said of this good woman, ' that her soul was bitter within her,' ver. 27. Elisha saw her agony in her looks, though he knew not the cause of it; and yet ' all is well.' When Job lost his substance and his children, and was smitten in his body with sore boils; when Heman, and when the church in the Lamentations were deprived of the consolations of God, when the Comforter, who could relieve their souls, was far from them; when David also was cursed by Shimei, and turned out of doors by his own son; can you think that in all this there was no feeling? Had there been none, there could have been no profit by any of the dispensations. Unless we realize our trials, and account them trials indeed, what are we the better for them? This would be to despise the chastening of the Lord, to be above correction. To be smitten and not grieve, is one of God's sorest

judgments,

judgments, and always argues a foul ripe for ruin; this *well* does not suppose us insensible of the evil of afflicting.

2. Though we believe all that befals us is well, this does not forbid our inquiring into the reasons of God's providential dispensations, and a searching out the cause for which they come upon us. Every rod hath a voice in it, and the 'man of understand-' ing will hear it,' and ' see the name of God in it,' Micah vi. 9. what God intends by it, what is his end and design in it, ' for he does not afflict will-' ingly, nor grieve the children of men,' Lam. iii. 33. There is a ' need be' in every dispensation that befals us: 1 Pet. i. 6. ' Wherein ye greatly rejoice, ' though now for a season' (if need be) ' ye are in ' heaviness through manifold temptations:' God acts with judgment in proportion to our needs; there is a conveniency and fitness, nay, there is an absolute necessity in the case; it must be that we are in heaviness, and that through *manifold* temptations. One single trial oftentimes will not do, to empty us of self, to wean us from the world, to shew us the vanity of the creature, the sinfulness of sin, &c. it must be repeated, or others joined with it, so fast are our affections glued to the things of time and sense. Now, what this needs is in *us*, what this intention and end is *in God*, the Christian will and ought to be searching out, and inquiring daily into. This was Job's frame, (and ye have heard, as says the Apostle, of the patience of Job), Job xxxiv. 31, 32. ' Surely ' it is meet to be said unto God, I have born cha-' stisement, I will not offend any more. That which ' I see not, teach thou me; if I have done iniquity, ' I will do no more.' Sin lies deep, it must be searched after in the deep and secret corners of the heart; there is so much self-love and self-flattery hid there, that a man cannot judge aright of himself or of God without divine teachings. ' It is meet to ' be said unto God, I have born chastisement.' Sirs! it is one thing to be chastised, and another thing to

bear

bear chaſtiſement, to behave aright under it, to be patient, ſubmiſſive, thankful, to have a frame of heart ſuited to the diſpenſation whatever it is. This is to bear chaſtiſement; and wherever this is, the language of the ſoul will be, ' That which I ſee not, ' teach thou me; if I have done iniquity, I will do ' no more:' When an affliction is ſanctified, it always begets godly fear and jealouſy. A man is then moſt afraid of his own heart, left that ſhould deceive him, left he ſhould come out of the furnace unpurged, unrefined, left the end of God's viſitation upon him ſhould be unattained. And this is well conſiſtent with our believing all that God does is well done. Once more,

3. A ſoul may ſay in a becoming frame, and in the exerciſe of ſuitable affections, ' It is well,' and yet long, and pray, and wait for deliverance from the trial. Submiſſion to the will of God, under awful diſpenſations, is not inconſiſtent with earneſt prayer for a gracious and ſpeedy iſſue to theſe very diſpenſations. ' It is well,' ſays this good woman in my text; and yet how does ſhe plead for the life of the child, *ver.* 28. ' Did I deſire a ſon of my lord? ' Did not I ſay, do not deceive me?' As if ſhe had ſaid, " I aſked it not, I could ſcarce believe it when " it was promiſed me; God raiſed my expectations " himſelf, he encouraged my hopes, and ſurely he " will not go back from his own word." It was a wonderful act of faith; but the promiſes of God can never lie long unfulfilled: When he has prepared the heart to pray, his own ear is open to hear. He has not called himſelf ' I am that I am' for nothing. Abraham ſtaggered not at the promiſe through unbelief, no more does this daughter of Abraham, here: It is bleſſed pleading, ' Did I not ſay, do not de- ' ceive me?' " May I truſt? May I venture? He " has given me the faithful word of God to rely on; " here my faith reſteth." And a ſon came in due ſeaſon; now ſhe looks to God the author of the mercy, and applies to the prophet who was the revealer

of it. He sends Gehazi with his staff, but this will not content her, except Elisha goes himself; she knew he was great with God; she will therefore have his prayers and presence: 'As the Lord liveth, 'and as thy soul liveth, I will not leave thee,' *ver.* 30. All this argues the strong desires of her heart after the return of the child's life, though still she says, 'all is well.' While we bear chastenings we may pray, and pray hard that God would take them off. 'If it be possible,' (says innocent aggrieved nature in the man Christ) 'let this cup pass 'from me,' Matt. xxvi. 26. Opening our mouth *against* God is our sin, but it is our duty to open our mouths and our hearts *to* him. In the former sense, says David, 'I was dumb, I opened not my mouth, 'because thou didst it,' Psal xxxix. 9. and yet with the same breath he adds, 'Remove thy stroke away 'from me: I am consumed by the blow of thine 'hand,' *ver.* 10. Was a child under the correction of a parent to intimate no desire of his forbearance, should we not rather account him stubborn than submissive? In like manner not to ask of God release from troubles, is as offensive as to murmur at them. It is a token of a proud heart and a relentless spirit; God expects other things at our hands: Even of the wicked he says, 'In their affliction they will seek 'me early;' much more shall his own people, who have known his name, and put their trust in him; who have known the advantage of prayer, and been so often set at liberty by it from all their fears. If these are silent, they cannot be sensible nor submissive. Only in all their prayers, when they are most earnest and vehement, " if it be consistent with the " will of God," and there will be no limiting him as to time or way.

These things are neither of them inconsistent with the soul's saying, under the most awful rebukes, 'All is well.'

Now what is included in this *well* in my text, or what is this submission to the will of God?

It

It takes in, as I apprehend, these three things;

1. A justifying God in all he does. ' It is well;' God cannot do amiss; he worketh all things after the counsel of his own will, to the praise of his glory; ' And after all that is come upon us' (says the church, Ezra ix. 13.) ' thou our God hast punished ' us less than our iniquities deserve;' thou hast not taken vengeance according to the desert of our sins. When sin appears to be what it is in itself, exceeding sinful, affliction will appear light, and not till then; wherefore says the church, Lam. iii. 39. ' Wherefore doth a living man complain, a man for ' the punishment of his sins?' So long as we are out of hell, God punishes us less than our iniquities deserve.

Whatever be our trial, it comes from God; he is the author, whoever be the instrument, therefore ' it ' is well.' He cannot do iniquity; David had not one word to say, by way of complaint, when he saw God's hand in the affliction; yea let him curse, for ' the Lord hath bid Shimei curse David,' 2 Sam. xvi. 11. We may puzzle and distress ourselves about instruments and second causes, but no quiet, no rest can we have till we are led to the first. ' He ' performeth the thing appointed for me;' that settles the soul, but nothing else will do it. ' Be still, ' and know that I am God,' Psal. xlvi. 10. If thy children are taken, thy substance fails, thy body is sore vexed, thy comforts, and even the presence of thy God leaves thee; yet be still, that is, do not say a word against the dispensation, do not fret, do not censure and condemn providence. I am God, who shall say, what dost thou? I will neither be questioned nor directed by thee. I know my own way, and I regard my promise and covenant: I am God, thy God in all; and a covenant God cannot do amiss. God will be glorified and exalted, that's enough for us. This, ' It is well,' implies in it, not in some things but in all.

2. This submission implies in it, our approving of all that God does; not only it is not amiss, but it is
right;

right; it is the best way, the only sure way to bring about our good: Therefore holy Job blesses God in all, *chap.* i. 21. ' Naked came I out of my mother's ' womb, and naked shall I return thither; the Lord ' gave, and the Lord hath taken away; blessed be ' the name of the Lord.' He had the same great and good thoughts of God as ever he had; God was his God still, and the God of his mercy. He should have an expected, a desired end, *that* he believed still, because God's thoughts were the same they ever were, that is, thoughts of peace, and not of evil. And this is the frame in which we find the poor saints, that were scattered up and down throughout the whole world almost, 1 Pet. i. 6. ' Who are kept ' by the power of God through faith unto salvation, ' ready to be revealed in the last time, wherein ye ' greatly rejoice,' *&c.* They were far from one another to avoid persecution, yet wherever they were, they met persecution, it was in their way; but none of these things moved them. There was joy in their expected rest and happiness at last, though there was great pain and heaviness in their way to it: The way was rough, but right; therefore they approved of it, they acquiesced in it, nay herein ' they great- ' ly rejoiced.' Thus the saints of old took joyfully the spoiling of their goods, and were tortured, not accepting deliverance, because they *knew* in them- selves, ' that they had in heaven a better, and an ' enduring substance,' Heb. x. 34. O that blessed knowledge! it comforts, refreshes, it fills the soul, and lifts a man above himself.

Every path which God takes is right then, it is safe, and the believer chooses to walk in it: His God, his Father has marked it out, and nothing goes so against the grain, but that ' all is well,' which his Father does: His will is brought to be one with God's; the soul approves of all God does.

3. This submission implies in it our cleaving to God in all. To be pleased with God as a friend, when he seems to be coming forth against us as an enemy;

enemy; to lean upon a promise, when all the ways leading to the performance are shut up; to rejoice in God when we have nothing left beside to rejoice in, and faith is hard put to it, to call God ours: Thus to cleave to God, when we do not find comfort from him, this is believing indeed; to love the hand that smites, that is true grace and great grace. A noble act of faith was that, Job xiii. 15. 'Though 'he slay me, yet will I trust in him.' So 'Abraham 'staggered not at the promises through unbelief,' Rom. iv. 20. He brought God's promise and faithfulness close together, and considered none of the difficulties, nay absurdities, which came between them: It was not——" Is this reasonable? What " probability is there in that? How can these things " be, &c." but being not weak in faith, he considered not his own body now dead, neither yet the deadness of Sarah's womb, but was strong in faith giving glory to God; he clave to him, abode by his promise in a way of faith and firm dependence.

This is the true nature of submission, and is contained in that expression in my text, 'It is well.' Upon what ground a believer says of every dispensation of providence towards him, 'It is well,' shall be considered in the next discourse. A word of use.

Use 1. Wonder not at your trials, be they never so strange, and grievous, and distressing; 'All is 'well;' some secret end is to be answered which you see not; God is in all; the hand and love of a Father is there. They are to purge from sin, to wean from the world, to bring you to the foot of God, to shew you that your rest is not here, that it lies beyond the grave. What though they make you smart, they do you the more good; this argues your sensibleness under the rod; that is not a rod which does not cause smart; the sharpest physic does most service, because it reaches the inward, hidden cause; not one of our many trials which we could well spare.

Use 2. Do not think any trial sanctified, till you have a suitable frame to the trial, whatever it be.

Are

Are you humbled? Are you prayerful? Are you submissive? Have you looked inward, and confessed your sins, saying, Take away all iniquity? If affliction has not brought you to this, it hath done you no good. For all you may have born, his anger is not turned away, but his hand is stretched out still.

Use 3. Do not think of other means, whereby God's end in visiting you might have been as well answered; that is in fact to quarrel with God in what he has done, or is doing. Have a care of your thoughts; unsubmission slips in at that door before one is aware. 'It is well,' is the only soul-quickening and God-glorifying frame. God that has appointed the end has settled, and he will order the means: Rest there, and 'all is well.'

SERMON XXI.

FAITH'S ESTIMATE OF AFFLICTIVE DISPENSATIONS.

2 KINGS iv. 26.

———*And she answered, It is well.*

TO have a frame of heart of a piece with these words, is one of the highest attainments of faith, and it brings to my mind the apostle's prayer for the believing Colossians, *chap.* i. 11. ' That ye ' might be strengthened with all might according to ' his glorious power, unto all patience and long-suf-' fering with joyfulness.' According to the degrees of that glorious power, which is communicated from God to the believer, so does his faith in God increase or decline. All our strength is from above, it is not lodged within. Our supplies are from God, not from ourselves. Be the affliction ever so heavy, be the continuance of it ever so long; if the Christian be favoured with the might of God's power, he is strengthened to bear it with all joyfulness. Whence is it else, that so great an example of faith as Jacob was, when he comes to part with his beloved Benjamin, for a while finds himself so exceedingly distressed? When he was turned out of his father's house with his staff only, he is submissive and content: And afterwards, when Esau came out against him with four hundred men, he acts with moderation and prudence, sets every drove in order, prepares his present, and gives every one a speech for his brother, Gen. xxxii. 16. surely at this time he believed all was well. But when ' Joseph is not, Simeon is not, ' and Benjamin is going after them, all these things ' are against me,' Gen. xlii. 36. God left faith alone there, and then it soon fails. If the arm of his power be withheld, the actings of our faith soon cease. Hence I conceive it is, that the Holy Ghost lays such an emphasis upon the story which my text is a part of. ' Through faith women received their ' dead raised to life again :' The emphasis lies upon the persons, not so much upon their faith, or the glorious effects of it, ' Through faith women,' &c. Such as had the warmest passions, and tenderest affections, and therefore the most aggravating sorrow, when all that was dear to them was gone, even they believed, faith conquered nature; there was submission under heart-rending providences, because they believed. The mighty power of God, when a believer rests upon that, all things are safe, ' All is ' well.' When Jacob lost but one son, ' he refused ' to be comforted,' Gen. xxxvii. 35. This good woman in my text had but one to lose, and no hope of another in his room, yet says she, ' It is well.'

So that the doctrinal observation raised from the words was this:

OBSERV. Faith in God's promise and power, will bring a man to submit to the sorest and most trying dispensations of providence: Or thus,

Faith, when it is in exercise, will teach a Christian to say of all God does, ' It is well.'

In discoursing on which, I proposed,

I. To shew you, what submission is; or how, and in what sense we are to understand the expression in my text, 'It is well.' This has been considered. And we come now,

II. To shew what are the grounds of this submission, or whence it is, that a believer says of all God does, 'It is well.' And,

1. The sovereignty of God is a ground of this submission. God has an absolute power, and right of dominion, over all his creatures, to dispose and determine of them as seemeth him good; he has a right to do what he will with his own. This quieted Aaron when fire from heaven consumed his two sons, Lev. x. 3. 'Aaron held his peace.' And Eli, when that tingling sentence was denounced against him and his household, 1 Sam. iii. 18. 'he said, It 'is the Lord, let him do what seemeth him good.' This gave David ease, when he was driven from God's sanctuary, and his throne usurped by his ungodly son, 2 Sam. xv. 26. 'Behold, here I am, let 'him do to me as seemeth good unto him.' In these instances the affliction was not only born, but *accepted*, as the word is, Lev. xxvi. 41. 'If their 'uncircumcised hearts be humbled, and they then 'accept of the punishment of their iniquity, then 'will I remember my covenant with Jacob,' &c. that is, willingly born, contently enjoyed; so Ainsworth renders it. O! It is a sweet frame when our trials are *accepted* ones; when God's chastening hand is esteemed a kindness, when physic, as well as food, excites our thankfulness. I do not say God's sovereignty alone, in our clearest views of it, will of itself bring our souls to this; yet this I say, that sovereignty works submission. How dare I repine that God takes away part of my substance, when he has a right to all? My children, my friends, my frames, were all but lent me. God gives us nothing to have and to hold but his Christ, (and we cannot always see our hold of him). Why should I object, why murmur, why gainsay? Doth he give any account of his matters? Is it befiting him, that has

absolute

absolute dominion over all his creatures, to be arraigned at man's bar? Or is it in my breast, by all my devices, reasonings and demurs, to change the purposes of his heart? Lord, I will puzzle myself no longer with *hows*, and *whys*, and *yets*; thou hast done it; I rest there: It seemed good in thy sight, that's reason sufficient. Thus God has left it; and I dare not bring in my " *yet*, Lord I would fain " have it otherwise." My friends! you bring in a bill of complaints against God and his Providence; this grieves you; the other is not right with you; a third thing you find hard to submit to; pray, where is there any one has a trial like Aaron, Eli, David? and yet the remedy was near, and it is a tried one: " It is the Lord, let him do what seemeth " him good." This never fails when it is well applied; if it be really taken, it will do you good; but it is not enough to look at the cup, and then turn away your head from it; or take it as children do physic, with their eyes shut; no, no, the more you weigh matters over, the better always. The more purely faith eyes God's sovereignty in all, the stronger are the actings of it: ' It is the Lord,' and Eli has nothing more to say. Let God choose my portion; best I am sure then it will be, and pleasantest in the end; for even when he acts as a sovereign, he forgets not his relation as a father; in his hands we are safe. Faith acts herein with the greatest reason, for it is the highest reason to leave all with him, who worketh, ordereth, over-ruleth all that befals us for his own glory and our spiritual good. This, therefore, is one reason or ground of this submission.

2. The justice and righteousness of God is a farther ground of submission, Job xxxiv. 31. ' Surely ' it is meet to be said unto God, I have borne chastise- ' ment, I will not offend any more.' If sin sits heavy, all afflictions will soon appear light; and the sensible Christian is for digging deep into his own heart; for the more spiritual sins, which are most offensive to God, are most secret and hidden. Bye-

ends and aims in duty, pride, vain-glory, carnal confidence, infenfiblenefs under providential rebukes, worldly difpofitions, lifelefs frames, creature love, and hopes, and expectations; where is the man wholly free from thefe things? And yet, when awful ftrokes come, where muft I look for the Chriftian who is patient and fubmiffive under them? Who if he does not fret and fume under the rod, yet is not apt to harbour thoughts within, as if God dealt hard meafures by him? Sirs, converfe more with the nature and perfections of God; converfe more with his holy law; converfe more with thy creaturefhip, and more with thy natural guilt and corruption; or elfe fubmiffion, as neceffary a duty as it is, will never be practifed by thee. When a Chriftian is in a right frame, his heart always goes with Ezra's words, *chap.* ix. 13. ' After all that is come upon us, for our ' evil deeds, and for our great trefpaffes,—thou our ' God haft punifhed us lefs than our iniquities de-' ferve.' The beft way to prize our mercies is to be affected with our fin; fcarce any trial comes, but a little heart examination will fuggeft what the caufe is: But where there is no fpecial fin for which God vifits, is it not enough to reconcile thee to the ftroke, that thou art fo unhumbled, fo unholy, that thy heart ftarts afide fo oft from God; that thou art fo far from him, fo unlike to him, fo full of plague-fores, from which thou haft not been thoroughly cleanfed? When once thy heart comes to be duly affected with thefe things; when God fpeaks, (as Zophar has it, Job xi. 5, 6.), ' when he fhews thee the fecrets of ' wifdom, that they are double to that which is,' that which appears to be; thou wilt have fenfible apprehenfions and knowledge of this, ' that God ex-' acteth of thee lefs than thine iniquity deferveth.' Juft thoughts of the juftice and righteoufnefs of God is another argument of fubmiffion.

3. The wifdom of God, as exercifing itfelf in all that befalls the Chriftian, is a farther ground of fubmiffion. To this holy Job has recourfe, *chap.* ix. 4. He is wife in heart, and mighty in ftrength; who
' hath

'hath hardened himself against him, and hath pro-
'spered?' The expression imports (says Caryl)
"That he hath infinite wisdom. His is not wisdom
"only in the tongue, or some flashes of wit, but
"deep, solid, rooted wisdom." He is God only
wise. From eternity he saw what we should need
in time, and our supplies were all wisely adjusted,
settled, and proportioned in the everlasting covenant;
and therefore nothing can be wrong which we meet
with in time, it is all the way to rest: The way lies
through thorns, and briers, and crosses, and snares;
the wisdom of God hath so ordered it for the best,
there is no getting any other way to glory. What
was said of Israel of old, is true of us now; 'And
'he led them the right way, that he might bring
'them to a city of habitation,' Psal. cvii. 7. We
know it was not the shortest way, nor was it the
smoothest, but it was the right way. It was the way
which God's wisdom had appointed, as best suiting
with their froward tempers, and the ends of his own
glory: Alas! till we get to see this, we shall never
speak the words of my text from the heart. If we
do not see God's wisdom in our trials, we shall never
be thoroughly brought to submission under them.
Look at them afresh; see, enquire, it may be you
have passed over some circumstances attending them
too lightly; whatever your burden be, it is suited
to your back, it is the proper trial of your faith.
'By these things' (says Hezekiah) 'men live, and
'in all these things are the life of my spirit,' Isaiah
xxxviii. 16. Every single circumstance attending
your trials has its use, and makes most surely for
your advantage. Perhaps you have a stout spirit.
God sees it proper to break your heart with reproaches, to lash you with the scourge of tongues;
or it may be your credit sinks, your reputation wastes;
or else it may be, strong pain upon your bed pulls
you down, till you look no higher than just yourself:
This was the very trial you needed, for by it the
end for which it was sent is attained. Or it may be
you are of a tender spirit, your heart has been wrapped

ped up in the creature, here you have settled, fixed, and nothing could move you from it; well, God will deal with that to kill your creature-love and delight, your all is taken away with a stroke. He rends the creature from you, husband, wife, children, friends; God removes them to bring your heart nearer to himself; or, it may be, you are of an ambitious, aspiring temper; but as you climb, so you fall: God unravels your schemes, breaks your plots, *advances* you to poverty; and a blessed advancement that is in your case; it is what best suits you; you could not bear to be rich, to be used tenderly, to be indulged. Again, others there be who are cross, rugged, who value no man; the world smiles, the creature they have, wife, children, lands, &c. all are with them; and they are of that unhappy temper, they think all no more than they deserve; but infinite wisdom has provided for them too; God will bring down their high looks. They shall be afflicted *in* the creature; their sorrows shall grow out of the root, in the fruit whereof they expected comfort; no stroke so heavy, no rod so smarting as this. Moses had his Zipporah; Abigail a Nabal; David had Absalom, Ammon, Adonijah. Better follow children to the grave, than bring them up for hell; the thought wounds as it enters the heart; yet here is wisdom in all this; because no other physic will reach the case, no other affliction will do you so much good, therefore God applies this: And then as to the time of an affliction, God's wisdom shines in that; when you began to grow weary of him, heartless in duty, proud of gifts, or fixed in some evil course, then was the time that the hand of God was lifted up, he would bear no longer. And, is there not also wisdom seen in making contraries work together for your good? That which is now your burden might have been your ruin; ' Out of the ' eater comes forth meat:' Joseph's seeming death was the way to save his father and his family alive;

our

our foreſt croſſes are often made the way to our ſweeteſt comforts.

Thus a believer cannot reaſon always; but finds it hard to believe ſo it ſhall be, when the trial is upon him; but he reſts here: ' Thy way is in the ſea, ' and thy path in the great waters; and thy foot-' ſteps are not known,' Pſal. lxxvii. 19. O! ſays the Chriſtian, my God is here; the diſpenſation is not ſo dark but I ſee God in it; he works deep; trace him I cannot, but follow him I will; it is my duty and my delight to reſign to him; I cannot *wade* in the ſea, it is out of my depth, but God can *walk* there; the reaſons of his dealings with me I ſee not, but they are laid in infinite wiſdom. I may believe him, truſt him, hope in him, though I cannot ſee him; he knows his own way, let that ſuffice: ' Why art thou caſt down, O my ſoul?' Be ſtill; ſay no more. God, a God of counſel and wiſdom, hath thee by the hand, and he will not fail thee: ' Thou leddeſt thy people like a flock, by the hand of Moſes and Aaron,' Pſal. lxxvii. 20. God's infinite wiſdom is a ground of ſubmiſſion to the darkeſt ſteps of his providence.

4. The love and mercy of God is a farther ground of ſubmiſſion: Theſe are always at the bottom of the ſoreſt trials; and when the believer ſees this, he ſays of whatever God does, ' It is well done.' If he chaſtens, he ſuſtains, and refines when he tries: ' He ' knoweth the way that I take; when he hath tried ' me, I ſhall come forth as gold,' Job xxiii. 10. Gold loſes nothing by the furnace but its droſs, it is not conſumed in the fire, but only made more pure. There is a ſparing juſtice, and a puniſhing mercy: Thus ſays God of the wicked, Ezek. xvi. 42. ' So ' will I make my fury towards thee to reſt, and my ' jealouſy ſhall depart from thee, and I will be quiet ' and will be no more angry;' enough to make one tremble at the hearing of it. If God corrects no more, he will deſtroy next; here is a ſparing juſtice: To the godly there is alſo a puniſhing mercy, 1 Cor.

xi. 32. 'When we are judged we are chastened of the Lord, that we should not be condemned with the world.' There is a blessing hid in the worst of things; better to be punished *now*, than to perish *for ever:* It is kindness in using the rod to prevent the child's ruin, Amos iii. 2. 'You only have I known of all the families of the earth; therefore I will punish you for all your iniquities:' Above all others, says God, I will see to you; and it is condescending love in him thus to punish. Why should he not give us up? He might say, as in Isa. i. 5. 'Why should ye be stricken any more, ye will revolt more and more:' But his love, his mercy holds out still. The believer, in the most dark and cloudy day, has light enough to read so far in the name of the Lord, as that he is JEHOVAH, merciful and gracious. Two things, when faith is ever so little helped, it will discern and rejoice in, namely, sparing mercy in this life, and saving mercy in that which is to come. It was a melancholy time with the church, Lam. iii. God had brought her into darkness, inclosed her ways, filled her soul with gall and wormwood; yet, when she bethinks herself, says she, *ver.* 22. 'It is of the Lord's mercies that we are not consumed, because his compassions fail not;' we are yet on this side hell; it is not so bad with us, but it might have been worse. God lives still, and his compassions are as full, as free as ever; in these is continuance, and we shall be saved. A full end is not made of us, be our trials what they will: 'In measure when it shooteth forth God doth debate with it.' Sparing mercy we see here; and saving mercy will follow after. Now, whatever comfort God renews, he does not take away his Christ, his great gift; our pains may be great, but his comforts are sweet, and infinitely overbalance them; though our bodies may be covered over with sores, our souls, our consciences are sprinkled with blood: 'Ye are come to the blood of sprinkling,' Heb. xii. 24. Blessed trial which brings us thither!

to be sure love is in it, or else Christ would never have been rendered precious by it. And then the rest remaineth for us, and it is well kept, for Christ hath possession of it, 'thither as our forerunner he 'is for us entered, Heb. vi. 19. not gone as a private person into the rest, but gone thither as our representing Head, to occupy our place against we come thither. It is a comfort to the saints, that in this world they have the worst place they shall ever have; things grow better with us every day, as every day brings us nearer to our Father's house. A traveller has but little concern that his money is all spent, when he has got within sight of home. What though there be no candles in the house, when we are sure break of day is near? The believer is looking for the mercy of Christ unto eternal life; and there is much mercy amidst all the trials which he meets with in his way to it. Every cross is sweetned with some mercy. This is another argument for submission. I should go on; but one word of use shall close at present. It is this,

Use. Observe providence, if you would profit by it. Experiments are reckoned choice things; they are to be laid by, and kept safe against a time of need. Psal. cvii. 43. 'Whoso is wise and will ob-
'serve these things, even they shall understand the
'loving-kindness of the Lord.' A Christian should be best versed in the history of his own life; there is always matter of instruction and entertainment there. Do not let signal mercies pass and repass, without taking account of them, Deut. viii. 3. 'Thou shalt remember all the way, which the Lord
'thy God led thee these forty years in the wilder-
'ness, to humble thee, and to prove thee, to know
'what was in thine heart, whether thou wouldest
'keep his commandments or no.' Some of the minutest circumstances of providence are the sweetest, because they are introductive to many others: Ahasuerus's not sleeping was the circumstance which led

the

the way to the salvation of all the nation of the Jews. Three things I would earnestly recommend to myself and you to be well studied; each of our pains in the work will be abundantly recompensed by the pleasure of it. One is the study of providence; the other of grace; the third of our own hearts. A Christian may find work enough there, to keep him employed all his life long. Observe providence, if you would profit and be instructed by it; ' whoso is ' wise and will observe these things,' &c. much spiritual wisdom it argues, and much of God's loving kindness will you discover by it.

But I add no more at present.

SERMON XXII.

FAITH'S ESTIMATE OF AFFLICTIVE DISPENSATIONS.

2 Kings iv. 26.

——*And she answered, It is well.*

WE see a Christian here in his best light, and in his sweetest frame. It is not always thus with a child of God, there is nature as well as grace in the best of saints, flesh as well as spirit, strong corruptions as well as strong faith and hope; wherefore strength must be communicated from God, or else, even under lesser trials, there will be no firm trust in him. Patience is not a mere endurance of trouble, but it is the exercise of those graces which are suited to a suffering state. To believe God, to love him, to delight in him, to resign over ourselves to his sovereign will and pleasure; and from a settled valuation of things eternal, above all that this present life promises or can give, to have the soul quiet and composed, chearful and dependent, even under the frowns and rebukes of Providence, keeping fast hold of the promise, the covenant of God; this is the faith, this the patience of the saints. Herein you best see its nature and use, and herein you

see

see the trial of it. Four things have been propoſed to be diſcourſed on, as God ſhould help.

I. To ſhew you, what ſubmiſſion is; or in what ſenſe, and with what limitations is this *well* in my text to be underſtood. Not as though there was nothing in trials, which to fleſh and blood appeared under the notion of evil: Not as though the cauſes of our troubles were not to be ſearched into: Nor yet, as if we had not a liberty granted us of God, to deſire and pray for the removal of them. But it conſiſts in theſe three things. A juſtifying God in all that befals us. An approving of all. And a cleaving to him in all. It was propoſed,

II. To ſhew what are the grounds of this ſubmiſſion; or whence it is the ſoul thinks and ſays of all God does, ' It is well' done.

1. It is becauſe he ſets before him the ſovereignty of God, as having a right to do what he will with his own.

2. The juſtice and righteouſneſs of God, which makes mercy of every thing ſhort of hell.

3. He conſiders the wiſdom of God, as exerciſing itſelf in all that befals him, for his own glory, and our ſpiritual good.

4 The love and mercy of God, as being at the bottom of the foreſt trials. I now proceed,

5. The faithfulneſs of God is a further ground of ſubmiſſion; this alſo the believer ſets before him under the ſaddeſt providences, and this puts a beauty and pleaſantneſs upon all: Pſal. cxix. 75. ' I know, ' O Lord, that thy judgments are right, and that ' thou in faithfulneſs haſt afflicted me.' The faithfulneſs of God appears two ways, and in both it works ſubmiſſion; in ſending an affliction, and then in guiding it.

Firſt. The faithfulneſs of God appears in *ſending* an affliction. This David acknowledges in theſe words. Not only that God was faithful *who* ſent his
trial,

trial, giving that measure of grace which was necessary under it; but he was faithful *in* sending it, *ver.* 67. The affliction itself was an act and discovery of God's faithfulness, he could not have been faithful had he not done it. A noble act of faith is this, to speak thus from the heart when afflictions come thick and close; when our dearest comforts are taken, such as credit, liberty, health, children, &c. that God is faithful in all; to know it, to feel it, and therefore to approve his way with us: This is true submission, but it is hard work; for it is one thing to be convinced in one's judgment of this, another thing to acknowledge and approve it in the heart, to find all still, composed and satisfied within, a cleaving, relying frame in all. *Then* says the Christian, " True, Lord! I needed this rod, my
" heart was stupid, secure, wavering, unhumbled;
" this rouses and fixes me. I know thee the better,
" I love thee the more for it; thou art an holy, a
" pure, a jealous God; sin shall not dwell with me;
" O this revenge and holy fear, which I now find
" working in me, it is the sweetest frame to serve
" my God in: My thoughts are raised: What is this
" world to a moment's communion with thee; what
" an empty nothing it is? My heart dies to it: Lord,
" I am weaned. My God will have an whole heart,
" and, Lord, it is thine; thy love is judicious, not
" fond. My *good*, not my *ease*, is what my Father,
" my God consulteth; and I now know, I now feel
" my wants; my prayers have a spirit in them;
" mercy is not asked for form's sake; I find I need
" it, and blessed be a covenant God, for such full
" supplies as I see in Christ. God commendeth his
" love and faithfulness to me, by this affliction;
" when I sit down and count the cost, I can pre-
" sently see, I am no loser; O it is good for me that
" I have been afflicted." God is faithful in sending afflictions, this works submission. And,

Secondly, He is faithful also in *guiding* them, 1 Cor. x. 13. ' God is faithful who will not suffer

'you to be tempted above what ye are able; but
'will with the temptation also make a way to e-
'scape, that ye may be able to bear it.' When
they fall too heavy, either they shall be removed or
you supported: 'My grace is sufficient for you, for
'my strength is made perfect in weakness,' 2 Cor.
xii. 9. God deals by his children as Jacob did by
his, Gen. xxxiii. 13, 14. 'The children are ten-
'der, and the flocks and herds with young are
'with me, and if men should over-drive them one
'day, all the flock will die.——I will lead on softly
'according as the cattle that goeth before me, and
'the children be able to endure.' Your Father
knows your strength and his own covenant better
than you do or can. What have you lacked yet
that your fears are so great, your cries and complaints so exceeding pressing? Wherein did he
leave you, wherein has he failed you? Say the time,
name the place, particularize the affliction. 'Ac-
'cording to this time may it be said of Jacob and
'Israel, What hath God wrought!' Numb. xxiii. 23.
Not only now, but upon all like occasions, God will
shew himself strong in your behalf, O ye that put
your trust in him. This and the other present salvation is but a pattern of what shall be, when your
needs and the ends of God's glory require it. And
is not this an argument of submission? O it is, it
composes, it settles the soul, and makes it to *glory* in
tribulation also.

6. The power and all-sufficiency of God are a
farther ground of submission; these have a tendency to work in the soul this blessed frame my text
speaks of, Isai. xl. 27. 'Why sayest thou, O Jacob,
'and speakest, O Israel, My way is hid from the
'Lord, and my judgment is passed over from my
'God? Hast thou not known? Hast thou not
'heard, that the everlasting God, the Lord, the
'Creator of the ends of the earth fainteth not,
'neither is weary! There is no searching of his
'understanding, he giveth power to the faint, and
'to

'to them that have no might, he increaseth
'strength.' Whatever thou losest, is there not e-
nough in God still? Are his consolations small? No,
but thy faith is weak. The fountain is as full as
ever: 'I am God all-sufficient,' Gen. xvii. 1. God
that is sufficiency, though this or that pipe, this or
that means of conveyance is cut off. Couldst thou
ever say this of any creature? Was there ever any
evidence of all-sufficiency in that? O with what
eyes do the best see God and the creature! Jonah
loses his gourd, and he must needs die too; Jacob
loses his son, and he can have no comfort more;
sure we have a patient God, as well as a mighty
Saviour! Had God taken either at their word, I
will not say, as David did of Abner's death, (one
was a patriarch, the other a prophet); but sure they
must have died martyrs to their own sinful creature-
affections. O Sirs, if you must have your props,
your comforts from the creature, woe to you. Ra-
chel must needs have children or die, Gen. xxx. 1.
And she died in her child-bearing. God gave her
a son, but it was a Benoni, the son of her sorrow,
her death; she never lived to have one moment's
enjoyment of him. If you suck at the nether springs
of creature-sufficiency, for satisfaction and rest, you
will not draw comfort, but poison. 'There is death
'in the pot.' God has not invested any creature
with his own all-sufficiency; it is dreadful to wrest,
what we fondly esteem blessings, out of God's hands.
I admire Hagar's faith, I adore the wisdom and
goodness of God in giving the occasion of it, Gen.
xvi. 13. 'She called the name of the Lord that
'spake unto her, Thou God seest me: for she said,
'Have I also here looked after him that seeth me?'
Do not faint under thy burden, poor distressed saint;
whatever it be, God, thy God seeth *thee* and *it*.
Thy Jesus is a tender-hearted friend; while thou
art looking after him, he will speak to thee, he will
be fond of thee; and love is in his lips, salvation is
in his hand; he is the God that liveth and seeth

thee. God's all-sufficiency is another ground of submission. It must be well when we have an interest in an everlasting and an all-sufficient God. Once more,

7. God's unchangeableness is another ground of Christian submission. Psal. cii. 27. 'But thou art 'the same, and thy years have no end.' But thou art the same: It is a blessed *but*. It comes in with a notwithstanding to all changes, not only which *have* been, but which *may* be. *My* health weakened, my days shortened, alas, what is this! these heavens themselves shall perish, they shall wax old like a garment, *but* thou, Lord, shalt endure, thou shalt stand eternally the same. The rock of ages is a sure dwelling-place. The believer's portion in God is perpetual and everlasting. No change in him, nor the least shadow of it. 'I am that I am,' says God; in all the revolutions of time, and distress of nature, when it shall be convulsed and wrecked, and the whole frame of it crumbled into nothing, he is still the same. What a stable foundation of comfort is here! What a prop for hope! What a blessed argument of submission! Look into the church, look into the families of friends, look into the world, look into thyself, what innumerable changes do we see on every side, in every circumstance and season of life. A week, a day, what an alteration does it make? And how can a Christian be easy with this? whence is it he can say, 'it is 'well! O it is because of God's eternity, God's unchangeableness, who is a tried God and a Saviour, a never-failing rock of refuge: Once a father (will faith say) and ever a father; once a friend and ever o. My God, my Jesus, my portion, changes not. His carriage may alter, his heart cannot; his expressions may vary, but not his affection. Everlasting love makes sure work, it reaches through all dispensations; God hath spoken peace, and he will never unsay it. I may lose my comfort, but not my interest. He has laid the foundation of it in his

everlasting

everlasting love, purpose, promise and covenant. Men shut their hands (as one well has it) because they *have* opened them; but because God hath once opened his, he will never shut them. He is of *one* mind, and who can turn him; good and gracious, wise and powerful; and his name JEHOVAH argues he is eternally and unchangeably so. Peace then, my soul, be still; thou shalt wade through this trial, as easily, as safely, as thou didst through the last. He is a rock, and his work is perfect. This God is thy God for ever and ever, he will be thy guide even unto death. Thus does God's unchangeableness lead to submission. And thus much as to the grounds of a Christian's submission, or, whence it is the soul thinks and says of all God does, ' it is well.' Which brings me to shew,

III. What are the blessed fruits and effects of this submission, or what benefit redounds to the believer, what glory to God, when he is enabled to think, and say of all God does, ' it is well.'

It would make the discourse very sweet to him that preaches it, could he bring every particular warm from his own heart. But alas! we are as low, as faint, as lifeless and unbelieving at times as you can be we preach to. However it is his desire and prayer, that God would bring his heart down to every particular, and that his own soul may be refreshed with those consolations, which he is seeking to administer to others; that he may say, ' I be-
' lieved, therefore have I spoken.' We live upon the same food we provide for you; and blessed be God! he often makes that word a comfort to ourselves, wherein we aim chiefly at the support and establishment of others.

Well! What are the blessed fruits and effects of this frame my text speaks of?

Four evils there are which it prevents, and as many real, positive blessings it procures.

1. What are the sins and evils which it prevents, and which, when they prevail, cost the Christian dear? I answer,

First, It prevents rash conclusions. Such was that of Jacob, Gen. xlii. 36. 'Joseph is not, and 'Simeon is not, and ye will take Benjamin away; 'all these things are against me.' Such was that of David, 1 Sam. xxvii. 1. 'And David said in his 'heart, I shall now perish one day by the hand of 'Saul.' And such was that also of the church, Lam. iii. 18. 'And I said, My strength and my 'hope is perished from the Lord.' "I give up all "for lost, I can stay myself no longer upon God "for support; my case is remediless, I have no en- "couragement, no hope." This is the language of unbelief, rash conclusions which arise from a bare looking to second causes, without bringing God's word of promise and his faithfulness together: Whereas he is of one mind, ever pursuing the designs of everlasting love towards his church and people, though the thought does not always possess their hearts. See Isa. xlix. 16. 'Behold,' says God, 'I have graven thee upon the palms of my hands, 'thy walls are continually before me.' "I see thy "ruined walls, I have the model of my own mercy "still in mine eye, my heart is not off thee, as de- "solate as thy circumstances appear to be." God will yet have mercy upon Zion, when the set time to favour her is come. Hence we read of him that believeth, that he maketh not haste, Isa. xxviii. 16. 'He that believeth shall not make haste.' He is not presently at his wits end, because a mercy which has been often asked and long expected is delayed. It is a metaphor taken from a person in some great danger, without any certain tried means whereby he may escape; he tries this way and that way, keeping constant to none; or else despairing of safety, he makes all the haste possible to quit the place where he is at present, though he cannot tell where he shall do better. Not so does the Christian,

ſtian, whoſe hope and whoſe refuge the Lord is. He waits the time of mercy. Can you not eaſily remember when the delay of mercy has been for thy advantage? God has been not only preparing the mercy for you, but alſo preparing your heart for the mercy. Iſa. xxx. 18. ' And therefore will ' the Lord wait, that he may be gracious unto you, ' and therefore will he be exalted, that he may have ' mercy upon you ; for the Lord is a God of judg- ' ment : bleſſed are all they that wait for him.' Had it come ſooner, it might have turned to your detriment, not your real good. Can you not call to mind how God's mercies were neareſt, when your own heart and hopes were loweſt, Zech. xiv. 7. ' At evening time it ſhall be light.' When dark- neſs is expected, light appears. Can you not look back and ſee faithfulneſs in ſending the rod, as well as faithfulneſs in removing it? The croſs which we met with trembling, have we not kiſſed at parting? That which occaſioned the trial was the means of ſome unforeſeen deliverance. ' God ſent me be- ' fore you,' ſays Joſeph, ' to preſerve you a poſterity ' in the earth, and to ſave your lives by a great de- ' liverance,' Gen. xlv. 7. Yet this is the ſon Joſeph, concerning whoſe ſuppoſed death Jacob refuſed to be comforted. But this believing ' all is well,' ſtills the tumults and riſing paſſions of the ſoul, ſtrikes it dumb when it is apt to murmur, and prevents theſe raſh and haſty concluſions againſt God and the ways of his Providence.

Secondly, It prevents ſinful ſtaggerings. Thus we read of Abraham, Rom. iv. 20. ' He ſtaggered ' not at the promiſe of God through unbelief, but ' was ſtrong in faith, giving glory to God.' Obſerve, unbelief lies at the bottom of all our ſtaggerings: It is not God's promiſe that fails, it is our faith ; we loſe our ſight and hold of the promiſe, that makes us ſtagger. Perhaps there is ſome particular pro- vidence we have prayed over and over again, God has fed our hopes by his promiſes, we have ſeen the fruit of our prayers, and all things go on according to our will; it is eafy believing then. But behold, when every way there feemed to be a revival, God on a fudden deadens and damps it, he makes an unexpected breach, as he did upon Uzzah, 2 Sam. vi. 7. and that at a time when his people, as David was, are rejoicing before the ark. How do we behave at fuch a time? I know how this affects me, though I would hope better concerning others. I am apt to ftagger at the promife through unbelief; to difpute matters; to confider and weigh things in my own mind, according to the mere dictates of flefh and fenfe, without paying that reverence and regard to God's word of promife which I ought. But Abraham ftaggered not at the promife through unbelief; he held no felf-confultation, to debate about it; did not allow himfelf to confider whether he fhould clofe with it or no; but by a refolute and peremptory act of his foul, ventured his all upon it: " It is right, it is " beft, it is the word of God that cannot lie, of a " God infinite in power, and of unchanging faith- " fulnefs; it will not admit of an argument, a de- " bate; I am at a point in it, and it is a ruled cafe, " I am fure I am fafe." 'He ftaggered not at the ' promife through unbelief.' This, my friends, this is the frame which gives glory to God, becaufe it takes God at his word, and gives him credit as God. Where we have to do with men, the more we weigh and confider matters, the better; but we know whom we have believed, when we truft God; there is the greateft ground of confidence and higheft affurance, that what he has promifed he is *able* to perform: Hence in the actings of Abraham's faith it is remarked, *ver.* 19. 'He confidered not ' his own body now dead, when he was about an ' hundred years old, neither yet the deadnefs of ' Sarah's womb,' οὐ κατενόησε. He did not dwell in thoughts about it, but caft it out of his mind, paffed it by. The ftability of the promife, and the faith-

fulnefs

fulness of the great promiser, he was swallowed up with the contemplation of these, nothing else had room in his heart. This is the way to be kept from sinful staggerings, to keep our eye fixed and steady upon God's promise. Had not this good woman, in my text, so done, her frame would never have been so sweet, and so exceeding becoming. It is the mere weakness of faith, says the great Dr Owen, which makes a man lie poring upon the difficulties, and seeming impossibilities that lie in the way of a promise; for an acquiescence in God's will, a resting upon his word, an eye to his wisdom, power, all-sufficiency and faithfulness in all he does, will keep a man from staggering, when the storms and waves of God's providence beat never so fast and strong upon him; because he hath God, 'I am 'that I am,' wherewith to answer every rebellious doubt and sinful fear. This is another of those blessed effects which flow from the frame in my text.

I should now proceed; but what remains must be left to the next opportunity.

SERMON XXIII.

FAITH'S ESTIMATE OF AFFLICTIVE DISPENSATIONS.

2 Kings iv. 26.

——*And she answered, It is well.*

THE doctrinal observation raised from the words is this:

Faith in God's promise and power will bring a man to submit to the sorest and most trying dispensations of Providence. Faith in lively exercise will teach the Christian to say of all that God does, 'It is 'well' done.

Sure this doctrine is never out of season; sovereign remedies are good to lay by against a time of need; but the use and value of them is best known when the time of trial is. It is a good hint which I have met with in a practical author of the last age, "We are perfect in no lessons so much as those into "which God whipped us;" nor can we speak of any argument so warmly and feelingly, as when we preach out of present experience. When a man feels his wants and his weaknesses, being ready to faint in the day of adversity; let a friend bring the

cordial

cordial then, which he has recommended before without fuccefs, and he is welcome, becaufe there is a fpecial fuitablenefs in the remedy to his prefent cafe and circumftances. Believers themfelves look at trouble too much as a diftant thing. It is needful that we be undeceived in this, for elfe God will have our heart lefs, and we fhall have lefs of the comfort which arifes from his perfections, his promifes and his covenant. Hence we read of the trial of faith, as being precious, 1 Pet. i. 7. A believer is a gainer by all the exercife, the conflicts and oppofitions of his faith; becaufe his faith honours God, God will maintain, eftablifh, and increafe that. Wherein faith honours God, and how it fupports, quiets and relieves the foul in all its dangers, and under all its fears, my text tells us. It teaches the Chriftian to fay of all God does, 'It is well' done. Four things have been propofed for confideration. What lies before me at prefent is the third general head, namely,

What are the bleffed fruits and effects of this fubmiffion.

Four evils (you have heard) it prevents, and as many pofitive bleffings it procures. The evils it prevents are,

Firft, Rafh conclufions; thefe are prevented.

Secondly, Sinful ftaggerings. We now proceed.

Thirdly, The frame which my text fpeaks of, likewife prevents immoderate forrow. 'It is well,' God-glorifying language! befitting the mouth of a Chriftian, whofe life, whofe refuge and truft the Lord is: It is not, " I am ruined and undone, I have loft " my all, my heart is overwhelmed, it is quite broke; " what good will my life do me? O! where is my " comfort, fure I have no intereft in Chrift and his " covenant, God would not elfe fhew me fuch great " and fore troubles as thefe." No, here is not one word, not the leaft fhew of this fort; fhe leaves her

son where she had ventured her soul, and because God hath done it, 'all is well:' She has nothing to object, no fault to find with God: In like manner David, when he was greatly distressed, and the people talked of stoning him, 1 Sam. xxx. 6. 'He en-
'couraged himself in the Lord his God.' As God had given him the promise of a kingdom, he will trust himself in his hands, and leave him to bring it about by what means he pleases. A little faith, when it is in lively exercise, will carry a man above great distresses. Why? Because it discovers an ordered covenant, a wise Providence, sure promises, and a faithful God. Little faith will make great improvements here. "Shall I, says the Christian,
" mourn immoderately for the loss of a creature,
" when my God, my Jesus lives? Is not my heart
" his? are not his love and covenant mine? Must
" I needs live upon my losses? If he has taken a-
" way, did he not first give? And what though *my*
" name dies, and is extinct in this only branch of
" my family, *his* name remains, my God is better
" than many sons."

Again, "My child is not lost, though he is ab-
" sent; I shall go to him; and wherein does there
" appear any thing hard, that one who is born from
" above, whose treasure is above, whose heart and
" whose conversation were above; that God should
" satisfy every desire at once, and take him to him-
" self? 'It is well;' he is taken from the evil to
" come, he is gone to be with Christ, which is far
" better than to be here; his race is soon run, his
" work is soon ended; but had he not been so soon
" ripe, he had not been so soon gathered. It is well
" for him, and well for *me*, for God will have more
" of my heart, my love, my trust, my praise now:
" The creature stole it away, and I perceived it not;
" now the creature is taken, I find how I loved it;
" Lord, I acquiesce." Thus the streams of the Christian's sorrows are stopped, at least they are turned another way; for if he laments, it is his sins rather
than

than his afflictions, and here there is always cause of mourning, and but little danger of excess in it. That is a third thing.

Fourthly, This frame also prevents heartless complaints. The Shunamitess, in my text, wholly looks over all second causes, and goes directly to the first. God hath done it, all events are appointed and ordered by him. 'My times,' says the Psalmist, 'are 'in thine hands,' Psal. xxxi. 15. "All that con- "cerns me thou hast the care of, and thou wilt per- "form it." There is nothing wherein believers shew a meaner spirit, and yet few sins beset them more easily, than an anxious concern and fretful care about some outward things, which have in themselves no power to do good or evil, any otherwise than as instruments in God's hands to attain his appointed end. Shall we quarrel with the sword because it suffered itself to be drawn? or be angry with the air because it is infected? No second cause can act without the direction of the first; there is no design in the instrument, as an instrument that acts, but as ordered by him who uses it. It has grieved me to hear Christians aggravate their trials, and debase their profession, by looking back to this and the other circumstance, dwelling upon that, as what gave rise to the whole affliction. "O! If I "had but had such advice—had I but thought!— "that I should consent my child should go to such "a place!—that I should not foresee," &c. And yet all the while the man believes God's purposes and decrees, and that 'he worketh all things after 'the counsel of his own will.' How beneath a Christian is this! Can you set aside divine counsels, or would you alter an ordered covenant? Use the means, but live upon God's power, wisdom, and faithfulness, who blesses or blasts them just as he pleases. To do otherwise is to make your burden a thousand times heavier than it is. 'It is well.' That is the only reconciling principle under the severest trials; and even under lighter strokes,

mere

mere casualities as they appear to us, the soul can have no rest till he issues his concern here. I have known little insignificances very vexing and grieving; and the more so, because one thinks how easily they might have been prevented. But the best way to quiet the soul is to eye God's hand. 'I was dumb,' says the Psalmist, 'I opened not my 'mouth, because thou didst it,' Psal. xxxix. 5. Well! these evils are prevented by the frame in my text. There are also four real, positive blessings, which it procures. As,

First, It gives inward peace, be the burden or trial what it will, Psal. xxvii. 13. 'I had fainted 'unless I had believed to see the goodness of the 'Lord in the land of the living.' But this cheered him, this revived, composed, and settled him, that God would appear on his side, and right his cause against the many that breathed out cruelty, *ver.* 12. So Isa. xxvi. 3. 'Thou wilt keep him in perfect 'peace whose mind is stayed on thee, because he 'trusteth in thee.' There is nothing but peace at such a time, because he has a God to over-balance every trouble; trust enters into the secret of his heart, his thoughts are full of it; he no sooner allows himself to think, but he begins to trust, and stay himself upon his God, and there is enough in God to bear him up: Can a soul sink that has almightiness, everlasting strength and faithfulness to lean on? Who has a rock underneath him, which has born it out against all storms, and will never fail till everlasting life comes? Hence David prays, Psal. lxi. 2. 'When my heart is overwhelmed, lead me 'to the rock that is higher than I.' This gives perfect peace; let whatever trial come, though it may shake him, it does not unsettle him; 'his heart is 'fixed, trusting in the Lord.' O! how deep are his counsels, how wise his designs! 'His thoughts 'are not as our thoughts;' our thoughts are of yesterday, but his are of old, even 'from everlasting.' We see but some ruder sketches of his work, but

faith

faith throws a beauty upon thefe, becaufe it gives a fubfiftence to things hoped for, and a convincing demonftration, even of things as yet not feen. More of which under the next head. As for God, fays faith, his work is perfect, let him alone with his own work, his own caufe, it is in the beft of hands. What! fhall his gofpel drop, becaufe we fee a flower, which we thought would have been very beautiful and adorning in his church, fade? Yea, let God choofe for himfelf, that you may know he is God; he will lay afide an inftrument, we thought ready polifhed for his work, and choofe and fquare another which fhall do equal, it may be, more fervice. He will appear God in all things; believe all to be well, and amidft the moft diftreffing viciffitudes of Providence, your foul fhall be at reft. This is one bleffing arifing from the frame my text fpeaks of.

Secondly, It gives an enduring patience. 'Behold,' fays the apoftle, James v. 11. 'we count them happy which endure.' Whence arifes this endurance, this long-fuffering which is the crown of patience? Paul tells us, Rom. v. 3. 'We glory in tribulations alfo, knowing that tribulation worketh patience.' It is from a review of the bleffed iffue of all former trials: Tribulation has worked patience, all things have worked together for good, and that unthought of to us; and why fhould the ftream of God's everlafting love, or the tenor of his covenant be now turned backwards? Why muft our God ceafe to be JEHOVAH now, any more than heretofore? What new trial can be fo fhoking, as to unrivet our faith, our truft, and affiance in him? Seeing there is no trial new to God, no trial for which he did not lay by fupport and comfort for us, according to his own purpofe and grace, which was given us in Chrift before the world began. Everlafting ftrength; what burden is fo heavy as to deprefs that! Everlafting confolation; what trial fo great as to fuck up the fulnefs and fweetnefs of that! A covenant ordered in all things and fure; what ftrefs of forrow can make a confufion there! Our
Saviour

Saviour knew the virtue and good of patience, as well as his diſciples need of it, when he commanded them, Luke xxi. 19. ' In your patience poſſeſs ye ' your ſouls.' A man cannot poſſeſs himſelf without this, he is at the beck of every trial, every mere inconveniency in life has power to depreſs him, and to hurry him away from himſelf. O! whither does a poor ſoul fly when he forgets his God! he wanders from mountain to hill, and comes back juſt as he went, finds no reſting-place. A Chriſtian cannot enjoy himſelf, if he does not at the ſame time enjoy his God, becauſe the ſprings of patience are all hid in him, and there is no waiting patiently for the Lord, if there be not a believing that God does all things well. This frame begets enduring patience.

Thirdly, It creates in the ſoul living expectation, Iſa. viii. 17. ' I will wait upon the Lord that hi-' deth his face from the houſe of Jacob, and I will ' look for him.' It denotes not only the ſoul's willingneſs to ſtay God's time, but a bleſſed expectation of ſome great fruit of his faith and patience. " He will come at laſt, ſays the Chriſtian when in " this frame, and ſalvation is in his hand. Unto " the Lord our God belong the iſſues from death; " even his rod ſhall bud and bloſſom, and I am " looking out to ſee the return of my long prayers; " how it is God will ſanctify and ſweeten this af-" fliction, and make it turn to my ſoul's good. It " ſhall be well; I can ſee ſo much of God in the " appointing, ordering, continuing this trial, that " I am ſure the end will be peace. It ſhall be well, " if he removes his hand; it has been a pray'd mer-" cy, therefore come when it will, it will be ſweet. " It ſhall be well, if he continues the trial; I ſhall " loſe the more droſs, and my graces be purer and " fitter for exerciſe in the ſervice of an holy Lord " God. And it ſh.ll be well, if I am removed by " it, for, Lord, thy time is mine; ſo I get ſafe to " glory, thou ſhalt chooſe the way. O my gra-" cious God, always chooſe for me, and ſpare not
" the

"the rod for thy child's crying, though this frame
"should not always abide; I have now living, pre-
"cious, increasing comforts, and these are not gi-
"ven for nothing; why not die and go to heaven
"now, when my heart is there already! I can tri-
"umph in the Lord, and why should not my next
"work be to rejoice eternally in his presence."
This is the height of Christian expectation, and this
also flows from the frame in my text.

Fourthly, It begets in the soul settled praise and
thankfulness. The Christian is in a frame in every
thing to give thanks, as the Apostle directs, 1 Thess.
v. 18. Can bless a taking, as well as a giving God;
he is assured, 'All is well;' and were God to put
the question, Wherein wilt thou have it otherwise?
With all cheerfulness he would refer the matter
back again to him; would dare by no means to set
up for his own chooser. Brethren, look back and
you will find your frames have usually been sweetest, when your trials have been sorest; when tribulations abound, comfort abounds too: 'Persecuted,
'but not forsaken, cast down, but not destroyed.'
This holds good of every Christian; and communion
with Christ is an heaven upon earth; to enjoy him,
is to enjoy every thing. Hence Job blesses God in
the loss of all things, and our holy reformers sang
praises in the flames. Nothing terrified, nothing distressed them; they knew that they had in heaven a
God, a Christ, a mansion prepared; they saw all was
well, and they were satisfied, they were delighted;
'They were more than conquerors' (as the Apostle
speaks, Rom. viii. 37.) 'through him that loved them.'
O how sweet, how becoming is a praising frame!
'Whoso offereth praise glorifieth me,' Psal. l. 23. In
your most afflicted state there is foundation for praise,
and then there will be a frame for praise, when looking into God's providential dispensations, you can
say with this good woman in my text, 'It is well.'

Thus have I considered, as God has helped, the
blessed fruits and effects of this frame. And this
brings me to the last general head.

IV. Whence

IV. Whence it appears, that this submission to providential dispensations flows from faith, as being in lively and vigorous exercise. For the Apostle lays the ground of this blessed becoming frame in faith, as drawn into exercise by the Spirit of God, Heb. xi. 35. ' Through faith women received their ' dead raised to life again.'

Now this appears from the four following considerations.

1. It is by faith we are helped to take a view of unseen things. This is what supports and refreshes the Christian under dark dispensations, that ' he ' looks not at the things that are seen, but at the ' things which are not seen, for the things which ' are seen are temporal, but the things which are ' not seen are eternal,' 2 Cor. iv. 18. God's everlasting love and sure covenant; Christ the Mediator, Surety and Trustee of the covenant; the wisdom, power and faithfulness of a covenant-God; and the purchased possession when the end cometh; by these faith makes its mark, and takes its aim. The believer knows this world is a world of trial; he expects, and would be taking up his daily cross; but then he sees something better beyond it; all will be well when he gets above, and he is for having as much of the comfort and happiness of heaven as he can in his way to it: He therefore looks at eternal things, endeavours to keep his eye and his heart upon the blessed place, where his treasure is; his life is hid with Christ in God. Thus his affections are set on things above; and this quickens and enlivens his patience, when trials lie long and heavy upon him; it takes off the bitterness which there is in the cup of affliction; it is like the tree which was cast into the waters of *Marah* to make them sweet and wholesome, Exod. xv. 23. ' And they went three days in ' the wilderness and found no water, and when they ' came to Marah, they could not drink of the wa-' ters of Marah, for they were bitter.' Creature-expectations God usually disappoints; that blessing

of

of which the Christian is ready to say, as Lamech did of his son Noah, Gen. v. 29. 'This same shall 'comfort us concerning our work, and toil of our 'hands;' there is the most bitterness, vexation and disappointment in. But when God is pleased to lead the soul higher, and to fix his hope and expectation upon himself, who is the living and unchangeable God, this infinitely preponderates and weighs down creature-crosses and comforts too. But what is it that gives us a sight of these distant and better things? Why, this is faith, Heb. xi. 1. 'Now 'faith is the substance of things hoped for, the evi- 'dence of things not seen.' Hope looks to future good things; for what a man seeth, why doth he yet hope for! but faith gives them a present subsistence; it mixes itself with the promise, and thereby tastes the goodness, experiences the power of it, and receives the first-fruits of promised blessings. Abraham saw Christ's day and rejoiced, because faith gave a present subsistence of it in Abraham's apprehension and judgment. There was as great a reality in it to Abraham's faith, as if he had lived in John Baptist's time; and accordingly there were suitable actings of his soul about it, 'he was glad.' Faith substantiates things unseen, it brings distant things near, and gives such an evidence, such a demonstration of them, as carries with it an answer to all objections to the contrary: It silences every objection of unbelief; so that the soul rests upon them, casts anchor on them, 'which anchor is both sure 'and stedfast,' because 'it enters into that within 'the vail,' Heb. vi 19. It keeps a man from being blown about with every wind or storm that rises. Faith it is which helps the believer to view unseen things, and hence it is the ground of his acquiescing and approving of all that God does as well done.

2. Faith it is that stills and composes the soul in every dispensation, because it shews it the blessed fruits and effects of all past trials. Faith is the believer's best remembrancer, when it is drawn into exercise by the Spirit of God. Thus Asaph speaks

when he comes a little to himself. Pſal. lxxvii. 10. 'And I ſaid, This is my infirmity: but I will re-member the years of the right hand of the Moſt High.' Before it was, 'I remembered God, and was troubled, I complained, and my ſpirit was o-verwhelmed,' ver. 3. But when faith revives, that ſets all to rights again, ver. 11. 'I will remember the works of the Lord, ſurely I will remember thy wonders of old. I will meditate alſo of all thy work, and talk of thy doings. Thy way, O God, is in the ſanctuary: who is ſo great a God as our God?' I will ſee whether I cannot find help given in a like extremity; whether there is nothing in my experience to match it; God's right hand hath done wonders, and his hand is not ſhortened that it cannot ſave. 'In the mount of the Lord it hath been ſeen.' I have been able to put an *hitherto* at the end of every diſtreſs and trial; 'hitherto the Lord hath helped me;' and ſhall I ever have occaſion to alter? I am well perſuaded it will never be, that I ſhall have occaſion to ſay, "He hath left me, he hath forſaken me." Pſal. lxxi. 18. 'When I am old and gray-headed, O God, for-ſake me not.' I cannot ſee thy path, but I ſhall ſoon glory in thy work. Thou leddeſt thy people like a flock, by the hand of Moſes and Aaron.

This is a great ground of patience and ſubmiſſion to the will of God, what God *hath* done; and this ſhould come oftener into our meditations, when we are looking on our preſent difficulties and trials of faith. Forgetfulneſs is a ſin, which eaſily beſets God's choiceſt ſaints; their need of paſt trials, their help under them, the bleſſed fruits and effects which have attended them, theſe are ſoon forgotten: But faith brings them to remembrance, it leads a Chriſtian far back, and ſo helps him to ſay of all God does, 'It is well' done.

This brings us to a third particular; but that, with what remains, muſt be left to the next opportunity.

SERMON XXIV.

FAITH'S ESTIMATE OF AFFLICTIVE DISPENSATIONS.

2 KINGS iv. 26.

—— *And she answered, It is well.*

THE doctrinal observation from these words is this:

OBSERV. Faith in God's promises and power, will bring a man to submit to the sorest and most trying dispensations of his Providence. Or thus,

Faith, when it is in lively exercise, will teach a Christian to say of all God does, 'It is well.'

In discoursing on this observation, I have shewn,

First, What submission is, and with what limitation this *well* in my text is to be understood.

Secondly, What are the grounds of this submission, or whence it is the soul thinks and says of all God does, that 'It is well' done.

Thirdly, What are the blessed fruits and effects of this submission, or what benefits redound to a believer, what glory to God, when he is enabled to think and say of all God does, 'It is well' done.

And I told you here, that there are some evils it prevents, and some real positive blessings it procures.

The evils it prevents are these four: Rash conclusions, sinful staggerings, immoderate sorrow, and heartless complaints. The blessings it procures, are inward peace, enduring patience, living expectations, and cheerful praise and thankfulness.

Fourthly, Whence it appears, that this submission to providential dispensations flows from faith, as being in lively and vigorous exercise.

This appears from the four following considerations:

1. It is by faith we are helped to take a view of unseen things.

2. It is faith which brings to remembrance the blessed fruits and effects of all past trials. So far we have gone; now to proceed.

3. It farther appears, that submission flows from faith, because this it is which leads the soul to God, and fetches strength from him under every new trial and emergency; there is no living upon past frames or past mercies; a *receiving* life is what every believer lives: 'And of his fulness have all we re-'ceived, and grace for grace,' John i. 16. There must be a daily coming to Christ for grace to help in time of need: 'To whom coming, as to a living 'stone, disallowed indeed of men, but chosen of 'God, and precious,' 1 Pet. ii. 4. to him coming for support, strength, subsistence; faith is one continued act in the soul, it is our daily, our hourly work; our life is in another, not in ourselves; and how is this life maintained? even as animal life is, by spiritual communications from Christ, who is the bread of life, and the rock who gives us drink, following us in the wilderness for this very end, 1 Cor. x. 3, 4. 'And did all eat the same spiritual meat, and did 'all drink the same spiritual drink: for they drank 'of that spiritual rock that followed them, and that 'rock was Christ.' All the grace his elect should need to the end of time, was put into his hands as their covenant-head, and he was made trustee for it, 2 Tim. i. 9. 'Who hath saved, and called us with 'an holy calling, not according to our works, but
'according

' according to his own purpose and grace, which
' was given us in Christ Jesus, before the world be-
' gan.' Faith it is that receives that grace from
Christ, whether it be pardon, righteousness, preparation for duty, strength under trials and temptations, peace, comfort, and the like. The Spirit
shews the believer first what his needs are, and then
directs him to Christ for the supply of them; faith
takes hold of, receives and applies what Christ gives,
and so feeds, supports and sustains the soul. Hence
the same things that are spoken of Christ are applied to faith, Gal. ii. 20. ' I am crucified with
' Christ, nevertheless I live, yet not I, but Christ
' liveth in me: and the life I now live in the flesh,
' I live by the faith of the Son of God, who loved
' me, and gave himself for me.' Never can we say,
' All is well,' when faith sinks; No! Then " All
" these things are against me." There must be a
revival before it comes to this. You know how it
was of old with Elisha's servant, 2 Kings vi. 15.
The king of Syria sends horses and chariots, a very
great host, to fetch the prophet; he found nothing
was to be done against Israel while he was there;
when the poor servant sees this, he was greatly distressed, and cries out " Alas, my master, how shall
" we do!" he thought of nothing but destruction,
till God opened his eyes, and then he saw a mountain full of horses and chariots of fire round about
them. So faith, when it sees God for us, God with
us, it bids defiance to the whole world; what are
trials, crosses, disappointments, when God lives, and
God is ours? They are ordered by him, and by him
shall they be over-ruled: His covenant-love and
faithfulness are the same now they ever were. Soul!
there is mercy laid by against this trial; the end of
it is peace; ' the God of all peace will stablish, and
' strengthen, and settle thee.' There is a ' rock
' that is higher than thee;' the foundation of God
standeth sure; thou wantest nothing but thy Lord
hath it to give, and ' he will withhold no good
' thing from him that walketh uprightly.' There

is grace laid up in Christ for every emergency; this faith receives, and thereby is a farther ground of patience and submission under every trial.

4. It appears that submission is grounded on *faith*, because it is that which teaches a Christian to abide by the promise when all promised supply fails. Thus says Jacob, when he was in danger of falling into the hands of an angry brother with four hundred men, 'Thou saidst, I will surely do thee good,' Gen. xxxii. 12. He had nothing to fly to but the promise; but that was hold enough, because that takes hold of God, the great, the faithful, the holy God: It is God's word, his word of grace; and grace, you know, is his darling attribute, the Lord God, gracious and merciful, abundant in goodness and truth; and thou 'saidst, I will surely do thee 'good.' The best thing we can say to God, is what he hath first said to us; promises are the sweetest grounds of hope, the sweetest pleas in prayer; God that knows all his purposes and designs, that knows how far his promise goes, God Almighty that can do all he hath promised, the true God, he that cannot lie, hath spoken it, who will therefore do what he hath said. O, says the soul, the promises will bring forth, the vision is for an appointed time; I do but credit God, and he is a tried God; it shall be well; mercy shall be built up for ever, though it does not yet appear to view, for 'all the ways of 'the Lord are mercy and truth, unto such as keep 'his covenant and testimonies,' Psal. xxv. 10. Hence Joshua pleads as Jacob did, Josh. vii. 9. 'O Lord, 'what shall I say, when Israel turneth their backs 'before their enemies! What wilt thou do unto thy 'great name?' Who can secure the glory of that, but himself only? But he is a God that *keepeth* covenant and mercy; surely then he will not lay it aside, he keeps it to shew it forth, to make it known; sooner or later, help will come: however, says faith, should it not come, I will die trusting. Hence said the three children, Dan. iii. 17, 18. ' Our God whom
' we

'we serve, is able to deliver us from the burning
' fiery furnace, and he will deliver us out of thy
' hand, O king; but if not, be it known unto thee,
' O king, that we will not serve thy gods.' If a
doubt may be made of this particular deliverance,
we will still perfevere in a courfe of duty; the Lord
he is God, and ' his name is a ftrong tower, the
' righteous runneth into it and is fafe,' Prov. xviii.
10. Thither, fays the foul, will I flee; if God cannot, or if he will not fave, I am ready to perifh;
elfewhere I cannot, I will not look, for ' this God
' is my falvation, and though he flay me, yet will I
' truft in him.' Faith hangs on the promife, and
fo it helps to fubmiffion.

Thus have we gone through the feveral things
propofed from the words; what remains is the ufe
and improvement of the fubject, in doing which, I
fhall confine myfelf chiefly to this fingle inquiry.

QUERY. What confiderations and directions are
there, which may be of ufe under the aids of the
Spirit, in order to our obtaining this bleffed frame
my text fpeaks of?

ANSWER. Firft judge nothing before the time.
When the end cometh, pafs a judgment on providential difpenfations; not before. Pfal. cvii. 43.
' Whofo is wife and will obferve thefe things, even
' they fhall underftand the loving-kindnefs of the
' Lord.' David's hafte might have coft him dear,
Pfal. cxvi. 11. ' I faid in my hafte, all men are
' liars.' " Samuel and all are liars, I fhall never ob-
" tain the kingdom, I fhall now perifh by the hand
" of Saul." It was well God did not take him at
his word, as he refufed to credit God. God works
often above means, fometimes without them; nay
fometimes contrary to them: But it is a fettled rule
with him, which every believer has found true in
experience, namely, ' He led them forth by the
' right way, that they might go to a city of habita-
' tion.' There may appear fome flaws at prefent;
but there will be none in the end, it will appear to
be

be the *right* way. Wherefore 'humble yourselves 'in the sight of the Lord, and he shall lift you up,' James iv. 10. Humbling providences are sweetest in the end, for they bring a man to himself; and till a man be thoroughly emptied of self, he can never, as he ought, improve Christ. What though God bereave you of children, friends, substance, health, ' All is well.' There is no empty, void space, but what he himself fills up. Surely, says one, " He dieth oft whose life is bound up in the dying " creature; as oft as the creature fails, his hope " fails, his heart fails; when the creature dieth, his " hope giveth up the ghost." He only lives an unchangeable life, that by faith can live on an unchangeable God. Do not say what his end is, till you see it. Many a saint has eat his own words for want of this: Psal. xxxi. 22. ' I said in my haste, ' I am cut off from before thine eyes; nevertheless ' thou heardst the voice of my supplications, when ' I cried unto thee.' These hasty speeches are seldom right ones.

Secondly, Bring the promise and a promising God close together; whatever be the promise, consider he is faithful that hath promised; all intervening difficulties should be viewed in the light of the promise. What is that? Why, ' all things are yours, ' and all things work together for good.' We *need* our crosses as well as our comforts. Are we ' through ' many tribulations to enter the kingdom?' Then we must have these tribulations ere we possess it. Abraham, you have heard, staggered not at the promise through unbelief: ' He against hope believed ' in hope;' he left out all *buts*, and *whys*, and *ifs;* he had God's word of promise, and he knew God's arm of power, and also that he ' was faithful, who ' had promised;' that is enough; but we shall never say, ' All is well,' till God's promise and faithfulness are brought close together. Faith sets all difficulties aside, removes them out of the way, never considering them but in the light of the promise.

Thirdly,

Thirdly, Confider the *grace* and *order* of the covenant, 2 Sam. xxiii. 5. 'He hath made with me 'an everlafting covenant, ordered in all things and 'fure.' Every thing is wifely adjufted there; the fending of trials, as well as the removal of them, come under the covenant and promife: 'My covenant,' fays God, 'will I not break, nor alter the 'thing that is gone out of my lips,' Pfal. lxxxix. 34. What that was, you have in *ver.* 30, 31. 'If his 'children forfake my law, and walk not in my judgments,' &c. 'then will I vifit their tranfgreffions 'with the rod, and their iniquity with ftripes.' And the Chriftian, when faith is in exercife, would have it fo, would have every crofs and every trial; 'that patience may have her perfect work, and be 'entire, lacking nothing.' Give me, faid the prodigal, all the portion of goods that falleth to my fhare; the believer would have the fame thing, though he afks it for different ends. 'Therefore 'behold,' fays God, 'I will allure her, and bring 'her into the wildernefs, and fpeak comfortably 'unto her,' Hof. i. 14. but wildernefs-frames attend wildernefs-difpenfations, and they are fweet frames: The duty of fome fore vifitations has been to many the time of fpecial love: There is 'a time to fa-'vour Zion,' a feafon of mercy, be it a time of affliction, adverfity, temptation, or whatever elfe, all *is well;* the covenant ftands fure, and everlafting love runs through every trial which befals you. Firft, blefs God for the grace of the covenant, and then for the order of it.

Fourthly, Weigh your fins and your mercies together, before you look at any of your trials. Never think of your fufferings, but at the fame time think of your fins; afflictions will fit light, where fin fits heavy. You will find then, that you have finned away this comfort, and over-loved the other bleffings, have abufed God's mercy, and ftood in need of his rod; for he does not afflict willingly, nor grieve the children of men; whatever be the temptation or affliction there is a need of it: And then have

have we no mercies under our strong temptations and sore trials? The Church upon consideration found it thus, Lam. iii. 23. Though God had written bitter things against her in righteousness; it 'is 'of the Lord's mercies we are not consumed, because his compassions fail not.' No trial is so grievous and bitter but it might have been worse.

Fifthly, Be much in the actings of present faith. Thou losest a child, a friend, a husband, or wife; but thou hast not lost thy God: Psal. xciv. 19. ' In ' the multitude of my thoughts within me, thy com- ' forts delight my soul.' " As much confusion as I " have within, I have comfort when I look above; " my thoughts are dark and doleful, intricate and " perplexing, and there is a multitude of them that " break in upon me, as if they would swallow me " up; but thy comforts are life, and light, and de- " light to my soul; my thoughts do not sink me " so deep, but thy comforts are a heaven to me." ' It is well.' God hath said, ' Leave thy father- ' less children, I will preserve them alive, and let ' thy widows trust in me,' Jer. xlix. 11. If they are God's care, they shall be well provided for. He that feedeth the ravens and clotheth the lilies, will he be less kind and bountiful to thee? ' The earth ' is the Lord's, and the fulness thereof, the world, ' and they that dwell therein,' Psal. xxiv. 1. Every heart is at God's disposal; rather than his poor shall want bread, God will feed them from their enemies table. You have a certain promise, God hath given his word, and there is no exception to it: Psal. xxxvii. 3. ' Trust in the Lord and do good, so shalt ' thou dwell in the land, and verily thou shalt be ' fed.' I had rather, says one, have God's *amen*, his *verily*, than a promise from all the princes and potentates of the world; if God has said it, it shall be well. Be much then in the actings of present faith; believe for this trial, believe to day; put not off till you see how things will go, that is to *know*, not to *trust*. Faith brings down general promises to a man's own particular case and circumstances: 'I will never leave thee nor forsake thee,' Heb. xiii. 5. "There is the promise;" says faith, "Lord, I trust in thee, I credit thee upon that word of thine; I am poor, but the poor committeth himself to thee; I am a widow and desolate as to outward comforts, but I trust in God." The Lord 'thy maker is thy husband, and fear not,' nor 'be dismayed, for he will help and uphold thee;' it is as easy for God to help me in these distressing circumstances as in any other. Thou art the holy One of Israel, and all thy saints have born testimony to thy faithfulness and truth; Lord, shall I be an exception? sure thou 'wilt not fail me;' I feel thou hast not; my 'cup is sweetened by thy presence and love, 'thou 'strengthenest me with strength in my soul.' I will believe, Lord, 'I do believe, help my unbelief;' it *is well*, Lord, it *is well*. Present faith must be acted when present trials come, and God, where he gives a promise, gives faith also to lay hold of it.

Sixthly, Be much in prayer. Prayer calls in God's help; almightiness itself can never be worsted; this was David's first and last refuge, and every saint has found it his best refuge: Psal. cxxxviii. 3. 'In the day 'when I cried thou answeredst me, and strengthenedst 'me with strength in my soul.' Prayer brought in God, and God brought in strength, and by this the Psalmist got the better of all his distempers and fears. It is said of Luther, "Whatever opposition he found, whatever "distemper in his mind, or distraction in his soul, "he presently carried it to the throne, and never "gave over praying, till he prayed his heart into "the frame he prayed for." Jacob, you know, got the blessing, but how? Why, he wrestled for it till break of day; that is, as the prophet explains it, Hos. xii. 4. 'He wept, and made supplication unto him.' He was importunate in his request, could take no denial from the blessed Jesus, but put in one plea, then another, till he had power over him, and came away a prevailer. Prayer sets every dispensation in a sweet light, because it brings in strength from God to the soul, whereby it is helped to wait to the end of it; when our eye and heart are up to God, fixed upon him, all *is well*. Be much in prayer, carry your difficulties, temptations, fears, unbelief to God, and leave them with him. Once more,

Seventhly, Be frequent in thoughts of heaven, your rest, your home, where all your sorrows will have a full end. 'There remaineth a rest for the 'people of God:' every one of our sorrows takes off one from the account; we are one step the nearer to glory; the same trial is not to come over again; and 'blessed are the dead which die in the 'Lord from henceforth; yea, saith the Spirit, for 'they rest from their labours,' Rev. xiv. 13. Christian! you shall rest from your labours soon; there is a heaven above, and the hope of it comforts and delights you here; it is well, it must be so, 'In thy 'presence there is fulness of joy, at thy right hand 'there are pleasures for ever more,' Psal. xvi. 11. and heaven will make you amends for every thing. What a blessed reckoning Paul made, and do not you account it so too? Rom. viii. 18. 'I reckon 'that the sufferings of this present time are not 'worthy to be compared with the glory which 'shall be revealed in us.' And you have them, not all at once; God proportions 'your day to 'your strength,' it is but here a little, and there a little, 'as you are able to bear it;' you have a wise and gracious God, which orders and over-rules all that concerns you; hitherto he hath done all things well, and he will perfect that which concerneth you.

These considerations are of use to beget and keep alive in the Christian this frame my text speaks of.

Two cautions upon the whole, and I have done.

CAUTION I. Do not think this great and sweet lesson is to be learnt at once. God teaches his children, as you do yours, by little and little, somewhat this week, and more the next, somewhat by this affliction,

affliction, more by another; and as our crosses, so neither do our comforts come all as once; the fruit of affliction is not gathered presently, Heb. xii. 11. 'Now no chastening for the present seemeth to be 'joyous, but grievous; nevertheless, afterward it 'yieldeth the peaceable fruit of righteousness to 'them that are exercised thereby.' The fruit is not gathered presently, it must have a ripening time; faith must be tried before it will come out precious as gold does out of the fire. Do not expect to learn this lesson at once, 'It is well.' Such knowledge and attainment is the fruit of long experience and observation.

CAUTION 2. Do not expect, if you are able to use the language in my text now, that you shall do it with the same ease and comfort always. 'Abra-'ham staggered not at the promise of God through 'unbelief,' when he received the tidings of a son; but it should seem afterwards he doubted it, when he went in unto Hagar. 'My mountain stands strong,' says David; but let 'God hide his face,' and immediately David 'is troubled.' A Christian is flesh as well as spirit. We hear not only of Job's patience, but of his impatience too. Observe it, we usually read of the failure of the saints in that grace for which they were the most eminent: The reason is this, to shew that no man is to be trusted in, no not to trust himself, or his own heart. A settled even frame of hope and trust, few Christians maintain here. When we come to be with God, we shall walk by *sight*, now we walk by *faith*, and this faith is often weak, therefore the Christian's trust often fails. But though moved he is, he shall never be removed; though he fall, he shall never fail; this is the foundation of every Christian's hope. O that it were more the rejoicing of his hope. May God the Spirit enable us so to do.

So much for this subject.

SERMON XXV.

GOD'S CHARGE AND CALL TO A BACK-SLIDING PEOPLE.

MALACHI iii. 7.

Even from the days of your fathers ye have gone away from mine ordinances, and have not kept them: Return unto me, and I will return unto you, saith the Lord of Hosts: But ye said, Wherein shall we return?

THERE are three things contained in these words, which well suit our times, and the occasion of our meeting together this day[*].

First, A charge or an accusation brought by God against his professing people: 'Even from the days ' of your fathers,' &c. All sin is a going away from God's ordinances, or a breach of his law. Whatsoever things God has described or constituted, let them regard his own worship, or our walk, man is to observe, keep and adhere to. The word is general, and relates to every thing which is appointed and commanded of God. 'Gone away ' from them,' supposes guilt 'contracted' by the commission of known sins: 'Not kept them,' implies the omission or neglect of known duties. To omit known duties, God construes as a commission of known sins; or else the people's sin is aggravated,

because

[*] This Sermon was preached on a fast day, October 31. 1745.

because they not only did not keep God's ordinances, but made nothing of them, trampled them under their feet, accounting it a vain thing to serve him; and this their sin of long continuance, 'even 'from the days of your fathers.' The longer a nation, or a professing people, lies in sin, the more provoking sin is, and the nearer such a nation and people is to ruin: God's patience will not last always. But 'for himself,' for 'his own name's sake,' they had been consumed before now. Nothing but pure mercy and sovereign grace could have kept them from ruin; 'even from the days,' &c. Neither example, custom, prescription, or antiquity, are pleas available for the excuse of any sin. This is God's charge against Israel.

Secondly, There is a solemn exhortation made to them, backed with an alluring motive: 'Return 'unto me, and I will return unto you.' God promises mercy, when he might execute judgment: 'Return unto me.' Sin turns a man backwards, it sets him in a way where God never walks: Repentance is that which sets the creature right again, with his face towards God, so that all his desires and expectations are from him. And turning to God's ordinances is turning to him, because his name is in them; nor will he be found by any soul in a way of favour and mercy, who neglects to seek him in a way of duty. The motive with which our return to God is backed, is God's return unto us, 'Return unto me.' Without some hope of mercy sinners would flee from God, not return unto him. 'I will return unto you;' not that God is far from any of us as to his immensity; he is in all places and fills all things: But then in scripture sense, God is said to return when he shews his face and favour which sin has hid; when he pardons, accepts, and blesses his people, and gives them special tokens of his reconciliation and love. It is as sweet to have God our friend, as it is dreadful to have him for an enemy.

enemy. He can arm the whole creation to save, or to destroy us.

Thirdly, In the words there is the people's reply: 'But ye said,' &c. This answer was either in words; then the import of them is, shew us wherein we have offended; we are not conscious of guilt, therefore we are not afraid of judgments. The deeper men are sunk in sin, the harder usually are they brought to conviction; none are nearer to a reprobate sense, than such as make a jest of the threatnings of the word, and who think lightly of awful, impending judgments.—Or else this was the language of their hearts and lives. Sin was loved in the heart, and held fast in the conversation, notwithstanding the repeated warnings which God sent them by his word and by his providence. God knows what are the returns of our hearts to the calls of his word; fasting and outward humiliation, without repentance and reformation, is but to say, as in our text, 'Wherein shall we return?'

Thus much may suffice for the opening of the words; would to God they were a less just description of all our hearts and all our frames: God has been calling us by his word, by his providence, by his mercies, by his judgments, for these six or seven years past, to return unto him: At first, England was but a looker-on, in that confusion and desolation which has been in other countries; now * she is become herself the seat of war and bloodshed: We are now threatned with the loss of our liberties, properties, laws, and the glorious gospel of the grace of God; and there is but one way left to retrieve them; it has been pointed too often, but as soon as heard of, neglected and forgetten: Sin is still kept in our bowels; every one of us have dealt too gently by this Sheba: It is this which ruins states, destroys kingdoms, and brings all that ravage and confusion

we

---

* The rebels at this time had defeated his Majesty's forces at Preston-pans, were in possession of Edinburgh, and daily expected to come forward.

we see in the earth. Here we are this day to begin our confessions against it, to unite with all our forces; and the more cursory and superficial has been our repentance heretofore, to see that it be the more sincere now.

Wrath we have deserved; but my text, if duly regarded, speaks peace; which, that I may open in some way suited to the present solemnity, as God shall help, I would endeavour the five following things.

I. Shew wherein we have gone away from God as a professing people and land.

II. How must our return to him be.

III. The blessings which will be in his return to us.

IV. Why he will not return to us, but in the way of our return to him.

V. In whom this vile frame mentioned in my text, is found; and so apply.

I. To enquire wherein we have gone away from God.

1. We have gone away from his truth. There has been a most dreadful itch after novelty, in the ears of many, concerning whom we hoped that their hearts were established with grace: And as to the generality of professors in the land, they scarce know what are the foundation-doctrines of the gospel, or what were the pillars of the Reformation. The doctrine of God's eternal election, the efficacy of grace in the regeneration and conversion of sinners, justification by the imputed righteousness of Christ, the perseverance of the saints in grace and holiness, our forefathers would not suffer a doubt about them; they were ' great without controversy:' Whereas, now the Godhead of Christ is denied; the personality of the Spirit is derided; and the authority of the scriptures, in many books, questioned even by some who call themselves Protestant Dissenters.

Thofe blefled truths, whereon the faith, the comfort, and hope of the faints reft, they are either too heavy, too common, too high and myfterious, fomething or other is difpleafing in them; men choofe to have water mixed with their wine; unadulterated truth, in many places, is unacceptable; it is grown fashionable to be wavering and unfettled as to doctrinals: But what fays our bleffed Lord? 'He that is not 'with me, is againft me.' Paul commands us to hold faft the faithful word againft thofe that would pull it away from us; and 'we are to contend ear-' neftly for the faith once delivered to the faints, Jude, ver. 3. In labouring to preferve the gofpel, you contend not for your own rights only, but God's, for what Chrift fhed his blood; for that which will bear its own charges; for a treafure that will abide with you when all other things leave you, and will make death and judgment precious. 'I have kept 'the faith,' faid bleffed Paul, 'henceforth there is 'laid up for me a crown of righteoufnefs, 2 Tim. iv. 7. It was a good faying of Luther's, "*Spiritus* "*fanctus non eft fcepticus*, God's holy Spirit doth not "lead to fcepticifm and uncertainties in matters of "faith." The more of God's Spirit, the greater affurance of underftanding to the acknowledgment of the myftery of God, even the Father, and of Chrift. We are gone away from God's truth.

2. As a profeffing people, we are gone away from his worfhip.

Primitive faints 'continued ftedfaftly in the A-' poftles doctrine and fellowfhip, and in breaking of 'bread, and in prayers,' Acts ii. 42. They could redeem many an hour in the week days, for godly conference and prayer; we can fcarce give God his own day, without bringing fome of our work or pleafure into it. Journeys, relations, new habitations, and bufineffes in life, all of them were begun and fanctified by prayer: Now families profeffing godlinefs are prayerlefs, unlefs one evening out of feven, or under fome fore affliction. Members of
churches

churches are unacquainted with the rules of fellowship, and would be ignorant even of the stated times of assembling together to commemorate the Lord's death, were they not given notice of in the public congregation.

There is a weariness of ordinances, and those that are purest are most burdensome: And look into the land, how full are the fields, how empty the sanctuary? Fasts and days of humiliation are become a ridicule; and it is thought a damp upon mens spirits, and a betraying our fears as a nation, when times are appointed for general confession of sin and for prayer.

3. We are gone away from our trust and confidence in God. God alone is not exalted in the soul. It is a complaint every one may bring against himself, Jer. ii. 13. ' They have forsaken me, the foun-
' tain of living waters, and hewed them out cisterns,
' broken cisterns, that can hold no water.' The counsels of men, the power and success of armies, the assistance of confederates; here have our hearts been, and God has been too little in all our thoughts. At other times we have trusted in friends; delighted in frames; made saviours of our past experiences, evidences, graces: Any thing naturally we had rather live by, than by pure faith. Sin is nothing else but a turning from one creature to another, to seek contentment and sufficiency short of God: Search thy life, soul! sift thy frames, and it will appear that thou hast been doing little else. The life of most, could it be obtained, would rather be of sense than of faith. Reeds of Egypt are rather chosen than the rock of ages.

4. We are gone away from God in conversation. Faith is nothing without fruit, nor gospel truth without gospel holiness: What our blessed Lord died for, was ' to redeem from sin,' not to give a licence to live *in* it. There's no walking with God, but by walking in Christ; and ' he that abideth in Christ,
' the same bringeth forth much fruit,' John xv. 5.

Are thy thoughts spiritual, thy speech savoury, thy mind and disposition heavenly, and thy outward behaviour without offence? Such are the fruits of the Spirit, and without them there is no walking with God. To walk in the ways of deceit, pride, oppression, uncleanness, this is to live without God, to walk like men, who know nothing of the truth as it is in Jesus. It is in the nature of truth to sanctify and cleanse the soul, John xvii. 17. O! it argues great declension in the churches, when the customs, conversations, and ways of the world allure and please them; when they can call upon God's name at one time, and take it in vain at another; can go with the saints on the Sabbath, and with sinners to places of sinful diversions in the week; can take Christ for their Saviour, and make Mammon their God; profess to walk in love when they sit at the Lord's table, and have little else but wrath and clamour at their own.

II. How must our return to him be?

1. *With deep humiliation.*—Sense of sin will beget sorrow and shame for it: 'Ephraim shall say, 'What have I to do any more with idols?' Hosea xiv. 8. When God touches the heart, sin will become the greatest burden we ever felt. It is easy confessing sin by rote; but to confess sin so as to feel the guilt of it, to see its filthiness and defilement, to have an apprehension of the holiness of God against which it is committed, and the dreadful wrath which it hath deserved, this is hard work. We are come this day to take part with the justice of God against ourselves; though justice be satisfied by Christ, God will have it owned and acknowledged by us. Benhadad's servants crept upon their knees, and fell prostrate at Ahab's feet, when they came but to ask the life of their bodies: We come to ask the life of our souls, the life of three kingdoms; the life and power of the gospel, and every thing that is dear and precious to us as men and Christians: O! how low should we lie, what an abhorrence of ourselves,

selves, what an indignation against sin, what affecting thoughts of the patience and long-suffering of God should there be here! It is just in God to destroy us, to give us up, to remove his candlestick out of his place; to make that nation our scourge, whom we have been following in its fashions and lusts; to bring the cruelty of Popish discipline upon us, when so many have paved the way so near to it in doctrine. Our return to God must be with deep humiliation.

2. With real reformation. God's anger is increased by *mock-turns*. We all declaim against the evil of the times, and too much continue the practices. It is one thing to confess sin with our mouths, and another thing to cast it out of our hearts. Our prayer should not be the voice of nature for ease, but of the Spirit for grace. First, pray that God would heal our land, and then, that he would save it.

Diseases are best cured at the root. Should the judgment we fear be removed, while sin remains, it would not be removed in mercy. Sense of danger begets speed and haste; sin and you cannot part soon enough. Think, God's hand is lifted up; the sword is drawn to avenge the quarrel of his covenant: Shall I linger when judgments make haste? 'That which I know not, Lord teach me; and 'wherein I have done evil may I do it no more. 'Look unto Jesus;' all strength and grace is in him; the 'author of your faith' will be 'the finisher of 'it.' Christ never yet did this work by halves. Our return to God, &c.

3. It should be with an eye to the blood of Christ: 'Without faith it is impossible to please God.' No mercy is to be expected for ourselves, or for our land, but through the satisfaction and intercession of our Lord Jesus Christ. The blessed Jesus in his person and righteousness, is the only meeting-place for lost and destroyed sinners. We read, Acts xii. 20. that 'when Herod was displeased with the men of Tyre 'and Sidon, they came with one accord unto him, 'and having made Blastus the king's chamberlain 'their friend, desired peace, because their country

'was nourished by the king's country.' This is our case; God is highly displeased with a sinful land, a degenerate church, and a backsliding people. What shall we do? Our country is nourished by the king's country; we cannot subsist without God, a God of Covenant and of Grace, as a church, or as particular believers: Therefore we come now to beg peace. Have we no friend in heaven, great with God? That has a name and interest of his own to use with the Father? Yea; we have. Christ and his blood are ever before the throne; he stands, as a Lamb that had been slain, both to receive our prayers, and avenge our enemies.—Jacob wrestled with the angel and prevailed, held God by his own strength. Christ alone can secure our souls and our land. This return, &c.

This leads me to shew in the third place,

III. The blessing which is in God's return to us. When God comes to a land or people, good comes with him; more particularly,

1. He comes with grace to pardon. 'Who is a 'God like unto thee, that pardoneth iniquity?' God can as easily forgive the sins of a land, as of a single soul; the vast ocean overfloweth both the lowest sands and the highest rocks: Pardoning grace removes smaller prevarications and grosser abominations. 'Take away all iniquity, and receive us gra- 'ciously,' Hos. xiv. 2. The blood of Christ washes out the foulest stains, and speaks good things to the chief of sinners. There were some sins under the law, that were capital; there was no being justified from them by ceremonial rites; but through the faith of Christ, 'all manner of sin and blasphemy 'shall be forgiven unto men.' Where God covers one sin, he covers all; scatters them as the rising sun does a mist or a cloud, so that in a way of vengeance and wrath there shall be no appearance of them more. Where God comes to a people or land, he comes with grace to pardon: 'Thou hast played the
'harlot

'harlot with many lovers, yet return unto me, faith
' the Lord,' Jer. iii. 1.

2. Where God returns to a people or land, he comes with grace to sanctify and renew. ' I will be ' as the dew unto Israel,' Hof. xiv. 5. No barren ordinances, nor barren hearts, where God is. God's Spirit, is ' a Spirit of grace and supplications,' Zech. xii. 10. He directs to pray, and supplies those requests, and satisfies those desires which himself dictates; and God has promised to pour him forth upon the house of Judah, and upon the inhabitants of Jerusalem. The great men and the common people shall both share in his gracious operations and influences; magistrates, ministers, parents, children, servants; there shall be a revival amongst all ranks and degrees of men. We think it a great blessing to have a revival in our own hearts, a revival in Christ's churches; but when God indeed returns to a people, he will heal their land. ' Then will I re-' turn to the people a pure language, that they may ' call upon the name of the Lord with one consent,' Zeph. iii. 9. God comes with grace to sanctify and renew.

3. When God returns to a people or land, he comes with power and strength to save and deliver. The presence of God with a people is the greatest terror and disappointment to their enemies that rise against them. ' I will be unto her a wall of fire ' round about, and the glory in the midst of her,' Zech. ii. 5. He will both keep off the enemy from an invasion or attack, and comfort and chear his people under their fears of it. Many may be against us, to *hate* us; but if God be with us, none can be against us to *hurt* us. Let France and Rome say with Pharoah of old, " I will pursue, I will overtake, I " will divide the spoil, my lust shall be satisfied up-" on them:" Let but our God return to us, they shall be broken; their counsels shall not stand; their decrees shall come to nought; and in the thing wherein they deal proudly, God will shew himself

above

above them. If there be *any* help or comfort against danger, in earth or heaven, God can command it: All his hosts are at his beck, he leads them forth when and where he pleases; if there be *none* he can *create* it. 'His eyes run through the whole earth, 'to shew himself strong in the behalf of him whose 'heart is perfect towards him,' 2 Chron. xvi. 9. God comes to a people, &c.

4. When God returns to a people or land, he comes with love to delight in them.—'Thy land 'shall be called Hephzibah, my delight is in her:' The heaven that believers enjoy here, lies in a gracious fellowship and intercourse between God and their own souls. It is sweet to be let into God's secrets, to be feasted with his fat things, to be taken into his banqueting house, and to see love, as a banner, under which every thing that befals us must pass. This is a blessing which attends God's return unto us.—But I pass on,

IV. Why God will not return unto us, but in the way of our return unto him.

It does not suppose any thing meritorious in the obedience of the creature; nor yet that the blessings of grace are suspended upon the condition of duty. God must first turn our hearts, before we shall have ability or a will to turn to him. But,

1. It is to justify his dispensations before men. The gifts of providence and grace come freely; 'who hath first given unto him, and it shall be re-'compensed to him again?' But though duty be not the ground of our claim, it is the warrant of our expectation and hope; the righteous God loveth righteousness; 'there are fruits meet for repentance,' by which it is evidenced, and demonstrated to ourselves and others; where these are not, God is not. His judgment is according to truth; and that men may see it to be so, he justifies none whom he does not renew and sanctify; and returns to none in a way of mercy, who are not made willing to turn to him

him in a way of duty. God will juſtify his diſpenſations before men.

2. He will ſlay preſumption and ſelf-confidence in his own people.——David muſt loſe his own peace, if he wounds his own conſcience; his nearneſs to God will not warrant his fellowſhip with ſin. Chriſt looks upon Peter, when he had forſook and denied him; but what bitterneſs his ſin coſt him, we all know. Sin ſhall not caſt a believer out of covenant; but it ſlays his comforts, dries up his ſpirits, and makes a dreadful breach in his communion. 'Abide 'in me, and I in you,' John xv. 5. To go off from Chriſt is to go off from the means of our ſpiritual growth and comfort. Our God is jealous: He will bear no rival in the heart, nor allowed ſin in the life: 'Return unto me, and I will return unto you.' This leads to conſider,

V. In whom is the ſad frame found, which is ſpecified in the text; 'wherein ſhall we return?'

This may ſerve by way of caution, and by way of trial.

1. We ſpeak as in our text, 'Wherein ſhall we 'return?' when we reſt in generals, in confeſſing ſin before God. Sin is a ſort of pack-horſe upon which every burden is laid: This and the other ſurpriſe, diſappointment, loſs, as to national affairs, it is alone of ſin. But, what ſin? Have you ſearched it out, prayed God to ſhew it you, humbled yourſelf for it before the throne, and aſked grace to avoid it? It is a good obſervation of Zanchy's on 1 John i. 9. 'If we confeſs our ſins, he is juſt;' he ſays not, if we confeſs we are *ſinners;* but if we confeſs *our* ſins. Senſe of ſin ariſes from the Spirit's ſetting ſin in order before the ſoul; every indictment is brought in in particular; and reſt cannot be obtained till all ſin is forgiven. It is a ſign of a ſtraitened, if not of an unſerious heart, where ſin is confeſſed only in the lump. This is to ſay, 'Wherein ſhall we re-'turn?'

2. This

2. This frame prevails where there is a transferring sin upon others. It is easy confessing other mens sins: But evangelical repentance begins at home. The nation is grossly wicked and profane; churches are sadly degenerated from the faith and order of Christ; but is there not a coming something closer than this on solemn days of humiliation and prayer? Ought we not first to say, what have I done? I a minister, I a church-member, a parent, a master? Have I filled up my character, adorned my profession, walked humbly with my God? We may suffer with other men in their sins; but we shall be condemned before God, but for our *own*. The windows of Solomon's temple were broad inwards, to shew that we must begin our search within. To transfer our sin upon others, is to say, ' Wherein ' shall we return?'

3. Men speak thus when they confess some sins, but not *the sin* which God *aims* at; we are all too partial with respect to ourselves; it may be we own this and the other *frailty* before God when we are guilty of dreadful *enormities;* complain of want of love to Christ, barrenness of frames, prevalency of temptations; when, alas! we have been wallowing in the puddle of some unclean lust, going in the way of sinners, courting their company, and delighting in their friendship; duty has been neglected; looseness of thoughts and speech indulged; holy duties have been engaged in with carnal frames or for selfish ends. Is not this the Achan in the camp, the Jonah in the ship? The sin which thou confessest may be a sin of which thou art guilty, but not that sin for which God visits. This is but to say, ' Where-
' in shall we return?

4. To confess sin with a secret liking of it in the heart, is in a notorious degree to say, ' Wherein shall ' I return?'—It argues little to confess sin, if thou dost not part with it. A returning penitent sets himself against all sin, and is most humbled for his own iniquity: Sin, regarded in the heart, makes all thy
confessions

confessions an abomination unto God. Repentance is the business of a man's whole life. Whosoever loves and holds fast sin, lies unto God in every prayer that he makes: 'Ye said, Wherein shall we return?'—The uses.

1. Are we thus gone away from God, and shall not we admire divine patience, that we are yet spared, both our persons and our land? That we have any room for prayer, any door of hope? England has long enjoyed and long abused the gospel; and the greater our mercies when abused, the sorer our condemnation. There is a power in God's patience; none but God could bear such enmity and rebellion against his sovereignty and his laws, as has been found in our land.

2. Adore grace. What! another call to return when we have backslidden so long! God seems by his dispensations to entreat your prayers; that he has made as though he was going away is, that you might constrain him to stay. Now is your love to his cause and his gospel tried: He will see what a value you set upon his word and ordinances.

3. We see what is the special duty of this day: It is to return to God. Our all is wrapped up in his presence and blessing. If God departs, woe to us! If he returns, all blessings come with him. Many in the land know nothing of God in a way of covenant and grace: You do; and can you let him go? What, God in whom your life, your help, and all your springs are? Rather no flocks, no herds, no houses, no vineyards, than no God. O! wrestle for yourselves, for your children, for the churches, for the land. Their best inheritance goes if they lose Christ and the gospel.

4. Beware of a double heart this day, and all your life after. Seek peace and truth; but Christ as the foundation of both: Grace for your souls, and safety for your land. Put away the stumbling-block of your iniquity from before your faces. Begin at your heart,

heart, then at your houses; and resolve with Joshua, 'As for me and my house, we will serve the Lord.' It is dreadful to sin against your own confessions and prayers. Pray for the Spirit; nothing is to be done in a course of duty or a way of holiness without his agency and operation. 'Uphold thou me with thy 'free Spirit,' must be the tenor of every day's prayer with them whose desire is to walk with God.

SERMON XXVI.

CAUTION NECESSARY IN THE BEST SAINTS AGAINST THE WORST OF SINS.

1 COR. x. 12.

Wherefore let him that thinketh he standeth, take heed lest he fall.

THE apostle's design in this context, is to set forth the danger and provocation of their state, who live in known acts of sin, and yet partake of solemn divine ordinances. To this end he refers the Corinthians to the judgments of God against such under the Old-Testament dispensation, and brings the several instances there specified close to their own consciences, as he goes along. They were idolaters, they committed fornication, they tempted Christ and murmured against him; though all the while they eat of the same spiritual meat, and drank of the same spiritual drink we do, 'For they drank of that spi-'ritual rock that followed them, and that rock was 'Christ,' *ver.* 4. The sacraments under the Jewish dispensation were the same for substance with those under the gospel; and like sins, under like ordinances and means of grace, call for like punishments. 'These things were our examples, to the intent we 'should not lust after evil things as they also lusted,' *ver.* 6. " God, says one, hath set them forth in his " word as buoys or sea-marks to warn us, that we " do not dash upon the same rock, Christ manifested

" unto

" unto us under like, but far more glorious ordi-
" nances." We serve the same jealous God, who
' will be sanctified by all them that draw nigh unto
' him.' Outward visible profession will not do, if
there be not inward spiritual grace; and this it behoves every one to look to, who is partaker of so high
and holy a calling. Special peculiar privileges call
for more than common and ordinary frames. The
blood of Christ, which we drink figuratively at the
Lord's table, puts a deeper dye into our sins, than is
in the sins of any others; if this be not a remembrancer *to* us to prevent our sin, it will be a remembrancer *against* us to aggravate our condemnation;
the cup of blessing, when abused, is turned into the
greatest curse. And are not these things written for
our admonition, upon whom the ends of the world are
come? ver. 11. to bring us to our right mind as the
word signifies? Have we no need of the caution,
who live in the worst as well as the last times? Have
we no ground, no call to fear, lest a promise being
left us of entering into rest, any of us should seem
to come short of it? It is easy living by a form, but
there is no dying by a form: O! set death and eternity ever before you. Brethren, be warned, be instructed by other mens falls, to search and ransack
your own hearts. My text is close and particular,
it comes home to every man's case; the Lord set it
home with power upon every one of our consciences.
' Let him that thinketh he standeth, take heed lest
' he fall.' The better your opinion of yourselves is,
the closer ought your search to be: It is not said, let
him that finds himself under sensible decays take
heed; nor he that has lately made a slip be more
cautious for the future; but let him that ' thinketh
' he standeth,' he that apprehends the ground he
stands on is firm, and there is no present danger, let
him take heed lest he falleth. And the exhortation
comes in with an awful solemnity, it carries a great
weight and force of argument in it, ' wherefore let him
' that thinks he stands,' &c. as if he had said, " This
" is

"is my aim and design in all I have been saying; take it for yourselves, lay it close to your own hearts, consider your own circumstances, your condition, your privileges, and your danger; see the awful concern you have all in it." 'Wherefore, let him that thinketh he standeth, take heed lest he fall.' Calvin, Beza, and others, think there is a metaphor in the expression, denoting that combat and conflict which every Christian has with his adversary Satan, the common enemy of our salvation. He lies in wait to gain an advantage against poor souls, desires to have them, ' that he may sift them ' as wheat,' so the expression is, Luke xxii. 31. that he may have pitched battle with them, and shews by this means that they are nothing of what they pretend to be, that all is notion, opinion, hypocrisy, &c. Now, in order to this, a person had need choose firm ground to stand on, that he may not slip; and advantageous ground, that he may have an opportunity of seeing into all his adversary's designs; which way he means to attack him, how he shall ward off the blow, and be most successful in resisting him; such an one had need to look about him, or he will soon be worsted, and that before he is aware of it. Take the words simply as they are in my text, or with this figurative gloss, they amount to the same thing, and afford us this awful, though profitable observation.

OBSERV. Such as think themselves most safe, as to their state God-ward, had need take great care lest they fall into those sins, which may appear to others wholly inconsistent with their profession. Or thus,

The best of saints ought to be ever upon their guard lest they fall into the worst of sins.

In discoursing on this subject, I shall endeavour, as God helps,

I. To consider what it is this *heed* refers to, or what is the nature of the duty to which my text directs.

II. Who are the persons it is directed to.

III. What are those motives or arguments contained in the term *wherefore*, to enforce the duty.

IV. The uses.

I. I am to consider what this *heed* is which my text recommends, or what is the nature of the duty which the words direct us to. 'Let him that think-'eth he standeth' take heed 'lest he fall.' The word here used is sometimes translated simply, *to see* or *behold*; at other times, *to look about*, to *consider*, *beware*, &c. because persons that are apprehensive of opposition or danger have their eyes every way, lest they should be overtaken with some sudden surprisal: This is the import of the word here; it denotes that heedfulness and circumspection a person would shew who apprehends danger to be near. In time of peace, if a man should leave the place where he is appointed centinel, no great harm would ensue; but it is death to do this in time of war, because an advantage, a pass, for instance, may be easily lost, but not so easily regained. More particularly, this circumspection and care relates to these four things:

1. To a man's outward circumstances and calling in life. We read, Rev. iii. 10. of the 'hour of 'temptation;' this is that particular season or opportunity, when temptation comes with advantage; when it most easily seizes the affections and enters the heart, so that the soul is hampered and intangled with it; this it always does, when a man's occasions and business in life cast him into such company as suits with his lusts and corruptions; when a spark of fire lights upon combustible matter, it is seldom but there is some flame. Hezekiah's pride was not discovered till the ambassadors of the king of Babylon came to enquire of the miracle done in the land, 2 Chron. xxxii. 31. Hazael's cruelty was a secret till he became king of Syria; he could not believe there was that barbarity in himself, which the prophet suggested, 2 Kings viii. 13. 'What, is thy
'servant

'servant a dog, that he should do this great thing?' His particular lust and a suitable occasion in life had not as yet met. So are there many whose conversation in life is amiable and free from blame, so long as they are free from temptations; but let an occasion present itself, and presently they are passionate, proud, frothy, neglectful of duty, or prone to revenge, as well as others. Temptation bores the heart, and lets out that corruption which lay hid within. Often have I pitied a wordly minded man, when trade has increased, and riches flowed in upon him from every quarter. It has grieved me to see a lovely youth imposed upon by fawning parasites, when his estate has come into his own hands; I have wished his temper was worse, unless his temptations were fewer. So to see a man drawn into company, and to the tavern by business, when his inclination and heart were there before; this, to a conscientious Christian, who knows something of his own heart, cannot but be very affecting: If a man does not strive against the stream in such a case, he is soon carried away by it into unknown sins. 'Lead us not into 'temptation,' is a necessary petition in every prayer; occasions of sin are more easily prevented than resisted: David prays, 'Keep back thy servant from pre- 'sumptuous sins, let them not have dominion over 'me,' Psal. xix. 13. Brethren, choose rather to be called unneighbourly, stiff, precise, and what not, than to sacrifice religion and conscience for a little wordly pelf, or a mere empty compliment: A mighty thing to have it said, yonder goes a good-natured, pleasant, facetious man, that will take his bottle and sing his song, though he is very strict on Lord's days, and belongs to such a church. O Sirs! till professors have a greater watch over their actions, no matter what are their sentiments; no matter where they belong, if religion be but a Sabbath day's work, it may be scarce that; as when they halve it with God for a little country air, because they have not leisure for that on week-days. Our fathers, where are they?

God's blessing was never sought by them, thus out of God's way. Take heed to your circumstances and callings in life, or else wherever your watch is besides, it will be fruitless and ineffectual.

2. This circumspection and care relates to a man's heart. Take heed of heart-sins: God complains of Israel, that his heart was divided, Hos. x. 2. 'Their 'heart is divided; now shall they be found faulty.' The true fear of God has always its seat in the heart: Jer. xxxi. 33. ' I will put my law in their inward ' parts, and write it in their hearts.' Hypocrisy loves and seeks a cover, but truth and sincerity begin here; if this be rotten, all your faith is vain, your hope is vain, ye are yet in your sins: It is not what I am in the esteem of men, but what does an holy and all-seeing God judge me? That the Christian regards; see then that your root be in Christ, or else your fruit will never be to the praise and glory of God by him. The beginning of their confidence; would to God professors would look more to that: Heb. iii. 14. ' For we are partakers of Christ, if we hold the be- ' ginning of our confidence stedfast unto the end.' A mistake in the foundation can never be cured, unless all the building be framed anew. Christian! you have to do with a jealous God, and you had need be jealous too, in all your watch and walk before him; sift more your principles, look into the springs of your actions; ask God and your own hearts, what are your intentions and aims in duty. David, while he communed with his *heart*, made his prayer to his God, Psal. cxxxix. 23. ' Search me, O God, and ' know my heart.' I cannot dive deep enough into it myself; I dare not trust it : ' Try me, and know ' my thoughts, and see if there be any wicked way ' in me.' Any way of grief or pain, the margin has it; that is, any purpose and design which, when it comes to be revealed, will bring pain. It is a great thing to have the bent and bias, the inclination and tendency of the heart right with God; a believer cannot be too careful about this. Peter was a great

saint,

faint, and yet miftaken here: 'Though all men de-
'ny thee, yet will not I.' But when matters came
to the trial, Peter's heart gave him the flip; inftead
of love to his Mafter, it bore him away to his own
eafe; the prefcription he had given to Chrift, he
takes himfelf, 'fpare thyfelf.' It is an awful word
in Hofea vii. 16. and yet it is a true reprefentation
of every man's heart: 'They return, but not to the
Moft High; they are like a deceitful bow.' They
made fome hopeful effays towards a return unto the
Lord; but when it came to the critical point, their
hearts gave back and falfely ftarted afide, juft like a
bow that flips the ftring when it fhould carry the
arrow to its defigned mark. Alas! how often do
our hearts fail us, when we have thought we took
them with us at the beginning of a duty? Prefently
we grow low and carelefs, and fo without life though
before enlarged; and when we come to enquire into the reafon of it, our hearts had flipped afide; they
were got into the world, fixed on fome luft or other,
or it may be hovering over nothing, when we had
been charging them to feek God, and thought them
engaged in fo doing. Take heed to your hearts, if
you would ftand your ground againft the evil one.

3. This circumfpection and care relates to the
way in which our enemies are oppofed and refifted
by us. Take heed *how* you walk, if you would
ftand your ground; *how* you fight, if you would
keep the field. You have the great law of arms
fet down, Eph. vi. 10. 'Finally, my brethren, be
'ftrong in the Lord, and in the power of his might.'
ver. 13. 'Wherefore take unto you the whole ar-
'mour of God, that you may be able to withftand
'in the evil day.' ver. 14. 'Stand therefore, ha-
'ving your loins girt about with truth, and having
'on the breaft-plate of righteoufnefs,' &c. ver. 16.
'Above all, taking the fhield of faith, wherewith
'ye fhall be able to quench all the fiery darts of
'the wicked.' There is nothing to be done without this; not a ftep to be taken, not a blow to be

struck without faith. The Christian must call in help from above; wisdom, and strength, and perseverance in the conflict; they are all the gifts of Christ, the great Captain of our salvation; take heed there. Some men go to their vows, their covenants, their resolutions, and what not: They will come no more near such a place, they will no more neglect such a duty, no, they will never be catched in such a fault more. This is striving, but it is not striving lawfully: 2 Tim. ii. 5. 'If a man strive 'for masteries, yet is he not crowned, except he 'strive lawfully.' The great statute-law of heaven is set aside: If you would speed well, you must begin with God, begin with faith and prayer. 'Whom resist, stedfast in the faith,' 1 Pet. v. 9. Satan makes a pish at every thing till you come to that; this is armour that is proof; it wounds your enemy, and puts him to the flight. Why? because it engages Christ on your side, and makes his strength yours. Faith looks first to the cross of Christ, and then to the grace of Christ; the one mortifies sin, and deadens the heart to the matter of temptation. Who can see his Saviour bleeding, and yet give him a fresh wound? The other strengthens and quickens grace, causing it to endure: 'My 'grace is sufficient for you,' says Christ, to tempted labouring Paul. 2 Cor. xii. 9. It is in Christ we stand, in Christ we walk, in Christ we conquer: Col. ii. 6. 'As ye have therefore received Christ 'Jesus the Lord, so walk ye in him; rooted and 'built up in him, and established in the faith, as ye 'have been taught, abounding therein with thanks-'giving.' O! take heed to this, whatever duty you engage in, interest Christ in it; first pray, and then speed; believe and be established; cast yourself upon Christ, commit your way to him, tell him his enemies are your enemies, his promises your support, and in his strength, and his only, you dare to go forth, expecting to conquer. Once more,

4. This

4. This circumspection and care relates to a believer's life and conversation after such a conquest; take heed to your walk after any advantages you have gained against your enemy. It is Peter's advice, and his experience cost him dear, 1 Pet. v. 8. 'Be sober, be vigilant.' Satan never is off his work; see that you be never off your watch; ever suspect danger, even though you have but just obtained a conquest. Pride and self-applause are apt to shove themselves in, though our own arm have not gotten us the victory. David had like to have taken a surfeit by his prosperity, and where had he been then? 'And in my prosperity I said, I shall 'never be moved,' Psal. xxx. 6. How other Christians may find it, they know best, but I have seldom had any signal manifestation from God, but some set temptation has followed afterward. Paul's thorn in the flesh was given to keep him humble: Take heed of a vain, wandering, loose conversation after sweet communion; pray that you may not fall from your own stedfastness; Satan gains vast advantage from the remissness of a Christian's life, after blessed views and discoveries of Christ, and interest in him. Remember thine adversary has always a sure party within; grace weakens, but it never wholly extirpates remaining lusts; our life therefore is but one continued warfare; when one skirmish is over, presently expect another onset. Well, these are things we are to take heed to, and so much may suffice for the first general. But,

II. Who are the persons the duty is directed to?

In general, it is to them that think they stand, them whose fall is least expected. Blessed Paul gives this special direction to Timothy, bishop or pastor over the church at Ephesus, 1 Tim. iv 16. 'Take heed unto thyself and unto thy doctrine, 'continue in them, for in doing this thou shalt 'both

'both save thyself and them that hear thee.' Ministers may soon pull down in their life and conversation, what they are building up in their doctrine. Paul was afraid of himself, though he had been so long a minister and an Apostle; great as his success had been, great as his grace was, yet he exercised this daily care and heed which my text speaks of, *lest*, says he, 'that by any means, when I 'have preached to others, I myself should be a cast-'away,' 1 Cor. ix. 27. A preacher of salvation may yet miss of it; he may shew others the way to heaven, and yet never get thither himself. An index or way-post directs travellers in the right path, but never moves a step itself: O! my soul, do thou take heed. You must pray, and we must watch, or else we may walk towards heaven in company, and yet, dreadful thought! part at the end of the road. 'Let him that thinketh he stand-'eth, take heed lest he fail.' It is very observable *who* are the persons that are sent to admonish and restore a fallen brother, Gal. vi. 1. 'Brethren, if a 'man be overtaken in a fault, ye which are spiri-'tual restore such an one in the spirit of meek-'ness; considering thyself, lest thou also be tempted.' Observe, the Apostle does not say, ye who are most gifted, most discerning, but ye who are (οἱ πνευματικοι) most in the Spirit of God; whose temper and frame, whose walk and conversation are most spiritualized; who are lifted above others in point of communion with God, do 'ye restore' such an one; (set him in joint again, it is a metaphor taken from a dislocated bone); labour to convince him of his sin, and turn him from the error of his way to God; and how must this be done? 'In the spirit of meekness,' with all that tenderness and bowels, which love to Christ and to one another, as also a sense of thy own danger and liableness to the same temptations will suggest, 'considering thyself lest thou also be tempted.' The direction in my text is to him that 'thinketh' he standeth. Good old Polycarp, angel of the

church

church at Smyrna, though he had endured much from Satan, and his works and tribulation were known, approved, and commended by God, yet had this word of caution sent, together with his comfort: 'Be thou faithful unto death,' Rev. ii. 10. Some that have stood it out manfully against the storms of persecution, have been easily drawn aside from their stedfastness in a calm of liberty. It is not without good reason, that our Saviour adds that important word, Matth. x. 22. 'He that endureth
' to the end shall be saved.' Many an ancient Christian has lost his first love and his first works, before the end of his faith has been come; a worldly spirit has made a deathbed uncomfortable to many a true and aged Christian: Hence the Apostle recommends it to the Hebrews, chap. xii. 15. ' Look diligently,
' lest any man fail of the grace of God, lest any
' root of bitterness springing up trouble you, and
' thereby many be defiled.' Let every one begin the search at his *own* heart, and let this discourse, and other things which might be named, be a fresh and lasting call to you to take heed. I come now,

III. To give some reasons why such as think themselves most safe, as to their state, should take heed lest they fall; or what are those motives and arguments contained in the term *wherefore*.
' Wherefore let him that thinketh he standeth, take
' heed lest he fall.' *Fall*, that is, into gross and scandalous sins, for in that light is my text evidently to be taken: We are not to suppose a man may fall from true grace; but he may fall into gross sins; and a mere outward profession a man may fall from, but not from a real saving work of grace upon the heart. Therefore it follows immediately upon this verse, ' There hath no temptation taken you, but
' such as is common to man: But God is faithful,
' who will not suffer you to be tempted above that
' ye are able, but will with the temptation also
                                            ' make

'make a way to escape, that ye may be able to bear
' it.' 1 Cor. x. 13. Whence is it therefore, that the
greatest saints, the closest walkers with God, should
take heed and use this greatest circumspection, lest
they be overtaken with any gross sin? To this I answer,

1. Because many have so fallen. 'Our fathers;'
so the Apostle styles them, and that not merely because they were ancestors, but members of God's
church of old, and some of them worthies in it;
yet, says he, 'with many of them God was not well
' pleased,' ver. 5. Where there are many cautions
and memorandums there must be great danger;
here a post and there a pillar, to give warning;
sure there must be some pits in the way, which we
are not well aware of. It is reported of a Grecian
commander, that wherever he went, though he was
alone, he was still considering all the places he passed by, how an enemy might possess them, and lay
ambushes in them to his disadvantage, should he
command an army there. O! that Christians were
half so cautious! 'A prudent man foreseeth the evil,
' and hideth himself.' We read of Demas, the Apostle's follower for a time; what sad havock the
world made of him afterwards? Demas hath forsaken me, having loved this present world, 2 Tim.
iv. 10. And yet how many are there amongst us
that *will* be rich? An estate they will have, if it is
any way to be come at; even though they fall into
temptation, into a *state* of temptation; for so I
apprehend the Apostle means, 1 Tim. vi. 9, 10.
' They that will be rich fall into temptation, and a
' snare, and into many foolish and hurtful lusts,
' which drown men in destruction and perdition.
' For the love of money is the root of all evil:
' which, while some coveted after, they have erred from the faith, and pierced themselves through
' with many sorrows.' We read how Peter fell in
the high-priest's hall, whither he went, out of mere
curiosity, to hear Christ's trial: And yet how many
professors

professors mix themselves with such as their business never calls them to converse with? Some go to feed their ears at consorts and balls, at operas, ridottos, &c. Others their eyes, at gaming-tables, cricket-matches, &c. that they may see who is the greatest artist, who fetches the finest stroke, and other such-like weighty inducements; and a third club it, it may be, twice or thrice in a week at a tavern, purely to pass away the evening in agreeable, cheerful, ingenious company; where they hear a story told, with some fashionable oaths to embellish it; or a song, it may be, is sung with its vile and filthy airs. And is this to take heed, to separate the fire from the tinder? Is it not rather to go in the way of temptation, and to give place to the devil? It is to turn tempters yourselves, that the enemy may have the most sure advantage over you when he comes against you. Brethren! do nothing which you cannot pray for a blessing on; be no where, where you cannot with pleasure remember, 'Thou God, seest 'me;' nay, where you would not willingly die and go to God. Take heed you fall not into gross sins, because many have so fallen.

2. Take heed, because there is nothing in your circumstances, gifts, station of life, experience, or attainments, that will of itself keep you from falling. Corrupt nature is corrupt nature in one as well as in another. Peter was a disciple, but his discipleship would not keep him from falling when he was in the way of temptation. David was a man after God's own heart; but all David's past prayers and past communion would not keep him from present sin, and that of the grossest kind, when he indulged sloth and the ease of the flesh. Would any have thought of Moses, that he should speak rashly and unadvisedly with his lips; 'When the man 'Moses was meek above all the men upon the face 'of the earth?' That patient Job would have cursed the day of his birth? Or, that Noah would have been drunken, who, by his upright conversation,

condemned

condemned the old world of this sin among others? But who can say what the power of temptation is, when an evil heart and a suitable occasion for sin meet? All considerations are nothing then; lust incorporates itself with the affections; and a man's reputation, his honour, nay his peace of conscience, and his loss of God's presence and Spirit, they are all forgotten and set aside for the present: Temptation meeting with approbation and acceptance in the heart, like a violent land-flood rushing down a steep place, carries all before it. When sin is committed, a man wonders he should be so overtaken, so sadly foiled; he can scarcely believe that it is he that has sinned. But thus the case too often stands, wherefore take heed. For,

3. Sin, when it is committed, hardens, whoever be the person sinning: Heb. iii. 13. 'Exhort one 'another daily, while it is called to day; lest any 'of you be hardened through the deceitfulness of 'sin.' Like causes produce like effects. When Samson lost his hair (which was God's ordinance to him, that he would be ever with him in the way of his duty) the Lord departed and he knew it not, Judg. xvi. 20. 'He awoke out of his sleep, and said, 'I will go out as at other times before, and shake 'myself. And he wist not that the Lord was departed 'from him.' His stupidity is as amazing as his sin; only sin hardens. Who would have thought David's tender conscience would have remained so long benumbed after his adultery with Bathsheba, had we not God's word for it? When he did but cut off Saul's skirt, his heart smote him; but no conviction now, though after so foul a sin; no confession of his sin, but in a worldly formal way, (no doubt he did that); no looking to Christ's sprinkled blood, no crying for his free Spirit, till Nathan the prophet was sent to him by the Lord, which was not till after the birth of Bathsheba's child. The deceitfulness of sin is such, it hardens the soul; every act of sin confirms the habit; and one sin allowed,

prepares

prepares for another; be a man's grace or experience what it will, sin, when it is indulged, darkens and dulls it; there is more Antinomianism in the heart of the best of saints, than any but God knows of: how common is it to think of Christ's blood, God's covenant, his preserving power and grace, &c. and at the same time this secret thought arises in the heart, " this once—you have an opportunity " now—confess afterwards—*the Spirit is a Spirit of* " *grace and supplication,* anon there will be *indigna-* " *tion, clearing yourself, vehement desire,* &c." And thus gospel-doctrines, through the corrupt tendency of an evil heart of unbelief, become abettors of sin. Take heed, O take heed, when such is the hardening nature and tendency of sin. I may read my text again and again, and yet not read it too often, nor enforce it too particularly, ' Let him that ' thinketh he standeth, take heed lest he fall.' Once more,

4. Should you be restored after your falls, the fruit of sin will be exceeding bitter. David complained of broken bones, Psal. li. 8. and of the arrows of God sticking fast in his flesh, Psal. xxxviii. 2. Peter carried the marks of his fall, as it were to the grave, and therefore always presses humility and godly fear upon himself and others. Will it not be a bitter reflection all your life long, O how have I dishonoured God, an holy, great and gracious God; how have I abused his mercy, despised his law, grieved his Spirit and his saints? I can never, by all my repentance, wipe off the reproach which I have brought upon his good ways, in the eye of the world; a pure and holy religion is become loathsome through my sin; here am I, but what have these sheep done? I cannot be called bad enough; but the church of Christ, to which I stood related, why must they suffer, when they dealt so impartially for Christ, so conscientiously, tenderly and brotherly by me? Would to God, these things were more thought of,

and

and more laid to heart by us all; sure there is a need that we do it. *Wherefore*, the word refers to us as a church, and it speaks to every one as members in particular, ' Wherefore let him that thinketh he ' standeth, take heed lest he fall.'

Many other reasons might have been added, but these must suffice, for it is time I hasten to a close. Therefore,

INFER. 1. If the heedful are in so much danger, what must become of poor heedless souls! If those who have such advantages to help them to stand, may nevertheless fall, O! how sad must be their case who have none at all, who were never built upon the rock of Christ, never knew what it is to walk heaven ward? Sleepy you are now, you are fast asleep; but if not awakened before, you must awake in hell. O Sirs! let me tell you, there is no such thing as a seared conscience there. There their worm dieth not, nor is their fire quenched. Your tempter will there turn your tormentor, and all the opportunities you have had of hearing of your danger and the means of recovery, come in against you, to aggravate your condemnation. ' And to whom ' sware he that they should not enter into his rest, ' but to them that believed not? Heb. iii. 18. Poor heedless souls, if mercy and grace prevent not, will be eternally ruined souls.

INFER. 2. Is he that thinketh he standeth in danger lest he fall? How humble should this make us in our own eyes! how pitiful and tender towards them that are fallen? ' God resisteth the proud, but ' giveth more grace to the humble :' Walk humbly, walk dependently, or else you will never walk safely: You may have faith and all knowledge to discern mysteries; it may be, you may be able to teach your teacher; but remember ' it is a good thing that the ' heart be established with grace, not with meats.' *That* is the soul's ballast, which keeps it poised; it is the soul's food which keeps it alive; grace imparted from Christ's fulness, not grace inherent in us, us, is the Christian's great preservative from all sin and temptation to it. When I see a professor read in philosophy, it may be, or the controversies of the day, that can talk glibly upon any subject, and give a reason (at least he thinks he does) to any question offered; what (I think presently) is the man's temper and frame? Does he know his heart? Is he conversant within? How goes the life of God on in his soul? Is he humble, watchful, given to prayer? Then he stands on firm ground, or else all his head-knowledge does but expose him the more to some strong blast of temptation. He falls sooner than another, because the ground whereon he stands is more slippery; and then the head being full, and the heart so empty, he is less poised, and so less steady than others of the common rank of Christians are. 'Be ye clothed with humility,' is Peter's direction; whatsoever other grace is hid, let this shine. And then be tender, pitiful and compassionate to others fallen. 'Thou standest by faith, therefore be not 'high-minded but fear.' Once more,

INFER. 3. What a blessing is the care and watch of a gospel-church, when so many are our temptations, so great our dangers. It was Cain's reply to God, but it was never adopted by Christians, 'Am 'I my brother's keeper?' We are all members one of another; and as it is in the natural body, so ought it to be in church-fellowship and relation: Are we not concerned that an eye do not go out, an arm wither, or a leg be broken? So ought we, that neither ourselves, nor any of our number, walk unworthy of our holy profession, or seem to come short of the rest set before them. Suspicious vain conjectures and evil surmises, as the Apostle calls them, are one thing; godly jealousy is another; this has for its end God's glory and the good of souls; and shews itself in love, tenderness, prayer and exhortation; the other rise from pride and envy, and open in whisperings, backbitings and slander. God forbid, *that* leaven

ven should spread so much as it does in gospel-churches; but it is the glory of a church when they watch over one another in the Lord, ' provoking ' one another to love and to good works.' And were I dying, I should recommend Jude's advice to the church as my last legacy, *ver.* 20. ' But ye, beloved, ' building up yourselves on your most holy faith, ' praying in the Holy Ghost, keep yourselves in the ' love of God, looking for the mercy of our Lord ' Jesus Christ unto eternal life. To him be glory in ' the churches, world without end. *Amen.*'

SERMON XXVII.

THE SAINTS IMPORTUNITY FOR ZION'S PROSPERITY.

Isaiah lxii. 6, 7.

I have set watchmen upon thy walls, O Jerusalem, which shall never hold their peace, day nor night: Ye that make mention of the Lord, keep not silence; and give him no rest, till he establish, and till he make Jerusalem a praise in the earth.

IT is a truth which holds good both in scripture and experience, that the care of Zion lies at the bottom of all God's powerful actings among the sons of men. All that he is and does, in the methods of his common and extraordinary Providence, is for the sake of his church and people, which is the principal cause and interest he has in the world. You will not think it therefore ill timed, if amidst our present apprehensions, dangers, hopes, fears, as a nation*, you are directed to a present immediate duty which concerns the church; which is indeed the substance, the security and glory of any land. In the former verses we have God's promises to raise his church out of a low afflicted state, into a condition so glorious, that she should be the admiration and joy of distant lands: 'The Gentiles shall see thy righteousness, 'and

---

* This Discourse was preached in the time of the late Rebellion 1745.

'and all kings thy glory.' Here we are told by what means and inftruments this great work fhall be brought about. 'I have fet watchmen,' &c. The thing is fpoken of as already done, to fhew its certainty; by thefe watchmen are meant, either godly magiftrates, or faithful minifters, whofe bufinefs it is, as men in public place and authority, to ftand centinel, and to difcover whatever might be of prejudice to the fafety and quiet of the church: Then may we expect glorious times to attend the churches, when magiftrates and minifters fet their fhoulders to the work of the Lord; when the fword is not held in vain, and vice does not triumph in the perfons and examples of them by whom it fhould be punifhed. Thefe watchmen are faid, 'never to hold their 'peace, day nor night,' to fhew that they confult, pray, and ufe all means to promote Zion's profperity, in good and bad times. Let the approach of the adverfary be open 'in the day,' they fee it; or if the accefs be more fecret and hidden, 'in the night,' they feek to God for the people; and they inform the people from God: 'I have fet watchmen upon 'thy walls.' It is not fo well agreed, who are to be underftood by the next claufe, 'ye that make men- 'tion of the Lord.' Some think there is a reference in the words, to a cuftom which prevailed among the kings of Judah and Perfia, who had their Mafki- rim or recorders, by whom they were put in mind of things which were neceffary to be done for the good of the commonwealth: It belongs to minifters from their office, to put God in mind of his people and of his promifes: 'We,' fays the Apoftle, 'will give 'ourfelves continually to prayer, and to the mini- 'ftry of the word,' Acts vi. 4. Others fuppofe, that God turns himfelf from them to the body of the people: Let every one that profeffes God and Chrift, that has an intereft in the promifes, a concern for Zion, not keep filence. The caufe of Chrift is a public caufe, wherein every true believer has intereft. In Zion's peace we have peace: Therefore pray for the

the peace of Jerusalem, and give him no rest or quiet. God is then said 'to be silent,' when he gives no answer to his peoples prayers; and 'to rest,' when there is a stop in those deliverances and salvations, which use to be wrought by him at the importunity of the people. 'Plead, cry, wrestle,' take no denial till you get what you are pleading for. Zion's establishment is what God has promised, and what he is pursuing by all his dispensations: what he loves to hear you concerned about: Therefore give him no rest till it is done. By Jerusalem is meant, not the *city* of Jerusalem, but the *church* which was in it: According to which the gospel-church is called, 'Jerusalem which now is;' and the whole collection of believers, when they get to glory, is called 'the heavenly Jerusalem,' Heb. xii. 22. God's promise to 'establish it,' supposes, that it is a building, weak and tottering in itself; and its being made 'a praise in the earth,' supposes, that it is an unregarded, contemptible thing to most men; or the meaning is, when God himself establishes Zion according to his own promise, his work therein will be so glorious, that all the world will admire it and praise him for it; she shall appear to be 'the perfection of beauty,' and God shall be renowned in her praise and glory, as the author of it all.

In the words there are three things:

First, That the church of Christ is liable to many shakings; there are some things which to present sense seem to loosen and weaken it.

Secondly, That God will settle his church, so as that she shall become 'a praise in the earth.' And,

Thirdly, That it is the duty of every one, who makes any profession of Christ, or who has any concern with him, to give him no rest, till this great event is brought about. In farther discoursing upon these words, as God is pleased to help, I would shew,

I. What are those shakings to which the cause and church of Christ are exposed here in the earth.

II. Shew when God may be said so to establish his own cause and church, as to make it famous and renowned among men.

III. What must be done by every one that professes Christ in order hereto. And so apply.

I. What are those shakings to which the cause and church of Christ are exposed in the earth. These arise either from outward violence, or inward decays. And they respect either the being, or the blessing and comfort of the churches.

1. There are shakings to which the cause of Christ is exposed, which arise from *outward violence.* 'The 'kings of the earth set themselves, and the rulers 'take counsel together, against the Lord, and a-'gainst his anointed,' Psal. ii. 2. As soon as ever Christ was born, he was persecuted. Abel, one of the first professors of religion, became a martyr for it. The princes of this world have a notion, that Christ's kingdom and theirs are incompatible: 'Therefore,' says Pharaoh, 'let us deal wisely with 'them, lest they multiply, and join unto our ene-'mies, and fight against us, and so get them up out 'of the land,' Exod. i. 10. And it has been a maxim of state-policy ever since, excepting in a very few instances, to oppress, and vex, and afflict the people of God, to prevent any danger or dread of an insurrection from that quarter; yea when God has employed any of the kings of the nations as instruments in their deliverance, the work has been carried through such a multitude of hindrances, oppositions, and dangers, that God himself has eminently appeared to have been the Saviour, by whose hand soever the salvation has been sent. As soon as the foundation of the second temple was laid by Cyrus, an edict was published by the same hand to stop the building; this must needs have been a great shock to the godly at that time. Afterwards,

in the reign of Artaxerxes, Tobiah and Sanballat conspired against the builders, so that they wrought with one hand in the work, and with the other hand held a weapon, Neh. v. 17. Sometimes the shakings, to which the church is exposed, arise from outward violence.

2. There are shakings which arise from *inward decays*.

A building will shake and totter, and grow ruinous, without any outward violence, if the foundation is undermined; or if the pins and fastnings, whereby it is held together, decay. This is the case,

First, When gospel-truth is perverted or denied. Christ is the foundation of every gospel-church: Not a stone in the spiritual building, but is laid on Christ, and derives all its life, growth, strength, and support from him. 'Other foundation can no man lay, 'than that is laid, which is Jesus Christ,' 1 Cor. iii. 11. To substitute other things instead of Christ for acceptance, such as moral righteousness, dispositions for grace, evangelical repentance, faith, holiness, &c. is to go off the foundation, or to lay some other foundation than that is laid. Can a building stand that is moved off the foundation? No more can any church which does not hold Christ the head; or which does not indeed grow, and make increase in him, Ephes. ii. 20. All gospel-doctrines centre in Christ: and so far as one is perverted, another neglected, and a third denied, so far there is a weakness, and decay in the foundation: The building must grow loose; one stone cannot support the other, if there be no foundation which sustains the weight of the whole.

Secondly, When gospel-holiness is neglected, sin eats out the strength which is in the pins and fastnings of the building; it makes ordinances useless, promises sapless, and leaves the house destitute of the presence of Christ, who is the great Master of assemblies. Shiloh itself became an hissing when God left it: Divine institutions have no more power to establish and keep a church together, than bare human appointments, when God withdraws his prefence and Spirit from them.

A church's ftrength and ftability lies in thofe two words, ' Ammi, ye are my people;' and ' Jehovah ' Shammah, the Lord is there.' Indulged, allowed fins, in a church, are like a weaknefs and diftemper in the bowels; when the vitals are touched, every part of the body feels it; either healing or death muft come foon. See, brethren, whether the prefent weak and tottering ftate of the church does not arife from a difeafe in our bowels, from fome inward decay. Eftablishment will not come to the churches till all grounds of controverfy between God and them be removed.

Thirdly, When love is not cultivated, and kept up among profeffors, the church is fhaking and growing ruinous. As there is a communion we all have with Chrift the head; fo there is a communion we all have one with another, on which the beauty and ftrength of a church in great meafure depends. Jerufalem is fpoken of as a city compact together, Pfal. cxxii. 3. ' And the body fitly joined together, and compacted ' by that which every joint fupplieth, according to ' the effectual working in the meafure of every part, ' is faid to make increafe to the edifying itfelf in ' love,' Ephef iv. 15, 16. Love is that which edifies and ftrengthens; it is like the cement of the building which keep the ftones together; without this, though the ftones lie upon the foundation, yet are they feparated one from another, which neceffarily infers weaknefs. A church full of love, is a church well built up; all parts, gifts, attainments, graces, will not edify and eftablifh without it: The enemies of Chrift know this; therefore it has been their fettled maxim, ' firft divide, then deftroy.' Happy difpenfation we are at prefent under, if in the iffue it brings profeffors, members of Chrift, and his churches, to abound in love one towards another. Divifions in affection loofen and fhake us, as well as divifions in judgment: Thus concerning our firft
general

general head, What are those shakings to which the church is exposed here upon earth? They are such that arise from outward violence, and inward decays. But,

II. When may God be said so to establish his church and cause, as to make it a praise in the earth? You may easily observe the words refer to a more glorious day than our eyes have seen: Nor does this glory consist barely in temporal, but in spiritual blessings. 'Arise, shine; for thy light is come, and 'the glory of the Lord is risen upon thee,' Isa. lx. 1. God *with* and *in* her, is the church's excellency. Christ in his churches makes Zion glorious. To make up this praise and renown which Zion is said to be, as the fruit of God's establishment, there are four or five things. As,

1. Abundance of light and knowledge. The foundation of Satan's kingdom lies in darkness; the beginning of Christ's, and the establishment of it, is in light. So far as Christ is known, relished and lived on, support and establishment are conveyed to the church, and every believer's heart: 'Abide in 'me, and I in you.' Hence believers are said 'to 'be rooted and built up in Christ, and established 'in the faith,' Col. ii. 7. Where there is a shaking in our faith, there will be a wavering and unsteadiness in our hope, love, zeal, and all other Christian graces. Therefore, says the apostle, 'Let your love 'abound yet more and more, in knowledge,' Phil. i. 9. And it is promised, when that glorious day begins my text speaks of, that 'the earth shall be full 'of the knowledge of the Lord, as the waters cover 'the sea,' Isa. ii. 9. There shall not be one corner of the heart empty, which this knowledge of Christ shall not fill: Our indistinct, uncomfortable apprehensions of Christ, and divine things, shall in a great measure vanish; there will be more of the Spirit of revelation in the knowledge of Christ. God will visit the spirit of his people in a more immediate

way than he now does; leading them into his secret, feasting them with his love, and causing them to know divine and spiritual things for their good; they shall see interest in them, and have as assured persuasion of them, as they have of the most sensible things. Then shall the church be so established as to be a praise in the earth, when God gives her abundance of light and knowledge.

2. When he gives her high degrees of holiness. Nothing makes a church more strong in itself, or more renowned before men, than this. The power our forefathers had with God, made them more the wonder and dread of the nations, than all the military force and conduct they had as men. ' Let us ' flee from them, for God fighteth for them.' There is a blessed day coming on, when the Lord shall have ' purged the filth of the daughter of Zion, by ' the Spirit of judgment, and by the Spirit of burn- ' ing,' Isa. iv. 4. God interests his people in holiness, that they may be interested in safety, that safety which is the fruit of his promise and covenant. Their inward corruptions shall be searched out and consumed, about which he has contended with them so often, and so sharply; ' and the Lord will create ' upon every dwelling-place of Mount Zion, and ' upon her assemblies, a cloud, and a smoke.' Yea, such shall be the spirit of believers at that day, that ' there shall be upon the bells of the horses, Holi- ' ness unto the Lord; and the pots in the Lord's ' house shall be like the bowls before the altar; yea ' every pot in Judah and Jerusalem shall be Holiness ' to the Lord of Hosts,' Zech. xiv. 20, 21. Men shall go about their civil employments in life with holy thoughts, desires, affections and aims: They shall be more spiritual and heavenly than we are in our attendance upon God in solemn ordinances. No infant of days shall be found; none weak in knowledge or grace. Christians shall not be full of doubts, fears, witherings, discomfort: ' The trees of ' the Lord shall be full of sap, and Zion shall no
' more

'more be termed forsaken,' ver. 4. Blessed time this! the church will verily be the praise and admiration of the nations, when God himself is 'her 'defence, her strength, and her glory.'

3. There shall be 'abundance of peace,' Psal. lxxii. 7. 'In his days,' (speaking of the time when the Messiah's reign shall be from sea to sea), 'shall the 'righteous flourish; and abundance of peace so long 'as the moon endureth.' Where there is growing holiness and fellowship, there will be peace. This is one of the first fruits of the Spirit, Gal. v. 22. Peace not only from outward persecution and trouble, but peace in their own consciences, and peace one with another. No disagreement in doctrine, no diversity of worship, no jealousies, or animosity of spirit, through pride, self-seeking, vain-glory, and other remains of the flesh: 'In that day there shall 'be one Lord, and his name one,' Zech. xiv. 9. Love to Christ and concern for his cause and glory, shall swallow up every other interest. Christ will be all to their souls in point of trust, fellowship, and complacential delight; and he will be in all their thoughts, converses, aims, desires, prayers, and praises.

4. There shall be a multitude of converts. In God's time there shall be no seat or office vacant in our churches. 'Who are these that fly as a cloud, 'and as the doves to their windows!' Isa. lx. 8. They came with such swiftness and eagerness, and in such troops and multitudes, that the church herself is filled with admiration at it. We look round about us now and think, should God take away this and the other member who seem pillars, that part of the church to which we belong must soon tumble down; it looks as if we could not be upheld except these abide with us: But 'God's thoughts are 'not like our thoughts.' Cannot he as easily create now, as heretofore? Regeneration was always creation work. 'The residue of the Spirit is with him.' It is Christ, not men, that bears up the pillars of the

the state and the church. The foundation of God's house is hidden and out of sight; it lies in Christ and the covenant, in God's own purpose and promise. When the day of Zion's help, establishment, and fulness comes, 'the righteousness thereof shall 'go forth as brightness, and the salvation thereof as 'a lamp that burneth,' it will be conspicuous and eminent to all.

5. When God so establishes his church, as to make her 'a praise in the earth,' she shall have a rich supply of all temporal good things. Mens natures shall be changed; their corrupt lusts and passions shall be subdued; and all their riches, honour, and power, shall be employed for the support of Christ's cause and kingdom. 'They shall not hurt, 'nor destroy in all my holy mountain,' Isa. lxv. 25. 'And thou shalt suck the breast of kings,' chap. lx. 16. The enemies of Christ shall either be converted, awed, or removed: Persecution and violence shall cease, when Babylon the great is fallen, and shall arise no more. Thou shalt be a crown of glory in the hand of the Lord. Thus shall God establish his church; till which time they that make mention of the Lord, are to give him no rest; which leads,

III. To the duty of such as make any profession of Christ, with reference to this great and glorious day. 'Ye that make,' &c.

1. This day of Zion's establishment and praise, should be uppermost in our *thoughts*. That which has no place in our thoughts and affections, will have very little in our prayers. The church of old deprecated this as an abominable sin; Psal. cxxxvii. 5, 6. 'If I forget thee, O Jerusalem, let my right 'hand forget her cunning; if I do not remember 'thee, let my tongue cleave to the roof of my mouth.' Absence did not lessen affection; many of them knew but by report the glory of Old-Testament worship, being born in Babylon: But their hearts were

in Zion. Things which are distant, are nevertheless desirable. Antichrist's ruin will be sudden, her plagues shall come upon her in one hour. All the changes we see or hear of in states, kingdoms or nations, prepare the way to Zion's advancement, and her enemies ruin. Let this great event be in the thoughts of all them that love Christ.

2. It should be continually in their prayers. The promise is the warrant of faith, and the rule of prayer, whatever difficulties lie in the way of it. God has chosen Zion, it is his own lot and portion; it is Christ's spouse; his body's fulness and glory. Men and devils are up in arms against it. What can be a more seasonable time, to be the Lord's remembrancers, than now? 'In the mount he has been seen;' in the mount he loves to appear; when every one seeks to destroy Zion, it is God's usual course to help her, Isa. lxiii. 5. 'And I looked, and there was none to 'help; and I wondered that there was none to up- 'hold. Therefore mine own arm brought salvation 'unto me, and my fury it upheld me.' When he begins to give mercy, he pours it upon us, so that there is scarce room to receive it: And terrible things are sometimes the way to eminent salvations. Psal. lxv. 5. 'By terrible things in righteousness wilt thou 'answer us, O God of our salvation.' Prayer helps the promise to bring forth: 'Go,' says Hezekiah, 'to Isaiah the son of Amoz, tell him this is a day of 'trouble, and of rebuke, and blasphemy; for the 'children are come to the birth, but there is not 'strength to bring forth; lift up a prayer for the 'remnant that is left,' Isa. xxxvii. 3, 4. God is, in this day, humbling us for our confidence and stupidity, and bringing us to our prayers. Prayer for Babylon's downfal, and Zion's glory, is the present duty of such as make mention of the Lord.

3. Prayer for Zion's establishment must be with an holy *importunity* and *constancy*. It is not the work of one day, but of every day; the blessing prayed for, has every other blessing and mercy in the bowels

of it. If God does but remove our sins, and quicken our graces, and settle our faith and confidence in Christ, doubt not but he will subdue our enemies. Is it not one cause, why God has suffered these *Popish* foes to prevail so far, that our prayers have no more been bent against the *Popish* cause? O! it is a time for fervent, importunate prayer. Enter into God's retirings; urge his promises; shew him, as it were, the person and blood of the dear anointed; take no denial. Jacob had power with the angel, and prevailed. In like manner tell him, you must lie at his feet, must be a constant suitor, till he gives some good word whereon he will cause your soul to hope. 'Keep not silence, and give him no rest.'

4. Zion's friends are called to pray and *work*. The former branch of the verse commands action: ' I have set watchmen upon thy walls, O Jerusalem.' It is hypocrisy to ask in private, what you would not be glad to do in public. Your time, gifts, substance and lives are God's. Can you encourage a gospel-ministry, a Protestant King, a faithful soldiery? Do it. Let every one look into his own heart, and see wherein he can help the church or state; you are called with these, as well as your prayers, to the help of the Lord against the mighty. The uses follow.

Use 1. Is the church exposed to many shakings? Then let not present troubles seem strange to us. Not our liberties so much as our religion is what the enemy is aiming at. *Popish* priests and Jesuits, by whom this vile rebellion has been stirred up, are set against Christ and his gospel. But a hard task they have to fight against him, ' who is the King of kings ' and the Lord of lords.' Zion has outlived every persecution and trial hitherto. The church is the safest part in the whole universe: ' Here am I in the ' midst of you.' Where Christ is, there may be danger; but there shall be safety in the end. ' And he ' shall be for a sanctuary: This man shall be the ' peace, when the Assyrian cometh into the land,' Micah v. 5.

Use

USE 2. We see why it is the church survives all dangers: It is because ' glorious things are spoken ' of her,' which are not yet fulfilled. So long as there is a promise unaccomplished, the church is invincible. When churches fail, there is a cause, and interest of Christ, carried on in the hearts of some hidden ones. Elijah thought himself alone in his profession and zeal, till God convinced him of his mistake. The glorious *inhabitant*, that is, Christ, secures the *house:* And as he is the owner, so he is the watchman or keeper of it: ' He that keepeth ' Israel, neither slumbereth nor sleepeth.' The whole world shall stand no longer, than till Christ hath fulfilled his promises made to his church and cause.

USE 3. Are all that ' make mention of the Lord ' *to* give him no rest.' Then let us lay aside all other smaller matters, and unite in this: Variance, heat, and resentment; it is no time for them: Count all believers friends, and let all your thoughts, prayers, and endeavours, be against the common enemy. Zion has been more shook and weakened by the dissensions of those within her, than by all the opposition of the world that is against her.

Ridley and Hooper could never agree about *black* and *white* in King Edward's days; but (as one of them expresses it), they could afterwards agree in *red:* When God puts them together into suffering, tears and blood, they could love and live and die together as brethren. Let us agree to humble ourselves before God, to put our prayers into one joint stock, to believe and cry, and wait, and give God ' no rest, ' till he establish, and till he make Jerusalem a praise ' in the earth.'

SERMON XXVIII.

THE GOOD-WILL OF CHRIST THE BEST OF BLESSINGS.

DEUT. xxxiii. 16.

——*And for the good-will of him that dwelt in the bush.*

THIS chapter contains an account of the blessing wherewith Moses the man of God blessed the children of Israel before his death: It is expressed partly in a way of prayer, denoting what his soul earnestly desired *might* be, and partly in a prophetic spirit, signifying what God had ordained *should* be. Moses was just now finishing his course, this was his last interview with the people, and his last act among them; he dies blessing God, and blessing them. How sweet is it for a faithful pastor, in this spirit and frame, to take his last farewell of those that have been committed to his charge by the great Shepherd of the sheep! But this is not every one's mercy; every one is not allowed thus to bless the people, and see the good land, and die as Moses the servant of our Lord did; however, the death by which we shall most glorify God, is more to be sought, than that with which we shall be most pleased ourselves.

The words now read are part of Joseph's blessing, wherein Moses prays for temporal good things in all

all their plenty, variety and sweetness: 'Blessed of
'the Lord be his land, for (or by reason of) the pre-
'cious things of heaven, for the dew,' &c. But these,
if compared with what follows, are small things.
'And for the good-will of him that dwelt in the
'bush.' This was the utmost Moses himself could
ask, or they enjoy. Take the words as referring to
Joseph's land as a nation, the observation is this:

God's grace and gospel are the greatest blessings
which a nation can enjoy: 'For what nation is
'there so great, who hath God so nigh them, as the
'Lord our God is in all things that we call upon him
'for,' Deut. iv. 7. The glory of a nation lies in
the presence and favour of God; how happy is Great
Britain in this respect, did we but know and improve our mercy!

But what I purpose from the words, as the Lord
shall help, is to consider them in a closer relation,
as expressive of the grace and good-will of Christ to
his church, and their great duty in valuing, prizing
and seeking this good-will above all other things;
for the tribe of Joseph may be considered in their
covenant-relation to God, and their fellowship with
him in ordinances, as expressive of the church and
people of God. It is not our number, or our riches,
or our judiciousness, or our love to one another, which
make us truly honourable, or necessarily imply in
them soul-prosperity; there may be these things
upon lower considerations. Knowledge and experience, and heart and conversation-holiness do not
always go together; and there may be by-respects,
for which members of churches may love one another; interest, agreement in principles and aims,
may promote this, abstracted from that love we bear
to Christ, and which we should have to one another,
as bearing his image. 'The good-will of him that
'dwelt in the bush,' if this be not amongst us, and
upon us, we may be left to leanness of soul and spiritual want, notwithstanding all outward prosperity,
beauty

beauty and order. So that the observation from the words shall be this:

Doc. The favour or good-will of Christ, who of old dwelt with Moses in the bush, is to be sought by believers, as the greatest and best of all blessings. Moses prays it may be amongst them, which shews how much they stand engaged to ask it for themselves.

In discoursing on this subject, I will endeavour,

I. To shew what this good-will is, and whose it is.

II. Why it is thus particularly described as the good-will of him that dwelt in the bush.

III. Consider how, or in what manner it is to be sought.

IV. Wherein consists the greatness of the blessing, which renders it so well worthy of all our seeking.

I. I am to shew what this good-will is, and whose it is. To this I answer in general, It is the love and free favour of Christ to all his covenant-people; that grace of his, in which there is continuance, which he ever bears towards them that are his. The best interpreters render the word 'favourable acceptation;' by which two things seem to be intended: *First*, That our Lord Jesus Christ ever bears good-will towards his people; his love, his whole heart is theirs. And, *Secondly*, This favour and good-will he is pleased to discover unto them for their edification and comfort: 'There (says he, speaking to his 'spouse) will I give thee my loves,' Solomon's Song, vii. 12. I will shew thee how full of grace and mercy I am.

First, Our Lord Christ ever *bears* a good-will towards his people. *He* is the glorious Person here spoken of; it is *his* love, *his* favour, *his* good-will; Jehovah God-man, who in his appearance in the bush gave the church a type of his taking our nature, and in his divine person dwelling therein,

(more

(more of which afterward). This is evident from Stephen's apology to the Jews, where he calls him *the Lord*, Acts vii. 31. 'The voice of the LORD ' came unto him;' and *ver.* 33. 'Then said the ' LORD unto him,' *&c.* And where we read of his appearance, Exod. iii. 2. he is reprefented as faying, *ver.* 6. 'I am the God of thy father, the God of ' Abraham, the God of Ifaac, and the God of Jacob. ' And Mofes hid his face, for he was afraid to look ' upon God. And the Lord faid, I have furely feen ' the affliction of my people—and I am come down ' to deliver them,' *&c.*

Now this bleffed and glorious Perfon always bears his people good-will; they are precious and honourable in his fight, they are highly favoured; his thoughts towards them are thoughts of peace, and fo they were from eternity, Mic. v. 2. 'Whofe go- ' ings forth have been from of old, from everlafting.' Then his heart ftood towards poor fallen man, and ' his delights were with the children of men,' Prov. viii. 31. All that he did afterwards in time, when he was 'manifeft in the flefh,' and all that he is doing now in his exalted ftate, proceed from his love and good-will; ftill he wears our nature, appears in our caufe, acts in our name, and reprefents our perfons: It is for this caufe, that the Father 'hath ' given him power over all flefh, that he fhould give ' eternal life to as many as he hath given him,' John xvii. 2. The church is his fpoufe, his body, his fair one; there is a gracious acceptation given to our perfons, and a gracious acceptation of our fervices: we are clothed in his garments, and made comely through his comelinefs put upon us; the graces which appear in our worfhip and walk, are his own fruits; not only what he has a right to, as our Lord, but what he works in us as our Saviour and Head. Every difpenfation of Providence is for our good; the foreft ftrokes that befal us come in love; when perfecuted, forfaken, made a fhame of before men, his heart ftands towards us the fame as ever;

' underneath

'underneath are the everlasting arms:' We endure the fire, and come purged and refined out of it. There is good-will in his heart, his purposes, and all the works of his hands, whatever the outward appearance of things may be. This is one thing intended by the expression in my text. But,

Secondly, This favour and good-will Christ is pleased to discover to his people for their edification and comfort. Solom. Song, ii. 4. 'He brought me 'to the banqueting-house, and his banner over me 'was love;' that is, *there* he shewed me all his fulness and glory as my Christ, my God. Believers have a fellowship with Christ: they partake, and, as it were, share with him in all his mediatory fulness; it is for their sakes 'God, his God, hath anointed 'him with the oil of gladness above his fellows,' Psal. xlv. 7. His love is a 'love that passeth know- 'ledge;' it is too great to be known, so as to be comprehended, but not so as not to be sweetly tasted and felt. 'Thy love is better than wine,' says the spouse, on account of a fresh experience of it given in Solomon's Song i. 2. 'Because of the favour of thy 'good ointments, thy name is as ointment poured 'forth, therefore do the virgins love thee.' Christ hath instituted special ordinances both under the Old-Testament and the New, on purpose to lead his saints into sweet and endearing views of his favour and good-will. What was the sprinkling of the blood of the Paschal Lamb designed for? The rock that followed them all along the wilderness? The ark of the covenant and the mercy-seat, with the cherubims covering it? What were all these things designed for, but to give Old-Testament saints a view of *his* good-will, who was their Surety and Mediator? Why did he so often assume a visible shape, and present himself before them in the form of a man, but that he might shew what a love he bore to their nature, and what a longing desire he had to the work agreed upon between the Father and him in the everlasting covenant? And why does he smile upon

upon thy soul in ordinances; cheer and comfort thee by promises; draw forth thy heart and affections towards him in duty? But that he may give thee a token for good, that he may covince thee that his heart, his love, his covenant, his whole salvation are thine? This good-will is carried from his heart into thine. This is one special work of the Spirit, even to reveal the love and good-will of Christ to thy soul 'to direct your hearts into it,' 2 Thess. iii. 5. that is, to guide into it by a straight line, so to persuade of it, as that the soul is overcome with it: Then thy heart is filled with joy unspeakable and full of glory; thou art compassed about with favour as with a shield; love, and grace, and truth, appear in all that befals thee; then God appears to be love indeed; that one perfection of his nature seems to swallow up every other. This is another thing intended by the phrase, 'The good-will of him that dwelt in the 'bush;' that is, the gracious manifestation of it to the heart, the precious experience of it in the soul. This leads to consider,

II. Why is this good-will thus particularly described, as the good-will of 'him that dwelt in the 'bush.'

The story which this expression refers to, you have Exodus iii. 12. 'Now Moses kept the flock of Jethro 'his father-in-law, the priest of Midian, and he led 'the flock to the back-side of the desert and came 'to the mountain of God, even to Horeb. And the 'angel of the Lord appeared unto him in a flame of 'fire out of the midst of a bush, and he looked, and 'behold the bush burned with fire, and the bush 'was not consumed,' &c.

Now the good-will of Christ is described by Moses in particular reference to this extraordinary representation, as I humbly conceive, on the following accounts:

First, Because the fire in the midst of the bush, was a type of the incarnation and sufferings of Christ.

To you this may appear a very dark and distant allusion; but though there were no analogy in the things themselves, I should credit the design of the representation to be, that God intended hereby to give Moses a view of Christ as God-man Mediator, who should appear and suffer in our flesh; because Moses in his last words lays so great a stress upon it, mentioning it as the chief of all blessings. Why did he not wish them the rock still to follow them; 'for that rock,' the Apostle tells us, ' was Christ?' Or that that spiritual meat might be continued to them, of which they all eat; for this manna also was a type of Christ? (as is clear from 1 Cor. x. 3, 4.) but, because though Christ was held forth by these things, yet there was not so immediate, clear and distinct a representation of his person and sufferings, as God in our nature, by *them*, as by the ' fiery bush?' Nor is the allusion so very dark and distant: For man's nature is a poor, despicable thing, like a dry bramble-bush that would be soon *fired*, as it were, and utterly consumed by the approach of God; but the Son of God dwells in this bush, and though the flame is seen, the bush is not burnt. ' The word
' was made flesh, and dwelt among us, and we be-
' held his glory, the glory as of the only begotten
' of the Father full of grace and truth,' John. i. 14.
' And Moses said, I will now turn aside and see this
' great sight, why the bush is not burnt,' Exod. iii. 3.
And is it not a sight which engages a poor soul to draw near, when he beholds in a crucified Christ all the wrath and indignation of an holy God, which like a flame of fire shall devour the wicked; all this wrath meeting on the person of Christ, and yet his human nature unconsumed? The blessed Jesus, as his surety, endured it all, and survived it; having died indeed once, but now living for ever, God and man united in his glorious person. This is it which taketh off all dread from the worshippers. ' And God call-
' ed to Moses out of the midst of the bush,' ver. 4.
The sweet words which believers hear from God,

are all spoken to them in the person, and by the mouth of his own eternal Son : ' No man hath seen
' God at any time; the only begotten Son, which
' is in the bosom of the Father, he hath declared
' him,' John i. 18. There is then a great and sweet propriety in the expression, ' the good will of him
' that dwelt in the bush.' Now the good-will, the favourable acceptation of this mediator ' Emmanuel,
' God with us,' Moses could not have desired another, so great a blessing as this is.

Secondly, Another reason why this good will is so emphatically described, as ' the good-will of him
' that dwelt in the bush,' is because God revealed his *covenant* to Moses at the time of this glorious appearance. He shewed Moses not only the glory of Christ's person, but also the glory of his grace in him, Exod. iii. 6. ' Moreover he said, I am the God
' of thy father, the God of Abraham, the God of
' Isaac, and the God of Jacob. And Moses hid his
' face, for he was afraid to look upon God. And
' he said certainly I will be with thee,' *ver*. 12.
' Moses hid his face :' God is awful in his very mercies. Sense of our own unworthiness fills the soul with dread, even when receiving from the hand of God his special and most distinguishing favours. Here you see God's covenant was renewed by the angel or messenger of it; all grace is contained in that, it takes in every blessing God means to bestow, even to the resurrection of these bodies of ours to eternal life. ' I am the God of Abraham, and the
' God of Isaac, and the God of Jacob; God is not
' the God of the dead, but of the living,' Matt. xxii. 32. The whole man, soul and body, shall for ever live with God. And when was all this grace revealed to Moses? Why, the Lord appeared in the midst of the bush, on purpose to do it : It is therefore good-will in a covenant-way Moses prays for; not the goodness or benevolence of God, as a pure and perfect being abstracted from his relation to Christ, and the respect he has to his sacrifice; it is

the good-will of Christ, the covenant of Christ, the fulness of Christ, which is here referred to. Our Lord Christ is a covenant to the people; all in the covenant is transacted by him; he is mediator, surety, head, trustee of the covenant, our Emmanuel is all. Sinners know not what they are about when they look to God without a Mediator: What peace can there be where there is no reconciliation? God is a fire to consume, not to enlighten, warm and refresh ungodly sinners, such as have not made a covenant with him by sacrifice. This is another reason why it is called ' the good-will of him that dwelt in the ' bush:' It is expressive of that covenant which was revealed at that time to Moses, and which God has established with his people through the blood of his Son.

Thirdy, This appearance of the angel in the bush sets forth the *love* and *care* of Christ to his church, even in their greatest troubles and dangers. This was the time of Jacob's trouble, emphatically so; the very name and remembrance of them was like to be cut off from the earth; they were sighing and groaning under great bondage, their children cast out, to the intent they might not live, and no deliverance came to answer their prayers and tears. But the Lord appears in a flame of fire in the bush, as Israel's preserver, upholder, deliverer, to strengthen Moses's faith in his promise and covenant. The bush burned with fire, and the bush was not consumed: The church suffered, was envied, persecuted, drove to the greatest straits, set on fire, as it were, by hell; but it was not destroyed, it still survived, Christ was in the midst of it, that is, her perpetual safety: ' Lo, I am with you.' The text says, he dwelt in the bush; this is the Lord's rest. Here his name, his honour, his glory are; and here his delight is. The glory he gets out of the whole world, is principally from his church, therefore he will not leave her. What a blessed encouragement is this to faith at all times! O how may believers in fellowship
plead

plead for the manifestations of Christ's presence in his churches! 'Concerning my sons, and concerning the work of my hands command ye me,' Isa. xlv. 11. All Christ's mercy, wisdom, power, love and grace are for us; yea his very life is on our behalf, 'Because I live, ye shall live also,' John xiv. 19. It is good to remember former deliverances even in the want of present mercies. This is another reason.

Fourthly and *lastly*, One reason more of this description is, because Moses had at this season the most special and sensible experience of the love and goodwill of Christ; it is one of the top manifestations of the Redeemer's fulness and grace to his own soul. There is a great deal of emphasis in my text, as the words lie in the original, that is, " And for the favourable acceptation of *my dweller in the bush*." As if Moses had said, " Then he revealed himself " to be mine, I saw his glory as my Surety, my Re- " deemer, my God manifest in the flesh, and to my " soul he sealed all the love and grace of the ever- " lasting covenant." Our first views of God and Christ, are often exceeding precious ones. This was Christ's first visible appearance to Moses that we read of; *now* the visions of God began; and what so sweet an introduction to his after-communion with him, as a sight of the second Person in the Godhead united to flesh, and in our nature transacting all the concerns of salvation? ' Thy time,' says God to the church, ' was the time of love,' Ezek. xvi. 6. Even this very time when their deliverance from the Egyptian bondage began. This appearance to Moses was so sweet, so glorious, so inviting, that he makes it the very pattern or rule of what he desired might be Joseph's blessing. Sirs! there are seasons, the sweet remembrance of which even death's awful face cannot wear of. In sickness, pain and age, when the senses are blunted, and desire itself fails, times of special communion are as often as fresh and as sweet as they were at first. Thus it was with dying Jacob,

Gen.

Gen. xlviii. 3. 'And Jacob said unto Joseph, God
'Almighty appeared unto me at Luz in the land of
'Canaan, and blessed me.' It was that vision of the
ladder set on earth, the top whereof reached to heaven, which he speaks of, Gen. xxviii. 12. When the
Lord 'stood, and said, I am the Lord God of Abra-
'ham thy father, and the God of Isaac: The land
'whereon thou liest, to thee will I give it, and to
'thy seed,' *ver.* 13. This first visit warmed his soul
still. O how precious to Old-Testament saints was
any view or representation of an incarnate God!
Hence he lays a special emphasis upon it, when he
blessed Joseph, Gen. xlviii. 15. 'And he blessed
'Joseph, and said, God, before whom my fathers
'Abraham and Isaac did walk, the God which fed
'me all my life long unto this day, the angel which
'redeemed me from all evil, bless the lads,' &c.
Just as it was with Moses here: And for the good-will of my dweller in the bush. Now Jacob and
now Moses can both willingly die. Nothing more
was wanting but to see him face to face. Precious,
signal, extraordinary manifestations of the grace and
good-will of Christ, are ever remembered by the
believing soul. For these reasons the inspired prophet seems particularly to describe this good-will, as
his 'who dwelt in the bush.'

Two words of use,

1. Let the saints plead former manifestations of
Christ to his church and people. Faith finds great
sweetness in them, when its eye is opened by the
Spirit of God. The church's deliverance from Egypt
is mentioned with thankfulness and hope in every
other trial. We give God the glory of past mercies,
when we plead them with him; thus far all providential favours and deliverances to the church in all
ages are a believer's own, for his comfort, his establishment, his good.

2. Labour to improve this good-will of Christ to
your own soul's advantage, maintain communion
with

with him in it. Go every day, and in every duty, for a fresh discovery of it: Press after the manifestations of it in greater frequency, and to greater degrees. We have too little fellowship in the actings of our faith on the person of Christ as distinct from the Father. His good-will, his grace, his love, should be every day the delight and food of our souls. But more of this, when we shew how this good-will is to be sought.

But I add no more at present.

SERMON XXIX.

THE GOOD-WILL OF CHRIST THE BEST OF BLESSINGS.

DEUT. xxxiii. 16.

—— *And for the good-will of him that dwelt in the bush.*

THE doctrinal observation raised from the words, is this,

DOCT. The favour or good-will of Christ, who of old dwelt with Moses in the bush, is to be sought by believers, as the greatest and best of all blessings.

In discoursing on which subject, I proposed, as helped,

I. To shew what this good-will is, and whose it is. And,

In general, you have heard, it is the free favour

and

and gracious acceptation of Chrift, who appeared to Mofes in the bufh; and it may be confidered in a double view, either as denoting that good-will and grace which is in his heart towards his people; or elfe it is expreffive of the manifeftation of it to their perfons, in a way of fellowfhip and communion.

II. We inquired, why it is called the good-will of him 'that dwelt in the bufh.' And,

This expreffion holds forth four things:

Firft, That the fire in the bufh was a type of the incarnation and fufferings of the Son of God. God dwells in our poor defpicable human nature, which is but as a low infignificant bramble-bufh, and his Godhead fupported the manhood under all the fufferings he endured as the finner's furety; all our communion with God comes in this way, even by that redemption which is through his blood.

Secondly, It is called the good-will of him that dwelt in the bufh, becaufe Mofes had a top-manifeftation at this time of God's covenant-grace and mercy, and all covenant-bleffings.

Thirdly, It is thus defcribed, becaufe this bufh burning, and not confumed, was a fweet emblem to Mofes's faith of Chrift's love to his church, and care of it under the greateft fufferings they can be expofed to.

Fourthly, It is thus defcribed, becaufe this was the firft and one of the fweeteft appearances of our Lord Chrift to Mofes; therefore he makes it the pattern of his requeft for Ifrael; " the gracious accepta-" tion of my dweller in the bufh." There was perfonal application of the grace and fulnefs of Chrift to his foul. Firft vifits of love and grace are ever fweet; extraordinary manifeftations leave an abiding favour. Thus, the Apoftle Peter, fpeaking of Chrift, fays, he received from God the Father honour and glory, when there came fuch a voice to him from the excellent glory, ' This is my beloved

' Son

' Son in whom I am well pleafed. And this voice
' which came from heaven we heard, when we were
' with him in the holy mount,' 2 Pet. i. 18. Still
the Apoftle had it in remembrance, as what warmed and refrefhed his foul, even now, juft before his
dying time ; for he wrote this epiftle, when he
knew ' that fhortly he was to put off this taberna-
' cle, even as our Lord Jefus Chrift had fhewn him,'
ver. 14.

I come now to the third general,

III. To confider how or in what manner this
good-will is to be fought. Surely, if Mofes prays
for it fo earneftly on Jofeph's account, it was no lefs
a duty in Jofeph's tribe to feek it for themfelves.

To this I anfwer,

Firſt, Seek this good-will of Chrift, his free grace
and favour, as a bleffing diftinct from, and over and
above what God the Father hath promifed on his
own part in the everlafting covenant. Believers
have a diftinct fellowfhip with God the Father, God
the Son, and God the Holy Ghoft. You are bleffed in each of their names, in that form of bleffing
which the Apoftle gives us, 2 Cor. xiii. 14. Each
glorious Perfon in the Godhead has taken a part in
your falvation. God the Father ' hath loved us,
' and hath given us everlafting confolation, and good
' hope through grace,' 2 Theff. ii. 16. This his love
fet him on work to determine good for us in eternity, to find out a covenant-head for us, a Mediator,
a Surety in whom he could fhew the higheft juftice
againft our fins, and the higheft mercy and kindnefs
to our perfons. Hence ' God is faid to be love ;' he
ever acts towards his people in a fatherly loving way ;
this is the inward principle by which he acts in all
outward difpenfations. Hence the Apoftle, fpeci-
fying the feveral parts of falvation, afcribes this pe-
culiarity to the Father, Eph. ii. 4. ' God who is
' rich in mercy, for the great love wherewith he lo-

' ved

'ved us, even when we were dead in sins, hath
'quickned us together with Christ,' &c.

The Holy Spirit is the Comforter, who, 'by taking
'of the things of God and of Christ,' and applying
them to the conscience, brings peace, hope, joy, &c.
into the soul, and works in it a meetness for glory.
His great work is confolation, therefore we pray for
the communion of the Holy Ghost; because considered under this character, he is the author of all
that communion which believers have with Father
and Son; by revealing the love of each Person, and
also drawing out believers hearts to the actings of esteem, faith, thankfulness, delight, rest, wherein communion consists on our parts.

As for the blessed Jesus, grace and good-will are
the great blessings believers eye in him, and are to
apply to him for. 'Ye know,' says the Apostle,
'the grace of our Lord Jesus Christ, who though he
'was rich, yet for your sakes he became poor, that
'ye through his poverty might be rich,' 2 Cor. viii. 9.
There is grace in his person, and grace in his purchase; our beloved has procured eternal life for his
saints, and all that mercy, help, provision and comfort which they need in their way to it. 'I sat down,'
says the spouse, 'under his shadow with great de-
'light, and his fruit was sweet to my taste,' Song ii.
3. These are blessings given from Christ as an husband, distinct from those given from God as a Father: There is no narrowness in the covenant of
grace, save what we make by our own unbelieving
frames. God is willing the heirs of heaven should
have strong consolation in their way thither; therefore he himself is our father, helper, saviour; all
his perfections in the various exercise of them, are a
believer's: Christ is also our head, surety, husband,
brother, advocate, &c. The Spirit is our interpreter that opens God's mind to us and ours to him;
our comforter, sealer; and distinct fellowship believers have with each glorious Person under each of
these characters. This good-will then is to be sought

over

over and above what the Father hath promised on his own part in the everlasting covenant; it is a prayer addressed to Christ, a blessing which comes from *him*, and as such is to be sought by every believing soul.

Secondly, This good-will of God-man Mediator is to be sought, as what alone can 'give life and liber-
' ty to the believer in all acts of gospel-worship.'
Moses as we have supposed, considers the tribe of Joseph not only in a national, but in a church capacity; and wherein consists believers fellowship one with another, the beauty, order, glory of a church of Christ in all acts of gospel-worship, but in the presence of 'him that dwelt in the bush,' in his gracious acceptation and good-will? This when experienced puts a power into ordinances, and life into the heart of worshippers. Take away the person of Christ as God-man, and the object of worship is as it were lost, for there is no going to the Father but by him. What can sinners do with an absolute God? Take away Christ's sufferings, merit, righteousness and intercession, what plea can there be for faith? And believers when they go in Christ's name, yet if their spirits are not taken up in the exercise of faith on his good will, grace and acceptation, there is no nearness to God. Christ's presence is our life, we have none in ourselves; gospel-liberty is Christ's purchase and gift: 'If the Son make you free, then
' are you free indeed.' With the Father you have communion in respect to his love, his free, eternal, unchangeable love; but the acceptation of your persons, and the sense of it, as well as the blessing itself, is given only in Christ the beloved; 'Who hath
' made us accepted in the beloved,' Eph. i. 6. Distinct communion with Father, Son and Holy Ghost follow, and desire to maintain; but a separate, two-fold foundation of a sinner's hope you never read of, one consisting in God's good-will as an absolute God, the other in Christ's redemption, through whom he is reconciled to sinners; the grace of Christ must be first

first known and laid hold of before there can be any access to the good-will of God; that, as a spring shut up, a fountain sealed, sinful man is not the object of it, but sinless angels, and they stand confirmed in Christ, though they were not redeemed by him. It is the good-will of Christ which gives life and liberty in all gospel-worship, church-ordinances, prayer, preaching, sacraments, censure: what are all without this? ' Lo, I am with you always.' There is the church's defence and glory, he hath set her as a seal upon his heart, and as a seal upon his arm; *hers* is his love: *hers* is his power. O! nothing cements a church together like this, the good-will of Christ drawn from his own heart and carried into theirs, into every one of them, so that, as it is expressed in Solomon's Song, iv. 2. ' Every one bear twins, ' and none is barren among them.' There cannot be a barren lifeless walk under the power and influence of Christ shed abroad in the heart.

Thirdly, This good-will is to be sought with great *expectation* and *hope*. The blessed Jesus loves a fear which produces watchfulness in the soul, but he hates those fears which breed torment. The good-will of my dweller in the bush, says Moses; the good-will of my Lord and God, say thou. Keep in view the sense thou hast had of past grace and favour under thy burden, and grief for want of present tokens of it. ' If thou wilt believe, thou shalt see the glory ' of God,' John xi. 40. says our Lord to Martha; not, if thou questionest, and doubtest, and canst believe nothing. When we go to a tried friend, and ask a new favour, we go to him as a friend, and presume upon his friendship, that we shall not be denied; experience gives boldness. Persons do not use to go to such an one, still questioning whether he is a friend, and saying, " It may be after all, " I am mistaken." But O, unworthy frame! in which we too often go to the Lamb of God, who bears us this great good-will; who hath loved us, and washed us from our sins in his own blood, and
in

in many a precious promise has spoken peace, and renewed his time of love to our souls. Believer, thou art come in the gospel, not to mount Sinai; there was a bound set about that to keep the people at a distance, but thou art come to mount Zion, and art called to draw near; thou art come to Jesus the Mediator of the new covenant, *thy* Jesus, who knows thy wants, and in measure feels them: 'We have 'not an High-priest who cannot be touched with 'the feeling of our infirmities,' Heb. iv. 15. His good-will arises from such a sense of thy miseries, weaknesses and wants, as is attended with feeling, and produces sympathy towards the object beloved. Our fellowship is with that Jesus, who was all beauty and suitableness in his person, all love, pity and fatherly affections in his heart; hence he is called the everlasting Father, Isa. ix. 6. who has redeemed his spouse with his blood, bought out of the hands of justice all she needs, and who has all power in heaven and earth, by right of sonship and suretiship; who has helped thee hitherto, and who has sent his Spirit into thine heart to set thee about praying this very prayer unto him now. Knowest thou not, that the throne thou art approaching is a throne of grace? God dwells in the manhood, the bush is not consumed, our nature is advanced in heaven, as a token how high our persons shall be soon also advanced. Well then, come and seek this good-will, not as a servant, but as a son, not in the spirit of bondage, but boldness. How sweet would ordinances be, was this more a believer's frame under them? Moses asks here as one who was sensible God would grant. He had done too much heretofore, to deny him now.

Fourthly, This good-will is to be sought in its higher manifestations, and a sweeter experience of it from day to day. Moses leaves the degree wherein this good-will should be shewn to Joseph, to the sovereignty of him in whom it dwells; but withal, the manner of expression he uses, shews that it was no small portion he asks of it for him, the good-will of

my dweller in the bush. It is as though he had said, "Did thy good-will bring thee down from heaven to earth, I may ask any thing now? Was the vision of my incarnate God so sweet in the wilderness, so wonderful, so exceeding precious? Thou art God still, and thy good-will is yet the same. Was the church preserved of old by thy good-will? Much more shall it be so now." It must be well with all such as have an interest in this great good-will, for God has added another pillar for their faith, and another obligation to his own faithfulness and covenant-mercy. Now how is it that believers have communion with Christ in this his grace? Surely by living upon it, by receiving of his fulness, and by living up to it too. 'With thee is the fountain of 'life,' therefore let thy desires be ever flowing. The image of Christ is what believers are to be changed into from glory to glory; then there is always matter for faith, foundation for hope, ground of comfort. Alas, many of us have no more peace, light, joy, holiness, because we sit down and rest in what we have, without looking farther; whereas we should go in every duty for a fresh discovery of Christ's good-will. The well is deep and full. There was good-will in consenting to covenant-terms, good-will in fulfilling them. Grace in Christ's humbled state, grace in his exalted state, good-will from the cradle to the cross, in all his sufferings, in all his temptations, in all his reproaches, for he suffered 'the 'contradiction of sinners against himself,' that by considering him when thou art in like circumstances, thou shouldest neither 'be weary nor faint in thy 'mind,' Heb. xii. 3. Grace in Christ's exceeding glorious state, for he is 'gone to heaven as our fore-'runner.' Now faith has a sharp eye, it sees distant things exceeding clear, it is a large hand of faith. But the believer never sees *all* that is in Christ; when he looks again, there is more to be seen, more to be received, more to be enjoyed: And the life of a Christian should be spent in receiving from Christ
and

and returning to him. Seek clearer, sweeter, more manifestations of this 'good-will of him that dwelt in the bush.'

I thought to have gone through the subject, but shall leave the last general, and instead thereof conclude with two things:

I. Shew when believers should more especially dwell on the good will of Christ in their meditations and prayers. And,

II. Shew what encouragements they have to seek larger manifestations of it, as Moses did.

To the first, I answer in three particulars.

1. When all men speak well of thee, seek this good-will. When all things go easy and well with thee, all men speak well of thee; look, inquire, where is Christ? Is he near? Lord, what of *thy* love do I see in this, what of *thy* grace in that blessing? Is the mount pleasant, purely because I am in the mount, lifted up something higher than I was before? or am I there hearing that delightful voice, and seeing that excellent glory I have heretofore seen and heard? Do not value comforts, frames, enlargements, for their own sake; but value them in their relation to Christ. If all men speak well of thee, and Christ answers thee not by Urim or Dreams, that is, hides his face in ordinances, at sacraments, in prayer and fellowship, what does all avail? Set up all the candles that were ever made, you cannot make a sun of them. Christ's grace and good-will, let these be first in every thing. It is sad, that the smile of a creature should so often occupy the room of Christ! That we should be so exceedingly glad because of the gourd, and forget the beauty, fulness, glory of the giver, who shews but his back parts in those outward, sensible representations of himself. Christ is a lily for beauty, a rose for fragrancy, a sun for light, &c. but remember he infinitely and eternally excels them all; wherefore seek his good-will above all.

Z   2. When

2. When men and friends speak evil of thee, then look to this good-will, and consider it as the good-will of him 'that dwelt in the burning bush.' Does Christ smile? Is there peace within? No matter then what thy reproach is from men. 'The reproaches of 'them that reproached thee fell upon me,' says Christ; therefore he will roll off thine, and 'bring 'forth thy judgment as the light.' Christ suffered reproach, therefore he knows feelingly how to comfort under it; the bush cannot be burnt up if JEHOVAH the God of Israel be in it. 'Fret not thy- 'self because of him who prospereth in his way, be- 'cause of the man who bringeth wicked devices to 'pass,' Psal. xxxvii. 7. Is Christ with thee? Sweet is the trial then, and his presence is sweeter than if thou hadst not endured it, for some of Christ's grace, his good-will towards thee, had then been lost. What a glory have some seen in these two texts! 'He endured such contradiction of sinners against 'himself.' The other is, 'Neither did his brethren 'nor kinsfolks believe on him.' Christ's enemies were those of his own house; the devil can make use of saints to grieve and distress thee, but does not thy beloved endure this every day from thee, and yet hath a good-will towards thee still? Think on my text under the ill-will of men, and even friends.

3. Think on this good-will when thou hast ill-will, or at least ill-thoughts towards thyself. Sure, says the soul, I am an hypocrite, I have no grace, how can it be? What was there in such a prayer, such a duty? Observe, Christ 'dwelt in the bush,' in the bramble, not in the cedar. Perhaps that duty thou despisest most, he respects most. Broken language is very sweet to him, when it comes from a broken heart. Sighs go a great way towards deliverance. 'For the oppression of the poor, for the 'sighing of the needy, now will I arise, saith the 'Lord,' Isa. xii. 5. Wo to the oppressor when God arises, be he either sinner or saint! Believers do not always act as such; but when thy frames are lowest

and

and thy troubles higheſt, Chriſt's good-will is yet the ſame: His righteouſneſs and the acceptation of his perſon and work in heaven are the ſame, and herein thou ſtandeſt, and in nothing elſe: 'And for the 'good-will of him that dwelt in the buſh.'

II. I am to ſhew what encouragements believers have to ſeek large manifeſtations of this good-will.

1. It is the good-will of God, and JEHOVAH's thoughts are not as our thoughts; he is *abundant* in goodneſs and truth; wherefore, always in prayer, put in for ſomething beyond what thou canſt ſee in the promiſe, for he will do infinitely beyond what his people can aſk or think.

2. It is good-will which Chriſt is reſolved upon ſhewing forth. He appeared to Moſes in the buſh for that end, that he might diſcover his great love and good-will to a poor, ruined, periſhing church. It is a thing pleaſing in his ſight, that thou ſhouldſt be ever 'receiving of his fulneſs.'

3. Your own unworthineſs is ſet aſide by him. What ſo deſpicable as a bramble-buſh, what ſo vile as man's nature now fallen? Yet Chriſt took upon him our nature at the worſt, with all its ſufferings, miſeries and weakneſs: 'The word was made fleſh,' to denote the aſtoniſhing condeſcenſion of the Son of God. As for 'your iniquities' therefore, 'he will purge them away.' Once more,

4. Why ſhould not thy God be faithful to you, when he has been ſo to all his ſaints? The fire did not conſume the church, ſhe throve in Egypt; and the more they were oppreſſed, the more they grew. Be your trials what they will, there is ſome light in them. Afflictions are for our profit; by them God tries us, by them we alſo try him; ſeek the good-will of Chriſt the more, and be it enjoyed but in one prayer, one ordinance, aſſure thyſelf thou art better by that affliction. All bleſſings are comprehended and ſummed up in this, 'And for the good-will of 'him that dwelt in the buſh.'

SERMON XXX.

THE GOOD-WILL OF CHRIST THE BEST OF BLESSINGS.

DEUT. xxxiii. 16.

―— *And for the good-will of him that dwelt in the bush.*

THE doctrinal observation from the words is this,

DOCT. The favour or good-will of Christ, who of old dwelt with Moses in the bush, is to be sought by believers, as the greatest and best of all blessings.

In discoursing of which, I proposed four things,

I. To shew what this *good-will* is, and whose it is.
II. Why it is called, ' the good-will of him that ' dwelt in the bush.'
III. How, or in what manner this *good-will* is to be sought.

First, It is to be sought as a blessing distinct from, and over and above what the Father hath promised, on his part, in the everlasting covenant.

Secondly, It is to be sought as what alone can give life and liberty to the believer in all acts of gospel-worship.

Thirdly, It is to be sought with great expectation and hope.

Fourthly,

Fourthly, This good-will is to be sought in the higher manifestations and a sweeter experience of it from day to day. It is said of believers of old, 'they 'go from strength to strength;' and it is as becoming a frame now, as it was then. In every duty, in every ordinance, you should go for a farther discovery and manifestation of this good-will: And I have also shewn, when believers should more especially dwell on this good-will of Christ in their meditations and prayers: As also what encouragements they have to seek large manifestations of it.

There is but one thing remains, which, as God helps, I would make the subject of the present discourse. Namely,

IV. Wherein consists the *greatness* of the blessing, which renders it so well worthy of all our seeking. And to this I answer:

First, The good-will of Christ, who of old 'dwelt 'in the bush,' lies at the foundation of every other blessing. 'Men shall be blessed in him, all nations 'shall call him blessed,' Psalm lxxii. 17. God the Father has not a single blessing to bestow, *out* of Christ, the Son of his love. All acceptation of our persons is in the beloved, and all spiritual communion is by him; 'through him we have an access 'by one Spirit unto the Father,' Ephes. ii. 18. True, there may be the precious things of the earth, and the fulness thereof, to them that know nothing of God or of Christ, but there is the curse in them. As many as are under the law, be their circumstances, conditions, relations in life what they will, they are under the curse, condemned men in law, reserved for execution a little while hence: And what would all this world avail a poor criminal under sentence of death, who knows not but the morrow may be execution-day? 'They that trust in their wealth, 'and boast themselves in the multitude of their 'riches; none of them can by any means redeem 'his brother, nor give to God a ransom for him,'

Psalm lix. 6, 7. The day is coming when none but Christ, an whole Christ, will be deemed a portion sufficient for an immortal soul. 'Seek first the 'kingdom of God and his righteousness:' This is the one thing needful. The good-will of Christ is the foundation of every other blessing.

Secondly, Every other blessing is comprehended in this. If Christ be thine, all is thine. Art thou at peace with him? 'He will make a covenant for 'thee, with the beasts of the field, and with the 'fowls of heaven, and with the creeping things of 'the earth;' all other things shall be at peace with you; at least, 'he will break the bow and the 'sword, and the battle for thy sake,' so that 'no 'weapon formed against thee shall prosper,' Hosea ii. 18. When God comes to bless a poor soul in Christ, he gives him all things. Ephes. i. 3. 'Bles- 'sed be the God and Father of our Lord Jesus Christ, 'who hath blessed us with all spiritual blessings in 'heavenly places in Christ:' pardon, and peace, acceptance, and grace, and comfort here, all blessings of a spiritual kind, such as *lead* to heaven and happiness, and eternal life, and glory itself hereafter. 'He that overcometh shall inherit all things, and I 'will be his God, and he shall be my son,' Rev. xxi. 7. so that there is no need to glean in another field: If God has given you all spiritual blessings in the gross, whoever will may take what is left: 'The 'earth he hath given to the children of men.' Let it go and welcome, says the saint, so long as the heaven of heavens is the Lord's, and this glorious and blessed Lord is mine. He is God 'all-sufficient,' or of 'many paps;' for thus some derive the word *Shaddai* in Gen. xvii. 1. he has paps of consolation for his saints to suck at to all eternity. The sum of all blessedness is wrapped up in this good-will and gracious acceptation of the Mediator; this is what Moses is express in here, and what Paul followed on to know, though it is such, he tells, us 'as passeth 'knowledge. And to know the love of Christ 'which

'which passeth knowledge, that ye might be filled
'with all the fulness of God,' Ephes. iii. 19.

Four things there are which make this love and good-will of Christ so precious to believers.

1. It is the love and good-will of *God*. Hence it hath in it an infinite fulness, it has heights and depths, and lengths and breadths, Ephes. iii. 18. It is beyond what thou canst ask or think : ' Fear not, thou worm ' Jacob, and ye men of Israel; I will help thee, ' saith JEHOVAH thy Redeemer,' Isa. xli. 14. ' I am ' God not man ;' this is the bottom of the sinner's consolation, JEHOVAH dwelt in the bush. Were there not everlasting righteousness, everlasting strength, everlasting grace, and consolation, in our dear Redeemer, that infinite guilt which there is in your sins and mine, would sink us into confusion and endless despair. How could our wants be known to Christ, or supplied by him if he were not the man, ' God's fellow ?' Zech. xiii. 7. possessed of *infinite* knowledge, grace and mercy. " If there were no " more grace for me, than can be treasured up in " a mere man, I should rejoice (says great Dr " Owen) my portion might be under the rocks and " mountains."

2. It is the love and good-will of him that is *man* as well as God, therefore there is in it infinite suitableness and sweetness. Not a circumstance of sorrow and distress the believer is in, but Christ felt it in his human nature, when he was fulfiling all righteousness: ' I am among you,' says Christ, ' as ' he that serveth ;' he knows our sorrows, by *bearing* them, and all our manifold temptations, by being ' tempted like as we are, only without sin.' Thy griefs are all, not only of his appointing but trying ; thy crosses of his measuring, as well as ordering and over-ruling ; and O that *feeling* which he has of thy infirmities, makes him very tender and compassionate, and full of bowels. ' Simon, Simon, Satan hath de-
' sired to have thee, that he may sift thee as wheat,
' but I have prayed for thee, that thy faith fail not,'

Luke xxii. 31. Fall thou muſt, to teach thee to be ſober and vigilant; but I'll recover thee again, thy faith ſhall not fail. 'JEHOVAH dwelt in the buſh;' our vile nature has God dwelling in it, that the glorious Perſon that aſſumed it, might give grace and mercy to help in time of need, as having been a fellow-ſufferer with us in his humbled ſtate: This makes the love of Chriſt precious to the ſaints.

3. This good-will admits of no change. The favour of creatures is a vain thing; they love to-day and hate to-morrow, but the favour of Chriſt endureth for ever. The God with whom, believer, thou haſt truſted thy all, thy ſoul, body, circumſtances, reputation, &c. is a tried God, and a Saviour. There is no living upon the ſmiles of a creature; they are like a ſummer's brook, they ſend him away deceived and aſhamed: The thirſty traveller comes to it with great expectation, but there is no water. Not ſo the good-will here ſpoken of: 'Peace I leave with 'you, my peace I give unto you; not as the world 'giveth, give I unto you,' John xiv. 27. Chriſt's affection is ever the ſame, beeſt thou on the mount, or in the valley; though the manifeſtation of it is reſerved uſually for times of ſpecial ſorrow, temptation, heart-reproaches, wherein the world and all creatures put together cannot help thee; yea, for ſuch times, when the world is ſet againſt thee; 'when my father and mother forſake me, then the 'Lord will take me up,' Pſalm xxvii. 10. This poor burning buſh is not conſumed, becauſe God is in it, the unchanging, everlaſting God, who is then readieſt to help, when poor humbled oppreſſed ſouls are moſt in need. The good-will of Chriſt is unto the end, he reſts in it, it is without leſſening or change, therefore ſo precious to the ſaints. Again,

4. The good-will of Chriſt is fruitful and communicative. No ſooner does the Chriſtian groan, than *he* hears: 'I have ſeen, I have ſeen the afflic-'tion of my people which are in Egypt, and have 'heard their cry by reaſon of their taſk-maſters;
'for

'for I know their sorrows,' Exod. iii. 7. A man may love another as his own soul, yet that love of his cannot help him; he may pity, and bemoan him in misery, but all his pity cannot give him ease. Abraham desired 'Ishmael might live before God,' Gen. xvii. 18. but he could not desire grace *into* his heart. But 'the good-will of him that dwelt in 'the bush,' always brings to thy heart the good it willeth, pardon, peace, strength, comfort, joy, and heaven itself at last. It brings sanctification and salvation too; every promise thou hast under any trial, it is the fruit of this good-will; every cleansing of conscience thou hast, after any filth gathered in thy walk, it comes from this good-will; every grace thou art quickened to the exercise of, hence it arises, even from the good-will of Christ. He first purchased it, and then wills it, and he lives to see his own testament executed. Whatever thou needest here, or hereafter, this good-will will give it in, in its season. Thy Jesus keeps nothing for himself, his favour is fruitful and communicative, he is head over all things to the church, which is his body; he fills all and every saint, in all their wants, hungerings, and expectations. 'Open thy mouth,' says he, 'and 'I will fill it,' Psalm. lxxxi. 10. 'I am the God of 'Abraham, Isaac and Jacob.' In speaking that one sentence, thy God says all things.

On these accounts, the good-will of Christ is so precious to the saints. I go on to a third thing, tending to open the *greatness* of this blessing, which renders it so well worthy of all our seeking.

Thirdly, Not only is this precious good-will of Christ the foundation of every other blessing, and that which comprehends every other blessing; but it is also *needful* to make our *other* blessings, 'blessings 'indeed.' The creature, in all its variety and abundance, has no sweetness, no blessing in it, save what the covenant puts into it. Therefore when Moses enumerates all the good things, which heaven and earth give, he adds this one, to make them all

of significancy and importance, 'and for the good-
'will of him who dwelt in the bush;' that which
denominates any thing we enjoy of the creatures,
a *blessing*, is the favour and good-will of God in be-
stowing it; if it come not from love, we have it only in common with the rest of the world, to whom
it may be a trap, a snare, and an occasion to fall.
Deut. vii. 12, 13. 'Wherefore it shall come to pass,
'if ye hearken to these judgments, and keep and do
'them, that the Lord thy God shall keep unto thee
'the covenant, and the mercy which he sware unto
'thy fathers; and he will love thee and bless thee,
'and multiply thee; he will also bless the fruit of
'thy womb, and the fruit of thy land, thy corn and
'thy wine, and thine oil, the increase of thy kine,
'and the flocks of thy sheep, in the land which he
'sware unto thy fathers to give thee. Thou shalt
'be blessed above all people.' It is God's covenant,
and hearty love, and good-will, which makes these
things blessings indeed. The whole world cannot
satisfy a soul without this: Men may be in straits in
the abundance of their possessions; have, and never
enjoy; be crying, 'who will shew me any good?'
when one would think all the good of the creature
is pressed out to them, and running over, yet 'who
'will shew me any good?' They see nothing worth
calling so, in what they have already: Now, whence
is this? It arises from a want of God, and Christ,
and covenant love, and good-will, to put a sweetness and relish into creature-comforts, and to make
up all creature-deficiencies. Ahab dies, though at
the head of a kingdom, because he wants Naboth's
vineyard; David, in the midst of a wilderness, has
no want, because 'the Lord was his shepherd.' Love
in the purchase, and love in the gift, let a believer
but see these, and creature-comforts always come
with a blessing. The world would be nothing in a
believer's inventory, were he not first to see Christ
his; this puts a value upon every other blessing.
Children, and friends, and health, and riches, and
honours;

honours; it is the good-will of 'Christ that dwelt 'in the bush,' which sanctifies and sweetens all; without this every thing that is good would be missing. Once more,

Fourthly, The good-will of Christ is a blessing infinitely *better* than all 'outward blessings,' and makes up 'the loss' of all. Paul had no friend left, when he most needed friends: What then was his comfort, his support? Why, ' the Lord was with him, ' and strengthened him.' 2 Tim. iv. 16. ' At my ' first answer, (before Nero) no man stood with me, ' but all men forsook me:—notwithstanding the Lord ' stood with me and strengthened me.' Believers of old ' took patiently the spoiling of their goods,' and the torturing of their bodies; now, what encouraged them so to do? Outward encouragements they had none; it was 'a looking to Jesus,' and his good-will towards them, who endured ' the contradiction ' of sinners against himself.' Hence also the church speaks in the strongest actings of faith; Habak. iii. 17. ' Although the fig-tree shall not blossom, neither ' shall fruit be in the vines, the labour of the olive ' shall fail, and the field shall yield no meat, the ' flock shall be cut off from the fold, and there ' shall be no herd in the stalls;' (though the streams of all creature-comforts be cut off), ' yet will I re-' joice in the Lord, I will joy in the God of my ' salvation.' Living and dying, God's covenant supports; the gracious acceptation and good-will of ' JEHOVAH that dwelt in the bush,' carries the soul far beyond distress and fear. If Christ do but reveal this his love, the wrath of all men on earth put together vanishes into smoke. ' Tribulation, dis-' tress, persecution, famine, peril, sword,' Paul glories in them all. ' In all things,' says he, ' we are ' more than conquerors,' but it is 'through him that ' loved us,' Rom. viii. 35. Believers are heirs under age; the children of a king under disguise; some are poor in circumstances; others low and mean as to their capacities and improvements; others in

pain,

pain, bondages or troubles; it may be the world owns them not, and their own mothers sons are angry with them, and look cool upon them; as to the precious fruits brought forth by the sun, and for the precious things put forth by the moon, they know little of them but by hearsay: However, that *soul* of blessings, 'the good-will of him that dwelt in the bush,' visits and revives them. No matter what the place be the soul is in: To this man,' says Christ, ' will I ' look, who is of a contrite spirit, and that trembleth ' at my word;' Christ has but few to shew his respect to, that are of Cæsar's houshold; but wherever the place is, there the blessing is, and none can say the greatness and sweetness of it, but such as have enjoyed it; it fills the soul with ' joy unspeak-' able.' The grace, and good-will of Christ to be wholly thine, and thine for ever; ' it passeth know-' ledge,' it is reserved for an hereafter, so to know it, as to be satisfied with it: ' I shall be satisfied ' when I awake with thy likeness,' Psalm xvii. 15.

Upon these considerations, ' the good-will of him ' that dwelt in the bush,' is worthy to be sought above and beyond all other things. A few uses shall close the whole.

Use 1. What a foolish choice do most men make! Christ and his good-will are last thought of by the natural man. 'The things which are seen,' these ingross the heart, and carry the whole stream of his affections after them: Man! pause a while. This world, is it as easily got, as it is greedily sought after? Or canst thou keep riches when thou hast them, that they fly not from thee? Or is there *rest* in riches, if thou canst keep them? Mayst thou not hear a voice, as thousands have done, ' Thou fool, this ' night shall thy soul be required of thee?' And what will this world appear, when thou art called to launch into eternity? Canst thou bribe or deceive thy Judge? or canst thou dwell with devouring flames? or hast thou a friend above? Think on these things before it be too late. Repentance is too late, when time is ended.

Use 2. Hence you see why Christ is so loved by every believing soul. It is because all that can be desired is in his person and good-will. 'He is fairer 'than the sons of men; grace is poured into his 'lips.' God and man in one person; a portion thou mayst live upon to all eternity. Who can see the Son of God bowing under God's wrath, or indeed united to man's nature, and not fall down and admire, and adore, and love him? He who has shewn his great good-will in his covenant-agreement, his coming into the world, his obeying and dying here as our Surety, yea our curse, for he was made a curse for us; who can, by an eye of faith, see all this, and not find his heart more firmly knit to the blessed Jesus? 'Whom,' says the Apostle, 'having not 'seen, ye love; in whom though now ye see him 'not, yet believing, ye rejoice with joy unspeaka- 'ble and full of glory,' 1 Pet. i. 8. And the Psalmist, upon a view of this his care and good-will, says, 'Whom have I in heaven but thee? And 'there is none upon earth that I desire besides thee. 'My flesh and my heart faileth; but God is the 'strength of my heart, and my portion for ever,' Psalm lxxiii. 25, 26. No wonder then that Christ is so loved by his saints.

Use 3. If this good-will be so great, let it be sought by thee, O sinner. Seek it, 'for it is thy 'life;' if thou hast not a Christ, thou art ruined for ever. The good-will of the creature goes but a very little way towards heaven; thy parents desires and prayers will not do, if thou seekest it not thyself. Religion is a personal thing; and remember this is *free* good-will, and sure that is encouraging to seek; 'This is the accepted time, this is the 'day of salvation,' 2 Cor. vi. 2. 'Behold, I stand 'at the door, and knock: If any man hear my 'voice, and open the door, I will come in to him, 'and will sup with him, and he with me, Rev. iii. '20.'

Use 4. Is this good-will so great? Do you also who believe make it your chief concern to know and enjoy more of it.

You have heard what precious encouragements are given you to this end. It is the good-will of God. It is what he is resolved upon shewing forth. Your unworthiness is set aside by him in this matter: And it is good-will which has been shewn to all his saints; and why should not thy God be faithful to thee, when he has been so to all his in their generations? To this good-will I leave you, and add no more on this subject.

SERMON XXXI.

THE WITHDRAWMENT OF GOD'S SPIRIT DEPRECATED AS THE WORST OF EVILS.

PSALM li. 11.

—— *And take not thy holy Spirit from me.*

THIS Psalm is David's penitential prayer after his great sin; and in it there are all the stirrings of holy affections that can possibly be expressed. It would carry me too far away from my design and aim in this discourse, were I to go over this psalm, verse by verse, and shew the actings of his Spirit in each, till I get to my text: This I shall therefore wholly wave, taking notice only of two or three observations which offer themselves from the title of it.

OBSERV. 1. The best of saints may fall into the worst of sins. Corrupt nature is the same in all. That it does not shew itself as vilely in us as in others, is not owing to any goodness in us, but to the preventing power and restraining grace of God. Grace is no self-acting principle; former experiences without present supplies of the Spirit, will not keep a believer from the grossest sins: We know not what we are till we are tried. When the wind of temptation comes, it blows off the ashes that were upon the coals, and presently the room is filled with heat. One sin leads on to many others: 'Let him that
'thinketh

'thinketh he standeth, take heed lest he fall.' David's sin is recorded as a caution to others.

OBSERV. 2. As the best of saints cannot keep themselves from falling, so neither can they raise themselves up again when they are fallen. 'Thou restorest my soul,' says the Psalmist, Psalm xxiii. 3. David lay stupid and secure, till Nathan the prophet came unto him. The heart grows hardened through the deceitfulness of sin. To sin against conscience, is the way to sear conscience. For smaller sins David's heart smote him soon, as when he cut off Saul's skirt, when he sent Joab to number the people, &c. but now he grows senseless; all tenderness of conscience is gone; there is no real heart-acknowledgment of it for many months: Some suppose there were nine months between David's committing the sin, and his repentance of it. O Sirs! Do not presume upon the favour of God, the stability of the covenant, the certainty of your recovery out of the snare of the devil, &c. when you venture upon known sins. It is easy falling into sin, but not so easy to rise again to repentance. Peter's fall cost him many tears; and David, for his sin, walked softly all his life after.

OBSERV. 3. Where repentance is sincere, a believer matters not what shame he takes, provided by his confession glory may redound to God. Before, David hid his sin, but now he can never speak of it too much. 'It is ever before me,' says he, ver. 3. And, as Bishop Patrick well observes upon the title of the Psalm, "To make himself as notorious an example of true repentance, as he had been of foul wickedness, he composed this penitential hymn, and sent it to the master of music in the tabernacle, to be used perpetually there, as a testimony of his unfeigned sorrow for what he had done, and of the miserable condition he thought himself in, without the infinite mercy of God." True repentance always breeds self-loathing. Public sins always call for public humiliation;
and

and the believer defires and approves, that God may be glorified, when his people are aggrieved though his means. Thefe obfervations arife from the title of the pfalm: The words which I have now read, do, as it were, bring both parts of the prayer together: " All my fin, in every ftep and degree of it, " fays he, arifes from hence; God has taken his " Holy Spirit from me; I was left to myfelf, that I " might know what is in my own heart; and, Lord, " what will become of me for the future, if thou " caftſt me out of thy prefence? If thy Holy Spirit " be taken from me, I am undone; I am unfit for " every duty; I fhall fall by every temptation; my " prefent fenfe of fin will foon wear off; David will " be found again in the mire. I cannot walk with " God, unaffifted by the Spirit of God. Lord, what- " ever thou denieft me, regard me in this. Let me " have thy prefence and Spirit with me, thy Holy " Spirit; how can the work of fanctification be pro- " moted and carried on in me, if his gracious, power- " ful, efficacious influences are denied me? ' Take " not thy Holy Spirit from me.' " Whatever elfe " thou takeft, continue this mercy. My children, my " crown, my life, I deferve to lofe them all, and I " can part with them; no part of the meffage which " Nathan hath delivered, but I can fubmit to: on- " ly grant me thy Spirit. Here, Lord, I muſt plead " till I obtain." David, as finful, as unworthy as he knows himfelf to be, can take no denial here. My all depends upon it:—' And take not thy Holy Spi- ' rit from me.' The plain obfervation contained in thefe words is this:

OBSERV No lofs is fo grieving to a child of God, as the lofs of God's prefence and Spirit. Or thus: Whatever other bleffing God removes, the fincere foul cannot bear that he fhould take away his Holy Spirit from him. In difcourfing on which, as God helps, I would do three things. As,

I. Shew you what it is for God to take away his holy Spirit, as expreffed in the text.

A a   II. For

II. For what reasons, or on what account he does this.

III. Why gracious souls are so earnest with God that he would not do it. And so apply.

I. I am to shew what it is for God to take away his Holy Spirit, as expressed in the text; or what does a Christian lose, when he loses the Spirit of God? To this I answer,

1. Not an interest in the favour of God, nor a standing in his covenant. Where the love of God is once fixed, it can never be taken away, 'his cove-
'nant is ordered in all things, and sure,' 2 Sam. xxiii. 5. There is a blessed *nevertheless* in the covenant which secures the love of God to a believer's person, notwithstanding the tokens of his anger against his sins, Psalm lxxxix. 30, 31, 32, 33. 'If his chil-
'dren forsake my law, and walk not in my judg-
'ments; if they break my statutes, and keep not
'my commandments: Then will I visit their transf-
'gression with a rod, and their iniquities with stripes.
'Nevertheless, my loving kindness will I not utter-
'ly take from him, nor suffer my faithfulness to fail.'
David's seed may be chastened, but they shall not be disinherited. God will bring them down by affliction, but will not cast them off under it: Why? Be-
cause how unworthy soever they are in themselves, they are loved in Christ, who is always worthy. His righteousness is 'an everlasting righteousness; he
'liveth ever to make intercession; the Lord is well
'pleased for his righteousness sake.' Though there be a rod in God's hand, and his people feel the smart of it; yet there is love in his heart. There is no change there. Nor,

2. Does the Christian lose the real presence of the Spirit, for this is constant and perpetual. In John xiv. 17. both these are included: 'He dwells with
'you and shall be in you.' The gifts and the call-
ing of God are without repentance. If the Spirit withholds his comforts, he does not shift his lodging;
where

where once he makes his abode, there he will settle it. Believers have the Spirit in this respect when they cannot discern him. Therefore,

3. For God to take away his Holy Spirit, is for him to withdraw his sensible gracious influences from the soul. The Spirit's residence is not altered, but his operations are interrupted. He feels none of the joys of God's salvation which he used to do; all is dark and dead within: his gifts are withering, his graces dried, and his comforts as if there were no such thing. 'Thou holdest mine eyes waking,' says Asaph, 'I am so troubled I cannot speak,' Psalm lxxvii. 4. As if he had said, " I can get no ease, no " quiet from my grief; and my soul is oppressed, " that I cannot tell God what it is." A man may look inwards, and upwards, but there is no peace, if the presence and witness of the Spirit is withheld. For when the Sun of righteousness hides his head, it is in vain for us to look for comfort to our own graces. These stars shine with a borrowed light. If God commands his clouds that they rain no rain, the choicest vine yields but sorry grapes. It is not the presence of the Spirit, as filling heaven and earth, that satisfies the Christian; he may be in terror and bondage, in misery and hell, for all this. It is the presence of his grace, as upholding, quickening, comforting, cheering, directing into the love of God, witnessing with his Spirit, sealing him up unto the day of redemption. This is the presence of the Spirit, which a poor heavy-laden soul needs, and seeks after. This presence David, in my text, had lost; and when God gives him to see his sin, he soon sees his need of it. Then all the world, for the return and presence of the Spirit. For God to take away his Spirit from the believer, is for him to withhold the sensible, gracious influences of the Spirit from the soul.

II. We are to enquire for what reasons, or on what accounts it is, that God acts thus towards his own people?

Among many others that might be mentioned, there are these four:

1. *Pride* and *self-confidence* in the performance of any duty. The Apostle seems to be most afraid of that little boasting pronoun *I*; 1 Cor. xv. 10. 'I 'laboured more abundantly than they all,' that is a great word for humble Paul to say, who counted himself ' less than the least of all saints;' therefore he qualifies it in the next words, and brings it to be more of a piece with the whole of his conduct, ' Yet ' not I, but the grace of God which was with me.' The more he laboured, the more he was a debtor to divine grace. Grace prepared him for service, grace assisted him in it, grace gave success to it, grace therefore has all the praise. Paul claims nothing to himself. He was but the vessel into which God's treasure was put. ' We have this treasure in earth- ' en vessels.' I have often observed it, when men have counted of doing some great thing most worthy of themselves, God has left them to act beneath themselves. Why? because their end was wrong; self lay at the bottom; not God's truth, his grace, and glory. God always finds some way to empty the soul he intends to fill. My friends, go to duty as you think *prepared*, and depend upon *it* in duty, and you will find yourselves straitned.

How was it with David, Psalm xxx. 6. ' In my ' prosperity I said, I shall never be moved.' As if he had said, " I have had a sweet time of it for a " long while; the visits of God's love are very pre- " cious, and they are oft repeated; I shall never be " in darkness, in bondage, in soul-distress more; " God has brought my feet out of the depths, and " set them upon a rock; it will be sweet walking " to heaven now." But what became of this elevated frame of his wherein the Spirit of God was so little concerned? O! he soon smarted for it: ' Thou didst hide thy face, and I was troubled.' It was high time it should be so, for he had almost forgot *him* from whom his frames came. This sudden

change

change brought him to his senses: 'Lord, by thy 'favour thou hast made my mountain to stand strong.' When the sun sets, night certainly follows, and the moon and all the stars cannot make day. The Spirit is quenched, when pride is indulged; when we think our good frames come of course, God shuts up the fountain; and where are all the streams then? To our sorrow, but to our trembling, we find them dried up.

2. Another reason why God withdraws his Spirit, is *negligence* and *sloth* in the discharge of duty. This was the spouse's frame, Cant. v. 2. but she paid dear for it: Christ comes and knocks, and sues for entrance; gives her all the endearing expressions imaginable: 'Open to me, my sister, my love, my dove, 'my undefiled; for my head is filled with dew, and 'my locks with the drops of the night.' Truly she is indisposed to receive him; her heart makes no answer to the kindness and love of Christ. Other things had taken up present possession. And how does her beloved take this? He resents it at her hands. Christ rebukes her delay with his denial; when she afterwards goes to open the door, ' her be-' loved had withdrawn himself, and was gone. Then ' she sought him, but she could not find him; she call-' ed him, but he gave her no answer,' *ver.* 6. The cause of his forsaking of us, lies in great measure in ourselves. Sure, if the presence of Christ is not worth seeking, it is scarce worth having. O! those formal lukewarm frames of spirit, our beloved loaths them. Give Christ your whole heart, or give him nothing. Do not think to put him off with bodily exercise; a cold petition or two, when you are half asleep and half awake; an ejaculatory prayer, when you are *dressing* in a morning to come to the worship of God, because this takes up all your other time. No! no! this is an offering his soul abhors. And if his presence is not endeared to you, you shall not enjoy it. The Spirit will carry away the message to some poor hungring soul, that sits by you,

whose clothes and dress it may be you despise; he needs it more, and will improve it better. 'I dwell, 'says the high and the holy One, in the holy place, 'with him also that is of a contrite and humble spi-'rit, to revive the spirit of the humble, and to re-'vive the heart of the contrite ones,' Isa. lvii. 15.

3. *Unimproved mercies* is another cause of the removal of God's Spirit. It is the blackest part of Solomon's character, that ' he sinned against the Lord ' that appeared to him twice,' 1 Kings xi. 9. God keeps an account of his gracious visits, whether we do or not. It is the heart he looks at, his eye is there: ' And the Lord was angry with Solomon, ' because his heart was turned from the Lord God ' of Israel which had appeared to him twice.' All outward duties are nothing, if the heart be not in them; see whether your heart be not humbled under humbling providences, your heart be thankful under encouraging ones; whether you render to the Lord according to what you have received from him. According to this it is God judges of you, and deals with you. It is a great blot upon good Hezekiah's character, 2 Chron. xxxii. 25. ' But Hezekiah ren-' dered not again according to the benefit done un-' to him: for his heart was lifted up, therefore there ' was wrath upon him, and upon Judah and Jerusa-' lem.' O, that same pride! it creeps in at little crevices; but pride and communion with God are two contrary things. Assure yourself if you are lifted up, that God will lay you low. Keep your distresses ever in view, if you would have an heart-affecting sense of God's mercies: ' Sure we had need be ' ever upon the watch.' If signal mercies will not melt us into humiliation and thankfulness, what will? Yet it had not this effect here. However, Hezekiah afterwards is humbled before God, and returns. Unimproved mercies are another cause.

4. *Present sins* are another cause of God's withdrawing of his Spirit: Sampson and David both failed here. Oh! what are the best of men when God

leaves them to themselves? and what a dreadful state do present sins, when committed, leave men in? 'Sampson would go out to shake himself as at other 'times, but he wist not that the Lord was departed 'from him,' Judges xvi. 20. David, a man so great with God as he was, to be indolent and careless under so long a want of sensible communion with him! What shall we say to these things? Sure we must admire God's patience, and adore his justice, as a God that taketh vengeance. No; he will not bear sin in his own people. He will not walk with them that walk contrary to him; and yet what amazing grace is here, that he devises means that his banished ones be not expelled. David is an elect vessel; a *child* still, though a sinning one. God sends his faithful messenger to reprove him, to bring sin to his remembrance; but communion he will not maintain with him, till he is brought to confession: 'Against 'thee, thee only have I sinned, and done this evil 'in thy sight.' God's Spirit is an holy Spirit; remember that. If you would walk with God, it must be in a way of conformity and obedience to all his commands. God will give an excuse to no sin, no not a little one. Neglect of duty always endangers loss of communion. But this leads to consider, thirdly,

III. Why gracious souls cannot bear the loss of God's Spirit without putting in their plea against it?

They pray, and cry for it; it is to them instead of all blessings. More particularly,

1. Because he is the Spirit of truth, and without his gracious teachings, all the knowledge that we have of God and of Christ, will do us no real good. Light in the head will be of little efficacy, if there be not life and heat in the heart. We may have a clear knowledge of divine things by reading, hearing, meditation, reasoning, &c. but a comforting soul-transforming knowledge of them we cannot have, but from the Spirit. Hence the Psalmist prays,

Psal. xliii. 3, 4. 'O send out thy light and thy truth; let them lead me, let them bring me unto thy holy hill, and to thy tabernacles. Then will I go unto the altar of God, unto God my exceeding joy.' The word signifies to send as an ambassador. The Spirit when he comes with a commission from Christ, to open the eyes of our understandings, and take off our natural darkness, how full and comprehensive, how sweet and glorious do supernatural truths appear? What a vast scope and suitableness, what a pertinency and power is there in gospel-promises? How close and how warm do they fall upon our hearts? There is a conviction goes along with the word, that God is in it. It is like a voice from behind us, or rather a voice within us, saying, 'This is the way, walk ye in it.' It is sweet reading, sweet studying, sweet preaching and praying, when the Spirit of truth is with us. 'He searcheth all things, the deep things of God,' shews a man what there is in a promise, infinitely beyond what he could conceive was ever in it. All things are plain and pertinent, all things are savoury and relishing. He both gives the appetite, and prepares the food; nothing will do us any real good without his gracious teachings.

2. He is the Spirit of grace and of supplication, and without his aid we shall be indifferent to duty, and lifeless in it. Zech. xii. 10. 'And I will pour upon the house of David, and upon the inhabitants of Jerusalem the Spirit of grace and of supplications, and they shall look upon me whom they have pierced, and they shall mourn for him as one mourneth for his only son, and shall be in bitterness for him, as one that is in bitterness for his first-born.' God has always some special blessing to give when he sets his people a praying; pours upon them, so that they cannot refrain from it. *O! Sirs*, you have reason to say, sure I have need of quickning *to* duty, when I have no quickning *in* it. Prayer is dull work then; matter, yea even expression

sion itself fails; but when the Spirit helps our infirmities, how is it at such a time? When he brings a promise, and as it were whispers us secretly, use, plead that; when he turns over the leaves of our experience, and shews us far back, and says, Has God done all this for nought? have you not found him a tried God? He will help still; 'his covenant is or-'der'd in all things, and sure;' then the soul mounts up as upon eagle's wings; such mourning, such a sense of distance from God, such self-abhorrency, and withal such holy freedom, and boldness before him; such a mixture there is of holy desires and affections, as cannot be felt or expressed, but by the renewed mind. 'The Spirit helpeth our infirmi-'ties;' it is a great word that συναντιλαμϐανεται, he heaves with us; helps *over-against us*, as we help one that is lifting a burden, by *lifting over-against* him; he maketh intercession for us, dictates our requests, indites our petitions, draws up our plea; and he does this 'with groanings which cannot be ut-'tered.' It is not the rhetoric and eloquence, but the faith and fervency which the Spirit works as an intercessor in us. Our minds may be so confused, our souls in such a hurry, through Satan's suggestions at this time, that we know not what to say, nor how to express ourselves. But the Spirit is present with his help; and our Father, our God, knoweth the mind of the Spirit. O! there is a 'running the ways of 'God's commandments, when he is pleased thus 'to enlarge our hearts;' till then we are slow of speech, and of a stammering tongue; first we bring out one word and then another; 'but where the Spi-'rit of the Lord is, there is liberty.'

3. The Spirit is a Spirit of holiness, and without his presence all our endeavours after sanctification in heart and life are fruitless, and in vain; 'and take 'not thy holy Spirit from me.' David knew he could never come at a *right* spirit, that is, a constant, even spirit, an heart thorough for God, unless it was created in him by the Holy Spirit. From

him

him come new principles, and all renewed acts; he forms and fashions the soul for holiness, and keeps it intent upon every thing which makes for sanctification. 'It is through the Spirit that we mortify the 'deeds of the flesh;' by his aid, as directing, fixing, strengthening our faith, that we are enabled to quench the fiery darts of the evil one. Hence we are said, 1 Thess. ii. 13. 'To be chosen to salvation 'through sanctification of the Spirit, and belief of 'the truth:' Or, as Peter expresses it, 1 Epist. i. 2. 'To be elect according to the foreknowledge of God 'the Father, through sanctification of the Spirit un- 'to obedience, and the sprinkling of the blood of 'Jesus:' That is the way in which the Spirit works, in order to the believer's sanctification; he prepares our spirits for, and assists in, and carries through all acts of holy obedience; and, by the sprinkling of Christ's blood, purges and washes away every thing in our obedience that is offensive and unholy. He fixes and purifies the thoughts, keeps the heart, stops or opens the door of the lips, and guides the feet in all ways of holiness. O! it is sad to be left without the Spirit; sin and Satan have easy access then. Our spiritual frame is wholly out of order, and every way temptation comes in and prevails. They that know the blessing of the Spirit's presence will be ever praying with the Psalmist, 'And take not 'thy Holy Spirit from me.'

4. The Spirit is the author of all consolation and joy; and without his gracious influences the believer will be ever sorrowing and cast down. John xvi. 7. 'It is expedient for you that I go away; for if I 'go not away, the Comforter will not come unto 'you; but if I depart, I will send him.' No comfort, no peace, no hope in believing, but it comes through the power of the Holy Ghost, Rom. xv. 13. Much power is required to satisfy the doubts, scatter the fears, and answer the accusations of a troubled conscience. It is the alone prerogative of God the Spirit. Isa. lvii. 19. 'I create the fruit of the lips;
'Peace,

'Peace, peace, to him that is far off, and to him
'that is near, faith the Lord, and I will hear him.'
There can be no hope till the Spirit works it; and
without hope, what foundation is there for joy?
The Spirit takes of Chrift's things, applies his blood,
brings to remembrance his promifes, fhews his love,
and fixes the foul upon the bleffed covenant. Alas!
what are all the encouraging promifes we read, the
fermons we hear, the fweet words of comfort we
have given us from one and another friend, all are
as nothing, till the Spirit fpeaks: And to live always
in terror and fear, is very diftreffing. A word by
way of Ufe; as,

Use 1. If the lofs of God's prefence here be fo
dreadful, how fad is it ever to be feparated from it
in the other world? Pfal. xc. 11. 'Who knows the
' power of thine anger, even according to thy fear,
' fo is thy wrath.' Let a man fear it ever fo much,
he is fure to feel it more, if he falls under the
weight of it. Poor fouls, did you know what it
is, you would not trifle with it, as many of you do.
You hear of hell, and that wrath which is to come;
but fure, if you believed what you hear, it would
have a more abiding effect upon you. You would
not dare to go on in the ways of fin, and harden
your hearts againft God. 'Becaufe there is wrath,
' beware.' There is a hell after death, where wrath
will come upon finners to the uttermoft. O! take
care you do not ftifle convictions. It is a fad judgment that, 'My Spirit fhall not always ftrive with
' man.' When men do all they can to harden themfelves, God in a judicial way gives them up to hard-
nefs. To be feparated from God, is to be feparated
from all good for ever.

Use 2. God has other ways to punifh his own people for fin, than cafting them into hell for it. He
takes away his Spirit, though he does not remove
his favour. Relation continues, but all fenfe of it is
wanting; and it is fad to be always in fear of death
and judgment, and wrath to come. 'Thou waft a
' God

'God that forgaveſt them, though thou tookeſt vengeance on their inventions.' Pſalm xcix. 8. 'Our God is a confuming fire; ſerve the Lord with fear, and rejoice with trembling'

Use 3. Have a care how you grieve the Spirit. Eph. iv. 30. 'And grieve not the Holy Spirit of God, whereby ye are ſealed unto the day of redemption.' Do not do that which is contrary to his nature and will. Embrace his counſels; ſubmit to his government; walk in all the ways of his appointment. Stand at the greateſt diſtance from all ſin. Avoid the firſt occaſions of temptation. Satan is to be reſiſted, not to be parleyed with. Apply to the Spirit every day. Seek his directions, his aid, his favour; not to pray to him, is to grieve him. It is ſad to be left without his preſence. Life itſelf will not make up the loſs of his preſence. Chiefly would I addreſs myſelf to *young ones*; Satan has his eye upon you; he will be ſure, if he can, to have you in his ſnare. How muſt this be prevented? Not by all your ſtrivings in your own ſtrength, that will not do; you muſt look up to the Spirit; and for your encouragement, take theſe *three motives*.

Firſt, He is a *free* Spirit; it is not for your worthineſs that he affords his aſſiſtance. No, he brings a *new* heart *with* him. Cleanſing and creating work is his work; new covenant bleſſings are given without upbraiding.

Secondly, He is a *promiſed* Spirit. Iſa. xliv. 3. 'I will pour water upon him that is thirſty, and floods upon the dry ground: I will pour my Spirit upon thy ſeed, and my bleſſing upon thy offspring.' Put God in mind of his own covenant; he loves to be reminded of his promiſes, though he is faithful to perform them: 'For all theſe things will I be inquired of by the houſe of Iſrael to do them for them.' You ſhall be welcome when you go to God the Spirit; he loves to hear your feeble voice, and he has an anſwer to your cries. Children, young men, and all that hear me this day, put matters to the venture.

Go and try God; 'feek, and ye fhall find.' He will not fend you away empty. And,

Thirdly, He is a Spirit that abides where he has once taken poffeffion. Though he may hide his face, he will not leave his houfe, his temple; you go to him under all clouds and darknefs, as well as at firft. Often he goes backward that you may follow after him; and if he gives ftrength to wait, he will give fuccefs to your waiting. ' For the vifion
' is for an appointed time, but at the end it fhall
' fpeak, and not lie: though it tarry, wait for it,
' becaufe it will furely come, it will not tarry,' Habak. ii. 3.

But I add no more.

SERMON XXXII.

BELIEVERS PARDONED, AND YET CHASTISED.

Psalm xcix. 8.

Thou answeredst them, O Lord our God: thou wast a God that forgavest them, though thou tookest vengeance of their inventions.

THE design of this psalm is to beget in his saints an awful sense and reverence of God's holiness in all their worship, and their walk before him. His name is holy, *ver.* 3. His ordinances holy, *ver.* 5. His dispensations holy, *ver.* 9. Carnal boldness in a customary performance of holy duties, without regard had to the majesty and glory of God, and to our own vileness and distance from him, can never be warranted by covenant-relation. God looks upon sin with another eye than men do; nor will he spare it, though it be found in his choicest favourites and friends. Moses and Aaron among his priests, and Samuel among them that call upon his name, must be called to account when they dare turn aside from God. They called upon the Lord, *ver.* 6. They kept his testimonies, and the ordinances which he gave them, *ver.* 7. These are evidences of their faith and of their holiness; but they had some inventions, some works or deeds of their own, for which

which they must smart, though a pardoned and beloved people. Dr Hammond and some others think these words refer to the children of Israel, to whom God was gracious or propitious for Moses's sake: 'Thou answeredst them,' namely, Moses and Aaron; 'and forgavest' (not *to them*, as it is in the Hebrew, but) *for them*, namely, at their intreaty and interposition; because they stood in the gap to turn away God's anger from a sinning nation; which is all one as to pardon for their sakes. This seems to be a going off from the main intendment of the Psalm; which is to shew, as in a glass, what are the dispensations of God's Providence towards his own people, who are as to the general course of their lives faithful and obedient, though in some things they come short. Towards their persons God acts in a way of goodness and grace; answering their prayers, and forgiving their trespasses: To their sins, in a way of holy justice and severity, 'Though thou tookest vengeance on their inventions.' The word is, *practices*, which are justly called here and elsewhere, *inventions*, because they are of man's own contrivance and seeking out; they are not commanded of God, but devised of man. All sins are of a man's own finding out, be they acts of omission, or commission, because hereby he seeks happiness in another way than God has appointed. It must be confessed, that the word *vengeance* sounds harsh, when at the same time we hear of pardon: But it must be understood with a mixture of favour. Whatever the vengeance be, it cannot hinder or lessen the blessing of forgiveness: Sentence of pardon once passed will never be revoked: God neither punishes to the extremity of the desert of any sin, nor does he bear an hatred to the person sinning, 'Thine anger is turned away,' Isa. xii. 1. The only meaning of the expression is this; God's dispensations towards his people carry a great deal of terror in them: They are so awful and affecting, that bye-standers see nothing in them but displeasure and wrath: Yea believers themselves,

were

were they not on other grounds assured of pardon, could think no otherwise than that God was coming out against them to execute judgment. Moses, after all his desires and intreaties, must die in the wilderness and not go over Jordan, because he sanctified not the Lord at the waters of strife. Samuel was partial towards his sons whom he appointed judges over Israel, so that to him the people were obliged to sue for a king to reign over them in his lifetime. Aaron the saint of the Lord joined with Miriam in murmuring and unbelief; and for fear of the people committed a trespass against God: God took vengeance on the sin, though he forgave their persons. In the words there are three propositions. As,

PROP. I. Those who are most faithful to God, have some sins and misdoings attending them, which need his pardon.

PROP. II. Notwithstanding the sins of his people, God is a God of grace towards them; hearing their requests and forgiving them, when they pray unto him, *Nevertheless*, &c.

PROP. III. Although God answers and *forgives* his people, he may see it necessary ' to take vengeance ' on their inventions:' Publicly to testify his displeasure against those sins, which yet unto themselves he has forgiven.

The method I shall take in handling the words shall be, as God shall help,

I. To shew, what are those inventions of his own people, for which he takes vengeance.

II. Why it is necessary for God to take vengeance on *their* inventions, whose persons he accepts, and whose prayers he hears.

III. Whence it is, that God answers and forgives his people, with a notwithstanding to all their sins, and to that displeasure which he is obliged to discover against sin. And so apply.

I. What

I. What are those inventions or evil practices of his own people, of which God takes vengeance? I answer: All sin is an offence to God: He 'is of 'purer eyes than to behold iniquity.' Whatever is contrary to his will, is provoking to his jealousy: But there are some sins in his own people, which he shews a particular displeasure against. Such are,

1. Those sins which concern the *worship* and 'the 'order of his house.' This was Aaron's sin, for which God was angry with him, to have destroyed him, had not Moses made intercession for him, Deut. ix. 20. 'A jealous God,' is the title God first gave himself with respect to instituted worship, Exod. xx. 5. Jealousy works indignation and revenge, it is the rage of a man arising from an apprehension or fear lest any other should possess that which they think peculiar to themselves. God can bear no partner with himself, in prescribing what shall be the outward form of worship, or with what affections and with the exercise of what graces he will be worshipped. Uzzah does but put forth his hand to touch the ark of God, and perishes in his error, 2 Sam. vi. 6. Our God will be worshipped after the manner he has appointed. Holy things require holy frames. If we are not graceless in our persons, yet if we are devoid of reverence and godly fear in our duties, God will deal with us as with them that worship him after their own hearts devisings. 'Even our 'God is a consuming fire,' Heb. xii. 9. No combustible matter can stand before devouring fire. 'The fear of the Lord' is ever an attendant of the 'comforts of the Holy Ghost,' Acts ix. 31. Alas! what have not the best of saints to fear, should God punish us in this case as our inventions deserve! With what wanderings, misapprehensions, unspirituality, and presumption do we often wait upon God? How is the closet, how are public ordinances filled therewith!

2. A secret *neglect* of *the honour* and *glory of God* in our behaviour towards *men*, is another of

those sins which God visits in his own people. It will be hard to find wherein Moses' failing was, for the sake whereof he could not see the finishing of his work, in leading the children of Israel into Canaan, if it lay not in this, Numbers xx. 10. 'Hear now, ye rebels; must we fetch you water out of the rock?' This God calls, *ver.* 12. a not sanctifying of him in the eyes of the children of Israel. There was a sinful distrust, and a secret uncertainty in his and Aaron's breast, whether water should issue forth out of the rock or not at their speaking. Dr Lightfoot's notion of their unbelief is, that they doubted whether now at last, when the forty years were expired, they should enter Canaan; and whether they must not, for the murmuring of the people, be condemned to another like fatigue, because a new rock was now opened for their supply, which they took for an indication of their longer stay; therefore God punishes *them* by keeping them out of the land, when the rest of the people entered in. As for others God deals with them visibly according to their outward actions; but in his own he takes notice of the springs of their actings: Of their inward fears, their jealousies, their unbelief, their self-seekings, how utterly contradictory are these to the many sweet manifestations which God has given them of his wisdom, power, love and grace in time of need. God has secret provocations from his choicest saints, which he will not pass over without some tokens of his fatherly displeasure, and the grief of his holy Spirit thereby. God's glory is very dear to him, it is the end of all his purposes, and of all his dispensations. He will be honoured, as well as loved, as a father. 'A son honoureth his father, and a servant his master; if I be a father, where is my honour? If I be a master, where is my fear?' Mal. i. 16. In every duty believers perform, love should be the principle of their obedience; 'herein they are sons:' yet should they look upon themselves as servants in respect of strict obligation to duty, and fear to offend. Love

and

and fear should season every duty; the Lord is high, though he has a regard to the lowly: 'Thou art great, therefore greatly to be feared,' Psalm lxxxix. 7. Set God before thee in all thou dost, and in all thou desirest. We are afraid in this and the other duty and dispensation, not that God's name, but ours, shall suffer reproach. It is a very great attainment, and what few arrive at, to say continually, 'Let God be magnified.'

2. *Unhumbledness* for the sins of an *unregenerate estate*, is another of those misdoings, for which God afflicts his people. When, with Jesurun, we wax fat, we are ready to kick, Deut. xxxii. 15. To take pride in our graces, instead of blushing and being ashamed because of our sins.

Corruption within takes occasion from our very mercies to make us heedless, proud and unthankful. Prosperity makes forgetful: It is said of Uzziah, 'when he was strong, his heart was lifted up to his 'destruction,' 2 Chron. xxvi. 16. David prays, 'Re-'member not the sins of my youth, nor my trasgres-'sions;' and flies to sovereign mercy for pardon, even when he can call God the God of his salvation, Psal. xxv. 5.

Any sin, unsearched to the bottom, be it before conversion, or since, will spoil all a believer's consolation. Hence Job complains against himself, chap. xiii. 26. 'Thou writest bitter things against 'me, and makest me to possess the iniquities of my 'youth:' The sins of youth will be the sufferings of age, if they are not brought forth often, and confessed before God. A gracious soul hath then the sweetest joys, when it hath the deepest wounds. Believer, ever art thou most humbled, when thou art most exalted. Sin and grace, under all thy sufferings and in all thy joys, should never be out of thine eye. God's covenant takes away the guilt of every sin, but not the remembrance of any. God will take vengeance for an unhumbledness on the account of the sins of unregeneracy.

4. Another

4. Another sin, for which God visits his people in a way of outward displeasure, is *partiality toward other mens sins*. Samuel himself was faithful to God, but too indulgent and favourable to his sons, 1 Sam. viii. 5. 'His sons walked not in his ways, 'but turned aside after lucre, and took bribes, and 'perverted judgment.' As the administration of justice was in his hands, he had the same power to turn out as he had to put in. It becomes such as profess godliness themselves, to wink at no sin in others. Jealousy for God's holy and reverend name should overcome all respects, which are easily shewn to the persons and circumstances of men. It is Levi's commendation, when acting in the cause of his God, Deut. xxxiii. 9. 'That he said unto his 'father and to his mother, I have not seen him, 'neither did he acknowledge his brethren, nor knew 'his own children.' God takes notice of every bow to Rimmon, and every knee to Baal. Not to reprove sin faithfully and conscientiously as for God, is to have fellowship with it: And sooner or later, in a way little thought of by us, God will take vengeance on such inventions. But so much for our first general.

II. Why does God 'take vengeance of his people's 'inventions,' though he accepts their persons and hears their prayers? I answer:

1. That he may *prevent* the *abuse* of his *covenant-mercy*. The price of redemption and pardon cost God dear, and he will not have the blessing of it esteemed common. There is in the best of saints that corruption of nature, which, without the power of divine restraints, would discover itself in the worst of sins. Samson went out to shake himself as at other times, relying upon God's promise, when he had profaned his ordinance. Peter presumed upon safety from temptation, though he went into the way of temptation. The tenor of the promise is,
'He

'He will keep thee in all thy ways.' Abounding grace has given occasion to some to have light thoughts of great sins. That freedom of access, which believers have to God through Christ, has not always been kept from degenerating into a presumptuous boldness. Therefore God so deals with his own people, as that 'their own wickedness shall correct 'them, and their own backslidings shall reprove 'them,' Jerem. ii. 19. Samson falls into the hands of his enemies. Peter, instead of owning him to the death, denies his Lord with oaths and cursing. If we are conformists to the world, we must take the world's lot. The punishment shall shew what the sin is, for which God takes vengeance. A holy covenant obliges to an holy conversation. If the people of God, like the men of Bethshemish, look into the ark with an unwarrantable curiosity and presumption, they must pay for their rashness. Vengeance is taken of the inventions of God's own people, to prevent the abuse of covenant-mercy.

2. To discover the *holiness* of God's *nature* and of his *law*. 'The Lord our God is holy,' ver. 9. There are some things becoming God, Heb. ii. 14. namely, That he secures his own glory in all that he does: That he dishonours not himself in any of his acts of mercy: That what he professes himself to be, he makes appear, that he is a God of righteousness, holiness and truth, before the whole world. Men see our sins, but they see not our humiliations, repentings, pardon: They see God dishonoured, and his law broken; but how this law is repaired by the obedience of Christ, or how the saints have interest in it, they see not. Therefore God testifies his displeasure against the sin, which is public, although he *forgives* the person, which is a more private and secret thing. Reproach must be rolled off from his own name, though it abides upon thine. Hence, says God to David, 2 Sam. xii. 14. 'Howbeit, because 'by this deed thou hast given great occasion to the 'enemies of the Lord to blaspheme, the child also

'that is born unto thee shall surely die.' God's awful dispensations, though to the saints they are no other than fatherly chastisements, are a public vindication of his holiness and justice before the world. By the 'vengeance which God takes of his people's inventions,' he discovers the holiness of his own nature and law.

3. This he does, to beget *watchfulness* and *circumspection* in all their walk before him. Sins which God condemns in the life, lead to a narrow search and examination into the sins of the heart. Job was falsely accused of his friends, but righteously corrected of God, chap. x. 2. 'I will say unto God, 'Do not condemn me; shew me wherefore thou 'contendest with me.' The very life of a believer lies in heart-holiness, and in an aim after conformity to Christ in every duty. 'Cleanse thou me from 'secret faults,' Psal. xix. 12. Those vain imaginations of the mind, such as no eye sees but God's; and those corrupt desires and affections which proceed from thence, pressing upon the will continually, resolutely: These are the things which cast the soul into a dead, lifeless, carnal, loose frame; by these God is grieved: And here begins a believer's humiliation, watchfulness and cares. If thou canst but walk humbly with God, no doubt but thou wilt walk honourably before men. God punishes sin in thee, some sins unknown to others, that he may bring thee into a closer walk, and more humbled frame and fellowship with himself.

4. God takes vengeance of the inventions of his own people, for the *reproof* and *warning* of impenitent *sinners*. 'If these things be done in the 'green tree, what shall be done in the dry?' Luke xxiii. 31. Cannot God endure provocations in his own, without testifying his displeasure against them? Surely then impenitent hardened sinners shall not go always unpunished. If the inventions of his own people call for stripes, what wounds will fall upon the head of the wicked? If the son be scourged,

the servant shall be turned out of doors. God's patience and long-suffering shall not last alway. 'Kiss the son, lest he be angry, and ye perish 'from the way.'

III. I am to shew whence it is, that God answers and forgives his people, with a notwithstanding to all their sins, and to that displeasure which he is obliged to discover against sin.

1 From the *relation* God stands in unto them; they are his own: 'Thou answeredst them, O Lord 'our God.' He loved and chose them from eternity; and if there be any blessing more than ordinarily sweet, it shall be bestowed on the men of his love. 'The secret of the Lord is with them that 'fear him, and he will shew them his covenant.' If he rebukes, he loves. The covenant subsists firm and invariable, when the dispensations of it change. Clouds and darkness may be before him now, but they will blow over in a little time. Thy God puts a sweetness into every dispensation. The everlasting covenant runs through life, and through death. He hath said, 'He will never fail thee nor forsake 'thee:' God will suffer thee to talk with him of his judgments, though he does not remove them; ply the throne of grace, and he will reconcile thee to them. Whatever becomes of himself, every believer is jealous of God's honour. 'I will,' says the church, Micah vii. 9. 'bear the indignation of the 'Lord, because I have sinned against him, until he 'plead my cause, and execute judgment for me.' Moses was answered in his prayer, though not in the very blessing he asked for: God took him to heaven instead of leading him into Canaan. Our God has better things for us, than the utmost of what we can ask or desire here. Communion, near and intimate fellowship with God, will make amends for the loss of any mercy. God will answer and forgive his people, though he takes vengeance on their inventions,

tions, because of the relation he stands in unto them as their covenant-God.

2. Because he hath received a *ransom* for them from the hands of their Surety. Their persons and their mercies are bought out of the hands of justice: and if a price be paid, it is unjust to detain the goods for which it is paid. God corrects his people, not for the satisfaction of his justice: The chastisement of our peace was upon another, by way of satisfaction: Christ hath born the burden of every sin: All God's corrections are for the display of his holiness, and that we might be purified and made holy thereby. Moses, Aaron, and Samuel were a people near unto God, even when corrected and reproved by him. Love to a believer's person is well consistent with indignation against his sin, so long as there is virtue in Christ's blood, and acceptableness in his person and work, as our Advocate before the throne; so long fear not, soul, the continuance of God's favour, as a pardoning and answering God. There is worthiness in the Lamb that was slain, though there be new guilt and defilement from day to day in thee. God has found, and accepted a ransom, therefore he will hear and pardon thee. Christ has more to say for his saints before God, than all their sins have to say against them.

3. God answers and forgives his people, because it is one of *his titles*, that so he will do. 'O! thou 'that hearest prayer, unto thee shall all flesh come,' Psalm. lxv. 2. And Nehem. ix. 17. 'Thou art a 'God of pardons.' Though he be a just God, he is also a Saviour. One part of God's name casts no reproach or dishonour upon another. If he prepares the heart to seek, will he not prepare his ear to hear? When he visits most sorely, on the account of sin, his visitations are all in mercy. Love lies at the bottom of all his dealings with his saints, and there are comforts prepared for the most afflicted state any of his saints can be in; God will not be called the God of all comfort in vain. If Moses

dies

dies upon the mount, he shall have comfort in dying, and honour afterwards. Some render those words which speak of his departure; so 'Moses the servant 'of the Lord died there in the land of Moab, upon 'the mouth of the Lord,' Deut xxxiv. 5. intimating, that when God had shewed him all the good land, his holy soul was resigned to God's will, who with a *kiss* of love separated the soul from the body, and he departed. The light of God's countenance and the love of his heart are two things; one may be wanting, but he never denies the other.

4. Should God mark iniquities and not forgive sin, there could be none among the children of men to serve him: 'All we like sheep have gone astray.' There is dross mixed with our finest gold; and some weeds to spoil the smell of our sweetest flowers. The Canaanite is left in the land to prove, but not to destroy us. There is corruption in the best of his saints to humble, but not to condemn: Grace and mercy are promised for a time of need. God would never be spoken of in our text as answering his saints, were it not that they might from hence have encouragement to seek it: 'Thou answeredst them, O 'Lord our God.' Some uses shall close all.

Use 1. Shall we marvel or murmur at any of our trials? Look inward, and you may see the cause of all. If sin be regarded in the heart, vengeance must follow in the life. God will not have Agag spared, though he be clothed delicately. *Secret* provocations his eye is most upon. Are our hearts so full of them? Our duties and dependencies so full? and yet shall we wonder when God visits for them? Consider who God is, and what sin deserves; then whatever be thy affliction, distress or sorrow, thou wilt 'be dumb and not open thy mouth, because 'God hath done it.'

Use 2. Does God answer and forgive, and yet take vengeance? Labour to have your affections suited to providential dispensations. The view of mercy is sweet. In prosperity rejoice: The appearance

of

of judgment strikes terror. 'Let them praise thy 'great and terrible name: for it is holy,' ver. 3. This should lead to deep humiliation and mourning. It is a beautiful frame of soul to be in, when all the affections are in exercise at once; a side wind fills all the sails; that providence which does this, for the *present*, may appear *awful*, but it will ever be found, in the *end*, to be advantageous. Thou speakest as David did, *in haste*, when thou concludest that 'all these things are against thee.' Labour for answerableness of spirit to providential dispensations.

Use 3. Bless God for Christ, whatever mercy thou wantest. There would be no pardon without a sacrifice; no person accepted but through Christ's righteousness imputed; no pardon given but what comes through his hands; no prayer heard, save in the virtue of his intercession.

Use 4. Admire God's patience. So many inventions, and no more vengeance; O! amazing. It is well for us, God does not take vengeance for every sin. Set God as an holy God before thee daily. 'Serve 'the Lord with fear, and rejoice with trembling.'

Use 5. Wo to such as were never interested in God's forgiveness. 'The wages of sin is death.' Without interest in God as a covenant God, there can be no pardon, no hope, no heaven: This is by Christ, 'in whom whosoever believeth shall not 'perish, but have everlasting life.'

SERMON XXXIII.

THE CHRISTIAN'S DUTY OF DYING DAILY.

1 COR. XV. 31.

I protest by your rejoicing, which I have in Christ Jesus our Lord, I die daily.

THE words with which this verse closes, in the original begin the sentence. *I die daily*, verily I do it, ' by your rejoicing, which I have in Christ ' Jesus our Lord.' There is an uncommon earnestness and vehemence in the expression, beyond what our translation can reach, as a learned writer observes upon the subject. Our great Apostle is speaking out his very heart, upon a most solemn and important occasion; his chief design and aim, in this chapter, is to evince the certainty and necessity of the resurrection, which he does by many incontestible arguments. Here he brings in the absurdity of his own conduct, and that of other Christians, upon any other supposition: ' Else what shall they do, which ' are baptized for the dead, if the dead rise not at ' all? Why are they also baptized for the dead? ' And why stand we in jeopardy every hour?' *Ver.* 29, 30. that is, as some interpret the words, "Why " are any baptized into the faith of them that die " in Christ?" Or as others, " Why are they bap- " tized into the name of Christ, who is dead, (so " putting the singular number for the plural) if the " dead

" dead rife not at all ; or, *why stand we in jeopardy*
" *every hour?* Why do we risk our comforts, and
" our lives, exposing ourselves every day to dangers
" and death, if there be no future resurrection? We
" are little better than fools or madmen to run all
" these hazards, if when we die we die wholly and
" revive no more." It can never be thus: You and
I have all of us an argument to the contrary in our
own breasts, which all the reasoning in the world can
never weaken the force of. There is a joy in Christ,
arising from a sense of interest in him, which we feel
the power and comfort of every day ; we have trusted our souls in his hands, lodged our eternal concerns
with him, and do we not also ' know in whom we
' have believed, and that he is able to keep that
' which we have committed to him, against that
' day?' The love of God is shed abroad in our hearts
by his Spirit given unto us ; we are so fully persuaded of it, that we can glory in it, in the face of all
those sufferings, which we are like to endure for his
sake ; nothing we can part with is too much for
Christ, for we have all things in him, he is ours in
life, at death, and ours when we come to judgment:
I am so fully persuaded of it myself, says our Apostle, that I am *in deaths often*, every day exposed
to die, and I suffer all that befals me joyfully ; or
otherwise, I am so confident of being raised up in
him, and by him, and of being with him, that I am
every day preparing for death ; I wait for it, as one
waits for a friend, who will bring me, by a short cut,
to that inheritance which life can never give me the
full possession of ; I am in readiness to meet death,
looking out beforehand for the kind messenger of my
Father's will, as one that will give him no room to
stay upon my account when he comes. *I die daily*,
I have, as it were, begun the work beforehand, that
I may be no stranger to it, when the appointed hour
approaches : ' By your rejoicing which I have in
' Christ Jesus our Lord.' According to this sense,
the participle, νη, seems to be a note, rather of strong
asseveration

asseveration than of juration or swearing. Their stedfastness and joy in Christ, was a quickning consideration to the Apostle in his views of death, and his preparations for it. Elsewhere says he, ' Now we ' live if we stand fast in the Lord,' 1 Thess. iii. 8. So here *I die daily*, I can willingly yield up my soul to God, because of that joy of mind which I see fulfilled in you.

Taking the words in this sense, they afford us the following observations.

OBSERV. Nothing is more comfortable to a gospel-minister living or dying, than to see the blessed fruits and success of his labours, in the spiritual walk, and holy confidence and joy of his hearers.

Or if we apply the words more closely to the Apostle, as exercising himself in his daily walk, with respect to the duty the text speaks of; we may raise from them this observation, which I propose chiefly to insist on.

OBSERV. The way to die comfortably, is to die daily.

In discoursing on this observation, I shall attempt only three things :

I. Shew you what the duty is.
II. Why we should be found in the practice of it.
III. How this redounds to our comfort, when death really comes.

I. I am to shew what the duty is, which the Apostle so vehemently pursues : ' I protest by your ' rejoicing, which I have in Christ Jesus our Lord, ' I die daily.' To die *once*, is a lot appointed for all ; to die *daily* is a duty practised, a blessing obtained by few ; most live as if they were never to die ; because the day is evil, they put it far from them ; and all the tokens of mortality within themselves, the many melancholy evidences they have of it among others, are no sooner seen than forgotten by them.

Alas !

Alas! saints themselves, who have hope in their death, are too forgetful of their dying time. Suffer me, therefore, in this great concern, to stir up your pure minds by way of remembrance, that whensoever your Master cometh he may not find you sleeping. What it is to die *really* I will not, I cannot say; the valley of the shadow of death, as it is a way whence we cannot return, so it is a way wholly unknown to us, till it is passed by us; but what it is to die *daily* may be learnt, under the Spirit's gracious influences, by a regular practice and due improvement of the following particulars. As,

1. To die daily, is to set death always before us as a change which ' will one day certainly come.' A time of affliction, temptation or desertion *may* come, but the time of our death *must* come. ' It is ' appointed for men once to die,' there is no way believers have into their Father's house but this; through dying we come to live. Our blessed Lord himself found no other passage into his own glory. ' Ought not Christ to suffer these things, and to en-
' ter into his glory?' Luke xxiv. 26. ' We see Je-
' sus, who was made a little lower than the angels,
' for the suffering of death, crowned with glory and
' honour,' Heb. ii. 9. and verse 14. It is pleasant to see death in Christ's hands; though it appear at a distance, we are for bringing it near, when we can read our names in the Lamb's book of life. And whence is it then believers are so much afraid of the stroke when the time comes? Is it not because they have thought so little of it beforehand? It has not duly engaged their thoughts, nor impressed their minds; it is rather looked upon as a possible occurrence, than a fixed, determined, and appointed thing. Man is apt foolishly to boast himself of to-morrow. because he is favoured with the comfortable enjoyments of the present day. Did they not live at uncertainties, few would die at so great uncertainties, as professors themselves often do. You believe you *shall die*, but do you live as if you were *dying?*

What! forget death in the midst of your cares and hurries in life? Not one thought what you shall be beyond the grave, when you lay so many schemes how you may be great and honourable in your passage to it! This was far from Job's case and practice: 'I have said to corruption, Thou art my father: to the worm, thou art my mother, and my sister,' Job xvii. 14. He took a turn to the grave often, as one that believed he should one day take up his dwelling there; he was no stranger to corruption and darkness, though he was at present in the light of the living. Thus also we hear holy David praying, 'Lord, make me to know mine end, and the measure of my days, what it is, that I may know how frail I am,' Psalm xxxix. 4. He was afraid to look to futurity, lest he should look at a thing that was not; his musings and the meditations of his heart were about the grave, the place appointed for all living. It is not, " Lord, make me to " know my stay, my abode here on earth, that I " may be useful and fruitful, whilst I am living:" No; but, 'Lord make me to know mine end, and the measure of my days,' that I may be ready for dying: 'Behold thou hast made my days as an hand-breadth, and mine age is as nothing before thee,' ver. 5. To die daily is to set death always before us, as what will *certainly* come.

2. It is to be ready to meet death, as a change which may *suddenly* come. How many are snatched out of time into eternity, without any manner of warning? In a moment they go down to the grave; and what is, of all others, the most awful word, 'Death has dominion over them.' Every one has a great work to do here, and a long journey to take afterwards, sooner it may be, by far, than he is aware of; the garment of mortality must be put off; perhaps even now, while I am speaking, God may be unclothing some of you. All are not young and healthy, prepared to resist the shock of a threatening illness. The pins of the tabernacle are already

loosened

loosened, by a long series of distempers; and who knows how soon the tabernacle itself may be wholly taken down? Is your living work done, before your dying time comes? Are you ready to wait upon your Lord, should you be immediately called forth to meet him? Is your heart chaste to Christ? Are your affections centering in him? Do you use the world, as not abusing it, for the fashion thereof passeth away? What! houses and lands, and children and friends, all left, and left willingly, in a Father's hands? This is a good evidence of readiness to meet your Lord, when he calls you to to do. Our Saviour uses two words, when exhorting his disciples to this duty, perhaps one may express the safety of our state, and the other **the agreeableness of our frame,** Matth. xxiv. 42. 44. ' Be ye also ready: for in
' such an hour as ye think not the Son of man co-
' meth: watch therefore, for ye know not what hour
' your Lord doth come.' Being ready, argues our state safe; watching, argues our frame suitable and becoming. Christians, though always warriors, are not always watchers; we sometimes forget our work, our way, and our journey's end; worldly thoughts produce worldly frames; and it is hard to leave the world, when we judge our treasure in a great part to consist in it. Do we expect our friend, and shall we not see to it, that all things are ready to receive him? Alas, my friends! is it not sad for Christ to call his own, when they are ashamed before him at his coming? Christians have lost their first zeal, and almost wholly lost their first love; secret faults and presumptuous sins, both lie upon the conscience unpurged, and a loose and careless walk, either in the church or in the world, begets bitterness and anguish in a dying hour. The sins of professors often cloud and darken the valley of the shadow of death when they pass it. Think every day your last day, and every duty your last duty, and see how you will act then. There must come one new morning which will have no night; or one night which admits no morning.

morning. When the fruit is ripe, it falls from the tree itself. Oh! to have our evidences for heaven clear in the views of death! This is a token for good; how pleasant, how easy it is, for those who are weaned from this world, and walk closely with God, to depart hence, and be ever with him, call when he will? But lamps will not do, if there be not oil in your lamps. Keep God and Christ and heaven and happiness in view, while ye are sojourning here, and blessed will be the surprise, though ye should in a *moment* die, and awake in glory: ' Bles-
' sed is that servant, whom his Lord, when he co-
' meth, shall find so doing,' Matth. xxiv. 46. To die daily, is to meet death as a change which may *suddenly* come.

3. To die daily, is to *wait* for our change, as what we *desire*, were it God's will, should come *speedily*. They are our Apostle's own words: ' Having a de-
' sire to depart, and to be with Christ,' Phil. i. 23. The word is expressive of an earnest, vehement, and continued desire; it is such a desire as cannot be satisfied, till full enjoyment comes; not a sudden passion which comes by fits, but a strong bent and lasting inclination; his heart was fixed upon Christ, who ' is the strength of the believer's heart, and his
' portion for ever.' Nothing less than this can work in the soul such an earnest desire to leave the body; for companions so long as these are, find it hard to part at last without a struggle; there is a natural love of life, and there is also a natural fear of death, even where there is no fear of the consequences, but only of the struggles and pangs of death itself. Now, what is it that conquers and dispels this fear? A view of Christ our risen Saviour, our trusty friend, who is gone to heaven already, to make all in readiness against we come there. The blessed Jesus! what will not the soul part with freely, to have and enjoy him? All our hopes are in him, and therefore our hearts are ever with him. The body is left in the grave, only to be purified, to be refined, that it may

be raised in glory when the resurrection comes. O! we can leave it there, under Christ's care, in whose sight our death and our dust are both precious. It is for him we are waiting, who is better than all; our life has hitherto been *in* him, now we are going to the fountain-head to be for ever *with* him. Christian, let me appeal to your experience, when you have freedom with God before the throne, and a view of Christ's conquest over death and hell, how do you find your spirit working? What are your thoughts, your hopes, and your desires fixed upon? Do they not work as our Apostle's did? Should death come, and take you upon your knees, would you desire a longer stay? Is there any thing here worthy your love? No verily, the sooner at home the better; long to be hid in the grave, that you may spend the residue of your life without clouds or fears, without trouble or sin, in the presence of Christ your living head: ' In his presence there is ' fulness of joy.' The body here cannot keep pace with the soul; it is a clog and a burden, therefore it is doomed to death; to death you yield it, and whilst your soul is mounting upwards, in contemplation of Christ, in communion with him, your flesh also doth rest in hope, and you wait with patience and holy joy, till you hear your Beloved say, ' Come, for all things are ready.' To die daily, is to *wait* for our change as what we *desire*.

4. To die daily, is to *resign* our souls *solemnly* into our Redeemer's hands, as those who know not whether they have another day to live. To leave them with his faithfulness, love and care, who hath said, ' I will not fail thee, nor forsake thee.' Thus the Psalmist exercised faith in God, Psal. xiii. 5. ' Into ' thine hands I commit my spirit: Thou hast re- ' deemed it, O Lord God of truth.' Many a promise he had received before, but now he needed the comfort of all. Thoughts of eternity are very awful. How it will be with our poor souls, when we leave the body, we know not; where they will be, how

how they will act, in what manner they are to be engaged, &c. Of these things faith gives us but dark and distant views; and yet all our hopes and happiness are wrapt up in our souls welfare; if our souls are safe, all is safe; we are blessed, infinitely blessed for ever and ever. Well, says the Psalmist, I am right in this great concern; I have left my soul where it cannot but be safe; it is left in his hands who redeemed it; I have solemnly committed it to him, who has ever hitherto supported it; it is in the hand of my covenant God, who will fulfil, in eternity, all the promises, on which my faith and my hope have been founded in time. 'Into 'thine hands I commit my spirit.' I have found him the 'Lord God of truth' in every other particular, and sure I may venture to trust him in this. In like manner, says our holy Apostle, 2 Tim. i. 12. 'I know whom I have believed, and I am persua- 'ded that he is able to keep that which I have com- 'mitted unto him against that day.' He speaks here like one that died daily. Nothing could move him from his hope, nor the confidence he had in Christ Jesus. Every day he made a new reckoning, counted up his sorrows, his joys, the blessed realities of the better state, and left all he had or hoped for in Christ's hands, and there he was sure to find it with interest. This was a trying time to Paul; he was called to stand before Nero, that persecuting Roman emperor, a second time, and he had no man to stand by him; but he was God's prisoner, and Christ's chains are precious chains. Many things he suffered of men, but he was in no wise ashamed of God or his gospel: 'For the which cause I also 'suffer these things, nevertheless I am not ashamed, 'for I know whom I have believed,' &c. As if he had said, "This is not the first time I have trusted "him upon the same account; I have often resigned "up my soul to him, and he has never failed me "yet; shall I at last draw back, what! now my de- "parture is so near? God forbid! Christ is the same "he ever was; 'I know whom I have believed;' "I am beyond doubts and fears, for 'I am persua-'ed he will keep that I have committed to him.' O Christian, 'this is an anchor of the soul, both 'sure and stedfast;' come death when it will, you may die cheerfully and comfortably, when your all is left daily in Christ's hands; no surprise can affright you, no fear shame you, if Christ be the rock of your heart, you can never be moved; your poor soul cannot be left naked, when Christ is your clothing. It is true, it is turned out of its old tenement, but not out of house and home; Christ has prepared an habitation for it in his own presence, in the bosom of his everlasting love; there shall it abide in the fulness of joy, till it be reunited to its former habitation in the resurrection-day. 'Thou wilt shew 'me the path of life; in thy presence is fulness of 'joy; at thy right hand there are pleasures for ever-'more,' Psal. xvi. 11. To die daily, is *solemnly* to 'commit our souls into our Redeemer's hands,' as not knowing whether we have another day to live.

Thus much for the first general, what is the duty itself. I proceed to consider,

II. Why are we to be found in the constant practice of it?

And let it suffice, that I mention only the three following things.

1. This redounds greatly to the *glory* of God. He is honoured by a lively frame and an upright walk. For the sons of God, and of glory, to live wholly strangers to death, or to be afraid of it; how does this fully their character, and shame their profession! This is to receive the spirit of bondage again unto fear, not the spirit of adoption whereby we cry Abba, Father. 'There is a walking worthy of the 'Lord,' Col. i. 10. worthy the obligations we lie under to him, and the blessed promises we have received from him; worthy of them that are called by his name, and chosen to his glory: And what must

must be done by us, in order to such a walk? Let the Apostle himself answer, 2 Cor. iv. 18. 'While we look not at the things which are seen, but at the things which are not seen; for the things which are seen are temporal, but the things which are not seen are eternal;' *then* we are thus walking. The word signifies so to *look*, as when one takes his mark or aim at any thing; his eyes were not presently on, and as soon off again; no, they were *fixed* on these things; by his views of them, he took his aim and scope, how he should walk here, and so brought the communion and joys of heaven into his daily walk and conversation on earth. How holily, how cheerfully and becomingly does such a Christian walk, who has Christ in his eye both as the author and the finisher of his faith! This redounds to the glory of God. The Lord increase the number of such walkers! But in our day, religion is little more than name; many talk well, but as for walking, that is left to others, who have more time or more conscience and grace than themselves.

2. It makes much for the *establishment* and consolation of *other* Christians. It greatly saddens the hearts of younger Christians, to hear those that are going off the stage of life mourning and complaining, as if they were wholly in suspence as to their eternal state. Sure, were you to converse more with God, you would speak more for him. What though your hopes for the present fail, the God of your hopes lives. Though you cannot read love in all things, the covenant, which concerns you in every state, 'is ordered in all things and sure.' If you are jealous of yourselves, you may confide in Christ; his left hand is under your head to support you, though his right hand does not sensibly embrace you. Press forward towards the mark; wait for God's salvation, as Jacob did, though you should not be able to say with Simeon, 'Mine eyes have

' seen it.' It makes much for the establishment of younger Christians.

3. This is a frame which is highly beneficial to our own souls. And so I am led to the third general.

III. How does the regular practice of the duty I have been explaining, redound to the comfort of our own souls, when death really comes? Or whence it is, that dying daily has so great an interest and concern in our dying comfortably? And,

First, They that die daily die comfortably; because by this means we make death *familiar* to us; and those we are well acquainted with, we are but little afraid of: Friends that meet often, converse without shyness or fear. Death is our friend through Christ; it is given to us through him, and that which is given to us for our good can never do us any real harm: 1 Cor. iii. 22. ' All things are yours, ' whether Paul, or Appollos, or Cephas, or the world, ' or life, or death, or things present, or things to ' come; all are yours, and ye are Christ's, and Christ ' is God's.' When we meet the stroke, we may bid it welcome, because it comes without a sting; Christ has received that into his own side, and by this means ' swallowed up death in victory.' What can death do, when it has done its uttermost? Have you never weighed things, and brought them to a balance; never conversed freely with your souls upon this head? The nature of death is changed, its ghastly visage altered; it may separate the soul from the body, but neither from our Lord Jesus Christ. The ship is broken to pieces in which our treasure is, but all that is precious gets safe to shore; though it cast you down, you shall rise, hereafter, the more glorious. If it be an enemy, it is a foiled one; and what hurt can our enemy do us, when he has both lost his strength and his weapons? The valley through which it leads the believer is dark; but Christ the Sun of righteousness is there to enlighten it; we have a

Captain

Captain of salvation to conduct us through it, and to welcome us to glory, when we come to the end of it. Have you never dwelt on these things, you that dwell in the dust? never viewed death the king of terrors, with Christ the Prince of life? It is high time, believer, to begin to familiarize these things now; else wonder not at the fearfulness of your spirits, nor the deadness of your frames, when death shall give you the awful summons once for all.

Secondly, **Dying** daily has a farther influence upon our comforts; because hereby we are ‘ weaned from ‘ the world,’ and all wordly enjoyments; and those things which we are weary of, we are glad to leave behind us. Christ known and enjoyed makes every earthly comfort tasteless and insipid. O! he can have no rival in *our* love, when he sets us as a seal upon *his* heart, as a seal upon *his* arm. Frequent meditation upon him in his excellencies and glory, is a means of transforming us into a likeness unto him. In this respect the knowledge of Christ, and him crucified, infinitely transcends all other knowledge; and he that knows and loves Christ cannot but desire to be with him. He is our all in heaven, and our all upon earth; but while we are upon earth, we cannot know the *all* that is in him, as we shall above in heaven. Here we see through a glass darkly; the sights we have of him we have by faith; but faith itself longs to cease, that we may see him face to face. True we must pass over Jordan, in order to our getting to Canaan the promised land, where our father and his friends all dwell; but who would stop at the swellings of Jordan, that has a good hope through grace that he shall be soon landed, and landed safe? The world is a sea of trouble; heaven a land of pure delight and uninterrupted rest. All our comforts are mixed with crosses here; but there no cross, no cloud, no sorrow, no sin, no fear, can ever enter; what have we here to pull us back? Do you never look within you, and about you; how many sins and corruptions within? how many snares and temptations without? Do you desire, or can you bear these for ever? What! have you lived forty, fifty, three or fourscore years, and not weaned from the world yet! Is death as great a stranger as ever it was? This cannot be, if you have lived in Christ, and lived to Christ. But rather, have you not resigned your soul to him, and your children into his hands, as a covenant God! Your affairs are all settled, being comprized in the everlasting and well ordered covenant; the messenger comes, and you are weaned from the earth, and ready for heaven: Your dying day then is your best day; you have been looking and waiting for it long; and now it is come, it is welcome. It is your marriage-day, and the prophet has given you a song ready composed for it; death gives an endless eternity to sing it in. Isa. lxi. 10. ' I will greatly rejoice in the Lord, my ' soul shall be joyful in my God; for he hath clo- ' thed me with the garments of salvation; he hath ' covered me with the robe of righteousness, as a ' bridegroom decketh himself with ornaments, and ' as bride adorneth herself with her jewels.' By dying daily we are weaned from the world, &c.

Thirdly, By dying daily, our ' accounts are clear- ' ly stated' between God and us; and what condemnation have we then to fear? ' Who shall lay any ' thing to the charge of God's elect? It is God that ' justifieth:' Rom. viii. 33. A man can hardly die well, who has any thing else to do than to die; the more careful and constant we have been as to our confessions, contrition, and daily obedience in life, the less advantage has Satan against us, to distress us, when death approaches; but sin indulged can never consist with communion enjoyed. ' The sting ' of death is sin, and the strength of sin is the law,' 1 Cor. xv. 56. This was a bar in the way, this was a gap which there was a necessity for making up, by the interposition of Christ's blood, in order to any comfortable walk in life; and now this is done, now iniquity is pardoned, and sin covered, who has
any

any further indictment to bring against the believer in Jesus? He sees death; but he sees Christ with it, who has been the death of death, and the grave's destruction; Christ has said to such, 'Fear not, I 'have the keys of hell and of death.' Rev. i. 18. Christ is Lord of both, and what can they fear, who have an interest in this living Lord? By dying daily our accounts stand the more clearly stated between God and us. Once more,

Fourthly, By dying daily, we learn to look *beyond* death while we are looking *at* it; and all is peace and joy there for ever and ever. To look always upon death, is dreadful indeed, but life without end follows immediately after; that life which Christ asked of his Father, for his many sons, Psal. xxi. 5. that life which he inherits as their head and forerunner in the presence of God. O! we are to be heirs above with him for ever; 'heirs of God, and 'joint-heirs with Christ,' Rom. viii. 17. Death brings us to a jubilee of rest; then our redemption day is come, and we enter upon our inheritance, never to quit our possession; there shall we see God in Christ, and ever enjoy him; no more taste of the streams of his goodness, love and grace, but drink at the fountain-head, till we are filled: Sips and drops we are to have done with there; we shall then 'be filled with all the fulness of God.' Happy souls that shall be counted worthy to obtain that world, and the resurrection from the dead. 'They shall 'hunger no more, neither thirst any more, neither 'shall the sun light on them, nor any heat. For 'the Lamb which is in the midst of the throne shall 'feed them, and shall lead them unto living foun- 'tains of waters; and God shall wipe away all tears 'from their eyes,' Rev. vii. 16, 17. These are some of the advantages which believers have in dying daily; from whence it appears, how great an interest and concern it has in our dying comfortably.

I.

I shall now close all with a few remarks. And,

REMARK 1. How dreadful is it for them to think of dying, who have not as yet begun to live. The youngest that hears me this day is old enough to die; life's longest lease is a short one; and how many sudden unforeseen events are there to make it shorter! Perhaps you may not think of death to-day, and yet launch into eternity some days before another Sabbath. Are you out of Christ? Wo unto you, if you die so. The sting of death will then wound you to the heart, and seal up your condemnation for ever and ever; all hope and help is past, when death comes; there is no discharge in that war, neither shall wickedness deliver those that are given to it; as death leaves you, judgment finds you; heaven or hell will be your endless portion, according to the state death finds you in; beware of uncertain promises and trifling delays in a matter of everlasting importance.

REM. 2. The truest wisdom is to be prepared against the greatest danger; our everlasting all depends upon our dying well. If a man miscarry in death, he is undone for ever; it is a step which can never be taken over again; while we live we are in time, and what is wanting in one duty may be confessed before God when engaged in another; but when we die, we leave time, and there is no changing in an eternal world; there our state is fixed, and fixed for ever, beyond the least hopes of an alteration. The greatest end of living is to prepare for dying.

REM. 3. Unless we know Christ savingly, we can neither die daily, nor die comfortably. He is the Lord our righteousness, and our strength. He is the foundation of our hope, and in him is all the grace we need to strengthen our hope in a dark day. All our peace comes from him, for it was made by him; all our comfort is his gift, because it was his purchase; he procured heaven for us; in our justification he gave us the right to do it, and he lives

above

above to keep it, till he has brought us at death into the full poffeffion of it. The believer, ftrong as his faith may at fome times be, never dares look at death unlefs he looks at Chrift alfo. Death is an enemy which keeps us captive till we are led to fee it an enemy conquered by Chrift: ' Through death he ' hath delivered them, who through fear of death ' were all their lifetime fubject to bondage.' There is the fpring of all our life, confolation and joy in a dying hour.

REM. 4. It is dangerous living, even for the Chriftian himfelf, without keeping his dying time ever in view; for a view of death is the greateft bridle upon indwelling fin, next to an immediate grant of mortifying grace from above: Who dares furfeit himfelf with the pleafures or cares of life, who knows not but that he may on the morrow go down to the grave? We all ' rejoice as though we rejoiced not, ' and weep as though we wept not, and ufe this life ' as not abufing it,' when we are helped to keep death in view, which will fpeedily put an end to all our forrows and joys.

REM. 5. Should we not make hafte with our living work, when we know not how foon our living time may ceafe? ' David ferved his own generation ' by the will of God,' Acts xiii. 36. Leave not your foul-concerns or your temporal affairs at peradventures, when even in the midft of life you are in death. ' To fet your houfe in order,' is a neceffary duty, more efpecially becoming the Chriftian, who fees death as his in Chrift Jefus. If you die daily, let this influence every action you are employed about in life; own God in all things, and endeavour that all may be at peace below when you are entered into reft above; be ready to go, though your matter fhould *prefently* call.

REM. 6. Learn hence the excellency and fweetnefs of the Chriftian's life. Intereft in Chrift makes life pleafant, and death joyful. All things are well with him

him that has peace with God through our Lord Jesus Christ. Such an one lives above in heaven, while he is sojourning here on earth; where his treasure is there his heart is, and the Lord is his portion here and hereafter. His soul takes up its rest in him, and dwells at ease; what is nature's aversion, grace delights in; the eye of faith sees life in death, and comfort in the midst of fears: It looks beyond the veil, and enters even on this side the grave into the holiest of all, ' where Jesus our forerunner is for us ' entered.' We shall be coming up from the wilderness, and hastening out of it, when we are found ' leaning on our Beloved,' looking to, and carrying on, sweet and daily communion with Christ Jesus our Lord; which the Lord the Spirit enable us more and more to do!

SERMON XXXIV.

THE BLESSEDNESS OF THEM THAT DIE IN THE LORD.

REVELATION xiv. 13.

And I heard a voice from heaven, saying unto me, Write, Blessed are the dead which die in the Lord, from henceforth: Yea, saith the Spirit, that they may rest from their labours; and their works do follow them.

AMIDST all the tears, and occasions of sorrow which are found upon earth, there is a voice from heaven which speaks comfort. Though sin has brought death into our world, Christ has put sweetness and a blessing into death. We have followed the precious remains of our dear deceased brother to the grave*: but let us not in our heart and affections stay there weeping. The man is where the soul and spirit is. Our God calls us to look upward. ' I am the resurrection, and the life,' is Christ's present language to every sorrowing friend. The precious saint, the dear and faithful minister

---

* This Sermon was preached to the church of Christ at Basingstoke, Hants, at the interment of their worthy Pastor the Rev. Mr William Moth, Aug. 24. 1744.

ster and pastor, in whose place I now stand, is with Christ. All his prayers, and your prayers for him, are now answered. He has done his Master's work, and is entered into his Master's joy. Shall we weep, that he is blessed? and that Christ, by a voice from heaven, declares him so? Rather let us see, and praise our God for his dying frames, and view, as far as we are able, the blessedness of his present state; that, as our God has been quickening and improving the graces of many of you by his life, you may also in some respects be gainers by his death.

'And I heard a voice from heaven,' &c.—These words, taken in their immediate connection, refer to the rage and persecution of Antichrist against the true church and people of God. Though her fall and punishment is spoken of *here*, as to the nature of it, *ver*. 10, 11. the time of it should not be till hereafter, chap. xviii. 1. Babylon's reign is to be long, though her destruction shall be certain and sudden. To some extraordinary season of corruption and persecution in the churches these words relate, because of the verse which goes immediately before, *ver*. 12. 'Here is the patience of the saints; here are 'they which keep the commandments of God, and 'the faith of Jesus;' that is, this is the time wherein it shall be remarkably tried. Now it shall appear, who are the chaff, and who are the wheat; what is dross, and what is gold. Upon this, a voice from heaven declares them 'blessed that die in the Lord, 'from henceforth:' Not as if such who died in Christ before were not blessed; but to be taken away in a time of so great trial, was a singular and special mercy, because there was an end of their grievous and intolerable labours and sufferings for the cause of Christ. The enemy should vex, torture, and oppress no more; and their works, that is, the fruit of their patience here upon earth, should be left behind, and follow them, as harvest does seed-time. There should be a succession of converts to Christ, through their sufferings. Hence to die *in* the Lord

is

is supposed, by many, to import chiefly, to die *for* the Lord, as the prepofition is often used; or, to die in the Lord's cause; not as Christians, but as martyrs. This voice John is commanded to write, that it might be of standing use and comfort to the church in all ages: And the Spirit, (as a Spirit of prophecy), who foresaw all events in their causes, circumstances, and effects, adds his testimony to this voice from heaven: 'Yea, saith the Spirit, that they may 'rest from their labours; and their works do follow 'them.' This seems to be the true sense of the text, but not the only one. There is a dying *in Christ*, when there is not, in a way of martyrdom, a dying *for him*. Even the bleffedness of martyrs lies not so much in their sufferings *for Christ*, as their 'dying in 'covenant-relation to him,' And where is the saint, that does not find this life a warfare, a painful and wearisome estate? so that when he dies in Christ, 'he rests from his labours, and his works follow 'him.' Therefore, in farther discoursing on the words, as God shall help, I would do three things. As,

I. Inquire what it is 'to die in the Lord;' for such are the dead, to whom a promise of blessedness belongs.

II. Shew what is that blessedness which belongs to the dead that die in Christ.

III. Why are those dead, 'who die in the Lord,' blessed from henceforth? And so apply.

I. What it is for any one 'to die in the Lord?'

1. It is to die in a state of union to Christ's person. Every true believer is a partaker of Christ, Heb. iii. 14. In the eye of the law, Christ and he are one. Therefore we read not of feeds, as of many, but as of one, 'and to thy feed, which is Christ,' Gal. iii. 16. God looks upon every believing sinner, who is in Christ, as a part of Christ; a member of Christ; and as such, deals out to him all the promi-

ses of the covenant, according as his needs are. The life of Christ dwells in him, because he is taken under Christ's covenant, and is in a state of union to his person. This union death itself cannot dissolve. ' He that hath the Son (it may always be said) ' hath life,' 1 John v. 12. Death, though it changes worlds, does not change states. If once in Christ, thou art ever so. God calls himself the God of Abraham, many hundred years after his body was crumbled into dust. Living and dying, believers are the Lord's; yea, their very bodies continue united to Christ, and sweetly rest in their graves, waiting his call at the great resurrection-day. This is the meaning of Job's words, chap. xiv. 15. ' Thou shalt call, ' and I will answer thee. For if we believe that ' Jesus died, and rose again, even so them also which ' sleep in Jesus, will God bring with him,' 1 Thess. iv. 14. Godly men die not as others do: a wicked man's hopes and his life go together; but in dying the believer lives. To die in Christ, is to die in a state of union to Christ's person.

2. It is to die in a profession of his faith. ' All ' these died in faith,' Heb. xi. 13. Faith is the last grace acted by a dying saint. It is this which anchors his spirit, and supports his hopes; because it shews him a faithful Christ, and a present God. It is not the lot of every believer in Christ to die triumphant; sometimes the clouds rise thickest about the saints, when they are nearest Canaan: Who can tell what the swellings of Jordan are, that has not passed them? But every child of God dies dependent. Oh! he bears up himself on everlasting righteousness, and an everlasting covenant. He can venture his soul and his salvation upon that record, that God has given of his Son, 1 Tim. i. 15. ' This is a faith- ' ful saying, and worthy of all acceptation, that Je- ' sus Christ came into the world to save sinners, the ' chief of sinners;' though he cannot, through present darkness, say, I am of the number of these saved ones. He believes, for himself, his seed, and the

dear

dear church of Christ, which is left behind; not from any present sense he has by way of enjoyment but purely on the word of a God, that cannot lie. Such as die in faith, die in Christ. Why? Because faith lifts up the soul to Christ, and fixes it on him, when it does, in a way of sensible manifestation and enjoyment, reveal Christ to the soul. To die professing faith in Christ, is ' to die in the Lord.'

3. To die in the Lord, is to die in obedience to Christ's will. ' He is thy Lord, and worship thou ' him,' is a command which runs through life and death. I own it, this is rather to die *to* the Lord than to die *in* him; yet it is the character of those blessed ones, who are said, in my text, to have died in the Lord. *Ver.* 12. ' Here is the patience of the ' saints, here are they that keep the commandments ' of God, and the faith of Jesus.' They died at Christ's call, and in obedience to his will. A believer, with good old Simeon, asks leave to die, as well as to live: Luke ii. 20. ' Lord, now lettest ' thy servant depart in peace according to thy word.' It is true, this world is a poor empty thing to one that has Christ in his arms and salvation in his eye. After such a sight we may well be content to have our eyes closed. But a believer's desires are regulated not by his own affections or joys: No; but by God's will. Perhaps Christ's cause is to gain more by thy pains and sorrows in thy flesh, than ever it did by thy praises, when most in the spirit. Thou art but a servant, though made ruler over all; allow thy Master, therefore, to set thee what work he pleases. Our times are in his hands, who is Lord of our lives, and of all our service. It is a great thing to give God's decree its full scope and time with respect to our persons, our sufferings, friends, and frames. There are seasons wherein the best of saints are ready to make haste. To die in obedience to our Lord's will! The world cannot do so, it is a dreadful *must* with them. Nature cannot do it: that is either too forward, or else it hangs behind:

but

but grace is ready to stay, and suffer; or to depart, and be with Christ, as the Lord himself pleases. To die in Christ, is to die in obedience to Christ's will.

4. To die in Christ, is to die in the exercise of those graces, which Christ acted when dying. In Christ there is grace of every kind. There are doing and suffering graces; there are living graces, and dying graces: when a saint exercises these graces, by virtue of his union to Christ, in the strength of Christ, and after the example of Christ, he may be said to live, and 'to die in the Lord.' A believer's strength, his faith, his patience, and resignation in a dying hour, are all in Christ. He is nothing in himself, with all his light, comfort, and joy unspeakable, any more dying than living. Therefore our Beloved is pleased often to hide himself 'behind the 'myrtle-trees in the bottom;' though nigh to us, he is unseen by us, Zech. i. 8. And he is pleased to do thus, after signal manifestations of his presence, that we may learn to glory only in the Lord. Christ is a believer's life, in doing and in dying. But how did Christ die? Calling upon God as his Father. Our blessed Lord died praying, Luke xxiii. 46. 'Father, into thy hands I commend my spirit.' He owns covenant-relation with his last breath, and dies yielding up himself into his hands, whose work he came into the world to finish; his last work, as man and as Mediator, was to give up himself into the hands of his Father and his God. Blessed dying! when all the tendencies and motions of a believer's spirit are towards Christ, who is the great centre of his soul, and his only rest! When he breathes the breath of heaven, and begins the work of heaven, before life ends! When he exerts his last strength in laying hold on the covenant, and with a quivering dying breath, can say, "*Into thy hands I com-*
"*mend my spirit, thou hast redeemed me, O Lord God*
"*of truth.*" There is no looking with comfort beyond time, if there be not first a looking to that redemption

demption which was obtained by a crucified Christ in time. So much for the first general.

II. I am to consider the blessedness which belongs to the dead, 'who die in the Lord.'

Our text describes it under two great branches. As,

First, They rest from their labours.
Secondly, Their works do follow them.

Resting from their labours implies in it,

1. Their being freed for ever from the sorrows, pains, and toils of life. The word signifies sore labour, such as wears away a man's spirits, and drinks up his very moisture; this present *evil world* at the best. The Spirit speaks of the life which now is, Gal. i. 4. Evil of affliction (though not of punishment and wrath) we are all exposed to here; and to make heaven sweet at last, our life is little more than a succession of disappointments. From wilderness to wilderness we are going, till we get to Canaan. Believer, thou mayst *change* thy sorrows and afflictions often, as thou art passing through Baca's vale; but thou never wholly *restest* from them. Every new state, circumstance and condition in life, has its cross: some labour and travail attends it: God will have thee taste the fruit of Adam's *sin*, though, as united to Christ, thou art perfectly freed from *his curse*. What were the racking pains and anguish that body endured, which now sleeps in Jesus, our God only knows, who appointed, ordered, and sweetened all: and what was the patience and resignation of spirit with which they were born: So sweet, so submissive, so yielding to God was his soul; so wholly wrapt up in his Father's will, that he seemed already to have rested from his labours, while he yet endured them. But now his rest is fully come, and he is in his Father's house, his arms, his bosom; where there shall be no more death, neither sorrow, nor crying, neither shall there be any more pain: Rev. xxi. 5. 'Write, Blessed

' are the dead that die in the Lord, for they rest from
' all outward affliction, sorrow, and pain.'

2. They rest from the being and indwelling of sin. In its guilt, it can no more depress and wound; in its adherency and stain, it can never further grieve. That fountain of corruption, original sin, which is the very Egypt of their souls, (as Dr Owen calls it), shall be perfectly dried up; and they shall never think a vain thought, never speak an idle word more. The best, the wisest, the holiest saint, is labouring and restless in this present life, because of this. The Apostle Paul himself, though he had been wrapt up to the third heavens, what a deep sigh does he fetch when looking into the plague of his own heart? ' O! wretched man that I am, who shall deliver me ' from the body of this death!' Rom. vii. 25. It is otherwise above; in heaven, with Christ, the saints are not only freed from actual sin, (as Adam was in his innocent state), but from all possibility of sinning: ' And to the spirits of just men made perfect,' Heb. xii. 24. There is nothing imperfect, nothing wanting in their obedience and graces; nor can any sin enter more, as often here it has done, by their imaginations, or by their senses. They rest from the being of sin.

3. The dead in the Lord are blessed, as they are at rest for ever from the assaults of Satan. These are common topics, but sweet ones. The adversary Satan came against Christ, to intimidate and affright him in his last hours, John xiii. 30. though he had nothing of his own in him: And often the saints follow their Saviour to heaven, through the same way of sufferings. It is awful seeing of sin through the devil's glass; because he always conceals Christ, and that redemption which is through his blood. But though Satan affrights thee now, thou shalt overcome him soon. No hissing serpent can come into the paradise above. We are then beyond ' the lions ' dens, and the mountains of leopards.' When thou diest to time, thou enterest into thy rest. All labour

and

and contention with self and Satan shall cease then for ever. It is a song begun on earth, which is continued in heaven; Rev. xii. 10. 'Now is come salvation and strength, and the kingdom of our God, and the power of his Christ; for the accuser of our brethren is cast down, which accused them before our God day and night.' They are free from the assaults of Satan.

4. The dead in the Lord are blessed, as they have everlasting satisfaction and rest, in the vision of God and of the Lamb. Here Christ is said to be with *us;* there the saints and followers of the Lamb shall be ever with *him.* 'So shall we be ever with the Lord,' 1 Thess. iv. 17. Free a believer from whatever labours you will, he has not rest, till this vast soul of his and all its desires are filled. Believers see God here as he is not: All their knowledge of him comes in by mere negatives, denying to God what imperfections are found in the creature: But thou soul, 'thou shalt see him as he is;' not by reflection, comparison, negation, as thou dost here, but by intuition, face to face, without one interposing cloud, for ever. There can be no satisfaction without perfect vision and enjoyment. Hence the believer, when he is leaving ordinances, frames, and friends, may justly take his farewel of them in the Psalmist's words, Psal. cxvi. 7. 'Return unto thy rest, O my soul.' We are aiming at rest, but it is unattained, till we are with Christ. 'I shall be satisfied when I awake with thy likeness,' Psal. xvii. 15.

So much for the first branch of that blessedness, which attends such 'as die in the Lord.' The second is, that their works do follow them. Either,

1. There are some works which the saints leave behind them on earth, to mellow and ripen, when themselves rest from their labours. Every prayer of faith shall have its answer, when these poor, vile bodies of ours lie rotting in the grave. Faithful martyrs see the seed which was sown by their blood, and faithful ministers the seals which God added to

their ministry, long after they have entered into their rest. Many a soul will own such hereafter for fathers, whom they were altogether ignorant of in this life as children. 'These where had they been,' will be a blessed surprise to many a faithful minister at the last day, who has seen but a little fruit of his labour here. God's word faithfully dispensed, is a fruit-bearing seed, though it may lie long under the clods. Often the enduring patience and triumphant deaths of godly pastors, are the very means of effecting what their hearts were most intent upon in life ; the Redeemer's glory, and the good and increase of the church to which they stood related.

Many of the fruits of your pastor's prayers went before him ; his children went first. But God is faithful : Ply the throne of grace hard, that you may see his works also following him. God did not try him so long, and so sorely for nothing. The fruits of the saints labours are left behind them to ripen. Or,

2. Their works follow them, as evidences of their right to Christ, and interest in him, at the last day.

There is a right of title which the saints have to glory, and a right of evidence. The righteousness of Christ alone gives the right of title : Rev. vii. 14, 15. 'These are they which came out of great tribu-
' lation, and have washed their robes, and made them
' white in the blood of the Lamb ; therefore they
' are before the throne of God.' But the graces of the Spirit give a right of evidence. Hence in the last day you hear Christ saying, ' Receive the king-
' dom prepared for you : For I was an hungry, and
' ye gave me meat,' Matth. xxv. 34. The *for* is demonstrative, not causal. The good works of the saints shall be produced, not as causes, or conditions of their salvation, but as evidences of their right to it, and their meetness for it. God will have it known to all the world, that his judgment is according to truth ; therefore his heaven shall be bestowed upon none but such as are holy, whose character and frame

fuits with the place to which they have a title. This is another sense, in which it may be said, of such as 'die in the Lord,' that 'their works do follow them.' This leads to consider,

III. Why the dead, 'who die in the Lord,' are said to be 'blessed from henceforth.' And,

1. Because hereby they are preserved effectually, from the corruptions of the times and places where they lived. It is a great and blessed truth, that a believer's soul is in paradise, before his body is in the grave; that as soon as his eyes are closed upon earth, they are opened in glory: Heaven is to be considered by us as a state, and not merely as a place: But this is not the immediate sense of the text; it speaks greater things than this with respect to the saints rest. As a special token of their Father's love, our God is pleased to take them from amidst those pollutions, which taint and defile others. Vile principles and ungodly practices (with which the age abounds) God takes them away from both; no longer shall Satan tempt, nor men ensnare. Alas! what are the best of men, when left to their own spirits! David's first days were his best: He was the man after God's own heart. Hezekiah, that zealous and successful reformer, soon grew proud after healing mercy. Peter, who would lay down his life sooner than leave his Lord, denies him with an oath. Many that were once zealous for the faith, have grown lukewarm and careless at the end of life. 'Blessed are the 'dead that die in the Lord,' from henceforth they are freed from all these temptations.

2. They are blessed from henceforth, because they are delivered from those 'vexations of heart' which attend evil, backsliding and degenerate times. It is said of Lot, that his righteous soul was vexed from day to day, with the vile abominations of the place wherein he lived, 2 Pet. ii. 8. Close walkers with God, Elijah-like, are very jealous for him, 1 Kings xix. 10. they cannot bear to see his name dishonoured,

noured, his ordinances flighted, his fabbaths profaned; and it may be, all by fuch as call themfelves profeffors, and think it hard they fhould not be efteemed believers. A tender heart grieves, and mourns in fecret for Zion's fins. We that are left behind live in a dark and dying time, with refpect to the precious truths of God, and the life and power of vital godlinefs in the fouls of men. While fome are ftealing away all the honours of the Redeemer's name; his friends are falling out by the way, as if religion lay in vilifying one another's characters, and expofing leffer flips and inadvertencies to a profane and ungodly world. Reft on, bleffed foul! reft from thy labours; thy God has taken thee to better company, to better and more glorious work. 'Bleffed are the dead that die in the Lord.' And,

3. Such are bleffed that die in the Lord, from henceforth; becaufe they are freed from the *afflictions* which attend evil times. God gathers his jewels, and houfes his faints, before wrath breaks forth upon a God-provoking people. Wo to the old world, when Noah enters into the ark; wo to Sodom, when Lot goes out of it; the next news we hear, is, that the Lord rained fire and brimftone from heaven, and confumed it, and all the cities of the plain, Gen. xix. 25. "Impending, feared, "temporal punifhments, (faid my dear brother, in "fome clofe converfe I had lately with him), God "hath, in meafure, delivered this nation from. But "we are left, we are left to fpiritual judgments, "which of all others are the foreft judgments." The miry places and the marfhes, where the waters of the fanctuary come, and they are not healed by them: They fhall not be healed, they fhall be given to falt. O! it is dreadful when God writes, Never let the gofpel come to that place; never let fruit grow upon that people, upon that foul more! Bleffed, 'bleffed are the dead that die in the Lord,' from henceforth fuch trials fhall no more afflict or affect them for ever. The ufes follow. As,

1. If

1. If the dead in Chrift are thus bleffed, how miferable muft their eftate be, who die out of Chrift, in a ftate of feparation from him; who know nothing of the Lord Jefus, but by the hearing of the ear. A foul that is difunited to Chrift, lies open to all danger; the wrath of God abideth on him. Man! as long as thou 'art under the law, thou art ' under the curfe;' thy mifery arifes from thy ftate. Thou art in fin; a ' ftranger to the covenants of ' promife;' therefore ' without Chrift, and with- ' out hope.' Till there be a change of covenant, there can be no change of ftate. If thou haft no Chrift to appear for thee, fin lies at the door: Thou muft wreftle it out with the wrath of God in thy own perfon. Not a drop of Chrift's blood fhall go to take off one fin, or one torment from thee for ever.

2. Are they ' bleffed that die in the Lord,' then who that is united to Chrift would be afraid of dying! It is a new way thou paffeft through to thy Father's houfe, as they faid of old, ' We have not ' paffed it before;' but it is a fafe one. Thou dieft *in* the Lord, and *to* him. Be comforted, believers, the ark of the covenant fhews you the way. Chrift will be with you dying. In the midft of Jordan his ftaff fhall fupport you: His power and grace will keep back the waves from overwhelming you. ' Blef- ' fed are the dead that die in the Lord.' Their Jefus is in heaven, waiting their arrival there, and he will welcome them to everlafting blifs, and to the mountains of fpices.

3. Are they bleffed that die in the Lord, from henceforth? then may we not from henceforth take up a lamentation againft ourfelves, who are left behind? Death is a lofs to us, though a gain to them. They die in a time of corruption, affliction, and temptation: That is the time when we moft need their lives, their doctrine and example, their prayers, and their tears. When Elijah dies, his fucceffor, though he faw him afcend in triumph to glory, yet

cries

cries out, 'My father, my father, the chariots of 'Ifrael, and the horfemen thereof.' *q. d.* All the ftrength of Ifrael is going, now thou art gone. Saints eminent in their day and generation, for our God, and religion, are the falt, the light, the pillars of the earth. It is for their fakes the earth ftands. Let me alone, fays God to Mofes, when *he* ftood in *the gap,* on behalf of finning Ifrael: But when Mofes, God's favourite, is gone, who fhall ftrive with him for a backfliding nation! Our God does not forbid our weeping, when fuch great ftrokes come; the children of Ifrael wept for Mofes, in the plains of Moab, forty days. It would be ftupidity, not fubmiffion, to do otherwife. Know ye not, that a prince, and a great man, is fallen this day in Ifrael? Such was your dear and beloved paftor, whofe place I now fill. Gofpel doctrines in their relation to Chrift's perfon, and the immediate influence they have upon all practical godlinefs, were the conftant drift of his preaching: And ye are witneffes, and God alfo, 'how holy, and juftly, and unblameably' he behaved himfelf amongft the Church, and all men. He was a living preacher; a burning and fhining light. His fermons were firft preached to his own heart, and then wrought into his life. Such as heard and converfed with him, either by word or by letter, could not but take 'knowledge of him,' from time to time, 'that he had been with Jefus.' The feed which he has fown, by the Spirit's help, amongft you, was fteeped in prayer firft, and followed with prayer after. And you know how he exhorted, and comforted, and charged every one of you, as a father doth his children, that ye would 'walk worthy of God, who hath called you unto 'his kingdom and glory.' A wife and holy God was pleafed to try him many ways; but from the mount of trials and ftraits, he always came down with his face fhining, though, with Mofes, he did not fee it himfelf. Your fouls were often lifted up by the cafting down of his. That long and un-

common

common trial of his faith and patience, which at last put an end to his life, you all know, and how he justified God through every part of it. When I was last with him, I asked him how his frame stood God-ward, when nature was racked and torn asunder with strong pain: His answer was, " I never " said, or thought (to my knowledge) any thing " more than, ' thou God art holy.' I have deserved " more than this from the hand of God in the pre- " sent life." An holy God did, indeed, towards the close of life, draw a veil over those sweet assurances, and pleasant tokens he had once given him of union to Christ and interest in him: Yet in his darkest hours this was his language, " I can go in- " to eternity, and appear before God, leaning on a " perfect righteousness and an everlasting covenant." But a gracious covenant God, though he tries long, will not try always. The cloud brake some days before life expired, and not a doubt or fear attended him after. Not only was he enabled comfortably to lean on Christ, but to rejoice and triumph in him. To one whom he heard saying, ' He is not like to ' live long, he is almost gone;' he answered, " I do " not desire to live; to be with Christ is far better. " From rivers of pain to oceans of glory. O! the " riches of free grace: I am so filled, that it is " ready to overcome me: Oh! taste and see that " the Lord is good. Love the Lord Jesus Christ " all of you." Being asked how he did when his last moments drew on apace, he answered, " I am " almost well. I know that my Redeemer liveth. " The doctrines I have preached are now a comfort " to my soul. Be sure you do not depart from the " doctrines you have been taught, nor from the or- " der of the church, and God will take care of you, " and I hope God will provide for you. Let young " ones take care they do not despise the hand of " the Lord: If they do, God will make them smart " for it." And having prayed, with many tears, and great earnestness, for this poor afflicted church

of

of Chrift, being heard firft to fay, 'Into thine
'hands I commit my fpirit;' he foon afterwards
fell on fleep. Such was the man whofe lofs we
mourn; fuch the frame in which he died. You all
know concerning him, that he lived long though he
died young: This God has given him as a fpecial
honour, that he died without an enemy, and in the
warmeft love and affection of every friend. His
name will ever live in your hearts, to whom he ftood
related as paftor, and whom he loved as a father;
and as one of whom the world was not worthy,
God has removed him to his upper houfe, where nothing filthy and unclean can enter. Bleffed are the
dead that die in the Lord; but wo to us, when God
is making fuch awful breaches upon us! wo to
them that are left behind!

4. Are the dead bleffed that die in the Lord?
What a reconciling thought is this to forrowing
friends and relations that are to ftay longer upon
the earth? To be with Chrift! is not this what you
are longing for yourfelves? O! why fhould you
grudge it them? Some of you, by this ftroke,
have loft many relations in one: A friend, a brother, a nephew, a fon, a paftor: But your Jefus fu-
ftains, and is able to fill all relations. Do not vent
thofe forrows upon your loffes, that fhould be fpent
on your fins. Our Chriftian forrows are not according to our Chriftian hopes, when our tears for one
enjoyment blind our eyes to all our other mercies.
Though 'Jofeph is not,' and 'Simeon is not, Jefus
'Chrift is; and he is the fame yefterday, to-day,
'and forever.' Blefs God you fee the fruit of your
tears and prayers early; and that it has ripened fo
foon into a bleffed harveft. You have buried a part of
Chrift's body, and a part of Chrift's fulnefs; Chrift,
as an head, would be incomplete without all his members. 'My flefh alfo fhall reft in hope.' Reft is after labour, and it is to fit the fpirits for further work.
Rejoice, one day you fhall meet again; meet and never part, meet and never fin.

5. Do

5. Do the saints rest from their labours, and their works follow them? Why should you not then, as a church of Christ, hope in your God, and your Jesus still! When the saints die, to us they do not die wholly; the fruits of their labours, patience, prayers, and examples are left behind. But though your pastor is dead, your Head lives. Christ, the King of saints, the Priest upon his throne, ever lives. Though he has put out one light, he can set up another; he holdeth the stars in his right hand. Moses led the children of Israel through the wilderness; but Joshua was appointed to settle them as a church in Canaan. God gives men of the most eminent abilities their dismission, at a time when the church can least spare them, that the dependence and trust of the churches may be wholly in himself. Josiah was cut off at a time when the reformation was but beginning; because the saints in that day built too much upon him, called him the breath of their nostrils, and thought under his shadow they should live. We usually break our props by leaning too hard upon them. 'God will be with you while 'you are with him.' Think of your dear pastor's last legacy, and dying command in your future choice: Take care of the doctrines and the order of Christ's house, and he will take care of you.

6. Are they 'blessed that die in the Lord?' But how can they expect a blessed death that live not unto him! Forgive me, if here, in a few words, I address my own conscience, and yours, who are my brethren, and fathers in the ministry. For whom do we live, but for Christ and for souls! O let us see that we live in him! This providence calls us to search our own hearts afresh; to look to the beginning of our faith and hope. Preachers to others may themselves be cast away. God has set us over others, as watchmen, overseers, and guides. But an abounding in public work will not excuse private neglects: That food we live upon, and digest daily ourselves, will prove most nourishing and

refreshing

refreshing to other souls. Stewards, above all men, ought to be often looking over their accounts. Our talents are Christ's, not our own. 'Be thou faithful unto death,' was Christ's charge unto Polycarp, angel of the church at Smyrna. We live in a dreadful day: Some have made shipwreck of faith; others spend all their strength about the extra-essentials of religion: Sanctification and heart-holiness is too little regarded by all. Well may we say, 'Blessed are the dead that die in the Lord.' But we must *live to* him, if we desire *to die* in him. Example goes beyond precept. I would lay it upon my own heart, henceforward to study these three things more closely than ever, Christ, my own heart, and other mens souls: And 'blessed is that servant 'whom, when his Lord cometh, he shall find so 'doing.'

Lastly, Are such 'as die in the Lord,' blessed henceforth? Then let them be henceforth remembered: 'Remember them who have spoken unto 'you the word of God,' Heb. xii. 7. You cannot again have them with you; but you ought to call to mind their prayers, exhortations, and reproofs, when they were among you. Young ones, remember concerning your dear minister, 'that being 'dead he yet speaketh.' He is gone to make his report to God, how his message was received here; and will be a witness for, or against you, in the last day. Let his last text and sermon be ever in your ears: 'As for such as turn aside to their crooked 'ways, the Lord shall lead them forth with the 'workers of iniquity.' You know with what earnestness and concern it was delivered amongst you. Some of his last words were to the young ones of his auditory. Wo to you, if you are shut out from that general assembly, to which he is now united! It is sad dying Christless, from a place where the pure gospel is preached. My dear brother 'is free 'of the blood of all men;' he has given up his

'accounts

'accounts with joy;' and 'bleffed and holy are
they, who have part in the firft refurrection; over
fuch the fecond death fhall have no power.'

'Now unto him that is able to keep you from
falling, and to prefent you faultlefs before the prefence of his glory, with exceeding joy; to the
only wife God and Saviour, be glory and majefty,
dominion and power, now and ever.' Amen.

FINIS.

www.ingramcontent.com/pod-product-compliance
Lightning Source LLC
Chambersburg PA
CBHW022148300426
44115CB00006B/395